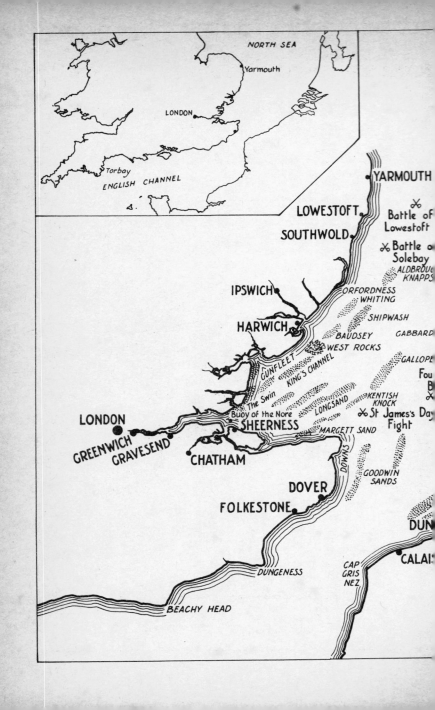

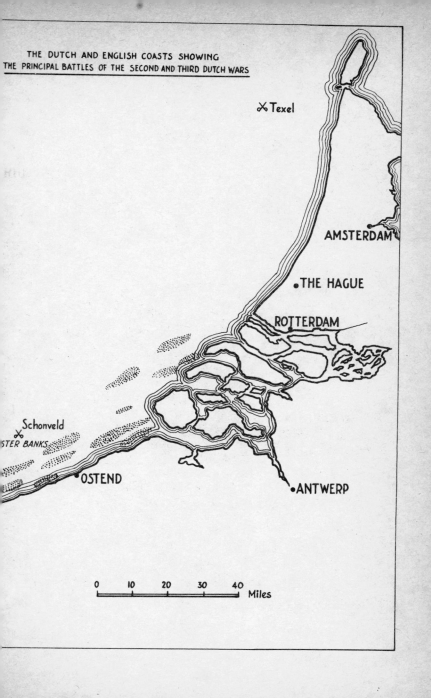

THE DUTCH AND ENGLISH COASTS SHOWING
THE PRINCIPAL BATTLES OF THE SECOND AND THIRD DUTCH WARS

✗ Texel

AMSTERDAM

•THE HAGUE

ROTTERDAM

Schonveld
✗
STER BANKS

OSTEND

•ANTWERP

0   10   20   30   40
                              Miles

Pepys

A Biography

Pepys
A Biography

RICHARD OLLARD

ATHENEUM *NEW YORK*

1984

TO PETER AND CHRISTOPHER

First published in 1974
Reissued with a new Appendix as a paperback in 1984

Preface to this Paperback Edition

When this book was first published in 1974 the definitive edition of the *Diary* still wanted two volumes of text. Since then Dr. Latham has crowned that magnificent contribution to Pepysian scholarship by publishing in 1983 the Companion and the Index volumes. Nothing of comparable importance has appeared or is likely to appear in any field of Pepysian studies. The index volume is necessarily confined to the actual text of the *Diary*. Yet to turn its pages is to open new vistas, to recognise hitherto unobserved associations of people and ideas. The most careless reader must have noticed for himself that there was a great deal in the *Diary*: the most searching will be astonished to find how much he has missed.

The Companion volume is not restricted to the nine years during which Pepys was keeping his journal. The many-sidedness of his interests and activities is elucidated in authoritative articles on music, science, finance, naval administration and much else that found a place in that crowded but never untidy life. Any deficiency of information in this biography may be more readily supplied there than in any other single work.

The errors of fact and interpretation that readers have been kind enough to point out to me were mostly corrected in the second impression of 1975. I have, however, taken this opportunity to rewrite a short passage on pages 136-7 dealing with the plague.

Finally, I have adopted the suggestion made by Dr. Latham in his review of the first edition of this book and have printed as an Appendix one of Pepys's great official letters. These documents are, to borrow his description, 'virtuoso performances' and their style is as revealing of the man as in its very different way is that of the *Diary*.

Richard Ollard
June 1983

Acknowledgments

The debts incurred in writing this book are many. For permission to quote from manuscripts in their possession I wish to thank the Master and Fellows of Magdalene College, Cambridge, the Curators of the Bodleian Library, the Warden and Fellows of All Souls College, Oxford, the Marquess of Bath, and the Trustees of the National Maritime Museum.

To the librarians and archivists who have made this material available to me I wish to record my gratitude. Those who have been fortunate enough to work in Duke Humfrey will know that the magic of the room is matched by the speed, efficiency and helpfulness of its staff. Without the privileges that the London Library extends to its members, writing this book would have been impossible.

For information and advice as to pictures I am particularly grateful to Sir Oliver Millar, the Keeper of the Queen's Pictures, Mr. David Piper, Director of the Ashmolean and to Mr. E. H. H. Archibald of the National Maritime Museum. I should also like to thank Messrs. Bell & Sons for their kind permission to reproduce the two maps of London in Pepys's time drawn by the late T. F. Reddaway for their new edition of the Diary.

Pepys is a subject of such extraordinary variety and richness that it would be difficult for me to express how and why in writing and thinking about him I have felt myself indebted to particular teachers, authors, scholars, friends (so often the four capacities are combined). To drop the names of the well-known, to call the roll of men whose memory lives chiefly in the minds of their pupils, would be either presumptuous or inept. No disclosure of such liabilities could be complete, yet to say nothing would have been ungrateful.

Associated with the institutions I have mentioned are people who have made research more than usually pleasurable. At Magdalene the Master and Mr. Richard Martineau both of whom taught me at school have been kindness itself: in the Pepys Library Dr. Robert Latham, Mr. Derek Pepys Whiteley and the late Dr. R. W. Ladborough have made every visit seem too short. To Dr. Latham indeed, a Pepysian scholar unrivalled in eminence as in generosity, I owe a large debt. To Professor Christopher Lloyd who read my typescript and improved it by his criticism I am most grateful.

There are debts too of a more obvious kind. Where would any student of Pepys be without the scholarship of the late J. R. Tanner, or without the transcriptions of Professor Matthews and the late Edwin Chappell? To the publications of the Navy Records Society as to the *Mariner's Mirror*, the journal of the Society for Nautical Research, anyone who writes on the seventeenth-century navy will be under many obligations. If I do not list the general works on the period it is not because I have not many reasons to be grateful to them. But there are several excellent bibliographies and I can see no purpose in listing all the works I have read.

Contents

Line Drawings

A Note on Dates and References

All dates given in this book follow the accepted compromise between the old and the new style, i.e. the year begins on January 1st, not March 25th, but the month date goes by the English calendar, then ten days behind that in general use abroad.

In citing references I have been more eclectic. Where my source is obvious from the context, easily accessible in print and precisely identifiable by use of an index, e.g. an entry in the Diary describing the Fire of London, I have not cited it. But where these conditions are not satisfied, e.g. an expression of opinion or emotion lacking any particular (and thus identifiable) application, I have. Unpublished sources are, of course, cited in full. I have further assumed that anyone in search of an authority will be acquainted with the printed materials, all admirably edited and indexed, of which I have given the short title in the left-hand column of the list given on pages 343–4.

Lastly, the facts and incidents of Pepys's career up to the end of his official career in the spring of 1689 are so amply documented in Sir Arthur Bryant's three volumes, *The Man in the Making* (1933), *The Years of Peril* (1935) and *The Saviour of the Navy* (1938) that it seems pointless to duplicate the clear and thorough scholarly apparatus there provided. Incorporating not only the fruits of the author's own researches, but the notes that Wheatley and, after him, Tanner, the doyen of Pepysian scholars, had each collected towards a biography, its signposts to the mass of material that confronts the student are invaluable. If I have here and there corrected a slip, I have kept in mind M. de Turenne's maxim: 'He that has made no mistakes has made little war.'

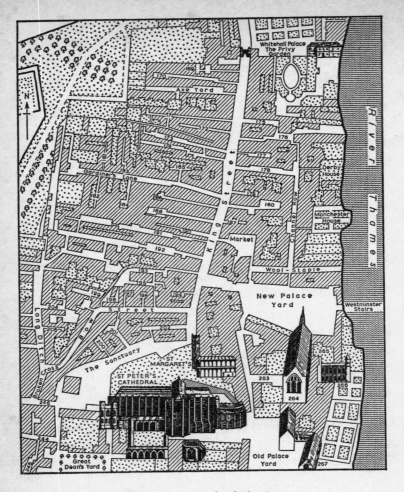

Westminster: Axe Yard and King Street.
Map prepared by the late Professor T. F. Reddaway from R. Morden and P. Lea, 'A Prospect of London and Westminster', 1682. Reproduced by permission of Bell & Sons.

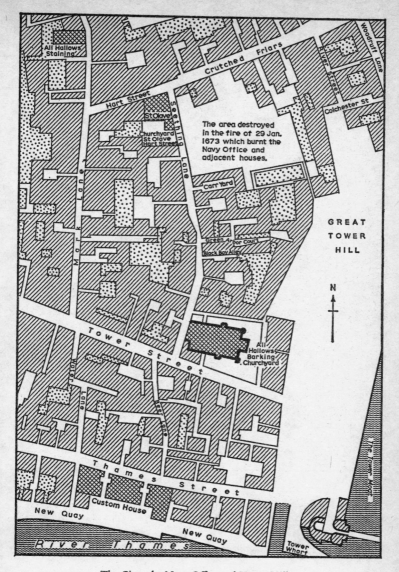

The City: the Navy Office and Tower Hill.
Map prepared by the late Professor T. F. Reddaway from J. Ogilby and W. Morgan,
'A Large and Accurate Map of the City of London', 1677. Reproduced by permission of
Bell & Sons.

I

Beginnings

———

To attempt a life of Samuel Pepys is to defy a prudent limitation of ends
to means. Several lifetimes would not suffice to master all the evidence that
could reasonably be described as relevant. And Pepys's mind is so many-
sided, his curiosity so rich, his achievements so substantial and so far-
reaching, his friendships so wide and so tenacious, his tastes so various,
his appetites so keen, his own consciousness so present to his mind, so
searchingly investigated and so carefully recorded, that a biographer who
felt himself competent to the task would himself be something of a pro-
digy. But books must have readers as well as writers; and the reader who
wants a life of this astonishing man may, like Pepys's contemporary,
Andrew Marvell, not have world enough and time for the coyness of too
nice a conscience.

It is the secret of Pepys's fascination that one never gets to the end of
him. The contrasts, not to say contradictions, of his character, emotions,
tastes, opinions, conduct and circumstances challenge our understanding.
Partly, no doubt, they can be explained by his extraordinary capacity for
absorbing experience and making it nourish the consciousness that neither
age nor disease could blunt or blur. Spiritually and mentally his arteries
never hardened; the process of growing up did not, as with most people,
end with the coming of middle age. His ear for the music of life always
kept him in time; he could make a harmony of the trials and infirmities

of old age as he had of the hot idleness of youth and the rush-hour traffic of middle age.

Partly the sturdy intellectual honesty of the diarist who wanted to see himself as he really was forced him to recognise the complexity of questions that most men in most ages never so much as ask themselves. But when all is said and done it is the very extent of our knowledge that shows us the range of our ignorance. We know more about Pepys than about any other individual Englishman of his time, far more than we know about Charles II or Clarendon, Sir Isaac Newton or Sir Christopher Wren, James II or Shaftesbury, to name but a few of the eminent contemporaries to whom he was more or less well known. Luckily for us he was one of the most observant and articulate men who ever lived; and by further good fortune his life covered the most exciting and eventful period of English history. And though he is that history's most vivid single witness (the account in the Diary of the Fire of London alone is one of the masterpieces of reporting in our language) he was by no means a spectator standing apart from the life of his time. He was at different times a Member of Parliament, a Fellow and President of the Royal Society, and, for nearly all his working life, both a confidential servant of men who were making policy and an expert government official. The Royal Navy owes more to him, is more his handiwork, than that of any other possible claimant from King Alfred downward. The passion for professionalism, the insistence on administrative discipline that his work for the navy exemplified in itself exerted a powerful creative influence on the civil service. Sea power and efficient bureaucracy were the means that had enabled the Dutch to overhaul and surpass the imperial predominance of the Spaniards and the Portuguese. In Pepys's early manhood England had challenged (he thought rashly) the Dutch title to the world championship. If it were to be made good, the same simple formula was required. Pepys more than any man of his time supplied it. In the words of J. R. Tanner, the great scholar, who has put all students of Pepys in his debt, he was 'one of the best officials England ever had'.[1]

It is easy to underestimate the historical importance of Pepys. We are too familiar with the randy bewigged figure whose name, as a symbol of a slightly *risqué* conviviality, has been appropriated by this wine-shipper or that restaurant. An irresistible air of bedroom farce clings to him, partly deriving from the candour of the Diary, partly from the bawdiness of Restoration comedy that gives so much life and colour to our picture of the age. As Mr. Tattle scampers across the stage, baulked of the seduction of Miss Prue by an unwelcome intrusion, we are reminded of the furtive and futile lecheries so vivaciously recorded by Pepys and for the moment

identify the great civil servant with a character described by his creator
as a half-witted Beau. It is not that we need to believe that great men have
no sex life, a feat of historical credulity possible to few: it is that greatness
seems incompatible with consciously making an ass of oneself. And yet
Pepys was — and did.

To have written the Diary clearly sets him apart from the ordinary run
of humanity which it reflects and judges with such piercing discernment.
Most men can brace themselves to the shock of self-knowledge provided
that they can look away again quickly. Moral and intellectual courage of
a high order is required for the sustained, relentless, clinical examination
of the private world of thoughts and emotions as well as the half public
one of actions and words. Why did Pepys keep his Diary? Did he know in
his heart of hearts that it would become one of the great books of our
language? Perhaps he did. But there is no evidence of it. Indeed as J. H.
Plumb has pointed out so accomplished a writer would not have plunged
his reader into a stream of consciousness that rapidly becomes a whirlpool,
as persons, places, allusions are dashed in his face with hardly a word of
explanation. Was his principal motive religious and moral? Pepys was a
Puritan by upbringing and, in the opinion of so great a scholar as J. R.
Tanner, always remained a Puritan at heart. Puritans set great store by
the keeping of diaries as a systematic form of self-examination. Or was
his ultimate purpose aesthetic, the artist's need to impose some order
on the untidiness of experience? Certainly this was among his deepest
springs of action. Was it accountancy on the grand scale, the apotheosis
of those close reckonings in which he took such evident delight? Very
possibly. Was it scientific curiosity, an attempt to establish the fundamentals of psychology by the study of the phenomena readiest to hand
— namely himself? Such a motive would not be inappropriate to a Fellow
and a future President of the Royal Society. Other reasons could be
plausibly advanced. As Robert Latham, the greatest Pepys scholar of our
day, has written in his introduction to his definitive edition of the diary:

After all is said, the origins of so deeply personal a document must
themselves be personal. One origin is certainly the vanity which is so
clearly marked a feature of Pepys's character. Another, equally certainly,
is his love of life. The diary is a by-product of his energetic pursuit of
happiness. The process of recording had the effect, as he soon found out,
of heightening and extending his enjoyment.

It would be surprising if there were an obvious explanation of anything
so extraordinary as the Diary. Everyone who reads it and who goes on to

find out more about its writer will form his own opinion. This in itself suggests something of the multiplicity of the man, the multiplicity that characterises a classic in which generations of readers catch echoes of sounds that they have heard when no one else was about. Variety, richness, depth: without these qualities no book could have lasted as long as Pepys's has. But how did they get there? Where do they come from? Not, surely, from that devious, shrewd Mr. Worldly Wiseman who is busily totting up his accounts or deceiving his wife in some liaison which by no stretching of language could be called romantic. Shallow, mean and monotonous would, at first sight, more aptly describe the preoccupation of the greedy, pushful, jealous little bureaucrat it reveals. True – as far as it goes. But Pepys possessed to a high degree the power of empathy, of entering into a mind or a milieu very different from his own and, as he did so, changing the colour and the tone of his mentality with the naturalness of a chameleon. Except that unlike the chameleon he was in some way changed and enriched by his experience. Rather, like Ulysses, he was a part of all that he had met. The combination of passionate curiosity about other people with an equally passionate interest in himself reminds one of Boswell. So does the tendency, most marked in early life, but still clearly discernible in old age, to set up a model of taste and conduct. 'Be Lord Kames!' Boswell's frenzied self-adjuration was carrying things too far. Pepys was at once too cautious and too self-reliant to tell himself to 'be' Sir William Coventry or, later in life, to 'be' John Evelyn. The phrase of the Psalmist 'when I awake up after thy likeness I shall be satisfied with it' comes nearer the mark.

If Pepys was in some respects like Boswell, in more important ones he resembled Dr. Johnson, notably in tenacity, decisiveness and independence of mind. The Diary and Boswell's *Life of Johnson* both owe to their method of composition an immediacy that transcends time. To both of them, with the necessary substitution, might be applied Stendhal's judgment of Cellini's autobiography: 'C'est le livre qu'il faut lire avant tout si l'on veut deviner le caractère italien.' The similarities of the two men, their moral seriousness, their political scepticism, their love of learning, their hatred of cant, their capacity for and need of affection, their kindness, are profound. Their differences are magnified or distorted by the fact that the close-ups we possess of each of them belong to opposite ends of their manhood. Johnson was fifty-four when Boswell met him and began that series of studies on which the great portrait is based. Had Pepys chosen that moment in life at which to begin his diary we should have had a self-portrait of the President of the Royal Society and Secretary of the Admiralty, Deputy Lieutenant for Huntingdonshire and Master of

Trinity House, a Member of Parliament and a great patron of learning and the arts — a very different person from the young man whom we first see dining at home in the garret off the remains of the turkey on January 1st, 1660. And had Boswell by some inspired tinkering with the time machine been enabled to meet Johnson at the corresponding period of life several years before his own birth he would have found a much more Bohemian and dissolute character than the monumental figure who squashed him flat in the back room of Davies's shop that May afternoon in 1763. This is not to deny the contrasts in temperament and talent that would have been marked at any stage in life. It is an attempt, crude but necessary, to put the Diary and its author into some kind of perspective, without falsifying the stature of either. The Diary is a great work, as literature, as history, as a psychological document and as a key to what has been known as the English character in an age of national cultures perhaps soon to become extinct. It is thus almost impossible to exaggerate its value and its importance. But Pepys's closest friends and most whole-hearted admirers would have been dumbfounded if they had been told that posterity would think of him as a diarist. They would not have been surprised that his name should still be as familiar as that of his great contemporaries Newton and Wren. But as a diarist! None of them even knew that he kept one. They did know him as a man of extraordinary parts and of outstanding achievements. It is almost as though we should be told that Sir Winston Churchill will be remembered by his country-men for a series of philosophical arguments unearthed among the Chartwell papers a century after his death.

The two facts, that Pepys wrote a diary and that its publication in a mutilated and bowdlerised version in 1825, a hundred and twenty years after his death made his name immortal, are common knowledge. Two other facts, that the Diary covers only nine years of a lifespan of seventy and that it was written in shorthand under the strictest secrecy, are perhaps less widely known or at least less often remembered. Yet to a proper understanding of the man they are not less important. Historically the Diary has been the making of Pepys; in real life the Diary was of his making. It is this paradox that helps one to allow for the magnetic pull into anachronism exerted by so highly charged a work.

Samuel Pepys was born on February 23rd, 1633, the fifth child of eleven children born to John Pepys and his wife Margaret in the house in Salisbury Court, under the shadow of St. Bride's, between Fleet Street and the river, where his father carried on his business as a tailor. Like so many families with legal and commercial connections the Pepyses defy any rigid social classification. Among the kinsmen of his name John Pepys

numbered two or three landed gentry, two lawyers, one of whom rose to
be Chief Justice of Ireland, a doctor, a don and a number of tradesmen
and artisans. It was the kind of family, commoner in our time than that
of our grandfathers, that ranged over the whole spectrum of class and profession. It traced its origins to the fenland countries of Cambridge and
Huntingdon in which its nuclei were still clustered. The first Pepys to
emerge from the collective anonymity of villeinage did so as a reeve, as
we should say a farm manager or agent, to the abbey of Crowland, a position in which he was succeeded by others of his name. By the time of the
Reformation the most successful members of the family were on the
fringe of the landed class. An advantageous marriage in Elizabeth's reign
was followed under James I by a further coup: Paulina Pepys, John's
aunt, married Sir Sydney Mountagu, brother of the Lord Treasurer whom
Charles I was to create Earl of Manchester. The lands, preferment
and connections of the Mountagu family made them one of the richest
and most influential in the kingdom. Nowhere was this more evident
than in Huntingdonshire, where the great estates of Kimbolton and Hinchingbrooke had recently passed into their hands, or in the University
of Cambridge which eagerly sought the patronage of such powerful
neighbours. The prospects that opened before the Pepys family were
hopeful.

John Pepys, the diarist's father, was not however well placed to exploit
them. At the time of his aunt's awe-inspiring marriage in 1618 he was
still serving his apprenticeship as a tailor. In 1626 he himself contracted
a marriage whose motive, whatever it was, can hardly have been social
advantage. Margaret Kight, Samuel's mother, was the sister of a butcher.
The glittering alliance with the Mountagus did not seem to be shedding
much radiance over Salisbury Court. In fact the fruits were reserved for
Samuel to gather.

What were his immediate family like? The Diary depicts his mother as
querulous, quarrelsome and feeble-minded. Granted she was by then old
and often ill. But her son was a compassionate man and would have made
allowances for her that we do not need to do for him. As for his father,
Mrs. Heath in her valuable and perceptive *The Letters of Samuel Pepys and
his Family Circle* prints enough letters from him to justify her estimate of
him as 'a father never quite equal to the occasion, always demanding or
receiving some type of aid'.[2] Nonetheless the courtesy, kindness and
patience which his son showed him in his old age seems as much the pro-
duct of natural affection as of filial duty. This at least suggests the possibility that John Pepys within the limits of a humourless and apprehensive
nature had been a good father.

Of his ten brothers and sisters only three survived infancy. His elder brother and sister both died when he was seven. Did he miss having someone older to play with or did he find his promotion to the status of eldest child exciting and enriching? We do not know. In fact we know very little indeed about his childhood and that little all from stray references in the Diary, prompted usually by some topographical reminder. A Sunday excursion takes him to the village of Kingsland, near Hackney, where he and his younger brother Tom were put out to nurse and where he remembers shooting with his bow and arrow in the fields. Prevented by violent weather from taking a boat he has to walk back from Deptford to London and finds himself passing through Horsleydown where he has not been since as a very small boy he went to inquire after his father, overdue and feared lost on a return passage from Holland. Another Sunday excursion to Islington prompts the memory of his father treating the family to cakes and ale at the King's Head there. And so on. There is no comment; no glimpse of character. An attenuated aura of placidity seems to hang for an instant over these recollections before they themselves dissolve in the strong consciousness of the present moment. So far as the indications go it would appear that Pepys's childhood was not unhappy.

His schooldays have left a sharper impress on his Diary. A single reference to 'one that went to school with me at Huntingdon' is the only evidence of his attendance at Huntingdon Grammar School, whose most distinguished old boy, Oliver Cromwell, retained Pepys's admiration in days when he could not publicly avow it. Probably Pepys was at the school during 1644–5: perhaps a little earlier. And probably he lived with his uncle Robert at Brampton, a small property a mile to the south-west which he and his father were to inherit. What is certain is that somewhere about 1646 he had returned to London and entered St. Paul's school where he remained until he went to Cambridge in 1650. St. Paul's in his time was a stronghold of Puritanism and classical learning. The High Master who set the tone of the place is not mentioned by Pepys but his successor, the then Sur Master, Samuel Cromleholme, clearly stimulated his intelligent and high-spirited pupil. A fine scholar and a collector of books (the destruction of his library in the Great Fire of 1666 is said to have brought on a decline) is it fanciful to see in him the first of many models on which Pepys formed himself? He evidently kept up with him after coming down from the University because he is still in touch with him during the period of the Diary. Even when he sees him the worse for drink in a tavern in the autumn of 1662 he prefaces his criticism of this indiscreet behaviour with the words 'though I honour the man and he doth declare abundance of learning and worth'. Two and a half years later this has become: 'Lord! to see how ridiculous a conceited pedagogue he is, though a learned man, he being so dogmatical in all he do and says. But among other discourse we fell to the old discourse of Paule's Schoole.' From the angle at which the graph of this relationship descends its peak it must have been a high one. The value that Pepys continued to set on the Latin and the Greek that he learned there is a measure of the teaching when he was a boy and Cromleholme was in his prime.

Like all good schools it endowed friendships. The Diary preserves the memory of half a dozen old Paulines whom its author still recalled with pleasure. Only one, Richard Cumberland, remained a friend for life and Cumberland's charming dedication of a learned work dates their friendship from their undergraduate days at Magdalene, Cambridge. Pepys left St. Paul's in 1650 with an Exhibition towards the cost of a University education. Cambridge was the obvious choice for someone of his connections, and Trinity Hall which numbered among its Fellows a first cousin of his father's seemed the obvious college. It had the additional recommendation of being in Dr. Latham's words 'very much a lawyer's college' and the law like the church, was a career open, or at least ajar, to the talents. Indeed in the revolutionary period of the 1650s when the whole form and constitution of the church was the subject of fierce political controversy the attractions of the law for a clever and ambitious young man must have been far superior. It was only six years since the Archbishop of Canterbury had been publicly executed. No Lord Chief Justice had suffered such a fate: and everywhere one looked, in politics, in administration, in diplomacy, the lawyers were riding high. Dr. John Pepys of Trinity Hall was himself a lawyer. When his young cousin's name was entered on the college books in June 1650 it would have been rational to predict a legal career.

But some other current was running beneath the surface. In October he was entered at Magdalene, came into residence there the following March and was elected to a scholarship a month later. Whatever the reason for the change, no association could have been happier for him or turned out more fortunately for posterity. Of all the scenes of Pepys's life, his college is the one that we can most nearly share with him. He himself saw the city of his childhood and schooldays destroyed by fire: the Whitehall and Westminster of his young manhood are changed out of all recognition: the house at Clapham where he ended his days is long since demolished: only the houses in Buckingham Street which he knew as York Buildings retain much of their original appearance although they have been in effect re-sited by the embanking of the river. But to pass into the front court at Magdalene is to see much of what Pepys would have seen when he came up as a freshman in the spring of 1651. And through the far passage is the library that enshrines him.

We know so little about Pepys's early life and education that it is unsafe to assert any reason for this happy change of plan. One possible explanation is a change of regime at Magdalene. Dr. Edward Rainbowe, the Royalist master who had brought himself to swallow the Solemn League and Covenant refused to sign the positive Engagement to support the Commonwealth government that was now required of all office-holders. He was replaced on August 31st, 1650 by one of Pepys's neighbours in Salisbury Court, a certain John Sadler who had forsaken a promising academic career at Emmanuel for a chancery practice in Lincoln's Inn. Sadler was a rising star in 1650. Only the year before he had been appointed Town Clerk of London and had been offered by Cromwell himself the lucrative post of Chief Justice of Munster. What more natural than that the new Master who continued to live and work principally in London should extend his patronage to a neighbour's son on the threshold of a Cambridge career, particularly as the boy was intelligent, lively and well affected to the Government? The dates fit: in June Pepys is entered at Trinity Hall; in August Sadler becomes Master of Magdalene; in October Pepys is entered there.

On the other hand it is possible that it may derive from the first unseen connection of his career with that of his rich and rising cousin Edward Mountagu whose patronage was to be the foundation of his fortunes. There are two clues, one very slender; Mountagu's chaplain was a Magdalene man: the other, obscure, but substantial, is Pepys's tutor, Samuel Morland, who was made a baronet at the Restoration.

Sir Samuel Morland's experiments in matrimony and the natural sciences, usually unsuccessful, sometimes disastrous and always expensive, bring him at frequent intervals into Pepys's Diary and correspondence. He personified to a high degree the bewildering versatility of his age, achieving considerable reputation as a mathematician and as a diplomatist, as a latinist and as an inventor, as a cryptographer and as a double agent working for Charles II in Thurloe's secret service. His skill in hydrostatics and hydraulics was such that both Charles II and Louis XIV employed him in the devising of those elaborate ornamental waterworks that to their eye so appropriately expressed the magnificence of kingship. He has undoubted claims to a place in the pedigree both of the computer and of the steam engine. He invented the speaking-trumpet and published a collection of documents concerning the history of the Waldensians. At the time when Pepys became his pupil, he had been a Fellow for less than eighteen months and must have been among the most talented dons of his time.

How and when Morland first came into contact with Mountagu is not known. But that it must have been round about the time of Pepys's entry to Magdalene is shown by a secret report on Mountagu's political complexion that Morland wrote for Clarendon and Charles II in the summer of 1659 when the tide was beginning to run for a restoration of the monarchy. He prefaced it by claiming to have been 'acquainted most intimately with the man for at least these seven or eight years'.[3]

Mountagu, a young Cromwellian colonel whose attachment to the person and family of the Protector was stronger than any positive ideological commitment, had been living at Hinchingbrooke since the execution of the King in January 1649. Coming of a naturally Royalist family he had been drawn to the Parliamentary side not only by the magnetism of Cromwell but by the moderation, tolerance and general good sense of the family into whom he had married, a refreshing contrast to the sour shut-in conservatism of his own father. Old Sir Sydney Mountagu had been a Puritan Royalist whose perceptions and sympathies had not mellowed or softened since their formation in the reign of Queen Elizabeth.* A generous nature could hardly fail to react against them. Equally it might be repelled by the exultation with which Pepys as a schoolboy greeted the execution of Charles I. Did the cousins meet while Pepys was at Cambridge? We do not know. In any case they must have met very soon after, as Mountagu returned to public life in the Barebones Parliament of 1653 and Pepys was acting as his secretary and man of business in London certainly by late 1655 and probably earlier. Both men evidently were shrewd enough to recognise congruities under different surfaces – the clever undergraduate fluent in fashionable views and the young man who had learned to keep his head and hold his tongue in the harder school of war and revolution.

What did Pepys do at Cambridge? The award of two college scholarships suggests that he must have done *some* work. But the only certain fact of his university career is that he was admonished in the presence of all the Fellows of the college then resident for being scandalously overseen in drink. This evidence that pleasure and conviviality were never too far away is supported by the few scattered references to his undergraduate days that come to mind. A day's outing to Aristotle's Well one hot day in summer was remembered twenty-five years later not, it is true, for its own sake but because it marked a turning-point in the agonising disease of the stone from which Pepys had suffered from his earliest childhood:

* His views on pre-marital sexual relations as quoted by his son (D. 7 Oct. 1660) cannot be criticised for excessive liberality.

I remember not my life without the pain of the stone in the kidneys (even to the making of bloody water upon any extraordinary motion) till I was about 20 years of age, when upon drinking an extraordinary quantity of conduit-water out of Aristotle's well near Cambridge (where some scholars of us were for refreshment in a hot summer's day walked), the weight of the said water carried after some day's pain the stone out of the kidneys more sensibly through the ureter into the bladder, from which moment I lived under a constant succession of fits of stone in the bladder till I was about 26 years of age when the pain growing insupportable I was delivered both of it and the stone by cutting and continued free from both (by God's blessing) to this day, more than what may be imputed to it of the aptness which I still retain to cold and wind and the pain attending the same in those parts.'[4]

How much of the mature Pepys is in that immense sentence winding its way through the easy open country of his mind. The exactness, the thoroughness, the judicial matter-of-factness: the intellectual manliness that refuses to disguise what is unpleasant or to indulge in self-pity over what is painful. And amidst all this careful historical documentation, scientific description and rational analysis there is the parenthesis irresistible to the artist 'where some scholars of us were, for refreshment on a hot summer's day walked'. In one stroke the divisions of time are cancelled. We can almost catch the talk of a group of young men drifting along in the sunshine as though the world belonged to them. The very structure of the clause with the word 'walked' pushed to the end renders the oppressiveness and lassitude of cloudless, windless heat. Pepys's mind when he wrote it was on a comprehensive assessment of his general physical condition at the age of forty-five, but he could allow his inner eye to bring before him a sudden brilliant image of his Cambridge days without losing the thread of his argument.

The artist in Pepys lies at the root of his nature. A passion for perception and a passion for imposing order on everything he perceived run through and through his life. He was an aesthete, if not after Walter Pater's own heart at least after his famous formula:

Every moment some form grows perfect in hand or face; some tone on the hills or the sea is choicer than the rest; some mood of passion or insight or intellectual excitement is irresistibly real and attractive to us— for that moment only. Not the fruit of experience, but experience itself, is the end. A counted number of pulses only is given to us of a variegated, dramatic life. How may we see in them all that is to be seen in them by the finest senses? How shall we pass most swiftly from point to point, and be present always at the focus where the greatest number of vital forces unite in their purest energy?

To burn always with this hard, gemlike flame, to maintain this ecstasy, is success in life.

The fineness of Pepys's senses might be questioned in the light of Pater's own standards but no one could deny the power, duration and range of his appetite for experience. By the time he is writing the Diary all the arts matter to him. And to some his responses are so highly developed that he has to take measures to prevent them from taking charge of his life. Plays, books, pictures, buildings elicit, generally, a reaction that is unself-consciously aesthetic. Pepys even seems surprised at this recognition of himself in the mirror — 'a strange slavery that I stand in to beauty, that I value nothing near it'.[5] The immediate context of this reflection was his susceptibility to pretty women. All the more appropriately, for in the most famous expression in the Diary of his deepest aesthetic response to his favourite art, music, he makes this identification explicit:

> But that which did please me beyond anything in the whole world was the wind-musique when the angel comes down [he had been to a performance of Massinger and Dekker's *The Virgin Martyr*] which is so sweet that it ravished me, and indeed, in a word, did wrap up my soul, so that it made me really sick, just as I have formerly been when in love with my wife; that neither then, nor all the evening, going home and at home, I was able to think of anything, but remained all night transported, so as I could not believe that ever any musick hath that real command over the soul of a man as this did upon me . . .[6]

'Musique is the thing of the world I love most.'[7] These words or their paraphrase run through the Diary. As there was so little in the world that Pepys did not love, the depth and ardour of his passion could find no stronger expression. It created his tenderest friendships; it hurt and healed his marriage. It was the only art in which he combined the four functions of patron, critic, executant and creator. It is impossible to doubt that he would have recognised his own profoundest perceptions in Pater's famous dictum: 'All art constantly aspires towards the condition of music.'

All of which makes it as certain as anything can be in the absence of explicit evidence that part of what Cambridge had to offer was the development, perhaps the formation, of his musical character. Probably the study of the subject and the learning of an instrument had no place in his academic curriculum. But music was a conspicuous feature of the

life and leisure of cultivated society in seventeenth-century England; and
two undergraduates who were up in Pepys's time, one at Trinity, one at
St. John's, provide specific evidence that music teaching was available in
Cambridge.[8] Singing and playing must have claimed much of his time:[9]
he was musical, he was pleasure-loving, he was young: it was not in
character for him to reject the advice given in an ode of Horace that he
must have construed as a boy at St. Paul's: *carpe diem:* make the most of
the present.

But what had the University to offer in its regular degree courses?
What was the particular intellectual and moral aura of the early 1650s?
What did one read? Who were the leading figures who might influence
an intelligent and impressionable undergraduate? Had ten years of civil
war and revolution culminating in a military regime reduced academic
life to the repetition of safe opinions and the avoidance of anything that
might prove controversial? The surprising fact is that both Universities
in this uneasy and uncertain period were confident, lively, stimulating
and, to an astonishing degree, tolerant of dissenting views and even
generous to political opponents. At Cambridge this civilised temper
perhaps owed something to the leading school of divines, the so-called
Cambridge Platonists, who were about as unlike the popular representation of Puritans as it was possible to be. 'Nothing spoils human nature
more than false zeal. The good nature of an heathen is more God-like
than the furious zeal of a Christian.' 'Men have an itch rather to make
religion than to use it.' 'Whosoever scornfully uses any other man dis-
parages himself.' To these aphorisms[10] of Benjamin Whichcote, Provost of
Kings' and Vice-Chancellor of the University, it is difficult to attach the
familiar labels of intolerant, humourless, gloomy, sour or self-satisfied.
Reason, common sense and courtesy are the great virtues, never more
needed than in periods where everything is to be put to rights, that
Whichcote and his friends and pupils brought to the religious contro-
versies of their time. Pepys was no theologian and not much of a philosopher: but his own precept and practice as an administrator was to
correspond exactly to the detachment, intellectual good manners and
absence of bigotry exemplified by the then Master of St. John's, himself a
strong puritan, who in elections to fellowships '. . . was determined to
choose none but scholars, adding very wisely, they may deceive me in their
godliness, they cannot in their scholarship'.[11] The tone and colour of an
institution often influence people in ways that they do not themselves
recognise and perhaps could not identify. Pepys probably learned from
Cambridge more than we can know.

The formal instruction offered at both Universities was still in essence the scholasticism of the Middle Ages. That is, by and large the limits and possibilities of knowledge and the means of apprehending it were what all the universities of Europe had for centuries taken them to be. The methods of teaching employed were, naturally enough, also medieval. The undergraduate attended lectures which he was often expected to take down, in their entirety — a practice known as 'diting'. No wonder that shorthand systems were much in demand among the more enterprising. Shelton's *Tachygraphy*, the system Pepys has immortalised by writing his Diary in it, was in such demand at Cambridge that the University Press had published three editions by the time he came into residence at Magdalene. The principal subject of the lectures was formal logic; the structure of rational argument and the technique of its application. But the most characteristic and effective academic exercise was the disputation, a gladiatorial display of logical virtuosity in which one had to prove and another disprove the truth of a given proposition. A disputation could be in varying degrees public or private; it might be a very grand affair but its everyday use was for the tutor, acting as part referee, part drill-sergeant, to put a group of pupils through the paces he had taught them. It was an educational device that must have been congenial to a person, like Pepys, of quick intellectual reflexes and of an aggressively competitive nature. As Father Costello points out in his admirable survey of the whole system. 'Such exercises in sharp and exact statement lie behind much seventeenth-century prose.'[12] The characteristic fault, noted by several contemporaries, was that it disposed the mind towards a tiresome plausibility in argument which we call sophistry and the spirit towards an instinctive contradictiousness which our ancestors thought ill-bred. No doubt this was even more conspicuous when, as in the seventeenth century, a university education generally coincided with adolescence rather than with young manhood. Pepys, who went to the University at the comparatively advanced age of eighteen, was perhaps less immature; but the vices and virtues of his intellectual training are discernible in the diarist.

Perhaps the most radical and pointed criticism of the scope and technique of Cambridge education had been delivered only two years before Pepys came into residence by a writer of his own generation:

> I could never yet make so bad an Idea of a true university, as that it should serve for no nobler end than to nurture a few raw striplings come out of some miserable country school with a few shreds of Latin that is as immusical to a polite ear as the gruntling of a sow or the noise of a saw can be to one that is acquainted with the laws of harmony? . . .
>
> Again I have ever expected from a university that though all men

cannot learn all things, yet they should be able to teach all things to all men . . . We have hardly professors for the three principal faculties, and these but lazily read — and carelessly followed. Where have we anything to do with Chimistry which hath snatcht the Keyes of Nature from the other sects of philosophy by her multiplied experiences? . . . Where any manual demonstrations of Mathematical theorems or instruments? . . . Where an examination of all the old tenets? . . . Where is there a solemn disquisition into history? A nice and severe calculation and amendment of the epochs of time? Where a survey of antiquities and learned descants upon them? Where a ready and generous teaching of the tongues? Free from pedantisme and the impertinencies that that kind of learning hath been pestered with?[13]

It is almost word for word what the Victorian Royal Commissions were to say about the universities and Public Schools two centuries later. It is also a very fair statement of the views that Pepys himself was to hold in later life.

What books he read, what authors he admired, what general stock of culture he brought back with him to London, we can only infer from the later days of the Diary. Presumably one could not be Morland's pupil without acquiring some inkling of the new experimental philosophy, some awareness of a new wind blowing from an unknown quarter. Clearly Pepys kept up and probably extended his reading of the Latin classics. Perhaps he formed that taste for plays, poetry and history that is so strongly developed in the Diary. We know that he began to write a romance which ten years later he came across in clearing out old papers: 'Reading it over to-night I liked it very well, and wondered a little at it myself at my vein at that time when I wrote it, doubting that I cannot do so well now if I would try.'[14]

There is nothing that suggests the anxieties or discomforts of the scholarship boy with his way to make in the world. Sir Thomas More remembered all his life the cold and hunger of his Oxford days and Dr. Johnson still felt the sting of humiliation when he told Boswell of the poverty that had blighted his time as an undergraduate. Not so with Pepys. All is spacious, sunlit, contented, tranquil. If there is silence it requires no explanation. From the first Cambridge was associated with happiness and when he revisited the place, as he often did, he found it there. Without advantages of birth or wealth, in the middle of a period of war and uncertainty, Pepys had made the most of his time at the University. It is the first instance of that genius for adapting himself to the positive possibilities of any situation: a genius that reflects the light striking the moving surface of his life.

2

Early life in London

When Pepys left Cambridge for the great world in the spring of 1654, Cromwell's regime had achieved an authority at home and abroad such as had not been known since the days of Queen Elizabeth. The Protectorate, as his dictatorship was styled, might be a constitutional dead end: but it was every inch as solid as it looked, and it provided its subjects with humane and sensible government. Abroad the transformation was even more astonishing. On the morrow of a long and exhausting civil war England had challenged the most formidable naval power in the world and had in a series of hard-fought, close-run battles won a complete and decisive victory. The early Stuart navy had been too decrepit and ineffective even to protect the channel coast from Barbary pirates, much less to maintain national sovereignty in home waters against the fleet of a European state. But Warwick's vigorous and professional handling of the navy in the Civil War had shown what a versatile instrument of policy had been rusting unused. In the early 1650s while Pepys was up at Cambridge its fullest potentialities were demonstrated in Blake's brilliant victories at the Kentish Knock and off Portland and in Monck's crowning success at the Gabbard.

The First Dutch War established the foundations of that permanent professional navy of which Pepys was to be the master-builder. The sound of the guns carried on the wind from those terrible tearing actions off the mouth of the Thames conveyed no overtones of personal significance to the unmilitary aesthete. It would be a very different matter in the year '66 when the distant thunder of the Four Days Battle brought anxious thoughts to the rising official of the Navy Board as he walked in Greenwich Park. But though Pepys had no reason as an undergraduate to identify himself with the navy, his keen interest in history and in contemporary politics must have made him alive to the importance and to the novelty of what was happening. Forty-five years before he was born the defeat of the Spanish Armada had shown that England could at a moment of supreme danger muster naval forces that could meet and repel an all-out attack by the greatest power in Europe. Besides that, it had confirmed that England could not be excluded from the oceans and the wealth that beckoned across them. This was a sufficiently remarkable achievement for a small country that had come comparatively late to the opening of the world but it was by no means equivalent to an aggressive assertion of naval supremacy. It was essentially a defensive victory. Even though Drake and Hawkins had achieved dazzling offensive successes against the Spaniards, it was no small part of their success that they had dared to take the offensive at all against an opponent so much bigger and stronger than themselves. And even Drake and Hawkins never succeeded in capturing the *flota*, the annual Treasure Convoy, as did the Dutch, or would have sought a set battle against the Spanish fleet. The forces they disposed of, the administration that manned and equipped and provisioned their ships, were simply not conceived on this scale. The navy of the Tudors was much more like a seaborne feudal levy, untrained, undisciplined, unintegrated, than like the specialised professional forces of a modern state. It was not expected to keep the sea for more than a very few weeks at a time, and that only when the country was either launching or expecting an invasion. It was an emergency service whose only wholetime officers were clerks or technicians, men who could look after ships and guns and stores and who could see that there were enough of them in the right place at the right time. All the men and most of the ships would be provided by commandeering the vessels and pressing the men of the merchant marine, reinforcing them with soldiers and other landsmen and entrusting the command to someone of conspicuous military talent and experience who had acquired the habit of being obeyed.

Fundamentally this was the feudal system, the system by which an agrarian society organised itself for defence, transposed from land to sea. It bore the marks of the society that produced it in that it was hierarchical, static and defensive. It would not have suited Attila or Louix XIV or Napoleon or Theodore Roosevelt because it excluded the concept of expansion. It was designed to enable people to hold on to what they had got. It made no allowance for technical developments in the art of war which might require specialised knowledge or training. This was no doubt adequate for the hand-to-hand butchery of medieval sea-fights but in the sixteenth century the coming of the great gun following on the improvement of the sail and rigging plan that dates from fifty years earlier offered opportunities of sophisticated tactics that were not to be fully exploited until Pepys's time. As is well known the Armada Fight was the first major sea action whose tactics were determined by the great gun. What is sometimes forgotten is that no ship on either side was sunk or even badly damaged by the incessant cannonading. The new weapon was still at an experimental stage.

What prevented further and rapid development was precisely the character of the navy as an expedient only to be resorted to in the direst peril. No English monarch except in extreme necessity was going to spend the huge sums necessary to fit out and victual ships and pay the officers and men aboard them. Charles I's Ship Money Fleets which might appear to contradict this, in reality confirm it. Had the sailors been properly fed and clothed and paid, had the officers commanded well-found ships, the Royal Navy would not have embraced the Parliamentary cause with the alacrity and the warmth that it did. The aspect of sea-power that interested Charles I, the greatest connoisseur of the fine arts in English history, was the visual. How beautiful a man-of-war can be may still be judged from the painting of the *Sovereign of the Seas*, the hundred-gun ship that Peter Pett built for him. Pepys spoke of her with particular admiration as 'a most noble ship' when he first saw her in 1661. But, as with the policy her name symbolised, performance did not match appearance. She played little part in the Civil War and next to none in the Dutch Wars. The number of men she required to work and fight her was out of proportion to her effectiveness. Her design, it is true, anticipated to an astonishing degree the ultimate potentialities of the sailing ship as an instrument of war. The function of a warship is however to fight in the battles of her own time. A superb military extravagance, she survived as a monument to the amateur in an age that encouraged professionalism.

Nowhere was this more true than in the great naval struggle with the Dutch. The victories that resounded through Europe while Pepys was a young man at Magdalene were won by superior professional skill, not by luck, or dash, or courage though these are of course as essential to success in war as oxygen is to human life. What Blake, the great admiral of the Commonwealth, did was to refine the natural courage and aptitude of his captains and crews by the scientific application of the lessons that he had learned from his experience of handling ships and fighting battles. As Clarendon the great Royalist historian pronounced: 'He was the first that infused that proportion of courage into the seamen, by making them see by experience what mighty things they could do if they were resolved, and taught them to fight in fire as well as upon water; and though he hath been very well imitated and followed, he was the first that drew the copy of naval courage, and bold and resolute achievement.' Blake's courage indeed deserves all that Clarendon says: but Clarendon knew more about brave men than he did about naval warfare as his somewhat airy, off-hand treatment of Blake's contribution reveals: 'He . . . was the first man that declined the old track and made it manifest that the science might be attained in less time than was imagined, and despised those rules which had long been in practice to keep his ship and his men out of danger . . .' There was more to it than that as J. R. Powell has demonstrated in his studies of a commander whom Nelson acknowledged as his superior.[1]

The transformation of the navy as a fighting force could not have been achieved without some corresponding changes in its administration. Here the moving spirit, certainly during the critical period of the Dutch War, was Sir Henry Vane. Pepys, who diligently collected all he could find about his predecessors in the Navy Office and at the Admiralty, must have known in later life how crucial Vane's part was. He may well have been struck by some remarkable parallels to his own career and to his own methods and policies. Yet he says surprisingly little about him, even in the privacy of his Diary at the very moment in May 1662 when he is searching through Vane's naval papers to find some shreds of plausibility for the judicial murder of a man whom the King considered 'too dangerous to let live'. Vane had come to his position of chief naval executive at the height of a major war by a route very different from that of the tailor's son. Rich and well-connected, Governor of Massachusetts at the age of twenty-three, appointed Joint Treasurer of the Navy in 1639 ironically enough by court favour, Vane served on the Parliamentary committees of the navy or the Admiralty or both from the outbreak of the Civil War. But it was not until the end of 1652 that the appointment of a small Admiralty Commission with powers to run the naval war gave Vane his chance.

Suddenly the creaking machinery of administration changes its note to that low purposeful hum that we associate with Lord Barham or with Pepys himself. Everything is to be done and everything will be done. Letters and instructions pour smoothly from the office when they are needed even if it is a Saturday or the hours are small. A drunken captain is replaced, powder and provisions are punctually dispatched, money is sent down to pay the seamen, conferences are arranged with the

Commanders-in-Chief: yet all this urgent work does not prevent the commission from initiating wide-ranging reforms to cover wages and prize-money, the care of the sick and wounded, and the codification of naval law. The overcoming of an immediate difficulty is not seized on as a pretext for postponing action on larger and more complicated issues. Rather it acts as a spur on an administrative instinct which has been roused to its fullest, clearest consciousness. *L'appétit vient en mangeant.*

There is a parallel even more striking. One of Pepys's supreme achievements, the Act of 1677 for the building of thirty new ships, was foreshadowed in the approval by Parliament in September 1652 for a construction programme of exactly the same size. Unlike Pepys's Act, Vane's was never carried out. In April 1653 Cromwell expelled the Rump and drove Vane out of public life.[2] Here again the mature Pepys, twice dismissed from control of naval affairs through a sudden shift in political power, might see a paradigm of his own experience.

Pepys, like everyone else, was much struck nine years later by the courage Vane showed on the scaffold. When the trial was read aloud to him he found it 'a very excellent thing, worth reading and him to have been a very wise man'. Why then does he say comparatively little about him, especially as a naval administrator?

Personal partisanship certainly must be taken into account. Two of his senior colleagues when he was first appointed to the Navy Office had been advanced and befriended by Vane. And in the two first and most serious attempts ro ruin him the attack was led by men who had had a hand in running the navy during the interregnum and challenged Pepys with the record of their own performance. It thus became a matter of self-preservation to establish the superiority of Restoration practice over that of the Commonwealth. Besides the personal there was also the political. Vane was a revolutionary. Unlike Cromwell, he had thought out his political position and was ready, in Cromwell's favourite description of doctrinaire republicanism, to put all things into blood and confusion. Like most Englishmen then and since Pepys preferred Cromwell's pragmatic approach. In the period between the death of the Protector in September 1658 and the Restoration of Charles II in May 1660 Vane had been a prominent and active promoter of daring constitutional schemes and desperate political coalitions. Pepys was by then a member of the political nation, even though a humble and junior one. Vane's political aspirations, empty though they proved, might therefore in Pepys's eyes have told against a fair acknowledgment of his work for the navy.

But this silent evolution of the service in which Pepys was to make his career did not yet concern him directly. The consequences, both immediate and distant, of England's sudden rising from the waves as a first-class naval power can hardly be over-estimated. In the short term it made Cromwell unshakable at home and abroad: in the long term it shaped so much of English life and policy and had such diverse and far-reaching effects on so many other countries as to overwhelm any attempt at concise statement. Pepys as a young man of intense curiosity about the world he lived in must certainly have been conscious of the enhanced power of government and of the military and diplomatic standing England now enjoyed among the great powers. It seems unlikely that even so intelligent a young man would perceive the underlying relation between cause and effect. Certainly we have no evidence that he did; and we know that his entry into the Navy Office some six years after he had come down from the University was not the fulfilment of some long-cherished ambition but the direct consequence of his employment as secretary to his cousin Edward Mountagu.

Mountagu, as has been briefly indicated, was the man who launched Pepys on his public career. He and his concerns run through the years of the Diary and provide the only direct evidence of Pepys's early manhood in London. Nothing whatever is known of what Pepys did from the time that he left Cambridge in the spring of 1654 until some references in Mountagu's letters and papers show that he was acting as a kind of resident steward — secretary would be almost too grand a word — to his cousin. He was expected to see that the maids behaved themselves, to make and receive payments on behalf of his master, to carry out any necessary errand and to keep an eye on things generally. The earliest evidence of this not very exalted or exacting employment dates from December 1655 but it seems likely that the arrangement really began when Pepys came down from the University. Answering a House of Commons Committee some years later Pepys described himself as Mountagu's secretary at this period, but such a context is the last one in which he could be expected to descend to personal particulars, especially if too detailed a reply might expose him to the sneers and the malice of his enemies. The truth is that Pepys, when we first glimpse him through a few fugitive references in accounts and letters, is a rather idle, perhaps somewhat disgruntled, inmate of the housekeeper's room who knows that his talents and education have fitted him for a higher place in society. If he was idle, it was not from choice. Like the vast majority of gifted people in an economically undeveloped society he knew the frustration of under-employment. Can anything else explain the exultant hedonism with which throughout his long official career he flung himself on work, any work, however tedious in itself? Only the active pursuit of pleasure could rival its attraction.

The transition from futility to fulfilment was made possible by Pepys's relationship to Mountagu, a figure whose importance to the subject of this biography can hardly be exaggerated. His mere existence shaped the strategy of Pepys's career. Had they never met the fact that he was what he was would still have influenced the life of his cousin, just as the existence of a fleet that may never see action or a bomb that may never be dropped may affect profoundly the direction of policy and the course of affairs. Mountagu's golden gift of reticence has concealed from posterity as it did from the less perceptive of his contemporaries how great a part he played in the peaceful transition – so easy and inevitable at three hundred years distance, so perilous then – from Cromwell to Charles II. What other politician of the first rank – a member of the Council of State under Oliver, Commander-in-Chief, ambassador and privy councillor under Charles II – was trusted and respected, even, it seems, liked by these dissimilar and by no means undiscerning masters? Sir Anthony Ashley Cooper, Earl of Shaftesbury, Mountagu's brother-in-law and a much more brilliant politician, held positions of at least equivalent importance under both but was distrusted and in the end defeated alike by Protector and King. Monck who shared with Mountagu the credit and rewards of the Restoration was a through-and-through military professional who served both regimes faithfully without displaying the least spark of interest in the politics of either. There were, of course, there always are, a host of smooth, sleek ingratiators who did well out of both the Protectorate and the Restoration, just as there were a number of able and conscientious public servants who, like Monck, were ready to work for any government that seemed to offer stability. But Mountagu occupies a unique position; a politician more of the Tudor than the Stuart type, guarded but daring, resolute but pliant, a man who could take an initiative but could not enunciate a principle.

In 1654 when Pepys came down from Cambridge Mountagu was already in the inner circle of government as a member of Oliver's Council of State, the fifteen-man executive whose wide powers were wholly independent of Parliament. In August he was made a Treasury Commissioner. As such he led for the Government in the crucial debates – crucial, that is, for the first Protectorate Parliament – on the financial provision for the navy and the constitutional control of the militia. Both debates took place about the turn of the year and both resulted in Government defeats. The open forum was not Mountagu's chosen field. This did not, in the event, matter much because Cromwell turned out the Parliament and retained the minister. Employed in a bewildering variety of Government business, Mountagu was finally selected by Oliver for the all-important assignment of understudying Blake, whose health had long been failing, in command of the fleet. Late in 1655 he was made a Commissioner of the Admiralty and early in 1656 he was appointed a General-at-Sea.

There is to our ears something agreeably informal and amateurish about this rank, held, from first to last, only by seven men. And so, in a sense, there was. One thinks of Monck delighting the sailors with his landsman's orders of 'wheel to the right' when he wanted the fleet to go about on the starboard tack. Of the seven only one, Sir William Penn, was a professional seaman. Yet a list of seven naval commanders that includes Blake and Popham, Deane and Monck, Penn and Mountagu has a ratio of success in action not easily equalled at any period in our history. This is the flavour of the age that Pepys was young in: and nowhere was it more pronounced than in the navy. Suddenly about the middle of the seventeenth century the clouds parted to reveal limitless prospects. It was not only in the furnace of politics and war, and not only Cromwell who

> . . . cast the kingdoms old
> Into another Mould.

Ideas and institutions that had been rigid for generations were melting into a miraculous pliancy. In science, in scholarship, in finance, in public administration, new techniques and fresh insights were transforming familiar views and discovering new horizons. The men who in the next decade would form the Royal Society were already active in the University of Oxford. The spirit of the age was expressed by its greatest poet:

> 'The World was all before them'.

It is difficult for the sceptic of the twentieth century, hag-ridden by the horrors of pollution and over-population, to conceive the optimism and self-confidence of men who had in general seen far more of violence and disease and starvation than most of us. Nothing explains Cromwell or Blake or Wren or Newton: but their careers and achievements, and those of many other brilliantly gifted contemporaries, both gave to and drew from the age that saw them flower. Without this awareness of enlarged possibilities neither Mountagu nor Pepys could have climbed as high as they did.

Mountagu, it seems, had matured young. To defy one's father at the age of seventeen in the choice of a wife and at the same time to range oneself on the opposite side in a civil war was no easy course for a young man bred up to succeed to the family estates. It was either recklessness or uncommon strength of character and independence of judgment. Everything about Mountagu's career shows that he was not reckless. And both the wife and the political allegiance proved well chosen indeed. So did the early, and steady, adherence to Cromwell.[3] Mountagu's withdrawal from politics over the trial and execution of the King confirmed that he had a mind of his own. His return showed his acceptance of the Commonwealth and, subsequently, of the Protectorate. Loyalty and decisiveness are useful qualities in a commander. So is tact. To share the command of a fleet with the towering figure of Blake and not to be either an irritant or a nonentity must have required a good deal. Yet in spite of attempts to make mischief, especially on the part of the Royalists, it seems clear from Blake's letters that he found Mountagu a valuable colleague. That Cromwell was satisfied with his choice is evident from his continuing to employ him until his own death in September 1658.

Mountagu's prolonged absences at sea inevitably increased the scope and importance of the business which he had to entrust to his confidential servants. Almost as soon as Mountagu steps on to his quarterdeck Pepys makes his earliest appearance in the Government offices that were to be his terrain for thirty years. At first he simply signs receipts or makes payments on behalf of his master. But he is so interested, so observant, so incurably sociable that he is soon beginning to be a useful source of political information. He still does the shopping and sends off parcels but he is rapidly becoming in fact the secretary that he has claimed to be all along. Somewhere about this time – certainly before Cromwell's death – Pepys also acquires a part-time job as a secretary to that formidable civil servant and diplomat George Downing, at that time employed in the Exchequer. This does not mean that he has done with his humbler domestic duties but he has at last embarked on his true career.

Not before time, since he had, most imprudently, married the fifteen-year-old daughter of a Huguenot expatriate. The wedding took place on December 1st, 1655, but perhaps owing to the extreme youth of the bride they did not begin to live together as man and wife until October 10th, 1656. That, anyhow, was the anniversary that Pepys, a great keeper of anniversaries, habitually celebrated as his wedding night.

Pepys's marriage, alone among his many and much canvassed sexual encounters, is undeniably romantic. Little as we know about their life together until the Diary opens, there is even then a strong tide of passion still running. Pepys married Elizabeth St. Michel because he found her captivating. No other explanation is thinkable. Judged by all the criteria of prudence, social, financial, professional, political, it was crazy. And these were precisely the criteria which Pepys systematically applied to the conduct of life, his own just as much as other people's. She was penniless and he had not got a proper job, not the most hopeful basis for marriage in any age. But this was just the beginning. She was half a foreigner, and, worse still, had acquired what education she had in a convent in Paris. In Puritan England it would be difficult to imagine more disadvantageous antecedents. True, her father had loudly renounced the Romish Church for himself and his children, and had lost a considerable inheritance in France by so doing. But, laudable as this might be in general, did it not show in this particular case a certain irresponsibility about property? Would one choose to be connected with people who acted in this head-strong way? Might one not oneself all too soon find that the cost of these grand gestures fell largely on the family of the man who made them? And it was not as though Pepys had not enough family commitments already. There were two younger brothers to be educated and given a start in life; a sister of disagreeable temper and no personal attraction to be provided for; the parents whose business this was were at best ineffective, at worst querulous and quarrelsome; little was to be expected, and with advancing years, much was to be feared from that quarter. To add anything to this formidable burden was rash. To add the St. Michels was besotted.

Pepys, we may be sure, realised all this. There can be few figures whose acuteness and objectivity a biographer would be more foolish to underrate. It is a measure of his passion for Elizabeth that he could contemplate, and having contemplated accept, the bizarre encumbrances of her father Alexander Le Marchant, Sieur de St. Michel, and her brother Balthazar, the 'brother Balty' who erupts so vigorously in the Diary and in Pepys's letters. But what to a contemporary eye would have been even more elo-quent proof of a high, romantic emotion is that he should have allowed himself to be impelled into marriage by the mere fact of having fallen in love. Such behaviour was not unknown among the aristocracy and the landed gentry who could afford to please themselves, though even there it was unusual. Marriage, with all that flowed from it, the transmission and amalgamation of property, the network of local and political alliances known comprehensively as 'interest', the connections that might accelerate or retard promotion, was a professional and economic option of crucial importance. To throw it away because one had lost one's heart to a girl would for someone of Pepys's class have been thought as eccentric as for a London bank clerk to buy a house in Switzerland because he had fallen in love with the landscape. A house, in the best-known modern definition, is a machine for living in: it must, even more obviously, be within one's means and within reach of one's work. So, in the seventeenth century, it was with marriage. A wife, to sustain Le Corbusier's bleak metaphor, was part of one's social and economic plant.

Viewed in this light Elizabeth Pepys might appear a questionable investment. And, since our knowledge of her derives almost entirely from her husband's diary, this is the impression that sometimes comes uppermost. But only sometimes. Much more often we catch echoes of shared anxieties and pleasures, of furious quarrels caused by her muddle or his meanness, of reconciliations which, since he was generally the aggressor, show her essentially affectionate and generous nature, above all of talk, without which any marriage is insipid. All this belongs to the Diary period when the marriage was already of several years standing. Of the first years all we know is that they started their life together in one room in Mountagu's lodging in Whitehall and that at some point during the first two years the marriage broke down and Elizabeth went to live with friends at Charing Cross. Perhaps the root of the trouble was sexual. All we *know* is that whatever it was it did not last long and that Pepys hated to be reminded of it. He was certainly a jealous husband and latterly an unfaithful one. Had there been infidelities before the Diary opens? We know too from the Diary that Elizabeth suffered from a gynaecological complaint that prolonged her menstrual periods. No doubt there were difficulties. But the significant fact is that both Pepys and his wife enjoyed recalling their early life together.[4]

Whatever Mountagu may have thought of his cousin's prudence he countenanced the marriage by providing the young couple with a lodging and a livelihood. He himself had married young, younger than Pepys, and against his father's wishes. But he had married into a family whose political connections helped him in the earliest stages of his career and had chosen a wife who had perfect manners, perfect sense and inexhaustible good nature. Even Pepys who at one time or another finds fault with nearly everyone never speaks of her with anything but admiration and affection. In any case the difference in rank and wealth between the two men makes Pepys's action, even supposing Elizabeth's qualities the equal of Lady Jem's,* much the more daring.

More immediately alarming than the consequences of an imprudent marriage was the state of his health. All his life he was troubled by pain or discomfort in his bowel and bladder, caused, as he correctly diagnosed, by the formation of stones in the kidney. All his life these and other symptoms were excited or intensified by cold weather and humidity. In the long, comprehensive and lucid minute on the state of his health which he drafted at the age of forty-five,[5] he summarises, classifies and explains his ailments with an objectivity that eschews self-pity and yet conveys the unmistakable personality of the patient. From the passage already quoted

* Short for Jemimah; the affectionate term by which Pepys usually refers to her in the Diary.

on page 27 we have seen that the chronic condition — 'I remember not my life without the pain of the stone' — was aggravated about the age of twenty and grew steadily worse until at the age of twenty-six its severity had become unendurable. Pepys prepared to face the ordeal by surgery, hazardous and terrifying as it was, that offered the only chance of ending present agony.

The chances of success in even the simplest surgical operation were inevitably slender in an age that was ignorant of sepsis. The certainty of pain, of extreme and prolonged pain in an operation such as lithotomy, from which there were no anaesthetics to give total or even partial relief, made most men recoil. Even those whose stoicism was equal to contemplating such a prospect could hardly be expected to undergo the actual experience in silence or without a struggle. The first essential of a surgeon's equipment was a length of stout cord with which the patient could be trussed to the operating table, or, as in the lithotomies that John Evelyn witnessed in Paris, to a high chair. Evelyn was appalled by what he saw: yet twenty years later when his own brother was advised that only a lithotomy could save his life, he had no hesitation in urging him to have the operation, and supported his arguments by bringing Pepys round to show him the stone extracted from his own body. Unhappily even these persuasions were unavailing.[6]

Dark though the prospect must have been there were glimmers of light. Lithotomy was one of the few branches of surgery that could report a recent advance in technique: and Thomas Hollier the leading surgeon at St. Thomas's Hospital had achieved a notable reputation for successful cutting for the stone. How Pepys prepared himself for what he certainly regarded as one of the most solemn and decisive occasions of his life we do not know, but from his subsequent commemoration of it it seems probable that he prepared himself for death. The house of his cousin, Jane Turner, wife to a lawyer, was larger and better suited to the surgeon's requirements than that of his parents. No doubt, too, the Turners would be less emotionally exhausting to the patient. Here on March 26th, 1658, Pepys underwent the operation with a success for which he never failed to give thanks. Whatever criticisms may be made of him he cannot ever be accused of undervaluing the gift of life. In a few weeks he was again attending to his business and enjoying better health than he had ever known. Sometime in August he and Elizabeth set up house for the first time in Axe Yard, not far from the present Admiralty building, and engaged a maid. Tuning up was finished: the overture was about to begin.

3

On the eve

The pursuit of pleasure and the love of life take in Pepys an added brightness from his conscious and articulate recognition of their importance to him, indeed as he thought to every rational man.

> The truth is, I do indulge myself a little the more pleasure, knowing that this is the proper age of my life to do it, and out of my observation that most men that do thrive in the world do forget to take pleasure during the time that they are getting their estate but reserve that till they have got one, and then it is too late for them to enjoy it with any pleasure.[1]

Such a perception can only have been intensified by the prolonged contemplation of death and the experience of extreme pain and fear from which he was now happily delivered. The world that received him back, his spirits disburdened, his health full and free, his appetites sharpened by denial, would in any case have appeared inexhaustibly fascinating. In the event reality was to exceed every expectation. For a young man of Pepys's social, political and intellectual tastes and powers of observation to find himself in London in the summer of 1658 connected with men such as Mountagu and Downing who were at the heart of things was to have drawn a high prize in the lottery of life.

The only certainty of England's political future at that point in time was that it could not be dull. Cromwell's adventurous foreign policy had raised the standing of his Government both at home and abroad. But the financial underpinning of a military regime was bound to produce political and constitutional problems. Sooner or later a Parliament of sorts would have to be called again. What would happen then was anybody's guess. In spite of doing his best to pack his parliaments with docile and well-affected persons Cromwell had three times failed to attain this objective. The nation was, as he realised better than some of his critics, far too fiercely divided in politics and religion to make government by consent a feasible proposition. The Royalists, the Republicans and the Levellers had all shown themselves more or less irreconcilable. And besides these rational, or at least intelligible, forms of political opposition there were yet higher and more thrilling peaks from which to look down on the kingdoms of the world, such as those scaled by the Fifth Monarchy men who believed that direct rule by the Ancient of Days was about to replace more conventional forms of government and who wished, like millenarians in all ages, to quicken the dawdling steps of history. On past form Cromwell should have been able to hold all these forces at bay. Only that spring he had sent his last Parliament packing without subjecting his regime to any visible strain. Rather the foreign observers best qualified to judge such as the French ambassador thought the Protectorate stronger than ever. So did Clarendon, the best informed and most objective of the Royalist exiles who advised Charles II. But Cromwell was beginning to feel his years. Two bereavements in the happy and affectionate family of which he was the centre drained his reserves. In August he was seriously ill. On September 3rd, the anniversary of his famous victories at Dunbar and Worcester, he was dead.

Suddenly political questions that had long been kept shut were unfastened and swinging in the wind. Were the Stuarts going to come in again? To judge by the pathetic failure of every Royalist rising, the latest still fresh in people's minds, it did not seem likely. Were the Republican Old Guard, men like Sir Henry Vane, at last to enter into the inheritance that Cromwell had denied them? Would they make common cause with the Fifth Monarchy men and light a real revolutionary bonfire? Would the Long Parliament return either as that final fragment of the original body popularly termed the Rump or in the somewhat larger edition that Colonel Pride had purged? Would the army endeavour to perpetuate themselves as the arbiters of political power which they evidently were when they lent their weight to Cromwell's dying wish that he might be succeeded by his amiable but ineffective son Richard? To a serious follower of politics such as Pepys these were all possibilities exciting beyond expression: and every scrap of evidence suggests that he discussed them with fascinated interest in the taverns and the new coffee houses where so much of his time was spent.

Where, politically, did he himself stand? It seems clear from the Diary that his sympathies lay with the Presbyterian party, that body of Parliament men and common lawyers who had originally taken arms against the King because they resented the policy of Strafford and the pretensions of Laud and the high-churchmen and saw in them the danger signals of absolute monarchy, perhaps even, under the influence of Queen Henrietta Maria, of Popery itself. But all that belonged to the 1630s and 40s. The surviving leaders of the Presbyterian party, men like Fairfax and Holles, had for years been Royalists in all but name. The execution of the King and the proclaiming of a Commonwealth had seemed to them as great a violation of the legality they had fought for as anything the Stuarts might have had in mind. Like all opposition movements their political existence was largely parasitic on the issue they wished to prevent. Once Charles I and Laud and Strafford were beneath the horizon they had no cause to which opinion might be rallied. Even the distinguishing mark of religious opinion from which they took their name became much eroded. Pepys himself had certainly begun to attend the Prayer Book services, still officially banned, that were all but openly conducted in private houses by clergymen ejected from their livings. Not that forms of worship or government were the kind of things for which Pepys would ever have risked martyrdom or even serious inconvenience. To his way of thinking these were matters of taste and preference, like food or clothes. One might have very pronounced likes and dislikes but at a pinch anything was better than starving or shivering.

It might be objected that Pepys's lively horror of revolutionary ideologues such as Vane or Milton flaws this perfect detachment. But it might equally be held to confirm it. If keeping still is the only way to stop the boat from turning turtle the principle operates independently of what course is being steered. Had Vane seized and established power it is hard to imagine Pepys conspiring against the regime. Yet it would be wrong to infer from this obedience to the powers that be either personal or intellectual timidity. We know that Pepys attended and enjoyed the meetings of the Rota Club where in the winter of 1659–60 the highest speculative intelligences controverted and criticised the fundamentals of politics. 'The discourses in this kind were the most ingeniose, and smart, that ever I heard or expect to heare, and bandied with great eagernesse: the arguments in the Parliament house were but flatt to it,' wrote the young

John Aubrey, a fellow member who shared Pepys's addiction to rational discourse.[2]

The pace of events outran speculation. Richard Cromwell succeeded peaceably enough to his father's position and in January 1659 summoned the Parliament that his father had been preparing to hold. But the slack rein on which he rode both alarmed the army leaders and invited them to unseat him. Richard and his Parliament were turned out by a bloodless *coup d'état* and the army officers, bankrupt as always of political initiative, recalled the Rump early in May. Whatever else that precious remnant of the much purged Parliament elected in 1640 may have lacked it was not spirit. Before the summer was out these fifty-odd veterans had shown that they meant to obtain political control over the Generals who had brought them back. Since this was precisely the same course of action of which Richard's Parliament had been suspected earlier in the year the Generals might reasonably be expected to react in the same way. The Rump promptly cashiered Lambert and Desborough, the two most vigorous army leaders, and vested the command in Fleetwood, the most senior but the least decisive of the Generals, assisted by six commissioners of a strongly Republican complexion. Lambert replied to his dismissal by marching his troops into Westminster and refusing the Rumpers admission to their house. The army was back where it came in.

This was in October. During the summer Lambert had crushed with contemptuous ease the Royalist rising led by Sir George Booth, a rich Cheshire landowner, on which so many hopes had been pinned. Charles II who had been eagerly waiting at Calais now set off for the Pyrenees where, on an island in the Bidassoa, Velazquez and others were setting the scene for one of the great diplomatic congresses of the century that was to negotiate the peace treaty between France and Spain. Cromwell had used the war between the two super-powers to advance his interests in Europe and the New World. Charles hoped to use the peace to secure diplomatic and perhaps military support for his restoration. In the event he obtained nothing. The autumn of 1659 was rock bottom for the Royalists. Hitherto however black the immediate prospect the King could always comfort himself with the thought that Cromwell was not immortal and could pull himself, as *émigrés* do, out of the pit of despair by the bootstraps of secret reports that his partisans were preparing for the great day. The great day had come and gone: the Royalist rising had fizzled out before it had even caught alight: and the powers of Europe were composing themselves for a period of slumber indifferent to the fate of the King of England.

But it was not only the Royalists who were facing a brick wall. So were the army. What were they to do next? How were they going to raise the money to pay the troops? The only known machinery for taxation needed a Parliamentary driving wheel to set it going. And on what possible basis could a Parliament of any kind be reconstituted by the men who had followed up the dissolution of Richard Cromwell's Parliament by ejecting the Rump? So incompetent were the Generals to answer these conundrums, so universal the dislike of military rule, that by Christmas time the Rump had returned to Westminster and to a nominal assertion of authority. The needle of history seemed to be caught in a scratched record.

Meanwhile the best hope of meeting the short-term demand for cash lay in the city. Merchants and financiers could always provide funds if the inducement offered was sufficient. For the immediate future the need to preserve the city itself from pillage by a large army mutinous from want of pay was a powerful incentive. But in the long run the citizens who were to be called on to act as the Government's bankers would want to have some say in the making of policy and the conduct of affairs. Hence at the point at which Pepys's Diary opens political interest centred on the recent elections to the Common Council of the city of London. These had shown a decisive swing away from both the army and the Rump and had strengthened the demand, voiced ever louder, for a new Parliament.

On the Scottish border George Monck, the General Officer Commanding, was edging his well-found, well-disciplined army closer to England. He had made no secret of his disapproval of army *coups* and of his belief that a soldier's function was to serve the legally constituted civil government. Facing him on the English side lay the troops of John Lambert, the General who had dominated events first by defeating the Royalist rising and then by turning out the Rump, to which he was still unreconciled. In mid-December Lawson, the left-wing Admiral in command of the fleet, had declared for the Rump and had brought his ships up the river to Gravesend. This was the situation when on January 1st, 1660, Pepys began his Diary and, unknown to him, Monck crossed the border at Coldstream. English history's supreme shorthand writer was ready and waiting.

This account of public events sheds no light on the activities of Pepys's two masters, Downing and Mountagu. In this it faithfully represents their own adept concealment of manoeuvres whose object would have been lost by publicity. Downing in particular was uniquely well placed to forecast the winner of every political race and to reinsure himself against unpleasant consequences. Besides his place in the Exchequer he was also English ambassador at The Hague under each successive Government and, as if that was not enough, a veteran of Secretary Thurloe's secret service.

Like Thurloe he therefore knew enough to be sure of powerful friends under any regime. There was nothing to be gained by early and steadfast adherence to any party. Downing could afford to wait and see.

Mountagu, however, was in a much more exposed position. He had identified himself with the house of Cromwell and had avowed his opposition to both the Republicans and the Royalists. The fall of Richard was a severe shock: he could expect nothing from the Rump and a great deal less from any Government headed by men like Vane or Hesilrige. Had he been in England he would have done his best to prevent the door being opened to such firebrands. But in the spring of 1659 as General-at-Sea he had been sent with a powerful fleet to the Baltic. The Swedes and the Danes having at last signed a treaty in 1658 were at each others' throats again and the Dutch, our great maritime rivals, were backing the Danes. To preserve the balance of power in a part of Europe that had a virtual monopoly of masts, spars, pitch, tar and other naval stores was a paramount English interest. Opposed in everything else both Dutch and English wanted a diplomatic settlement rather than a resumption of hostilities. The conduct of such negotiations backed by the presence of a fleet was all in the day's work for a seventeenth-century admiral. Mountagu was within sight of a satisfactory settlement when a frigate arrived with news of Richard's overthrow.

It was a situation that called for coolness of judgment, calmness of manner, complete self-reliance and an exact sense of timing. Everyone knew that the Commander-in-Chief was no friend to Republicanism, the Good Old Cause, whose star was now ascendant. Everyone knew that the exiled Stuarts would go all out to enlist his support now that his loyalty to the Cromwells was no longer an obstacle. Everyone knew that the new Government in London would watch his every move, would surround him with military and diplomatic nominees of their own, would eavesdrop on him, intercept his correspondence, would leave him unsupported while he was abroad, and would at the first opportunity dismiss him summarily from all his appointments. Certainly Pepys knew all this: he even came out to the Sound to bring and take back confidential correspondence and, no doubt, to report to his master on what was being done and said at home. Yet even from so trusted and discerning a servant Mountagu kept inviolate the secrecy of his actions and intentions. A year later when everything was over Pepys confesses his astonishment at hearing from Mountagu's own lips that he had been in correspondence with the King at this very time — 'and I do from this raise an opinion of him to be one of the most secret men in the world, which I was not so convinced of before.'[3]

Pepys was right to be astonished: and those who have smiled at his innocence betray a want of insight. Not only did the Government suspect Mountagu of negotiating with the Stuarts, they sent three commissioners over to keep an eye on him. Not only did one of the commissioners share these suspicions, he was actually present when Mountagu was approached by a Royalist agent ashore one day in Copenhagen. Not only did he report his findings, he openly charged the Commander-in-Chief in the presence of a number of senior officers and diplomats both English and foreign. Not only did he charge him, it was all perfectly true. The whole performance was a triumph of the straight face. When at the end of August 1659 Mountagu brought the fleet home against the wishes of the commissioners and without orders from the Government, the suspicious coincidence of Sir George Booth's abortive rising would have embarrassed or flustered any but a master of impenetrable bluff. But Mountagu carried it off. He lost all his military commands: he was superseded as General-at-Sea; he had already been deprived of his regiment; but he kept his head.

> Much suspected by me
> Nothing proved can be.

The lines that the young Elizabeth scratched on the window-pane epitomise the technique of political survival so successfully practised by Pepys's patron.

The excitement and uncertainty of that autumn were part of what Pepys and his contemporaries knew as London. To us the affairs of the nation are as present in Westmorland or Cornwall as within a stone's throw of the palace of Westminster. Either in London or out of it we can choose whether to contemplate or to ignore the public issues of the day. But what is a matter of choice for us was a matter of geography for our ancestors. In English history not all the world was a stage: only London. The disproportion in wealth and population between the city and the next largest town was so huge as to constitute a difference in kind not in degree. The tension of affairs could be felt there as nowhere else, and felt the more keenly by contrast with the immemorial calm of a countryside that changed only with the seasons. Only in London could Pepys's most characteristic qualities, restlessness, curiosity, competitiveness, multiplicity of consciousness, have grown to the height they did. In his lifetime London was never quiet for long. The sinking of the barometer in 1641, the storm of civil war, the unpredictable yawings that followed the death of Cromwell, the plague, the fire, the Dutch fleet coming up the Medway, the Popish plot, the attempt to exclude James Duke of York from the succession, the punitive reaction that followed, the Glorious Revolution

1659
60

Axe yard — ... Jane —

... Lamb. ... Lawson ...

River — Monke ... Scott

... Lamb ...

... Monke ...

... Mr Downing ...

The opening page of the Diary. See page 52.

that turned out James and ended Pepys's own career, the louring of Jacobite conspiracy that more than once darkened a dignified retirement with the shadow of arrest, this is a record of experience by no means confined to the tranquil and the serene. Pepys, the supreme observer of his age, saw it as turbulent and uncertain. He was a Londoner looking at London.

It is there that he comes before us in his own introduction to the opening entry of the Diary, begun on January 1st, 1660, just as the renewed momentum of events promised an exciting and perhaps decisive turn in the affairs of state. With a masterpiece, the reader in his eagerness to see what all the world says is so wonderful is apt to flash past the opening phrases. Much can be learned from their content, their manner and above all the order in which Pepys, most systematic of men, arranged them.

> Blessed be God, at the end of the last year I was in very good health, without any sense of my old pain but upon taking of cold.
>
> I live in Axe-yard, having my wife and servant Jane, and no more in family than us three.
>
> My wife after the absence of her terms for seven weeks, gave me hopes of her being with child, but on the last day of the year she hath them again. The condition of the State was thus. *Viz.* the Rump, after being disturbed by my Lord Lambert . . .

So matter-of-factly, like the screech of a sash-window being thrown open, begins one of the greatest texts in our history and in our literature. The subject of this biography turns his head to us across the centuries and addresses us as though we were only across the room. Not to be moved is to be deficient in humanity. All the easier not to notice exactly what he is saying.

The Diary opens (and closes) with the invocation of God. A man who had been born and brought up in the time of Charles I and Cromwell had had his bellyful of theology. Is this just a conventional gabble, like grace in an Oxford college, or does it tell us something about the place taken by religion in Pepys's view of things? Both. Pepys's religion, unlike almost everything else about him, seems dry and uninteresting, but it was not unreal, still less unimportant. Except for an intermittently uneasy consciousness of sin there seems to have been little specifically Christian about it: no perception of the beauty and simplicity that George Herbert had found and expressed: no outgoing of the heart towards the person of Christ: no love or forgiveness for man as a brother for whom Christ died. This is not at all to say that Pepys was lacking in compassion or benevolence, but that he practised these virtues either from impulse or from general principles of a moral and religious, but not noticeably Christian, nature. Moral principle and religious observance lay at the heart of Pepys's understanding and conduct of life. To argue that he was a hypocrite because he was unchaste or that he was an unbeliever because he was worldly is to take up a position that would have been thought extreme in a Victorian academy for young ladies.

God, then, came first. But hard on his heels came health, the over-whelming preoccupation of the inward-turning mind. Writing about a country clergyman of Pepys's time who also kept a diary, a modern scholar comments on the '. . . high incidence of physical distress arising from the many incurable diseases of pre-industrial society. Only a reading of the actual diary will bring home to the reader the constant almost obsessional discussion of pain and sickness.'[4] The same concern is abun-dantly evident throughout the Diary we are considering. No doubt it is true that twentieth-century medicine could have saved Pepys much pain and more anxiety: but to believe that improvements in drugs and surgery will ever stop humanity from droning on about its ailments is to close one's mind to what all too often one would have wished to close one's ears. Pepys's ills were far from imaginary but they did leave him with a some-times too exalted sense of the duty he owed to his bladder and his colon.

After health came social statistics – a word that only a dozen years later was to make its début on the linguistic stage.[5] And after social statistics comes his wife Elizabeth and *her* state of health. The vagaries of her gynaecological disorder had given them hopes of children but these had been dashed. (Almost certainly the knife that had relieved Pepys of his stone had cut off his posterity.)

These matters established and for the time being disposed of we are free for a tour of the political horizon after which we return to the point from which we started, the circumstances of the diarist himself:

> My own private condition very handsome; and esteemed rich, but indeed very poor, besides my goods of my house and my office, which at present is somewhat uncertain. Mr. Downing master of my office.

Pepys has drawn a quick sketch-map of his world that significantly omits all mention of its most conspicuous feature: Edward Mountagu. That he, not Downing, was the true centre of hope and interest, of activity and reward, is clear from the lightest skimming of the first few entries in the Diary. But in the New Year of 1660 he was lying doggo at Hinching-brooke. So successfully had he effaced himself that even his most

intelligent and sharp-eyed servant had for the moment forgotten his existence. Such a withdrawal was certainly easier in the days before the car and the
telephone but even then its completeness was sometimes deceptive. Pepys
and others kept Mountagu informed of what was reported in London.
Early in January it was known that Monck had crossed the border at
Coldstream and that Lambert's army was melting away. A month later
Pepys watched him march past Whitehall at the head of his troops and
recorded his impression of a well-found, well-disciplined military force.
What was Monck going to do with it? All the signs were that he would
support the Rump who regarded him as their rescuer from the military
satraps like Lambert and Desborough and their defender against the
resurgent royalism that had taken so dangerous a hold in the City. On
February 9th he was sent there to arrest some of those who had challenged
the Rump's authority and, as Pepys heard, 'clapped up many of the
Common Council'. To teach the City a lesson the Rump further ordered
him to destroy the posts and chains and gates and portcullises by which the
Corporation asserted its ancient freedom and privileges. This Monck
began to do; and the next day, to quote Pepys, 'The city look mighty
blank and cannot tell what in the world to do.' Pepys himself solved this
problem by lying in bed and going late to his office where he spent what
remained of the morning reading a Spanish guidebook to Rome.

At noon I walked in the Hall [i.e. Westminster Hall] where I heard
the news of a letter from Monke, who was now gone into the City
again . . . and it was very strange how the countenance of men in the
Hall was all changed with joy in half an hour's time. So I went up to
the Lobby, where I saw the Speaker reading of the letter; and after it
was read, Sir A. Haslerig came out very angry; and Billing* standing at
the door, took him by the arm and cried, 'Thou man, will thy beast
carry thee no longer? thou must fall.'

Pepys's eye had caught the tide at the instant of turning. He went on
to make the approach of the Restoration his own stretch of history. Ever
since the Diary was first published in 1825 it has coloured and shaped the
view of those few weeks like the sun coming up on a winter morning.

And endeed I saw many people give the soldiers drink and money,
and all along in the streets cried 'God bless them' and extraordinary

* The Quaker who with some of his congregation had been roughly handled by Monck's
soldiers on the day of their arrival in London. It was an apt indeed epigrammatic summing
up of the situation, but one does see why people often found the Quakers exasperating.

good words. Hence . . . to the Star tavern . . . where we drank and I wrote a letter to my Lord from thence. In Cheapside there was a great many bonefires, and Bow bells and all the bells in all the churches as we went home were a-ringing. Hence we went homewards it being about 10 a-clock. But the common joy that was everywhere to be seen! The number of bonefires, there being fourteen between St. Dunstan's and Temple-bar. And at Strand bridge I could at one view tell 31 fires. In King-streete, seven or eight; and all along burning and roasting and drinking for rumps — there being rumps tied upon sticks and carried up and down. The buchers at the maypole in the Strand rang a peal with their knives when they were going to sacrifice their rump . . . Indeed it was past imagination, both the greatness and the suddenness of it. At one end of the street, you would think there was a whole lane of fire, and so hot we were fain to keep still on the further side merely for heat.[6]

No wonder the young Macaulay was entranced: no wonder that this passage is quoted at length in the most detailed and technical account of the restoration by a modern scholar who can certainly not be criticised for leaning towards the lush or the picturesque.[7] Mountagu was well-served by his London correspondent.

There were other letters reaching Hinchingbrooke, secret from Pepys and all the world beside. Mountagu was in indirect touch with the Stuarts through one of his kinsmen.[8] Within three weeks of Monck's letter to the Speaker telling him to admit the secluded members and setting a date in May for a dissolution and fresh elections, Mountagu had been restored to the colonelcy of his regiment, joined with Monck in the supreme command of the fleet as General-at-Sea, appointed a Commissioner of the Admiralty and elected to the Council of State. His coyness towards the King's advances vanished, though his discretion remained impenetrable. It was reported that he would try to bring back not Charles II but Richard Cromwell. Clarendon analysing the news across the channel did not believe it for a moment. Pepys who was closer to the scene of action seems to have felt less confidence in his own powers of prediction. In the first brief private conversation on politics that he records after Mountagu's return to London in the first week of March: 'He told me he feared there was a new design hatching, as if Monke had a mind to get into the saddle.' He at last showed his hand, or part of it three days later, on March 6th, that ever-to-be-remembered day on which Mountagu 'called me by myself to go along with him into the garden, where he asked me how things were with me', and went on to invite Pepys to go to sea with him as his confidential secretary and promised to support him in any application for a permanent post in the Government service.

'He told me also that he did believe the King would come in.' That this opinion was conveyed in no ringing tones of royalist fervour may be gathered from the expanded version of these remarks which Pepys found room for later on in his entry for the same momentous day:

> My Lord told me that there was great endeavours to bring in the Protector again; but he told me too, that he did believe it would not last long if he were brought in; no, nor the King neither (though he seems to think that he will come in), unless he carry himself very soberly and well.

It is all very cool, detached, pragmatic. Pepys did not guess that the speaker had, like Monck himself, called in his hedging bets and staked everything on the Stuarts. In any case Mountagu had committed himself unequivocally on a far more interesting question: the future of Samuel Pepys; '. . . and in discourse thereupon my wife and I lay awake an hour or two in our bed.'

Between Monck's *coup de théâtre* and Mountagu's return to London Pepys had paid a brief and bibulous visit to Cambridge to see his brother John settled in at Christ's. The sudden change in the political wind provided an opportunity of combining a private jaunt with a business journey since Hinchingbrooke was only a short ride from Cambridge. Indeed Mountagu's father-in-law, one of the members now readmitted to his place in Parliament, told Pepys on February 21st that his master ought to be sent for at once. On the next day James Pearse, a surgeon whose unusual abilities and connections were to make him into a lifelong friend and colleague, suggested that they should ride down together as he had to rejoin his regiment then stationed at Cambridge. Pepys gladly agreed and they set out early on the 24th 'the day and way very foul'.

Love of travel was a passion that grew stronger as the means of satisfying it grew less. The eagerness with which Pepys in old age planned, directed and vicariously followed the European tour of his stolid nephew John Jackson is part affectionate solicitude, part wistfulness for chances gone beyond recall, but mainly the random avidity of the addict. In young manhood even the mud and the rain of a February day could not quench the exhilaration. At Puckeridge they were very merry over a fried loin of mutton: and when both the day and their horses were spent some six miles short of Cambridge they passed an agreeable evening at an inn playing cards while supper was prepared. Early next morning the two friends parted but by a strange reversal of roles, Pearse went to Hinchingbrooke, 'to speak with my Lord before his going to London', while Pepys went straight to Cambridge to join his brother and his father who was staying at an inn in Petty Cury. Why did Pearse go to call on Mountagu? Does the ease with which he and his pretty wife moved in the circles of the Restoration court and the official appointments subsequently showered on him — Surgeon-General of the Fleet, Surgeon to the Duke of York — afford a clue? We do not know. But it is odd. And it is odd, too, that Pepys, with his way still to make in the world, should join his father and brother for an incessantly convivial weekend before reporting on the latest developments to his patron. Two or three years later he would have treated anyone guilty of such a frivolous misordering of priorities to a severe and ponderous lecture. In the spring of 1660 he had hardly begun the transition from the indolence and self-indulgence of under-employment to the brisk bustle of the rising executive, from uncertainty of his social position and professional future to the confident self-importance of the administrative Prometheus born to bring order and system into the Chaos and Old Night of the Navy Office.

Perhaps Cambridge, for ever associated in his mind with enjoyment and good fellowship, exerted a sympathetic attraction. Certainly no opportunity of either was neglected in a whirl that leaves even the reader of the Diary feeling a little fuddled. Party succeeded party in tavern and college, most notably in Magdalene where Pepys was sumptuously entertained by those very members of the governing body who had previously reproved his alcoholic excesses. There was one faintly ominous moment on the Sunday afternoon when he was called away from a comfortable fireside in Christ's by a message that Pearse was waiting for him at his inn 'who told us that he had lost his Journy, for my Lord was gone from Hinchingbrooke to London on Thursday last, at which I was a little put to a stand'. But only a little. Another drink restored the situation and the rest of the day was spent in heroic tippling.

Not that this seems to have blunted any of Pepys's usual faculties. He records the frequency with which the King's health was drunk; he is amused by the alacrity with which the grave and reverend signiors of his own college liquidated their Puritanism; he buys a book or two; he makes advances to the chambermaid. He rises without apparent discomfort at four o'clock on the Monday morning to ride back to London, breaking the journey at Saffron Walden to see round Audley End. His metabolism was clearly adjusted to hard drinking. In view of what lay before him it was perhaps as well that it should be so.

4

Restoration

———

Pepys arrived back in London on the Tuesday to find all the shops shut and one of the militia regiments in arms. A day of public thanksgiving for the return of Parliament had been ordered. Riding straight to St. Paul's he left a travelling companion to hold his horse while he went in to hear the preacher and to pick up the latest news. Only then did he return home to his wife and a change of clothes before going to pay his respects to Mountagu, who was most affable. A week later, as has been mentioned, Mountagu declared his readiness to underwrite Pepys's career and invited him to come aboard his flagship as his confidential secretary.

It was the prospect of the silken ladder lowered from the parapets of officialdom that excited Pepys. Next morning he heard of a legal opening in Westminster; and then it seemed there might be something falling vacant in the Exchequer. Pearse the surgeon reappeared with his Cheshire Cat-like ubiquity and 'gave me great encouragement to go to sea with my Lord'. And later that afternoon Pepys met his father, hotfoot from Cambridge, or rather from Brampton, the near-by village where his childless brother Robert, the diarist's uncle, had a small estate. This he had declared his intention of bequeathing to Samuel, no idle statement as according to Pepys *père* 'his leg [was] very dangerous and he doth believe he cannot continue in that condition long'. What was a life on the ocean wave compared to landed proprietorship and a snug place in the civil service? If things went on at this rate the future was assured.

Next day there were disturbing reports of the officers turning nasty and refusing to let in Charles Stuart. Monck asserted his authority and the rumbling died away. Still it was a warning. Pepys resolved to accept the sea secretaryship, the more readily because he had been told how easily he could make money by pocketing the wages of the servants to which the position would entitle him.[1] Two problems flowed from the decision: what to do about the clerkship in Downing's office, which was a personal, not an official position, and what was to happen to Elizabeth while her husband was at sea. The first was easily settled by providing a substitute and the second with rather more anxiety by arranging that she should go to live in the household of a senior Exchequer colleague near Iver.

Elizabeth was very much upset at this sudden disruption of their life together. She was much more dependent on him than he was on her. In what was still a man's world, she had no money, little education and no evident talents or interests to occupy her when she was on her own. Separation, for her, meant suspended animation, which it certainly did not for him. Even her youth and her beauty weighed against her because her husband, as mindful of his own proclivities as of her lack of sophistication, would prescribe a rural seclusion that he would never have tolerated for himself. It is characteristic of Pepys's view of their relationship that he should consult first Mountagu, who suggested the plan, and then his own father, who approved it, before saying a word to his wife. No wonder she was often pettish; and, treated as a child, behaved like one.

Pepys himself, still now in the springtime of their marriage, may have felt a stirring of sympathy, perhaps even a twinge of guilt. At any rate he does not censure her or confide to his Diary the exasperation he found it ever harder to check at such natural distress. But there is no disguising the fact that he was a selfish husband. As Dr. Latham has pointed out, *his* birthday is impressively celebrated in the Diary but *hers* is not even mentioned. There is a strong tincture of *A Doll's House* about the marriage. Cheerful and companionable as he was, Pepys could never take naturally to the idea of partnership or equality.

He was himself both agitated and exulting at the prospect opening before him. Hard drinker as he was at this stage of his life, he began to drink even harder, until sleepless nights and other symptoms warned him to take care. But once the decisions had been taken and accepted, his equilibrium was soon restored. Even a ride down to Iver in lashing rain with a nasty cold on the chest seems to have revived his spirits. And the news that his rival John Creed who had been Mountagu's secretary at the Sound was now to be made Deputy Treasurer of the Fleet acted as a powerful stimulant on his competitive nature. Creed was a man to be watched. He and his brother Richard, who had been Secretary to the great Blake,[2] had naval connections and experience far superior to Pepys's. Probably their social standing was higher too, since Creed was considered a suitable match for Mountagu's niece, herself the daughter of an important and well-connected Parliamentarian. For several years Pepys hob-nobbed with Creed without ever really liking him, fascinated by his cynicism and envying his craftiness. From start to finish he is seen as a competitor, and a dangerous one, in the great race of life. To have supplanted him in the secretaryship was one up to Pepys. There was no doubt about that, least of all in Creed's mind, as Pepys himself had heard at the Navy Office. But did this new appointment put the score level again? It was the kind of question that keyed Pepys up to his keenest and most alert.

What with packing his traps for sea, settling Elizabeth's departure, closing the house, making his will, briefing himself for his new responsibilities and (sweetest of all) engaging a boy and a clerk, supernumerary no doubt, to the shipborne servants whose wages were to be their sole *raison d'être*, Pepys had little time for jealousy or anxiety. In any case the shower of small bribes that had already begun to patter on him whispered delicious intimations of what might be in store. He was wined and dined and flattered and solicited. Best of all, Mountagu continued to distinguish him by marks of particular respect. Bad weather and floods delayed embarkation but at last on March 23rd Pepys and the rest of the Admiral's personal staff went abroad the *Swiftsure* lying at anchor in the river. 'As soon as my Lord on board, the guns went off bravely from the Ships; and a little while after comes the Vice-Admirall Lawson and seemed very respectful to my Lord, and so did the rest of the Commanders of the frigates that were thereabouts.' This was a great point gained. Mountagu had begun his naval career by superseding Lawson, a brave and popular commander, whose advanced Republican views had rendered him suspect to Cromwell and to Blake. Again only a few months earlier it had been Lawson's initiative in bringing the fleet into the river in support of the Rump that had checked the army leaders. Lawson's hold on the loyalty of his officers and men was undoubted. Why should he be content a second time to be passed over in favour of an officer whose professional qualifications were much inferior to his own and whose political inclinations were certainly not towards the left? If we knew the answer to that question we could perhaps explain why English political history has been so much less disastrous than anybody else's.

Pepys was very pleased with the cabin allotted to him. Any discomfort was more than compensated for by the fact that it was 'the best that any had that belonged to my Lord'. Indeed he could hardly believe the deference shown to him. In the great cabin at formal meals he took precedence over everyone except the Captain. And even the Captain went out of his way to distinguish the secretary with unheard-of marks of civility. He came to drink a bottle of wine with Pepys in his cabin to celebrate the hallowed anniversary of his lithotomy, staying till eleven o'clock at night 'which is a kindness he doth not usually do to the greatest officer in the ship'. A few days later after the Admiral had transferred his flag to his old ship the *Naseby* 'the Captain would by all means have me up to his cabin; and there treated me huge nobly, giving me a barrel of pickled oysters, and opened another for me, and a bottle of wine, which was a very great favour'. No wonder Pepys was charmed by the hospitality and comradeship of naval life. Even a day or two's seasickness when the fleet moved down to the mouth of the Thames hardly spoiled the fun – 'every day bringing me a fresh sense of the great pleasure of my present life'.

He got through a great deal of work, attacking it with the vigour, method and thoroughness that he was to apply throughout his professional life and increasingly to his personal affairs and intellectual pursuits. He records for the first time his pleasure in having cleared his mind by the efficient discharge of business. He had, at last, been given a job that took some doing and had found that he could do it easily. To the discovery of his own powers was added the approval of his superiors, the deference, the compliments, even the substantial *douceurs* of important people, and the infinite agreeableness of living in a well-mannered society. There were only two flaws in the perfection of existence: separation from Elizabeth and (occasional) reunion with Creed. Even these were only passing clouds. Creed had come aboard the *Swiftsure* the day after Pepys 'and dined very boldly with my Lord', but mercifully there was not an empty bed left on board. When the Admiral shifted into the *Naseby* Creed, not to be caught the same way twice, had had his things sent aboard beforehand but to Pepys's glee Mountagu's personal steward resented Creed's high-handedness and had him sent ashore.

The incessant comings and goings aboard the flagship made up both the business and the pleasure of life. Sailors are sociable people and the hospitality of the State's ships seems to have been worthy of the standards subsequently maintained by the Royal Navy. A large fleet at anchor keeps its boats' crews busy. Pepys dined on successive days with Lawson in the *London* and with Captain Clarke in the *Speaker*. Invitations such as these were a distinction indeed. And not a day went by but Lawson or Stayner, Mountagu's old colleague now appointed Rear-Admiral, or some of the senior captains came over for a conference and stayed for a meal and a private talk with the Admiral at which Pepys was often invited to remain. Some of the captains were suspected of dangerously Republican sympathies and were sent off out of harm's way to escort a convoy to the Straits. It was a situation that demanded the closest possible personal contact between the Commander-in-Chief and his captains. A division in the fleet would expose the country to incalculable risks. Whatever they did they must do together. And as the country waited for the new Parliament to meet it was overwhelmingly clear that a Stuart Restoration was the direction in which everything was moving. Even before Pepys left London the exultant inscription on the empty niche of Charles I's statue at the Royal Exchange *Exit tyrannus, regum ultimus* . . . had been painted out by a man who came with a ladder and a brush during working hours when the floor was buzzing with merchants and jobbers. Not only had no one questioned the man's authority but 'there was a great bonefire made in the Exchange and people cried out "God bless King Charles the Second"'. Ever since the fleet had moved down the river there had been a stream of Royalist agents and sympathisers coming aboard for passes or even for orders for passage in State's ships.

To spend one's days talking on terms of equality with the captains who had won the great victories of the Commonwealth against the Dutch and the Spaniards or receiving the respectful addresses of rich and important Royalists in need of a passport or a passage was to pass from the cinders of everyday life to the pumpkin coach and the glass slippers of fairyland. Pacing the quarterdeck under the stars with Captain Cuttance it was pleasant to be instructed in nautical terminology. And with all the bustle of business and the courtesies of social life there was still plenty of time for music and plenty of people, including Mountagu himself, who shared Pepys's enjoyment of it.

Those happy spring days aboard the *Naseby* breathe in the Diary the freshness of the season, the sharp tang of the sea air, above all the delight in being alive that makes Pepys like Falstaff a favourite in every age. They also introduce us to a number of the principal characters in his life. One of the very first to put in an appearance was Pearse the surgeon. Like Pepys he combined to an uncommon degree astuteness in promoting his own career with a conscientiousness in discharging his duty. He was to be one of that select circle, Sir John Narbrough the Admiral was another, of professional colleagues whom Pepys both respected and liked. All these men belonged to what was virtually a new social category — the expert permanently employed in Government service. It was appropriate that some of them should meet aboard the ship that was to be freighted with the new age.

Next day three figures from a past that was by no means dead and buried came over the side of the *Naseby*. Colonel George Thomson, the veteran whose wooden leg had taken him from the battlefield to the Parliamentary Commission of the Admiralty and Navy, was to infuriate Pepys by his pertinacious criticism of the Navy Board in the Second Dutch War. William Penn, who accompanied him, was to be even more of a menace. With Mountagu and Monck he was the only survivor of the seven Generals-at-Sea, and as a sea officer he outclassed them both. Neither, after all, could handle a ship, much less a fleet, without professional assistance. Penn could. It was Penn whose tactical brilliance had earned Blake's highest praise at the battle of the Kentish Knock, Penn whose bold initiative had rescued the great Admiral from a very tight corner at Portland. Worse still from the point of view of a competitor such as Mountagu he had long been suspected of Royalist sympathies and had been left unemployed for several years. Once the Restoration was assured he was a much more formidable rival than Lawson. How much Pepys feared his superiority is evident from the abuse heaped on him in the Diary during the years that they were colleagues at the Navy Office. The last of the trio Robert Blackborne held the post of Secretary to the Admiralty Committee and had an awkward, shy nephew, Will Hewer, who was to grow up into Pepys's right-hand man and closest friend.

Two days later appeared the bizarre figure who was to put Pepys's strong sense of family obligation to its longest and severest trial — Elizabeth's brother Balty. If Balthasar St. Michel had not existed only Dickens could have invented him. The character revealed in his letters to Pepys has much of the roseate irresponsibility of Mr. Micawber, much of the unctuous craftiness of Uriah Heep, but remains, like all the highest flights of imagination, unique and unmistakable. Strutting, protesting, wheedling, cadging, whining, once or twice, when the mask drops, snarling, Balty is always voluble, always larger than life, always, somehow, sham, as if his troubled spirit recognised that it had been classified under the wrong category. On this his first appearance as in so many subsequent ones he was in search of a job that would not depreciate his social pretensions. As his understandably irritated brother-in-law was to write when these applications were repeated a few weeks later, 'I perceive he stands upon a place for a gentleman that may not stain his family; when God help him, he wants bread.' Pepys who had only just got a toe-hold himself was embarrassed. What might not Balty do or say? What would the senior officers who had treated him so civilly think of him for bringing so strange a relation on board? And how was he to get rid of him without offending Elizabeth? Balty wanted to stay aboard the flagship as a Reformado, that is a supernumerary officer without regular duties, a terrifying prospect. The only hope of relief was an appeal to Mountagu who had, at dinner, shown his usual courtesy to his secretary's uninvited guest. Mountagu promised a letter recommending him as a Reformado to a Captain whom, a few days later, he confessed to disliking. Pepys breathed again and sent Balty early to bed in a cabin whose regular occupant was sleeping ashore.

Two days later the flagship sailed out of the river to join the fleet in the Downs. The weather turned rough and Pepys felt squeamish. But walking on deck and eating and drinking soon put him right. He was much pleased by his first sight of the French coast and perhaps even more by seeing Balty safely off the ship on his way to Deal and back to London with fifteen shillings for Elizabeth. It was now early April and the spring flowers of Royalist revival scented every breeze from shore. Mountagu was chosen M.P. for Weymouth and was offered the honour of representing the University of Cambridge. Even the news that Lambert had escaped from the Tower on April 10th, presumably to head a last stand against the restoration of the monarchy, hardly signified. The tide that Pepys had seen turn only a few weeks earlier was running now in overwhelming strength. By the 18th he had concluded 'that it is evident now that the Generall and Council do resolve to make way for the King's coming. And it is now clear that either the Fanatiques must now be undone, or the Gentry and citizens throughout England and clergy must fall, in spite of their Militia and army, which is not at all possible I think.' Events proved him right. On the 24th he heard that Lambert had been taken in Northamptonshire. The last guttering flame had been snuffed out.

On May Day the King was proclaimed in London amid scenes of rapture such as the Stuarts especially inspire in those separated from them by space or time. Two days later Pepys at the Council of War aboard the flagship read the King's letter to the assembled commanders who accepted the Restoration with markedly less enthusiasm than the sailors who were subsequently mustered on the quarterdeck to hear the same message. Perhaps the seamen recognised a welcome opportunity for plenty of free drink where their officers saw a threat to their own employment. Pepys anyhow enjoyed himself being rowed from ship to ship while the men cheered and the bullets hissed overhead from the flagship firing her salute. The days that followed were an ambrosial foretaste of the joys that Pepys was to find in an official career. Work was always at high pressure, letters to be drafted, orders to be sent off, commissions to be made out, either on the spot or against a tight deadline. And when work had been dispatched, social life succeeded at the same brisk pace. Oysters and wine and barrels of ale, songs and music and half-tipsy horseplay, ninepins and gossip and wearing a new fine cloth suit, here was every pleasure life could afford except the company of women and the enchantment of the stage. Most delectable of all was the consciousness of being on the inside: to be shown private letters from the King and the Duke of York, to hear Mountagu's private opinion of Monck 'but a thick-skulled fellow' and to know which of the important people around one were on the way up and which on the way down. And to be paid for all this, paid to enjoy oneself; surely the world had nothing more to offer except to prolong and to extend this state of affairs.

On May 12th the flagship weighed anchor, bound for The Hague where she was to embark the King and his brothers for England. On passage the tailors and painters set about changing the flags and other emblems from those of the Commonwealth to those of Charles II. Two royalists who came aboard from another ship told Pepys that his old employer Downing was in bad odour with the court and had been sent home in disgrace. This, as Pepys soon found out, was a mistaken report, but they had more accurate news of his old tutor at Magdalene, Samuel Morland, who had been knighted by the King that very week for his activities as a double agent in Thurloe's intelligence service.

On the 14th Pepys on waking looked out of the scuttle and saw the Dutch coast close to. In spite of the big sea that was tumbling the boats and soaking their occupants he was one of the first to obtain leave to go ashore in the afternoon. The weather was filthy: the landscape nothing but sand-dunes: and supper — for ten — consisted of a salad and two or three mutton bones. A traveller less resolved to admire might have growled: but Pepys was delighted with the neatness of the town, the civility of its inhabitants, the prettiness of the women. Returning on board next day he found that his old tutor, now Sir Samuel, had put in an appearance but had been treated with contempt by Mountagu and the other senior officers. Neither he nor Downing, soon, like him, to be knighted and to appear aboard the flagship, could even in that far from censorious age expect to be thought of as men of honour. It was one thing to change sides: public life could not go on if people did not. It was quite another to betray one's friends.

Preparations for the reception of the royal party were accelerated by the arrival of Peter Pett, the Commissioner of Chatham Dockyard, that rich administrative fief over which his dynasty had held sway since the time of

James I. Pepys and he were to wrestle many a fall without either securing a lock on the other. But for the moment all eyes were turned towards the King and his brother James, Duke of York, newly appointed Lord High Admiral.

Pepys, who had gone ashore with Mountagu's young son Edward, was introduced into the royal presence by the agency of a convivial royal chaplain whom he had met in an inn. He kissed the hands of both brothers and records his first impression: 'the King seems to be a very sober man'. The Chancellor, Hyde, later Earl of Clarendon, although in bed with the gout 'spoke very merrily to the child and me'. The merriment seems to have communicated itself to Pepys who, casting responsibility to the winds, spent the next three days in an alcoholic whirl of sightseeing and party-going, during the course of which he twice lost the child committed to his care. It was fortunate that Holland was the most orderly and civilised country in Europe even if the pubs were full of 'Duch boores eating of fish [in] a boorish manner'. Indeed it was the boy's zest for seeing the country that caused these anxious separations. On the first occasion he accompanied a party to Delft, where Pepys pursued him and met him on the road. On the second he disappeared, leaving no message, so that Pepys, looking out of a picture dealer's shop at The Hague next day was not a little relieved to see his young charge among a crowd of passengers landing on the quay at which the Leiden boat had just made fast. Twice was enough. Pepys made sure of his child-minding arrangements that evening before going out with friends in search of nocturnal sport.

What did the young Pepys, already an inveterate book-buyer and soon to be a patron of artists and a collector of prints, make of his first visit to the Holland of Rembrandt and Ruisdael, of Steen and Van der Velde, the centre not only of living artists but of the fine art trade as it had long been of publishing and bookselling? He bought two or three books 'for the love of the binding', he went to picture dealers and visited famous rooms in famous houses where famous paintings were hanging, but he does not describe them or name the painters. On his visit to Delft he is much struck with the realism of a sea-battle carved on Van Tromp's monument but says nothing of the paintings of Vermeer. What really takes his fancy are the echoes artfully achieved in various great houses which he tests by singing or playing the flageolet: or the *faits divers* with which guides have regaled tourists from the dawn of the industry, such as the story of the lady whose stinginess was punished by a pregnancy terminating in the birth of 365 children. Pepys's artistic taste like his genius was an addition to, not a substitute for, the curiosity and susceptibility of everyman. Appetite preceded and subsequently accompanied discrimination: he was *gourmand* before he was *gourmet*. And at all stages of his life he was a chameleon. Had he been travelling with John Evelyn, whom he had not yet met, we should have a very different story. His company on this occasion, apart from Master Edward Mountagu and Will Howe, the steward from Hinchingbrooke, consisted of shipmates ashore, chance encounters in inns, odd acquaintances from Cambridge or London who were heading the goldrush for jobs under the new Government. Conducted tours, hearty jokes, tippling and titillation filled a round of pleasure which Pepys could enjoy to the utmost.

Blearily he scrambled back aboard the *Naseby* with a hangover such that he slept the clock round 'and rising to piss, mistook the sun-rising for the sun-setting on Sunday night'. He therefore returned to bed and slept for a further five hours until woken by the Captain's boy with a present of four barrels of Breton oysters, sent by another captain who desired his favour. Luckily there was a lull in the work to be done, since Mountagu thought it tactful to defer all to the new Lord High Admiral, who was expected on board directly. On May 22nd late in the forenoon James and his brother the young Duke of Gloucester were received with a general salute. After they had been shown over the ship 'upon the Quarter Deck table under the awning the Duke of Yorke and my Lord, Mr Coventree and I spent an houre at allotting to every ship their service in their return to England'.

One day, says a Latin quotation familiar to Pepys, contains the whole of life. That hour on the quarter-deck contains the best part of his. Here joined together for the first time in the conduct of naval affairs were the men who through nearly thirty years constituted the directing intelligence of the service, planning, administering, commanding. With these three Pepys was to rise and, at last, with James, the sole survivor, to fall. Their opinion was the constellation by which he shaped the course of his life. All of them were by social and political position so far superior to Pepys that his relationship to them, even when he had long been accepted as an intimate and indispensable colleague, could never be hurt by the violent competitiveness of his nature. James, as a royal duke and later king, belonged to a species still generally accorded more divinity than it claimed: even Pepys after years of day-to-day contact with the royal family still recorded his amazement at the King's being a man like other men. Such a divinity was, as in the ancient world, perfectly compatible with lechery, frivolity and idleness. But Coventry and Mountagu, aristocrats who were at home in court or camp, were in Pepys's mind always mortals, even if mortals of a higher order. As such they could properly be taken as models in habits, manners, opinions and taste. And it was William Coventry, in this inconspicuous entry dwarfed by James's height and Mountagu's bulk, who was to have far the deepest influence on Pepys's mind and character.

The principals are completed by the entrance of the King, amid the huzzas of the whole cast. The *Naseby*, now renamed the *Royal Charles*, weighed anchor and sailed on a fresh breeze for England. The pleasant weather encouraged the King in two favourite activities that his courtiers were to find penitential: walking up and down (he was a tall man and walked fast) and telling the story of his adventures as a hunted man after the battle of Worcester. Pepys was entranced. He loved a good story (and it is one of the best in English history); he had too the yearning for first-hand evidence that turns a man into a historian, an activity to which both Coventry and Evelyn were later to urge him and which he recognised to 'sort mightily with my genius'. Twenty years later he took down in shorthand the full account that the King dictated to him while at Newmarket for the races. This he supplemented with other narratives of those who took part, some of whom he further questioned about discrepancies and gaps in the various sources to which he had access. So the grave and reverend Pepys of the Kneller portrait and the Cavalier medallion sustains the curiosity and imaginative sympathy of his younger self.

So the voyage passed, a Watteau-esque voyage to Cythera, the decks paced by persons of honour, the weather glorious, the conversation smart. On May 25th, two days after setting sail, the King landed at Dover amidst scenes of rejoicing that defeat even Pepys's vivid powers of description. From there he went on to Canterbury and London while Pepys and Mountagu returned to their ship: 'My Lord almost transported with joy that he hath done all this without any the least blur and obstruccion in the world that would give an offence to any, and with the great Honour that he thought it would be to him.'

And well he might be. As a Commander-in-Chief, as a politician, as a courtier and *chef de protocol* in an age that took these minutiae with maniac seriousness, he had not put a foot wrong. After so long a winning run it was time to cash the chips. Pepys, too, by the terms of that memorable conversation in the garden, stood to collect a share of the winnings. Even before the King had left, largesse had been distributed on no contemptible scale. One way and another Pepys had managed to put by as much in the two months of his secretaryship as he had in the preceding five or six years. But what both he and his patron wanted, at different levels, was office. Discussing the future in the Admiral's cabin Mountagu was reassuring: 'We must have a little patience and we will rise together. In the meantime I will do you all the good Jobbs I can.' It all looked hopeful. And on the very day that the King landed the Duke of York had spoken to Pepys by name and had promised his future favour.

It was thus natural that Pepys should see in the rewarding of his patron some indication of what might be in store for him. By the first post Mountagu received an earldom: by the second the far rarer honour of the Garter. What might not be had for the asking if only master and man were at Whitehall? But Mountagu was a serving officer and could not leave his post until ordered. At last after dinner on June 7th the longed for summons arrived. Early the next morning Pepys took horse at Deal, dined at Canterbury and went round the Cathedral, resumed his journey by Sittingbourne and Chatham and Rochester to Gravesend, dismounting hot and tired, but not too tired to kiss 'a good handsome wench, . . . the first that I have seen a great while', nor to stay up late drinking huge quantities of beer with a naval captain. Next morning the whole party travelled to London in six boats. Although it was a Saturday and about midday when they disembarked at the Temple stairs, Pepys spent the whole of the afternoon and evening in attendance on Mountagu, accompanying him to Whitehall to wait upon the King. He slept at his father's house still not having seen Elizabeth from whom he had been parted for nearly three months. In the morning he again went first to Mountagu's lodging and after that to church. Only when he returned to his father's house for dinner was he reunited with his wife. In the afternoon they went for a walk by themselves in the grounds of Lincoln's Inn. For all the public boisterousness and the drinking of loyal toasts, for all the gallantry which Pepys records in his Diary after each visit to Court, the Restoration was for him a time of tension. A great opportunity might offer itself at any moment and might, if he were not vigilant to seize it, slip away never to recur.

That Mountagu's star was still rising no one could doubt. Within a week he was given one of the most important and supposedly one of the most lucrative household offices, the Mastership of the Great Wardrobe. The post carried with it a large house and a large establishment: besides these there would be contracts for clothes, robes of state, hangings and such like that could yield handsome fees and commissions. Even during the first few days back in London people were constantly pressing sums into Pepys's hand either to secure his recommendation to Mountagu's favour or to repay him for having forwarded their business when he was Admiral's secretary at sea. How was this happy state of affairs to be put on a permanent footing? This is the thought that hammers through the June entries in the Diary, drowning the raptures of reunion with Elizabeth (though he did find the night she went to Buckinghamshire to collect her things 'very lonely') and confining to one terse phrase the heartfelt relief of returning home to their little house in Axe Yard.

In fact Mountagu could hardly have acted quicker or more effectively. On the 18th he told Pepys 'that he did look after the place of the Clerk of the Acts for me'. Pepys makes no comment. Yet it was one of the four senior posts in the administration of the navy, and probably the only one to which a young man who was neither an expert nor an aristocrat could aspire. On the 23rd he told him that he had obtained the promise of the place 'at which I was glad'. Indeed from that moment it dominated his consciousness. On the 25th he asked and received William Coventry's promise of assistance. On the same day he had a civil meeting with a Mr. Turner of the Navy Office who was a rival candidate for the job, supported, it seems, by Monck, who had asked Mountagu to give way.[3] Mountagu refused in crisp terms. Next day a merchant offered Pepys £500 to withdraw his candidature. Pepys prayed for divine guidance. On the following day Mountagu and Pepys went to see the Duke of York who as Lord High Admiral ordered William Coventry 'to despatch my business of the Acts, in which place everybody gives me joy as if I were already in it, which God send'. (Presumably he had advised against accepting the £500.) On the 29th Pepys secured his warrant for the place from the Duke of York – the first obstacle in the bureaucratic assault course. But that same afternoon a friend in the Admiralty told him 'that Mr Barlow my Predecessor, Clerk of the Acts, is yet alive and coming up to town to look after his place – which made my heart sad a little'. And well it might. But the imperturbable Mountagu informed of this the same evening told Pepys to make sure of his patent – the final stage in the administrative process initiated by the warrant – 'and he would do all that could be done to keep him out'.

How Pepys struggled over the nightmarish barriers erected by the capricious and extortionate freeholders in public administration, that happy band of licensed highwaymen whom he most ardently wished to join, has been so well told by Sir Arthur Bryant and can be so fully reconstructed from the Diary itself that no further account is necessary. Offstage the infirm but inexorable steps of old Barlow totter menacingly nearer while the distraught Pepys rushes up and down Chancery Lane to find an engrossing clerk, pulls every string to have his warrant turned into a bill and the bill into a patent, until, after a fortnight of frenzy, punctuated by hard bargaining with his rivals and consoled by reports of Barlow's age, ill-health and disinclination to resume the life of a civil servant, the patent is, on July 13th, signed and sealed by the Lord Chancellor himself. It only remained to negotiate a financial arrangement with Barlow in exchange for his renouncing all future claims. This was easily and amicably achieved. Barlow turned out to be a nice old man who obligingly died five years later without having caused any further trouble. Pepys was in.

5

The Navy Board

Only a few weeks before his appointment Pepys had known very little about the Navy Office. He had, as he records, seriously considered accepting a lump sum of a few hundred pounds to abandon his pursuit of the Clerkship there. Yet the pride with which Pepys presented his wife with the patent certifying his appointment and the joy with which she received it still glow in the Diary. Why had he warmed so suddenly to what was to be his life's work? What was the Navy Office? Who were its other members and what was its standing in the hierarchy of Government? What was the pay? What were the opportunities of supplementing it by open or furtive corruption?

Pepys did not yet know the full answers to these questions on July 13th, 1660, the date of his patent, but he knew quite enough to justify his enthusiasm. He had, in the first place, discovered that the Navy Office in Seething Lane, north-west of the Tower of London, contained handsome private houses for its four Principal Officers of whom the Clerk of the Acts was one. A man who lived in such a house maintained at the public charge would belong to a different world from that of Axe Yard. And evidently a Government department which accommodated its chief servants in such grandeur must be a very important department indeed. This had been confirmed by experience only the previous week. Pepys had been approached by a man who wanted to buy a place as one of his assistants. Assistant clerks in Government offices made their living by charging private individuals fees for the transaction of public business. The cost of a place was thus an excellent indicator of the level of activity. Pepys named £100, a very large sum in such a context. On the same day he had discovered that the salaries of all the Principal Officers were to be substantially increased. The Clerk of the Acts went up from £182 p.a. to £350. The others, the Surveyor, the Comptroller and the Treasurer, already higher were raised in the same generous proportion. Indeed the Treasurership at £2,000 p.a. became one of the best-paid posts in the public service. And like their assistants these senior officials stood to make even larger sums out of the glorified system of tips that traditionally stimulated the discharge of their functions.

Were these functions really proportionate to their rewards? Surely old Barlow even in his palmiest days had never cut much of a figure in the service of his country? True. But the navy Barlow had known was the old navy of the Tudors, dwindling by his time into the decrepitude of James I and Charles I. The navy Pepys was heir to was the large, modern, well-found force that had, arguably, won the Civil War for the Parliament and had, beyond any possible dispute, taught the proudest nations of Europe to treat Cromwell with respect. If such a fleet was to be kept in being the Navy Office would be the largest spending department of all. And everything pointed to that intention. Sandwich (as Pepys's patron Mountagu had now become) was an aggressive partisan of overseas expansion. Monck believed in foreign war as the sovereign remedy for disunity at home. The city wanted a strong navy to protect its growing merchant fleet from the piracy of the North African ports and to check the lawlessness of the European powers. There was even a more hawkish element that wanted the Dutch dealt with once and for all. The new navy was beginning to look indispensable.

The Navy Board as an administrative institution was both old and new. Old in that it could show a pedigree of continuing existence from Henry VIII to the Civil War and could plausibly trace an even more distant ancestry to the medieval Clerk of the King's Ships. New in that Charles II in reconstituting the Board after the twenty years of Parliamentary and Protectoral interlopers known as Navy Commissioners had improved not only the pay but the status and the calibre of its members. Pepys, though he would never have admitted it once he had shaken down into his clerkship, had joined a strong team.

The Treasurer, Sir George Carteret, was one of the best qualified men ever to have held that office. After long and varied service as a sea-officer he had joined the board as Comptroller five years before the outbreak of the Civil War. During the war he had reconquered his native island of Jersey for the King and had used it as a base for a privateering fleet which he organised and commanded with notable success. Such was the skill and resolution with which he defended the place when all else was lost that it was not until December 1651, more than three years after the end of the Second Civil War, that Blake at last compelled him to capitulate. Both Charles II and Clarendon had been sheltered by him when every man's hand was against them so that in the shifting sands of the Court no man's position was more firmly founded than his. Such a combination of proved efficiency as a sea-officer, as a naval administrator and as an independent Commander would have been remarkable enough without the special access to the King and the Chancellor that his past services had won him. It was reinforced by a passion for hard work that made little allowance for the susceptibilities of colleagues and none, as even his enemies admitted, for his own ease and pleasure.

The Comptroller, Sir Robert Slyngsbie, was another old Cavalier of high professional competence. Born into the navy (his father had been Comptroller) his sea service was even longer than Carteret's, but unlike Carteret he knew how to enjoy himself. Pepys found him the most congenial of his colleagues and was much distressed by his premature death in the autumn of 1661. Both the old Royalist and the young clerk wanted to institute radical reform in the navy and both chose a historical and comparative approach. Slyngsbie's *Discourse upon the past and present state of his Majesty's navy* states briefly and well many of the criticisms and proposals that Pepys was to spend the better part of his life in pressing. Their natures had marked affinities, including the vanity proper to an author. Turning over the sheets of the *Discourse* Pepys recorded in the Diary that 'he doth seem to have too good an opinion of them himself'. Slyngsbie's successor, Sir John Mennes, who had an even longer record of command at sea, was something of a man of letters and good company over a bottle of wine. But of his work he had no grasp at all.

The Surveyor of the Navy, Sir William Batten, was an old seaman of a very different type. Carteret, Slyngsbie and Mennes had been made sea officers as Gentlemen, Batten as a Tarpaulin. This distinction, differently phrased and variously interpreted, can be discerned at every stage of naval history from the remotest beginnings to the days of Queen Victoria. Its explanation lies in the fact that sailing a ship and fighting a battle are two different sorts of activity for which English society could supply two different sorts of men. Sailing was a skilled trade: fighting, or at any rate leading men into battle, was supposed to be the function of the aristocracy. In the Middle Ages when the art of sea warfare consisted in grappling the enemy ship and fighting it out hand to hand the military facts bore some crude relation to this social analysis. The seamen manoeuvred the ship alongside and the soldiers did the rest. But even then the division of labour was not quite so neatly defined. The sailors could hardly stand aside as neutrals or non-combatants since horrid experience taught them that the vanquished, unless rich enough to be worth a personal ransom, would all be butchered in cold blood. From its origins, then, the distinction was easier to maintain in theory than in practice. With the coming of the great gun and the almost coincident development in sail-plans and rigging, even the theoretical basis was largely knocked away. A naval ship became a special kind of ship designed exclusively for fighting other ships (by means of guns carried on her broadside) and the art of handling her became a skill of its own, drawing on but distinct from the arts of the navigator, the seaman, the gunner and the soldier. We can see this through the long perspective of hindsight. Pepys and a few others had the penetration and the insight to grasp it against the received ideas of their time. The Gentlemen versus the Tarpaulins was an antithesis that was to occupy his mind one way and another for most of his official life. It is a topic which must be enlarged later in this book. But though it has burst in unannounced in the person of Sir William Batten it must not be allowed to obscure him.

Batten, as Pepys never tires of making clear, was not a gentleman. But in knowledge of ships and in experience of sailing them in peace and war, above all in the variety, duration and extent of his experience of command he outranged even such formidable competitors as Carteret and Slyngsbie. And beyond that he was easily at home in territory where they could not follow. Batten had been bred to the sea. His father had been a master, that title, far older than captain, which designated the officer responsible for navigation and sailing.

'Very well, sir, very well. You have done your duty by making this remonstrance. Now pray let me do mine by laying me alongside the French admiral.' Hawke's reply* to his master who had demurred at taking the fleet among the reefs and shoals of Quiberon Bay in the fading light of a November afternoon with a gale rising from seaward is the classic definition of responsibility between the military caste (admiral, captain and lieutenant) and the civilian (master, boatswain and mate).

---

* Hawke's latest biographer (R. F. Mackay, *Admiral Hawke*, Oxford: Clarendon Press, 1965) concludes that the story is apocryphal. Accepting his arguments, I have therefore not felt obliged to follow either of the two variants he prints, since there can be no authority for a remark that was never made. The historicity of the incident is of course irrelevant to the point it illustrates.

Batten knew everything a seaman knew: and he had himself made the transition to military status by obtaining letters of marque, that is legal protection for privateering, when in command of a whaler. The extent of his success must be judged by his appointment in 1638 as Surveyor of the Navy against hot competition from a number of well-placed courtiers. It was confirmed by Warwick's retention of him as Vice-Admiral of the Parliamentary fleet throughout the Civil War. When in 1648 he was replaced by Colonel Rainborough half the ships revolted and sailed over to Holland to join the Royalists in exile. Here Batten had joined them with a privateer, reputed the fastest sailer of her day, in which he owned a substantial share. The true-blue Royalists however neither liked nor trusted him. There were mutters about taking bribes from the London merchants to let their ships go free instead of carrying them into continental ports as prize-of-war. It was remembered that Batten's squadron had forced the Queen to take cover in a ditch after he had chased her into Bridlington Bay and had opened fire on the military cargo she had landed for her husband's army. Compromised with both sides Batten took advantage of an amnesty to return to England, restoring his fine frigate to the Commonwealth in exchange for his freedom as a private citizen.

The hard life aboard a whaler or a man of war had by no means blunted Batten's appreciation of the comforts and pleasures of life. Pepys, who was often censured by himself and others for his love of luxury, speaks of his living 'like a prince' at his country house at Walthamstow. He was certainly a very rich man, avaricious and corrupt even by the unexacting standards of his day. His meanness in defrauding the seamen of what little pitiable provision had been made for them against sickness and poverty is odious in an old sailor.[1] But he had been brought up in a hard school that left compassion and justice to those who could afford them.

The Treasurer, the Comptroller, the Surveyor and the Clerk:* these are the historic four Principal Officers of the navy. But Charles II's board was strengthened by Commissioners whose authority was no less and whose influence was greater than that of the traditional quartet. During the years that Pepys was learning the business of the office it was dominated by two men of very different backgrounds and very different professional abilities, Sir William Penn and Sir William Coventry. Both men have, briefly, appeared in this biography: both will be familiar to all who have read the Diary: Coventry as the pattern of a brilliant and well-bred public servant, high-minded, witty, informed, lucid and incisive, Penn as the almost direct antithesis, low, crafty, lumpish and

---

* 'Of the Acts' simply means that he recorded what was done at the Board: what we should now call a Secretary.

absurd. If the portrait of Coventry is a little heightened by hero worship that of Penn hardly reaches the level of caricature. It seems odd that Pepys's vision, as revealed to us in the Diary, is so distorted. It is even odder, on a close reading, that Coventry, the shrewd superintelligence on whom no one could impose, should give no sign of being aware how worthless and wicked Penn was. Pepys of course is writing a diary, not giving sworn evidence before the bar of history. He can there purge his mind of fear and jealousy, he can let his prejudices rip, he can abandon himself to the delights of unreason without hurting himself or anybody else.

But it is the function of reason, if it can, to unravel the irrational. Why did Pepys come to hold such violent opinions about Penn who, on the clear evidence of the Diary itself, went out of his way to make himself agreeable to a junior whose cocksure and aggressive behaviour must often have been trying? Penn's whole record shows him to have been a firm disciplinarian but an easygoing, perhaps too easygoing, colleague. If he had been a little sharper to the valetudinarian Venables with whom he had been joined in command of the expedition against Hispaniola both his own career and Cromwell's imperial policy might have benefited. If he had been less self-effacing the credit for the great English victory off Lowestoft in 1665 would have been given to him rather than to the Duke of York. But Pepys, as the years went by, became bitterer and bitterer, his scurrility verging at times on the hysterical. What lies behind this?

Jealousy. Rivalry. Or rather a double rivalry. Pepys was a member of the Navy Board because Lord Sandwich had put him there. But both Penn and Coventry represented a grave threat to Sandwich's naval influence. Sandwich's claim to power and office and all that went with it was that he was a Cromwellian General-at-Sea who had seen the light in 1659. But Penn was an infinitely more distinguished naval commander, also an ex-General-at-Sea, who, it was generally believed, had seen the light a lot earlier. Penn was therefore a potential rival to Sandwich, and thus at one remove to Pepys. In addition as a colleague at the same board, as a neighbour in a Navy Office house, sharing the Navy Office garden and the Navy Office pew at St. Olave's Hart Street, he was a direct competitor: a competitor for power, for patronage, for perquisites. And a competitor, a dangerously well-equipped competitor, for the good opinion of William Coventry.

For Coventry too was no friend of Sandwich's. He had fought for the King in the Civil War: he was detested by Clarendon, the great minister with whom Sandwich had close political relations: and, worst of all, he was the steady advocate of the personal and professional merits of Sir

William Penn. Pepys's relations with Coventry, the burgeoning love of one born administrator for another, the ardent courtship, the bliss of requited professional respect, nourished his genius. But Penn, blackened in the pages on which Coventry glistens, is no less important to the understanding of Pepys.

Penn, like Batten under whose command he had served at sea during the Civil War, was a tarpaulin inasmuch as he was a seaman born and bred. The son of a Bristol merchant who traded to the Mediterranean in his own ships, he belonged like Blake to a class that would have been reckoned certainly superior to Batten's and perhaps to Pepys's. As a fighting sailor and a fleet commander his record was unrivalled. As a young captain in the Civil War he had matched seamanship with the military qualities of boldness and initiative in the conduct of combined operations in Ireland. His share in Blake's great victories over the Dutch has already been indicated. And the credit for snatching the valuable prize of Jamaica from the fiasco of the expedition against Hispaniola belonged to him. Carteret, Slyngsbie and Batten were veteran sea officers as well as naval administrators but none of them had commanded a squadron in a fleet action or knew what the Dutch meant when they attributed the English victories in the recent war to their tactics of fighting in line. Penn was the only man who had and did and could do it again.

These considerations were clear to the King and to the Duke of York both of whom have been allowed by their harshest critics to be outstanding judges of naval affairs. They must also have been clear to Pepys. Yet to run the eye over the index entries under Penn, Sir William, in Wheatley's edition of the Diary is to see accusations of knavery, deceit, cheating and cowardice leaping from the page. Pepys could not bear a rival. Even in his Diary where he opens his mind and scrutinises his conscience with a candour that hurt his self-esteem, the antennae retract. The shell clamps shut at the approach of a possible competitor. It is a reflex anterior to any intellectual process, an animal instinct of fear and self-preservation. The acute powers of analysis, the detachment, the observation that make Pepys's mind perpetually refreshing are drowned under a dark rushing torrent of cheapness and silliness and plain untruth. Can he really have believed, as he implies as late as 1667, that Penn's whole career from first to last was maintained by bribing a clerk at the Navy Board who was junior to them both? It is difficult to escape the conclusion that when Pepys is agitated by jealousy he can convince himself of anything. He lets his will cook accounts that only the mind can audit.

The Navy Board that Pepys attended for the first time at the beginning of July 1660 was a body of men much older, tougher, and in every point except native genius more formidable than himself. Yet it is characteristic that he never for an instant seems to have felt out of his depth. What these grizzled veterans thought of their soft rather overdressed young colleague can, to some extent, be inferred from the Diary. All of them except perhaps Carteret understood the proper use of conviviality. Slyngsbie was from the first the easiest and most congenial, but there are other cheerful scenes in the early months of the new board's existence in which the unsteady figures of the young clerk and the two old Parliamentarian commanders can be discerned giving that support that the one ought to have of the other as they return from an evening's tippling. But as day by day they take decisions, award contracts, grant requests, make appoint-ments, the occasions of conflict multiply. At first Pepys hardly knows enough to have a point of view. He watches, he listens, he records. But not for long. Soon, indeed, the very Navy Board itself is too narrow a compass for the full exercise of his administrative talent. The project outlined over dinner by the Lord Chamberlain's secretary 'for all us Secretaries to join together and get money by bringing all business into our hands'2 might appear over-ambitious but it had the root of the matter in it. Within a month Pepys added to his new appointment the favour of acting as Sandwich's deputy as a Clerk of the Privy Council. Clerks took it in turn to do a month's duty at the Privy Seal Office, a mere administra-tive tollgate that yielded quick and easy money. Delightful as this was it offered no scope for the exercise of intelligence or curiosity. After a couple of years Pepys gratefully abandoned it (for various reasons it had anyhow become less profitable). But in 1665 he added two new provinces to his administrative empire: the Treasurership of the Tangier Commis-sion and the Surveyorship of the navy's victualling. Each of these by itself would have been enough for a man of energy and professional skill. To combine them with the work of the Navy Board at the very moment when the country had embarked on a war with the greatest naval power in Europe is a dumbfounding display of self-confidence and of appetite for business.

The distinction between the work of the Navy Board and the duties of the Lord High Admiral corresponds pretty well to that between Tarpaulin and Gentleman. It was the Navy Board's business to provide the ships and everything that was needed to sail them, spars, masts, cordage, sails, flags, anchors, and the whole range of ships' stores together with the experts who knew how to use them, master, boatswain, carpenter, cook, gunner and purser. It was left to the Lord High Admiral to recruit, appoint and promote the officers, to issue instructions as to tactics and discipline and to advise the Government on the use of the navy as an instrument of policy. It was difficult for a Lord High Admiral even for so lordly and high a fighting admiral as James, Duke of York, to discharge so many and such complicated functions, which is why the office has since his time been almost continuously delegated to a Commission of Lords of the Admiralty. But before that was done it was natural that he should lean very heavily on the exceptionally strong Navy Board that his brother had appointed, and therefore natural that a Navy Board officer should become familiar with what was strictly Admiralty business. And since the Duke's secretary, Sir William Coventry, was also a member of the Navy Board it was inevitable that Pepys should form the habit of looking at a proposed course of action as a man informed by the views of experts and by the practice of the department rather than limited by them.

Pepys soon came to have still grander visions of naval administration. Even if, some day, he were to control both the Admiralty and the Navy Board there were matters still more essential to sea-power that would lie outside his authority. Where were the men to come from? Who was to be responsible for feeding them? Or taking care of them if they were wounded or fell ill? What about the guns and powder and shot? And where was the money to pay for all this? This last question remained unanswered. Public finance was unsophisticated: public honour was not exemplary. Experience taught that if people were left unpaid they would in time die. Those who like Pepys could not bear untidiness and preferred to be honest were disturbed by this state of affairs and, intermittently, cogitated possible remedies.

The question of pay was the root of the question of manning. Men were unwilling to serve, and this in an age when unemployment was always high and starvation never remote, because they had good reason to believe that they would be cheated of their wages. The provision of funds was for the King and Parliament to settle. Part of Pepys's job at the Navy Office was to brief his Parliamentary colleagues – Coventry, Carteret, Penn and Batten were all M.P.s – when they were trying to obtain more money from the House or to defend themselves from uncomfortable inquiries as to what they had done with what had already been granted. But financially the main concern of the office was in making payments, or, more often, failing to make them. When a ship was to be paid off one or more of the Board had to be present. When there was no money, or not enough, to pay the seamen's wages, tickets were issued which were in theory redeemable in cash at the Navy Office. Brokers bought up the tickets at a heavy discount and, knowing their way about, made large profits. Starving seamen who knew their rights and nothing else sometimes besieged the office or attacked the prosperous-looking officials. Of those requiring payment the seamen were only one class, and in some ways the easiest to manage. They could as a last resort be kept at sea. The workmen in the dockyards could not be conjured away so painlessly. And the merchants who supplied the timber and the hemp, the tar and the sail-cloth, were reluctant to supply goods on credit until their past accounts had been settled. Round the neck of Charles II's navy hung the huge debt incurred under the Commonwealth.

Manning was a problem for which the Navy Board shared responsi-bility with a number of other bodies, local government officials for instance, or even more the sea officers in the ships. But the other questions raised two or three pages back did not, in July 1660, come within the purview of the Navy Office at all. Guns and powder and shot were the responsibility of the Ordnance Board. Feeding the seamen was the province of the Victualler. Looking after the wounded was nobody's business, once a man had been discharged from his ship. To all these matters Pepys was, with varying success, to address himself. From the first day of his connection with the navy the searching, generalising scientific bent of his mind disposed him to acquire information pell-mell, to elicit principles of efficiency and to embody these in a scheme of administrative reform. The wide-ranging curiosity, the need to impose order and the instinct for business run through and through Pepys from young manhood to old age. Like Luther he could no other. 'Would to God,' he wrote to Coventry on August 22nd, 1662, 'you could for a while spare two after-noons a week for generall debates; . . . Contracts . . . ye many old Rates to be enquired into, Tickets. . . . regulating ye slopsellers practices with forty more scandalous errors . . .'[3]

Coventry was in all these matters his ally and his pattern. Of the three men who dominated his life Sandwich raised him, Coventry formed him and Evelyn refined him. It was the cutting edge of Coventry's mind, the wit, the clarity, the force that captivated Pepys and that still retains the power to delight. What a colleague to find on a committee, incapable apparently of being dull, devious, timid or obtuse. How accurately and gracefully he says what he has to say and how perfectly the swift unstudied beauty of his hand conveys the character of the writer. That he talked as well as he wrote, the Diary abundantly confirms: 'very good discourse . . . most excellent discourse . . . in short I find him the most ingenuous person I ever found in my life'.[4] And as a man of business in Pepys's considered judgment: 'the best Minister of State the King hath'[5] leaves nothing more to be said. That Coventry also thought highly of Pepys we are left in no doubt. His words as reported by Sandwich 'that I was indeed the life of this office'[6] are happily chosen: and ten years later Coventry wrote to his nephew who had just succeeded to his own old post of Secretary to the Lord High Admiral 'you may receive more help and learn more of the Navy affairs from him than from any man living'. Pepys was so pleased by this compliment that he began to copy the letter that contains it in his own hand.[7]

Coventry did not join the Navy Board until Pepys had been there for two years. But from the first as Secretary to the Lord High Admiral he bulked large in the affairs of the navy. Alone of all the senior officials he had a policy and the qualities needed both to articulate it and to carry it out. He believed that England must have a large permanent navy and that she could afford it if only she would abandon slapdash methods of administration and finance. In support of such a policy he was willing to forego the handsome sums that officials such as he received by way of presents for each appointment they made. The sale of places, as it was called, was corrupt in principle and corrupted the service by example. Since he could not in the event induce his colleagues to abolish the practice he did in fact accept and profit by it. But of the sincerity of his desire to end it as of his personal honour there seems no doubt. Like Evelyn but unlike Sandwich he was against graft.

All this strongly appealed to Pepys. His mind recognised the force of Coventry's arguments; his conscience, well developed by his Puritan upbringing, swelled within him; his passion for order pressed him forward. But there were inhibitions. Bribes, presents, call them what you will, are pleasant things to an impecunious young man with an appetite for enjoyment. Deliberate dishonesty such as charging for goods that had never been supplied or claiming pay and allowances for people who had never existed was one thing. But when an officer whom one had helped to advance – on grounds of merit naturally – showed his appreciation by a gift of money or plate was there anything wrong in accepting it? Or put the case that a merchant had tendered for better quality masts beneath the going rate, should the King be denied the advantage of a contract with him just because the generous fellow had presented the Clerk of the Acts with forty gold pieces in a glove? Readers of the Diary will recognise the tune. Even in moral questions Pepys instinctively favoured a commercial approach. He was, in most cases, ready to do a deal. Treachery, disloyalty, cringing were unthinkable. But everything else was relative and therefore up to a point negotiable.

One enriching influence of Pepys's work at the Navy Board was that it brought him into close and regular contact with the great London merchants. Determined to know his job thoroughly he soon started inves-

tigating the markets and methods of production and supply of the principal commodities needed by the navy. Hob-nobbing with hemp importers,
mast contractors, canvas merchants and the like he learned the price structure of half a dozen trades. He also made some profitable contacts and
some true friends. These, perhaps, were the men with whom he was most
at home: cultivated citizens of the world, citizens not aristocrats, men
who carried their urbanity even into their country retirements. It is
hardly too much to say that Pepys saw in them the highest type of civilisation, a dislike of force, a tolerance, a range of curiosity and a well-
proportioned, high-minded worldliness that answered to his own most
characteristic aspirations. Such were the Houblon family, Flemish
refugees with extensive interests in the Mediterranean trade, and such was
Thomas Hill, the music-loving Lisbon merchant whose portrait hangs in
the Pepys Library.

Sir William Coventry however held firm views about merchants.
Pepys hankered after injecting brisk and businesslike habits into the
unsystematic and discursive transactions of his colleagues. But Coventry
would have none of it. When in November 1664 it was decided to
strengthen the Navy Board by the appointment of another Commissioner
the choice lay between Lord Brouncker, the mathematician and first
President of the Royal Society, and Sir William Rider, the great hemp
merchant. In a letter to Pepys telling him that Brouncker had been chosen
Coventry wrote:

My Lord Brunkard is a very ingenious and honest person and I hope
may bee usefull. Sir William Rider is able but a Merchant, and if the
Merchants come in to rob the office of its reputation I am sure they
shall take the burthen of it alsoe, and I will content myselfe to act as
some others of my fellowes, for I never expect reputation by acting
there, after a Merchant hath soe donne there.[8]

It would be easy to find other indications of the low opinion that he held
of what his age called merchants and ours calls businessmen. He thought
their reputation for efficiency overvalued: 'the laziness of the merchant'
he affirmed to Pepys was the principal reason for our poor performance in
competing with the Dutch. He had been brought up as a member of a
noble family in the service of Charles I and could hardly divest himself of
the standards and prejudices of his time and place. And he reinforced
these with a strictness over money that Pepys found uncomfortably
fastidious.[9] Coventry heightened and extended Pepys's ideas both of
public service and of the aristocracy whose justification was supposed to

lie in undertaking it. Coventry's tastes, appetites and affinities were, at first sight, far less congenial than Sandwich's. Though a man of the world he lacked the avidity for easy money and obvious pleasures that Pepys shared with his patron. On the other hand he touched chords in Pepys that Sandwich could never reach. He was witty; he was well-read; he enjoyed argument and preferred his ideas clear, sharp-edged and un-ambiguous; he took a pride in doing whatever he did as well as it could be done; he had style.

So vivid a figure could not but make enemies. It is safe to assume that the merchants liked him as little as he liked them. Clarendon and Sandwich recognised him as an enemy; Sir George Carteret, who soon ratified his political allegiance by marrying his son to Sandwich's daughter, resented him; cunning old professionals like Batten and pompous old fuddlers like Sir John Mennes saw him as a threat. For all his brilliant gifts and for all his high position, Secretary to the Duke, a prominent figure in the House of Commons, he was not so safe and so prudent an investment for an ambitious follower as Sandwich was. But it is the argument of this book that Pepys's deepest springs of action were artistic. 'An artist,' wrote Jane Austen, 'cannot do anything slovenly.' It was this divine dis-content with the serviceable second-best that recognised in Coventry the master it had been looking for.

6

Style of life

In Restoration England, as in most unindustrialised societies, obverse sides of life, the public and the private, work and play, interpenetrated each other. The shape of the day will not fit a twentieth-century pattern. Office hours, for instance, seem irregular and idiosyncratic. Even so relentlessly methodical a man as Pepys was surprisingly free from the servitude of the clock. Indeed he did not acquire a watch until the spring of 1665 and, like the Chinese on their introduction to clockwork, was rather fascinated by its potentialities as a toy than awed by its power to dismember the continuity of existence. Pepys's readiness to take the afternoon off to go to a theatre, or, should the weather prove irresistible, to embark with his wife and her maid on an expedition on the river, seems by twentieth-century standards irresponsible. After one or two narrow squeaks with authority, particularly as personified by Sir William Coventry, Pepys eventually begins to think so too. But he recognised this as a change in himself, in his way of looking at life, more precisely in his calculations as to how to extract the maximum of enjoyment from it: 'My mind, I hope, is set to fallow my business again, for I find that two days neglect of business doth give me more discontent in mind than ten times the pleasure thereof can repair again, be it what it will.'[1]

Adaptable as he was, the transition from semi-menial under-employment to a chief place in one of the busiest and most important Government offices required time for adjustment.

This was true in private and domestic matters as well as in habits of work. Indeed as has been suggested the two went together more closely in those days than in ours. Company and tastes which were perfectly acceptable in one of Sir George Downing's clerks or in a member of Sandwich's household would not do in a Principal Officer of the Navy Board. The move from Axe Yard, Westminster to Seething Lane in the City marked an end and a beginning socially and intellectually, even if the dividing line was not so immediately discernible as in the comforts and graces of life. Which leads straight to what the poet has called:

> That topic all absorbing, as it was,
> Is now and ever shall be, to us — CLASS.

What did Pepys think about it? How did he react to its manifestations? Was he a snob?

In a sense, and that not a snobbish one, Pepys remained all his life a tailor's son. He was for ever trying on new clothes and seeing how he looked in them. Fashions and materials and styles and novelties fascinated him. No one can read far in the Diary without recognising his passion for clothes and his knowledge of them. 'This day I put on first my fine cloth suit'[2] made of a cloak that had been overtaken by an unfortunate accident when first worn the preceding year. 'This morning came home my fine Camlott cloak with gold buttons — and a silk suit; which cost me much money and I pray God to make [me] be able to pay for it.'[3] Four days later his brother Tom, who had joined his father in the shop, brought round 'my Jackanapes coat with silver buttons'. And Elizabeth's taste in dress was scrutinised with no sentimentally indulgent eye. No wonder that in one of their sharpest quarrels when he taunted her with having brought him no dowry she replied by calling him 'prick louse', a pointed allusion to the needles from which he had sprung.[4] But it is the metaphorical rather than the literal application that perhaps yields some insight into the questions of snobbery and class. Pepys put on the clothes of recognised and approved types — the man of fashion, the man of informed and fastidious taste, the man of affairs. To look the part required, in each case, an air and an attitude that must be studied by imitation. Hence the crucial importance of such models as Sandwich, Coventry or Evelyn. Hence, too, the readiness to pick up hints from colleagues whom his jealousy led him to despise or dislike such as the rich and exquisite Mr. Povy or the shrewd and knowing Creed. Pepys was too much of a realist not to see how society worked. But, strangely for so impressionable a man, he was too little of a romantic to be swept off his feet by the glamour of aristocracy, just as he was never taken in by the mumbo-jumbo of nationalism. Measured against Dr. Johnson, himself neither a snob nor a flag-waver, Pepys is cooler and more detached. The poet in Johnson was stirred by the idea of ancient loyalty: 'I am quite feudal, sir'[5]; and his views on the natural superiority of England to the constituent nations of the auld alliance are too well known to bear re-stating. Pepys, on the other hand, spent his best energies in resisting aristocratic pretensions unsupported by profes-sionalism 'the commanders, the gentlemen that could never be brought to order, but undid all'.[6] And of his objectivity towards his compatriots this is but one of many examples:

> The nature of the English is generally to be self-lovers, and thinking everything of their own the best, viz. our beef, beer, women, horses, soldiers, religion, laws, etc., and from the same principles are over-valuers of our ships.[7]

Pepys accepted the class structure of society as he accepted the nation state. But he appears to have been unmoved by the mythology with which some have felt it necessary to invest them. That he loved, as he undoubtedly did, being taken up by the great is no argument that he took them at their own valuation.

If Pepys did not romanticise the facts of the social system it was not because he had a soul above such considerations. Almost as soon as he has established himself in his new situation he begins to feel ashamed of the low connections and boorish behaviour of his own family and to criticise Elizabeth for not running the house in an appropriate style. But there were, as he recognised with unflinching self-knowledge, aspects of his own conduct that called for some alteration. Chief among these was drink. Conviviality, as we have seen, was not second but first nature to Pepys. As a hard-up young clerk he and his fellows used to meet for a weekly club at a tavern in Pall Mall. His diary shows what use he could make, on still very slender means, of the opportunities offered by a visit to Cambridge or a spell afloat. Now that he was master of an assured income and in a good way to make a great deal more he could afford to drink as hard as he liked. His colleagues at the Navy Board were for the most part glad of an excuse to ply the bottle. And the host of people who came into the office, merchants seeking contracts or settlement of unpaid bills, petitioners for places and pensions, boatswains and gunners in search of a sea billet, found it easier to press their causes by adjourning them to a wine house. Drun-kenness was not generally regarded as disgraceful. The Court, the City companies and the world of fashion made it hard to do so. But beastly habits exact a price in health, efficiency and dignity, three topics on which

Pepys was, all his life, acutely sensitive. Dignity was affronted when he was, to quote his own expression, too foxed to read family prayers 'for fear of being perceived by my servants in what case I was'. Efficiency suffered through headaches, lassitude, indisposition: even, so his surgeon Hollier suggested, to the extent of impairing his memory. But the gravest threat to health that Pepys saw was to his sight. The first of many references in the Diary explicitly identifies this cause: 'I was much troubled in my eyes, by reason of the healths I have this day been forced to drink.'[8]

The diagnosis, as Pepys himself later came to realise, was wrong. But this did not reduce its urgency as a motive to action. And action was, in Pepys's view, at once the test and purpose of moral and intellectual consciousness. He would certainly have shared Dr. Johnson's contempt for professions of generosity or sympathy unaccompanied by practical effort. 'They *pay* you by *feeling*.' He had recognised alcoholism as an unacceptable risk and he set about taking measures against it in the same way as he would have tackled some abuse in the methods by which boatswains accounted for their stores. He pressed all sides of his nature into the service: the residual Puritanism of his upbringing, the fiercely competitive ambition and the passion for good order; he said his prayers and took solemn vows; finally, as J. R. Tanner happily puts it, he hit upon 'the ingenious idea of enlisting a lesser vice to destroy a greater. Pepys was careful about money and he attached money penalties to the breaches of his vow, thus fining himself into sobriety.'[9]

With what distaste the aristocrat averts his gaze, with what audible superiority the Marxist sniffs at this deplorable triumph of middle-class morality. The conception and the execution are so characteristically bourgeois; the readiness to do a deal (even with one's lower nature), the reluctance to rely solely on principle, so inescapably English. And what aggravates the offence to such *bien pensants* is that Pepys actually managed to extract pleasure from the process of disciplining himself in this low, commercial fashion: 'I drank but two glasses of wine this day, and yet it makes my head ake all night, and indisposed me all the next day — of which I am glad.'[10]

Boozing had been overcome but drinking remained a pleasure. How could it be otherwise to a man who took nothing for granted? He enjoys the cup of cider or the bottle of beer that refresh his frequent walks between the dockyards at Deptford and Woolwich just as, even when cold and tired, he enjoys the weather. 'And I walked with a Lanthorn, weary as I was, to Greenwich; but it was a fine walk, it being a hard frost.'[11] Wine he bought with care and drank with discrimination. The cork, without which wine cannot achieve the subtleties that come from bottle age,

only began to come into use about the time of his death so that his taste
lies on the medieval side of that dividing line. Writing in 1677 when his
mature habits had long been formed he sums them up thus:

> . . . I never drink to excess and seldom or not at all but at meals and
> thereto at dinner principally now, but then I drink liberally (with a
> temperance still) and for the most part of the wines that are reckoned
> strong, viz — Greek, Italian, Spanish and Portuguese and at the small
> Bordeaux claret.
>
> The thin French wine, flying presently into my head, occasioning
> a moisture . . . I rarely meddle with any of these sorts where any other
> coarser or stronger wine can be had.[12]

The same taste is evident in the purchases mentioned in the Diary,
especially in the cellar inventoried with some pride on July 7th, 1665,
claret, canary, sack, tent,* Malaga and white wine. Haut Brion, the only
claret at this period to bear the name of the estate on which it was made,
is, on another occasion, particularly commended: 'a sort of French wine,
called Ho Bryan, that hath a good and most particular taste that I never
met with'. Pepys kept his wine in cask and was duly impressed by the
novelty and splendour of Povy's cellar management: '. . . where upon
several shelves there stood bottles of all sorts of wine, new and old, with
labells pasted upon each bottle, and in that order and plenty as I never saw
books in a bookseller's shop.'[13] As he grew richer Pepys provided better
and better wine for his guests, reaching the heights at a dinner given for
Sandwich and the Earl of Peterborough, together with two or three
important members of the House of Commons on January 23rd, 1669:

> . . . dinner was brought up, one dish after another, but a dish at a
> time, but all so good; but above all things the variety of wines, and
> excellent of their kind, I had for them, and all in so good order that
> they were mightily pleased and myself full of content at it; and indeed
> it was, of a dinner of about six or eight dishes, as noble as any man need
> to have I think; at least all was done in the noblest manner that ever I
> had any, and I have rarely seen in my life better anywhere else, even
> at the Court . . .

Such a passage, drowsy with good living, hardly suggests the angry
upbraiding of Elizabeth for her inadequacies as a hostess, the pitiless
scrutiny of her kitchen accounts ('and there find 7s. wanting — which did
occasion a very high falling out between us'), the basting of maids with

* *tinto.* Dark-coloured Spanish red wine.

broom-handles and the other unedifying scenes through which the pair of
them had passed on their pilgrimage. But it does sound a note, deeply
characteristic of its author, of disgust at grossness, even of disapproval at
elevating eating and drinking into topics of polite conversation. Dining
with the Lieutenant of the Tower and the distinguished soldier and colonial
administrator Colonel Norwood he remarks on the 'strange pleasure they
seem to take in their wine and meat, and discourse of it with the curiosity
and joy that methinks was below men of worth'.[14] The judgment gains in
authority from being passed on men whose birth and breeding were better
than his own.

Food and drink, as any casual reading of the Diary shows, were in the
first place direct and primary pleasures like sunshine or starlight. Their
secondary importance was of two kinds. First as an indicator of social
position; a hashed pullet, a roast sirloin of beef and a jowl of ling are
delightful in themselves but even more for the cachet they confer. Second
as a social emollient: 'strange it is, to see how a good dinner and feasting
reconciles everybody'.[15] Such pre-eminently was the function of the great
banquets given by the Brethren of Trinity House, or by the Clothworkers'
Company to both of which Pepys was admitted during his years at the
Navy Office.

These years are the centre of Pepys's life, personally, professionally and
intellectually. Professionally he entered the office as a barely known young
hanger-on of Lord Sandwich — 'Chance, without merit, brought me in' —
and left it as unquestionably the ablest naval administrator of his time.
Personally and intellectually the transformation is less dramatic, but still
considerable. Some aspects of his character, and those among the most
likeable, remain unchanged. His loyalty to, and care for, his generally
tiresome and sometimes embarrassing relations does not falter. Privately
he finds their oafishness, their stupidity, their discourtesy and their
unreliability harder to bear as he strives to root out the lurking remnant
of such qualities from his own manners and conduct. But he does not
make them feel this. He may decline an invitation from one of his
mother's poor connections 'where I should have been, but my pride
would not suffer me';[16] he may find his cousins the Joyces, his uncles and
aunts Wight and Fenner disgusting in their habits and tedious in their
table-talk. He says so so often and so vehemently that it is easy to believe
that he had good reason. But what is distinctive about this familiar reaction
to sudden social and professional success is that Pepys recognises it as a
shortcoming of his own at least as much as of theirs. 'But I do condemn
myself mightily for my pride and contempt of my aunt and kindred
that are not so high as myself, that I have not seen her all this while, nor

invited her all this while.'[17] Even more remarkable is the kindliness and indulgence of so irritable and exacting a man towards his brother-in-law, Balty. Balty, like Captain Grimes, is of the immortals. Across the centuries he distils an aura of dud cheques and ingratiating fecklessness. Pepys had already perceived that Balty looked at jobs in the light of his own social pretensions rather than as a means of earning a living. By January 1664 he had concluded that he was idle. Yet after Balty's only recorded effort at self-help, a year's service in the Dutch army, Pepys obtained him an appointment in Albemarle's troop of the Life Guard under the command of the fashionable and exquisite Sir Philip Howard.*
In March 1666 he sent him to sea as a muster-master, an official appointed by the Navy Board to check the corrupt practices of the Captains and Pursers. Both posts entailed considerable risks for Pepys. Albemarle was no friend of his: and the one quality for which Pepys and Coventry admired him was 'that he never would receive an excuse if the thing was not done; listening to no reason for it, be it good or bad'.[18] And to employ one's brother-in-law to keep an eye on the muster books was to lay oneself open to the counter-charges of an unscrupulous or resentful sea officer.

Pepys's own family, his father, mother, sister and his two brothers, had cause to bless his good fortune. All of them were generously helped when they needed money; all of them found the time and trouble of the busiest bureaucrat in England always at their disposal; all of them were treated with a kindness and consideration that must sometimes have been heroic. Only between him and his father was there strong affection:

> . . . it joys my very heart to think that I should have his picture so well done — who, besides that he is my father, and a man that loves me and hath ever done so — is also at this day one of the most careful and innocent men in the world.[19]

His mother was sliding into senility. At her death in March 1667 Pepys was evidently moved, but this was the re-emergence of a stream that had long run underground. His feelings for his brothers and sister were less tender. Tom, who was only a year his junior, seems to have aroused little affection and much anxiety. When their father retired to the small estate at Brampton which Samuel inherited on the death of his Uncle Robert in 1661, Tom was left to run the tailor's shop. Samuel doubted if he had either the intelligence or the industry needed and set about finding him a wife whose dowry would at least provide some working capital. Three

---

* The style in which he discharged his military duties (D. 21 Nov. 66) might have commended itself to the Duke of Dorset in *Zuleika Dobson*.

times he came near success but Tom cannot have been much of a help —
indeed one of the young ladies declined on the grounds of the imperfection
in his speech. Was there perhaps some congenital or glandular disorder?
By the autumn of 1663 the business was on the rocks. In the winter Tom
fell ill and died the following March.

The sequence of entries in which Pepys records his reactions to his
brother's deathbed is one of the most remarkable in the Diary. When
first told that his brother is 'deadly ill' he is shocked. But when he hears
that it is venereal disease he is horrified. It is only fear of what people may
say that induces him to visit the dying man, whom he finds delirious
though capable of recognising him. Talking to the housemaid he finds that
his brother is deep in debt: and, as if humiliation were not already complete, she hints strongly at homosexual relations with a neighbour in Fleet
Lane. 'So that upon the whole I do find he is, whether he lives or dies, a
ruined man. And what trouble will befall me by it I know not.'

On his next visit the same piercing candour reveals an entirely different
yet equally real facet of the diarist. 'He talks no sense two words together
now. And I confess it made me weep to see that he should not be able
when I asked him, to say who I was.' But, looking in later in the day it is
the extent of Tom's debts that dominates his brother's thoughts. Next
day, however, a second opinion pooh-poohs the diagnosis of venereal
disease, upon which Pepys sends for a barrel of oysters 'and we were very
merry'. After dinner he visited the patient, who was still delirious, and
conducted with the doctor an examination that satisfied them both that
Tom was free from all taint of the pox. He was by then very near death so
that when Pepys 'began to tell him something of his condition, and asked
him whither he thought he should go' the spiritual curiosity seems as
ghoulish as the physical. Yet when the death rattle began Pepys could not
bear to see him die. Returning a quarter of an hour later he fell into paroxysms of grief. When at last he and Elizabeth went up to bed, 'I lay
close to my wife, being full of disorder and grief for my brother that I
could not sleep nor wake with satisfaction.'

A few days later Tom was buried with six biscuits a-piece and abundance of burnt claret for the mourners (120 were invited but nearer 150
turned up) followed by an even more magnificent spread for the family.

. . . being too merry for so late a sad work; but Lord to see how the
world makes nothing of the memory of a man an hour after he is dead.
And endeed, I must blame myself; for though at the sight of him, dead
and dying, I had real grief for a while, while he was in my sight, yet
presently after and ever since, I have had very little grief endeed for him.

The self-revelation is as profound as the understanding. The egocentric and the unfeeling are shot through with touches of compassion and flashes of insight into the depths and shallows of the human heart. The mind has been cleared of cant.

Tom left behind him a number of debts (which Samuel had to pay), an illegitimate daughter (towards whose fostering further expense was to be incurred) and a pile of letters. Among these were several from the youngest brother John which referred to Samuel in most offensive terms. Worse, there was clear evidence of collusion between the two brothers to deceive their benefactor and some suggestion that their father might have guilty knowledge though himself innocent of any malicious intention. Two days after the funeral Samuel called both father and brother into his study and read the letters aloud. His father's evident contrition and his brother's obstinate churlishness confirmed his reading of their characters. His brother was stupid as well as underhand. In the anger of the moment Pepys swore not to let him have any more money and vowed to remember his ingratitude to his dying day.

John had seemed the one member of the family who might, in a modest way, fit himself to share in his brother's success. Like Samuel he had been educated at St. Paul's and Cambridge (scholar of Christ's: and there was even talk of a fellowship) but in spite of his brother's encouragement and assistance he wasted his time. The coolness that followed Tom's death did not last long. Two years later when he decided to take orders Samuel gave him money, brought him a smart clerical outfit, and tried to find him a benefice. In 1670 when these hopes had been abandoned he was made, through Samuel's wire-pulling, Clerk of Trinity House and in 1673, by the same agency, joint Clerk of the Acts at the Navy Office. He was still holding both these positions on his death in 1677. By then his elder brother had long come to regard him as to some extent competent and trustworthy;[20] but of affection or sympathy there appears no trace.

The last of Pepys's immediate family, his sister Paulina, played a much greater part during the years of his rise to wealth and position. Not that she can have been anything but a handicap to the pursuit of either. The unattractiveness of her person and the disagreeableness of her temper are palpable across the centuries. Right through the Diary period Pepys busies himself with negotiations for her marriage, ultimately going as high as five or six hundred pounds in the dowry he was prepared to provide for her. At last in the spring of 1668 she was married to a Huntingdonshire neighbour, 'Mr. Jackson, who is a plain young man, handsome enough for Pall, one of no education nor discourse, but of few words, and one altogether that I think will please me well enough'. His taciturnity remained his only recommendation. But in fathering two sons, one of whom, John, survived to be the hope of Pepys's old age, he contributed more than the rest of the family put together to the happiness of their benefactor.

Pall, her brother thought, was improved by marriage; and in her widowhood when Pepys was the victim of a political conspiracy that might have cost him his life she proved staunch and true. But in the Diary she rarely if ever appears in an admirable light. Almost as soon as the Pepyses were settled in to their handsome new house they decided to kill two birds with one stone by taking on Pall as a servant. She arrived in January 1661 and her brother showed her her place in the household by pointedly not inviting her to sit down at table. In spite or, perhaps, because of, hints of this kind Pall became insufferably proud and idle. By the end of July it was clear that she would have to go. Early in September she was packed off to Brampton to live with her parents, 'crying exceedingly'.

This attempt to harness family obligation to domestic convenience was not repeated. In January 1663 Elizabeth was in want of a lady's maid and suggested that Pall might be better suited to this than to housework. Pepys was very pleased indeed with his wife for proposing her but even though he groaned at good wages going outside the family he could not bear the prospect. Only once again did he think of mixing the two worlds of servants and relations. In January 1667 after so many disappointments a marriage had been arranged for Pall, but the bridegroom upset it all by dying. Growing desperate, Pepys offered her to his most valued secretary, Will Hewer, who pleaded a preference for bachelorhood. It is doubtful if anything could have deepened or strengthened the bond that formed of itself between the two men. Marriage with Pall might have blighted its growth.

Servants were one of the principal causes of friction between the Pepyses. Elizabeth had neither the temperament nor the experience to manage them. How, indeed, could she be expected to possess either, married so young and brought up so oddly? Pepys, who had been a kind of servant himself, understood matters better and became, in his official capacity at least, the object of loyalty, even devotion, to most of those who worked for him. Elizabeth, uncertain of herself, oscillated between over-familiarity and sudden bouts of petulant assertiveness. At least that is the impression conveyed by the Diary, our only source but hardly a disinterested one.

Pepys does not disguise his own irritability nor the cowardly violence he sometimes used against people who could not hit back. He kicks the cook and is mortified by being caught in the act by Sir Willian Penn's footboy. He bastes his maid and even, on one occasion, locked 'our little girle' into the cellar for the night. Boys, naturally, were treated much more roughly. One in particular Wayneman Birch was several times thrashed so energetically that Pepys complained of exhaustion and an aching arm. Such harshness long remained the rule. In the next century Dr. Johnson, kind and tender-hearted as he was, believed firmly in the moral and intellectual benefits of the rod. Even in the nineteenth century Dr. Keate the great headmaster of Eton who raised the standard of scholarship and introduced debating societies into the school once flogged eighty boys in a day and stood astonished at his own moderation. There were men in Pepys's time, John Aubrey was one, and before, such as the Ferrars at Little Gidding, who thought such proceedings uncivilised or unchristian. By the end of his life Pepys might well have agreed with them. Even when he was punishing poor Wayneman, whom both he and Elizabeth liked best of all their boys in spite of his naughtiness, he had his doubts: 'I am afeared it will make the boy never the better'.[21] After boxing Will Hewer's ears in annoyance at being contradicted, Pepys records a sense of shame or is it a sense of impropriety? The words '. . . which I never did before, and so was afterwards a little troubled at it'[22] bear either interpretation. From the start Hewer was in any case partly an apprentice to the business of the Navy Office, in which he rapidly became Pepys's right-hand man, and partly a domestic. Probably Hewer, unlike Wayneman, belonged by a narrow margin to a class of people that one did not knock about. He was the nephew of Robert Blackborne who had been secretary to the Admiralty under Cromwell and was to become secretary to the East India Company, an important and useful man to know. Had anyone dared to box Pepys's ears when he began life as a servant to Mountagu? It is difficult to imagine such an outrage.

If master and mistress sometimes applied a discipline that seems to us ferocious or unreasonable they also admitted their servants to a degree of equality that the polite servants of succeeding centuries would have thought rustic. Pepys loved horseplay and so, when she was in health, did Elizabeth. The round games and frolics of Twelfth Night were enjoyed by the whole household: the summer parties of pleasure by coach, or on the river often included Elizabeth's maid or Will Hewer; and one of the first recommendations to any post in their domestic service was musical ability. The new house gave Pepys opportunities of singing in the garden or on the leads which he was anxious to enhance with a soprano or an alto to balance his bass. There were, too, other qualifications; youth, charm and beauty. But these inviting vistas deserve the opening not the closing of a chapter.

7

Licence and morality

———

Those who see in Pepys a forerunner if not an exponent of the view, seminal to modern advertising, that sex will cure us from all ills in this world and the next are under a misapprehension. Sex as such was not a concept or even a word with which he was familiar, except in the narrow sense of physiological gender. The deity venerated by D. H. Lawrence and to which chantries of strange dedication are still served was unknown to him; and, on the evidence, if known, would have been abhorrent.

It seems important to state this point, if only to disentangle it from two others cardinal to any understanding of the man: first that he was lecherous and second that his opinions and attitudes, his philosophy if that is not too pretentious an expression, anticipate to a remarkable degree the kind of questions that perplex us. Both are true: but neither has the slightest connection with the other. Still less is it possible to infer from them any mystical or even giggling enthusiasm for sex *per se*. On the contrary:

> . . . Sir J. Mennes and Mr Batten both say that buggery is now almost grown as common among our gallants as in Italy, and that the very pages of the town begin to complain of their masters for it. But blessed be God, I do not to this day know what is the meaning of this sin, nor which is the agent nor which the patient.[1]

It is difficult to discern here so much as the glimmer of approaching dawn. Taken with his reaction to the insinuations about his brother Tom the passage hardly suggests that its author held any view of the sexual urge as a liberating force or of the sexual act as a fulfilment of the personality.

In all these matters Pepys was both in theory and in practice thoroughly conventional. He believed firmly in marital fidelity and lost, as he himself admits, all sense of proportion when he began to imagine without a shred of evidence that Elizabeth was having an affair with her dancing master. So far from regarding his own infidelities as a matter of pride he records them in the Diary in an absurd macaronic jumble of languages that would hardly have deceived Elizabeth had she *per impossibile* mastered his shorthand and broken the lock under which he kept those dangerous volumes. The only gaze from which he was disguising them was his own.

Except for one or two letters written by other people all the surviving evidence on this aspect of Pepys's life comes from the Diary. It is difficult for anyone who is not either an exhibitionist by temperament or a clinician by training to be candid, still less objective about a subject so private and so sensitive. Nothing can staunch the flow of sexual reminiscence: but in all reminiscences the varnish of a lifetime's self-satisfaction is apt to produce effects that seem, somehow, too good to be true. Fresh, direct, undoctored evidence given at the time with a real attempt at truthfulness is rare. It is hard for a man, particularly a vain, fastidious and conventional man, not to suppress matter necessarily known only to himself that exposes him to derision or contempt. The *soi-disant* successful sexual athlete has a compelling motive to tell all: so does the professional breast-beater. But Pepys was too sensitive, too subtle and too clear-headed to be open to such inducements. No topic in the Diary reveals its author in so unheroic a light: and that is the true measure of the heroism required for so unswerving a pursuit of truth.

Pepys's self-revelation on the subject epitomises the Protean quality that makes him slip for ever through fingers stretched to catch him. He boxes the compass of humanity, so that almost every reading of him is true. Even the too familiar representation of the naughty, bottom-pinching bounder of musical comedy can be adequately documented. But so can many other interpretations. Where so much, most of it apparently irreconcilable, can be maintained, it is perhaps best to start with what every reader of the Diary must have observed, namely appetite. Its crudest manifestations are so often described that some have thought Pepys's sexuality exceptional. But what is the exception and what the rule and on what evidence can we arrive at either? Sir D'Arcy Power, the surgeon, suggests that both Pepys's kidney condition and the post-operative consequences of his lithotomy combined to excite his sexual desires.² Whatever the explanation the fact is explicit. And simply by contrast with the general reticence on this subject Pepys, at first, may appear to some highly sexed. There seems no evidence that he himself thought so. What he did notice in himself was a diffused romantic feeling towards the opposite sex as a whole (women, not a woman) akin to that which Sterne elaborates in *A Sentimental Journey*.

In the physical satisfaction of his appetite it is the cautious and calculating side of his nature that rules all. So far as we know Pepys never attempted an affair with anyone who came near to his own station in society, let alone with those above him. Servants, shopgirls, barmaids, prostitutes; there is a chilling prudence about the choice. And yet there was sometimes a real tenderness, particularly in his relations with the young girls who came to live in the house as companion to Elizabeth. The fact of their femininity, their innocence, their simplicity and sweetness of nature enchanted him. Perhaps they roused sleeping affection for the children that he had once wanted but had reconciled himself to not having. Gosnell, Ashwell, Mercer and last, most poignant of all, Deb Willett touched emotions very different from those which the diarist records in his transactions with the shifty and unprepossessing ladies he was accustomed to pick up in Westminster Hall. And different from either was the long liaison between Pepys and the pretty wife of a subordinate, which throws light on so many contrasting aspects of his character.

On a wet afternoon in July 1663 Pepys ended a not very strenuous day by having himself rowed down to Deptford:

> . . . and there mustered the yard, purposely (God forgive me) to find out Bagwell, a carpenter whose wife is a pretty woman, that I might have some occasion of knowing him and forcing her to come to the office again — which I did so luckily, that going thence, he and his wife did of themselfs meet me in the way, to thank me for my old kindness; but I spoke little to her, but shall give occasion for her coming to me . . .³

What the old kindness was we do not know. Bagwell was at that moment carpenter of the *Dolphin*,⁴ a fifth-rate captured from the French,⁵ so that it is possible that Pepys had in some way helped to obtain the place. But the conscious use of official position and an official pretext, the admission even if only conventional, of guilt, and the frank intention to deceive leave no room for speculation. Whatever heats of passion might follow this is a fairly cold-blooded opening.

A week later Pepys was again down the river visiting the yards when the Bagwells saw him:

> . . . and they would have me into their little house: which I was willing enough to, and did salute his wife. They had got wine for me and I perceive live prettily; and I believe the woman a virtuous modest woman.
>
> Her husband walked through to Redriffe [Rotherhithe] with me, telling me things that I asked of in the yard; and so by water home, it being likely to rain again to-night, which God forbid.[6]

Pepys, it appears, was touched by the friendliness of the young warrant officer, by the care taken to offer generous hospitality, and by the knowledgeable enthusiasm of a young man who wanted to succeed in his career. At any rate the divine aid was only invoked to improve the weather, which suggests a more temperate and decent state of mind. Indeed he seems to have taken no further initiative in the matter. But on an evil day some six months later Mrs. Bagwell sought him out at the office to ask his help in finding a new appointment for her husband. Pepys chucked her under the chin 'but could not find in my heart to offer anything uncivil to her, she being I believe a very modest woman'.[7] Another three months passed without any sign of the Bagwells but on May 31st

> . . . a great while alone in my office, nobody near, with Bagwell's wife of Deptford; but the woman seems so modest that I durst not offer any courtship to her, though I had it in mind when I brought her into me. But am resolved to do her husband a courtesy for I think he is a man that deserves very well.

But early in October Bagwell's professional merits were still unrecognised. On the 3rd Pepys met Mrs. Bagwell at the office:

> and there kissed her only. She rebuked me for doing it; saying that did I do so much to many bodies else, it would be a stain to me. But I do not see but she takes it well enough; though in the main, I believe she is very honest.

A turning-point seems to have been reached on October 20th when

> . . . I to my office, where I took in with me Bagwell's wife; and there I caressed her and find her every day more and more coming, with good words and promises of getting her husband a place, which I will do.

Easily enough, one would have thought, with a full-scale war against the Dutch on the point of breaking out. But on November 3rd he made an assignation with her in Moorfields:

> . . . and there into a drinking house — and all alone eat and drank together. I did there caress her; but although I did make some offer, did not receive any compliance from her in what was bad, but very modestly she denied me; which I was glad to see and shall value her the better for it — and I hope never tempt her to any evil any more.

These resolutions proved infirm. Twelve days later he seduced her in the same unromantic surroundings to her evident distress and his great pleasure. Just before Christmas he went to great trouble to repeat the performance and was vexed when she resisted him. However the next day, December 20th, he found a pretext to visit Deptford yard and:

> . . . walked, without being observed, with Bagwell home to his house and there was very kindly used, and the poor people did get a dinner for me in their fashion — of which I also eat very well. After dinner I found occasion of sending him abroad; and then alone avec elle je tentoy a faire ce que je voudrais, et contre sa force je la faisoy, bien que pas a mon contentment.

And so, both trust and hospitality betrayed, he took leave and walked home.

The affair, for want of a better word, went on for two or three years. A month later Pepys was shaking his head over female virtue:

> . . . and there I had her company toute l'apres dîner and had mon plein plaisir of elle — but strange to see how a woman, notwithstanding her greatest pretences of love a son mari and religion may be vaincue.[8]

Smugness greased the slipway of routine: routine led to boredom: boredom to distaste: and distaste to active repulsion. Eighteen months later Pepys arranged to spend the night at the little house in Deptford.

> . . . but though I did intend para aver demorado con ella toda la night, yet when I had done ce que je voudrais, I did hate both ella and la cosa; and taking occasion from the uncertainty of su marido's return esta noche, did me levar; and so away home late . . .[9]

None the less Pepys still continued to avail himself of her services for another six months. He had at the beginning of the war obtained a better post for Bagwell — carpenter of the *Providence*, a fourth-rate — and as it drew towards its close he had him appointed to a new third-rate building at Harwich. He continued to watch over his career with a headmasterly sententiousness, in the circumstances more than usually revolting. Twelve years later in a long letter announcing his promotion from the *Resolution*, a third-rate, to the *Royal Prince*, a first-rate fitting out at Bristol he urges:

> . . . the study of the Art of ship-building as well as the Common prac-tices which as your friend I would advise you to apply some of your present leisure to, the King being one that understands it soe well as makes it unsafe for any shipwright to approach him that is not a Master of the Theory of the Trade, as well as of the ordinary labour of it.[10]

Four years later still, when himself out of office and only two years beyond the Tower and the threat of execution, he wrote to Lord Brouncker, his old colleague at the Navy Board, to solicit a dockyard appointment for Bagwell.[11] Restored to power he was not able to reward his protégé as soon as he desired and wrote him a firm, perhaps rather too magisterial letter, explaining that Mrs. Bagwell's constant visits to the office would in no way promote the end in view.[12] Finally as the curtain fell on his own official career after the Revolution of 1688 and the scene-shifters were jostling round him, one of his last acts was to recommend Bagwell for a vacancy in Chatham Dockyard.[13]

How deeply the whole story bears the impress of Pepys. And how sharp and distinct are the contrasting flavours of his personality. Like the Impressionists he disdains the neutral tints. The actor-narrator provides insights of his own that could support a Marxist indictment of bourgeois exploitation, a Christian exposition of sin, and the more cynical view that morality consists in what one can get away with. But for all its univer-sality of application it does draw lines of perspective in which class domi-nates the scene. Pepys sometimes desires Mrs. Bagwell, sometimes pities her, sometimes despises her. There is no suggestion of love or tenderness, no talk of standing in strange slavery to beauty, no comparison to the enchantments of music, no hint, however distant, of romance. These higher feelings were inspired by women of a higher class. Lady Castlemaine, for instance, or even the Queen, Catherine of Braganza, were the objects of Pepys's cerebral lust, issuing sometimes in dreams of ecstasy. The wives and daughters of colleagues and friends frequently elicit a response, part aesthetic, part sexual, that corresponds more closely to the ideas of Plato than to the actuality of Mrs. Bagwell. The nearer Pepys approaches to particularity, the lower burns the flame of romance. A shop girl seen in passing could retain her status as part of the feminine ideal and inspire feelings generally reserved for her social betters.[14]

To all this must be added a touch of the *voyeur*. He feels a vicarious thrill at seeing two 'gallants' dragging a pretty girl out of her stall on Ludgate Hill with the evident intention of raping her: and the cavortings of the King and his mistresses sometimes excite these susceptibilities. More often, it is true, they provoke an outburst on Charles II's frivolity or a denunciation of the wrath to come upon a nation that has forgotten its purer traditions.

For Pepys found no difficulty in combining a self-indulgence that he never pretends to condone with a strong moral and social code which he never hesitates to proclaim. On this account he has often been accused of hypocrisy. He might more justly be admired for integrity in refusing to deny principles he believed to be right simply because he did not live up to them. Certainly he was prepared to take extraordinary risks in maintaining the proprieties, whereas in defying them he was notably timid.

The most striking example of his boldness is the famous episode of what Pepys called 'my great letter of reproof'. The story, astonishing enough in itself, becomes even more amazing when it is remembered that it took place at almost exactly the same time as Pepys was making the opening moves in the Bagwell campaign.

Early in 1663 Sandwich who had been in poor health through most of the winter fell very ill. On his recovery in the spring he took lodgings in Chelsea, then a pretty village on the Thames, where he remained for several months to recruit his strength. At the beginning of August Pepys heard from his old fellow-servant Will Howe that their master had become infatuated with the daughter of the house in which he was staying and was behaving in the most indiscreet and scandalous manner. The story was soon corroborated by the other senior members of Sandwich's household, Moore and Creed, and heightened by the lurid account given by Ned Pickering, a young kinsman of his patron for whom Pepys usually had little time.

. . . he telling me the whole business of my Lord's folly with this Mrs Becke at Chelsy, of all which I am ashamed to see my Lord so grossly play the beast and fool, to the flinging off of all Honour, friends, servants and every thing and person that is good, and only will have his private lust undisturbed with this common whore – his sitting up night after night alone, suffering nobody to come to them, and all the day too — casting off Pickering, basely reproaching him with his small estate which is yet a good one; and other poor courses to obtain privacy beneath his Honour — with his carrying her abroad and playing on his lute under her window, and forty other poor sordid things; which I am grieved to hear, but believe it to be to no good purpose for me to meddle with it; but let him go on til God Almighty and his own conscience and thoughts of his Lady and family do it.[15]

Pepys was always quick to prefer the colourful to the humdrum. Provided the story were good enough he was ready to suspend his critical faculties. Whether Sandwich, that portly, cool, reserved figure, was likely to behave in a way that suggests the undergraduate Pepys he did not stop to wonder. He had had, at this point, no opportunity of meeting the lady and judging for himself whether Howe's description of her 'a woman of a very bad fame and very impudent' or Moore's 'a common Strumpett' in any way fitted the facts. Sandwich he considered 'a man amorous enough' — had he not attempted Elizabeth's virtue? — and it was not surprising that he 'now begins to allow himself the liberty that he sees everyone else at Court takes'. But he had already, as the passage quoted makes clear, considered and rejected the course of speaking to his patron for his own good.

A few days after this conversation both families adjourned to Huntingdonshire, Pepys to view his property at Brampton and Sandwich to enjoy the beauties of Hinchingbrooke in early autumn. For the first time Pepys derived pleasure instead of vexation from his inheritance. Riding with Elizabeth in his own woods and gathering nuts he thought himself a lucky man. She looked well on a horse and conscious of being, for once, admired and approved of was excellent company. On Sunday the two families met at church, walking back afterwards to Hinchingbrooke where a large party sat down to a noble dinner. Before the meal Sandwich took his guests round the garden, distinguishing his dependent by asking his opinion, in front of all the company, as to the re-designing of a wall that closed the perspective of the walks. Soothed by such characteristically beautiful manners, relaxed by fresh air and exercise, happy and contented in body and estate, away from the wrangles of the Navy Board and the irritations of a busy life, Pepys let his anxieties fall away. Whatever anyone might say there was no denying, once one was among them, that the Sandwiches were a most affectionate and united family. Official duties called Pepys back to London immediately but Sandwich spent another four or five weeks in the tranquillity of the country. When the two men met again in London at the end of October Pepys's mind was full of a host of other things — the effectiveness of the Emperor in resisting the

Turk, the results of his interminable litigation with his co-heirs, the need to get more money and the imperative necessity of spending it. Sandwich, helpful as always, undertook to see about getting Pepys a place on the Fishery Commission, another of those opportunities of being paid for doing nothing which in those days relieved the hard-pressed servant of Government. So matters went on until, on November 9th, just when Pepys's new periwig had so transformed his appearance that the Duke of York declared that he did not recognise him, up bobbed Pearse the surgeon. Did Pepys know anything of Sandwich's being out of favour with the King? His absence from court was the subject of much adverse comment. To judge from the moral diatribe which Pearse at once launched into, the Court would have seemed an admirable place to stay away from — 'nobody looking after business but every man his lust and gain'. But the alarm bells were ringing in Pepys's mind. If Sandwich lost the royal favour his dependents could expect short shrift. As Pearse turned to go, up came Creed and Ned Pickering. They dined together at the King's Head where Pickering's criticism of Sandwich shocked and disgusted Pepys by its extravagance.

For two days he did nothing, but on the 12th, dining with Moore, they talked of nothing but Sandwich's absence from court, its incalculable consequences and its scandalous cause. At last Pepys resolved on immediate action. He took a coach to Sandwich's lodgings, determined to have it out man to man. He was met by Will Howe who went over the same ground in long, lugubrious detail. After some time Sandwich appeared. Pepys began 'to fall in discourse with him, but my heart did misgive me that my Lord would not take it well, and then found him not in a humour to talk; and so after a few ordinary words, my Lord not talking in that manner as he uses to do, I took leave . . .' Rejoining Howe he told him that he thought it would be better done in writing, a decision which Howe applauded.

Was it chance that made Sandwich, usually so approachable, discourage his cousin from plunging into some topic about which he was evidently agitated? Men do not survive in the politics of civil war and revolution unless equipped with antennae. If Pepys's emotions had not been roused, his own skill in handling people would surely have enabled him to read the signal then made to him. But he bustled on. By the 16th he had drafted, not without pain, his letter of reproof. On the 17th he read it over to Moore who received it with rhapsodies and offered to send a duplicate signed by himself, a proposal which Pepys still retained enough sense to refuse. On the 18th he had it personally delivered by Will Hewer with orders not to stay for an answer.

Why had Pepys acted in this reckless if heroic manner? If he himself was not only planning the seduction of Mrs. Bagwell but habitually deceiving his wife with his doxies in Westminster, why should not Sandwich 'a man amorous enough' partake also of pleasures that flattered their sovereign by imitation? Even had they been equals it would have been in a high degree presumptuous to issue such a warning. To write on such a matter to a man far above one in social position, wealth and political power was to defy the rules of prudence and the deference to social order that Pepys held all but sacred. Strangest of all he had rushed into this course on the hearsay of Howe, Moore, Creed and Pickering, all of whom, in his heart, he either distrusted or despised. He had not so such as set eyes on the lady whose feral attractions were wreaking such havoc. When he did, several months afterwards, he found her charming, intelligent and well-bred, the exact opposite of what she had been represented 'one that hath not one good feature in her face and yet is a fine lady'. With a lame show of bluffing it out he concludes 'and I dare warrant him she hath brains enough to entangle him'.[16] Why did he persist in taking so grave a risk on such frivolous evidence?

A number of reasons might be given. Certainly Sandwich seemed to be withdrawing from public life — Pearse the surgeon had emphasised this. And Pepys as one who was both professionally and financially involved in Sandwich's affairs knew that he was heavily in debt. It was essential to bring him back into the game if all was not to be lost. But why should Sandwich, hitherto so adroit a performer, have abandoned the field? A woman. Of course it must be a woman. Look at the King. Look at the Duke of York. Look at — but without multiplying examples beyond necessity, the report from Chelsea explained everything.

This pragmatic explanation of Pepys's conduct is possibly true as far as it goes. But it does not go nearly far enough. Pepys was shocked by what he heard, shocked socially and morally. Peers of the realm ought not to misbehave in a notorious manner. And morally an action was not less wrong because it was common. Behind these feelings lay other springs of action. Pepys was a busybody by instinct. Both by taste and education he had in him much of the teacher and of the lawyer. Naval administration, as his bulging files still show, was to give both faculties almost unlimited scope. To show someone what they ought to do and how they ought to do it and to analyse a case were among his greatest pleasures and commonest duties. These aptitudes were not happily applied to the moral and caution-ary instruction of one's patron. One further element may here have played its part — vanity. Pepys fancied himself — and with reason — both as a letter writer and as a man who could draw up a brief. The urgency,

the concern and the distress of 'my great letter of reproof' are palpable
It conveys exactly what its author intended. Was it not too well written
to throw away?

Sandwich's reception of it mystified and alarmed Pepys. No thunderbolt
flashed from the sky; but equally there was no invitation to intimate discussion. Pepys had been expecting anger or gratitude: embarrassment
seems not to have occurred to him as a possible reaction. Agonised
inquiries of those about his patron, Moore and Howe, were met with
comforting reassurance that the letter 'hath wrought well upon him', the
phrase Pepys habitually employs to describe the effects of purgatives.
After four days of suspense the two men met on Sunday morning as
Sandwich was preparing to go to chapel at Whitehall. Sandwich was firm
and brisk but not unkind: since Pepys had reported these allegations he
must disclose his sources. Pepys broke down and wept. As soon as Sandwich
had obtained the information he wanted he closed the subject and 'began
to talk very cheerfully of other things, and I walked with him to Whitehall and we discussed of the pictures in the gallery'. Pepys was so upset
that he missed the whole drift of the sermon and was only brought to
present-mindedness by the anthem composed by one of the choirboys. It
was some months before he felt the same ease in Sandwich's company as
he had before. Indeed was it ever quite the same ease? The impassive
surface of Sandwich's nature disconcerted Pepys's vivacity. But within the
month Sandwich had had him put on the Fishery Commission.

At first sight these two episodes seem to illustrate two opposing sides
of Pepys's approach to these matters at this stage of his life. And so, in
many ways, they do. In the first he is selfish and calculating; in the second
wildly rash. In the one he plays the lecher, in the other he champions what
Mr. Doolittle would dismiss as middle-class morality. What imposes the
unity of his personality on these evident contrasts is that unlike the
generality of mankind he is rash in defence of respectability and staid in
pursuing his amours. It is, further, perfectly clear from the account of his
relations with Mrs. Bagwell that he felt ashamed of himself. Perhaps the
contradictions are more superficial than profound.

8

Taste and curiosity

The years at the Navy Office saw the flowering of that universal curiosity that Pepys himself recognised as indivisible from his consciousness. 'But I, as I am in all things curious . . .' 'A liberall genius, as I take my own to be, towards all studies and pleasures.'[1] So deeply did he admire this faculty in himself that he devoted the better part of a Sunday to trying to celebrate it in verse before abandoning the attempt. But the judgment hit the mark even if the lines fell short. The work of the office itself opened fresh vistas of practical and theoretical study. He began, naturally, by mastering day-to-day technicalities, who did what, how much things cost, by what standards they were judged or measured. Such questions touched on a host of specialised skills whose practitioners could not always give a lucid or coherent account of their mastery — 'their knowledge lying in their hands confusedly' as Pepys himself brilliantly expressed it in a survey of the leading shipwrights of the 1680s. Pepys's hands, like ours, acquired their knowledge by turning the pages of books.

Not that he disdained or even underrated the educative value of apprenticeship. On the contrary his greatest single achievement, the professionalising of the naval officer, rested on this foundation. In his own life a true passion for learning the job always got the better of vanity and self-importance, qualities which were at no stage negligible. He was never too proud to begin at the beginning or to take instruction from a man of simple qualifications. When he had been two years in the office, calculating

wages, measuring tonnage and striking bargains of many kinds, he engaged
a mathematics master to teach him the multiplication table.

The arrangements with old Barlow had been reached partly through
the agency of Sir William Petty, whom Pepys had seen at Harrington's
Rota Club, and John Graunt, who was deputed to receive Barlow's share of
the salary. Graunt's *Observations on the Bills of Mortality*, edited by Petty
and published in 1662, is still on Pepys's shelves at Cambridge. A pioneer
work of social statistics it is the foundation both of life insurance and of
scientific demography. These were the kind of people and the kind of questions that fascinated Pepys. Petty became a lifelong friend whose views on
religion or plans for constructing a double-bottomed vessel Pepys carefully
preserved among his own papers. In the breadth of his curiosity as in his
good nature and in his unblushing readiness after greatly enriching himself
as a Government servant to utter piteous cries of destitution, he had
obvious affinities with Pepys. But in originality and intellectual power he
outclassed him. Anatomist, physician, land-surveyor, naval architect and
above all political economist Petty personifies the age of the Royal Society
to which he was elected on its foundation. No doubt his scepticism and
his humour delighted Pepys. Aubrey tells us that 'He can be an excellent
Droll (if he haz a mind to it) and will preach *extempore* incomparably
either the Presbyterian way, Independent, Cappucin frier, or Jesuite.'[2] But
it was in his insistence on numeracy and his determination to quantify
that he made his impact on the minds of his time. No one else argued so
tirelessly for statistics as the prerequisite for policy. Did Pepys, consciously or unconsciously, learn this lesson from him? It certainly characterised his own administrative practice.

John Evelyn, that other great virtuoso whose influence on Pepys can
hardly be overestimated, did not enter his life until after the outbreak
of war in 1665. It is strange that Pepys should owe his election as a Fellow
of the Royal Society not to his close friends Petty or Evelyn but to Thomas
Povy, a man whom he first envied or despised and seems, ultimately, to
have hated.[3] The elegance of his cellar management has already been described. Elegance, indeed, was Povy's long suit. His house in Lincoln's
Inn Fields was 'beset with delicate pictures'; his stable contained 'some
most delicate horses, and the very racks painted, and mangers, with a
neat leaden painted cistern and the walls done with Dutch tiles like my
chimnies'.[4] Dazzled by this splendour, irritated by Povy's incompetence
as a colleague in Government service, jealous of the rich appointments
that, for no discernible merit, had been showered on him, Pepys reluctantly
admired his taste, even, on occasion, enjoying his company. But it was
the possessions not the man that formed a model:

. . . his room floored above with woods of several colours, like, but above the best Cabinet-work I ever saw – his grotto and vault, with his bottles of wine and a well therein to keep them cool – his furniture of all sorts – his bath at the top of his house – good pictures and his manner of eating and drinking, doth surpass all that ever I did see of one man in all my life.[5]

Like Povy, Pepys was already, in a much humbler way, a collector of books and engravings and a patron of artists. But it was music and the theatre that, at this period of his life, provided his keenest aesthetic excitement. Music, the thing he loved best in the world, had always been with him. But the theatre was a new pleasure, one of the indisputable advantages of the Restoration. Pepys went to a play with the uninhibited expectation of pleasure that owed a great deal to the novelty of the experience. By the end of the Diary he is becoming more critical or more jaded. In the years before the war he is forced to take the same measures of self-discipline against playgoing, fines and vows, as against drinking. That the plays he saw fired his imagination and held him rapt we cannot doubt. But what it was he saw in them, why for instance, he admired Massinger's *The Bondman* to such an extravagant degree, why he thought *Romeo and Juliet* 'the worse I ever heard in my life' or considered *A Midsummer Night's Dream* insipid and ridiculous, or why he should be moved by *Hamlet* and *Othello* (which he none the less rated below a trivial and forgotten comedy translated from the Spanish) are all questions that must puzzle more than they enlighten.

That Pepys's taste was unsure, that it leaned towards the conventional, his literary judgments strongly suggest. If one enjoys Fuller's racy and entertaining *Church History of Britain* how could one endure repeated readings of Bacon's sententious *Faber Fortunae*, which at this period was Pepys's favourite piece of prose? He read widely, prose and poetry, Spanish and French and Latin, history and law, plays and books of travel. If we can discover no unifying principle in his opinions and cannot understand why he should like some books or dislike others, it is at least manifest that he thought about what he read and made up his own mind about its merit. Twice he bought Butler's *Hudibras* because everyone else told him how amusing it was and twice he yawned and threw it away. For this, as for his Shakespearian judgments, he has been generally patronised by later writers. Sir Sidney Lee[6] confidently attributes it to his being a bone-headed businessman with no imagination, an explanation perhaps more baffling than the phenomena to be explained. To convict him of crass materialism because he was perceptive enough to identify an uncomfortable seat as prejudicing him against a play, or, conversely, the appearance of a pretty and favourite actress as predisposing him to enjoyment seems perverse. It would be impossible to make out a case for the originality or the inherent interest of his taste. As in every other department of life he unashamedly enjoyed much that was commonplace.

The Diary years are years of appetite, not digestion. A taste would form, an outline would harden. But it would come through the multiplicity of life. Like a child in a toy department at Christmas, Pepys's eye was for ever absorbing him in some new prospect of delight. And like a child he continued to notice what other men of his age generally take for granted. What Londoner has ever extracted more pleasure from the weather or found more to enjoy in the routine journeys entailed in the day's work? '. . . and there it begun to be calme and the stars to shine', '. . . a most fine bright moonshine night and a great frost' — the language is suddenly lyrical, with no changing of gear from a matter-of-fact account of, it may be, some dubious commercial transaction or an ugly scene with Elizabeth. As in childhood all experience comes in through the same front door. Pepys understood the use of a tradesman's entrance as well as any man. His filing system, his personal and official accounts, his determination to master all relevant knowledge from the multiplication table to the best methods of measuring and storing masts attest a mind whose power to specialise and subdivide would be approved by an industrial consultant. What raises a mentality in its component parts so often commonplace to the level of genius is a capacity to keep this intellectual gadgetry in its proper place. Pepys does not anticipate his own responses. Ordinary things, a pot of beer, a walk through a dockyard, a night journey on the river, are apprehended as though they were being offered fresh on the first day of creation, instead of for the hundredth time in a busy life.

This applied equally to ideas as to the impressions of the senses. Sermons, books, tavern gossip, professional interchanges and the conversation of learned men tumble pell-mell into the Diary. Sometimes a quick and summary judgment is passed but more often the idea is examined, squeezed between finger and thumb, and put aside without comment or commitment. Except in practical affairs Pepys liked to defer judgment. Predisposed to a rational explanation of phenomena he by no means closed his mind to the mysterious or the magical. Even in a matter of such concern as his health he could write, 'But am at a great loss to know whether it [his unusually good state of health] be my Hare's foote, or taking every morning a Pill of Turpentine, or my having left off the wearing of a gowne.'[7] Three weeks later, within a fortnight of his election to the Royal Society, these doubts were refined

. . . Mr Batten in Westminster hall . . . showed me my mistake, that my hares-foot hath not the joint to it, and assures me he never had his cholique since he carried it about him. And it is a strange thing how fancy works, for I no sooner almost handled his foot but my belly begin to be loose and to break wind; and whereas I was in some pain yesterday and tother day, and in fear of more to-day, I became very well, and so continue.[8]

If detachment and empiricism characterised his view of nature, what, in that highly theological age, of his religion? So far as he dared he maintained the same stance. To eschew the dangers of Popery to the right or Fanaticism to the left came easily to him. So did regularity of attendance at public worship. Some churches — St. Dionis Backchurch in particular — offered an exceptionally fine range of female beauty in the congregation. Others — notably Captain Cooke and his choirmen at the Chapel Royal — maintained a high musical standard. All offered sermons, good, bad or indifferent, whose texts Pepys usually misremembered but whose arguments, if properly thought out, he would listen to in the spirit of a tutor appraising an undergraduate's weekly essay. Yet little as religion interested him his easy conformity had its limits. During the Diary years he never received the sacrament, an omission that could have caused him trouble if any malicious person had made use of the fact. Indeed when, many years later, he was accused of being a secret Roman Catholic both he and his parish priest at St. Olave's swore that he had been a regular communicant during this period. Although he had, to his mother's sorrow, accepted the restored liturgy of the Church of England, he had not yet come under the influence of that learned circle of High Churchmen and Non-Jurors to whom he was drawn after the Revolution of 1688. Sympathising with the Presbyterians and detesting the bishops he occupied the conventional position of the educated non-partisan. He seems to have been faintly shocked, or was he merely surprised at finding Sandwich '. . . plainly to be a Scepticke in all things of religion and to make no great matter of any-thing therein'.[9] Agnosticism was by and large congenial to his own temperament. But atheism, especially if publicly professed, he found offensive. Interested in and tolerant of other people's religion he is one of the first Englishmen to have left on record a description of a visit to the synagogue of the recently readmitted Sephardic Jews and he frequently attended Mass in the Queen's Chapel.

It was against the grain of his nature to isolate abstract questions. Religion, like politics, much more often presented itself to his mind in the form 'who whom'. Religion, in its public manifestations, was indeed an

GRANA ANGELICA:

OR,

*The rare and singular Vertues and Uses of those Angelick and
innocent PILS, discovered and left to posteritie, by Doctor
Patrick Anderson, late Physician of* Edinburgh.

A Mongst the most eminent Physicians of this age, the late famous Doctor *ANDERSON* is most deservedly to be esteemed; for he spared no Travel nor Study, that he might be serviceable to the Diseased of his Country; and returning from his Travels, with a mind fully enriched, an use of other things, he brought from *Venice* this inestimable Jewel; whose Vertues and Uses are these.

I. They exceedingly comfort and strengthen the Stomach; they restore the lost appetite; they purge Choler and Melancholly; but chiefly Phlegm and waterish matter; they cleanse the same of all putrid, gross and thick humors; they comfort the Intrals, open obstructions, and disperse all the pain of their places.

II. They strengthen the head and all the senses, but chiefly that of hearing and sight, whose weakness and pale they remove; they help the giddiness thereof and the Megrim; and as they comfort and purge the Stomach, so they do the like both to Head and Heart, and have this excellent faculty, that being as red with other Physick, they correct its malignity, and make it unhurtful to the Stomach, and are therefore to be preferred to all other gentle and easie Medicines.

III. They are wonderfully helpful to all diseases of the womb, and all other maladies belonging to women, that proceed from coldness by chance or constitution: for they safely and easily purge and empty the Belly, without pain or grippings, and carry out by their proper passages, all those vicious humors and other dregs that are stopped on a woman after her delivery; and they much help barrenness that proceedeth from uncleanness of the Womb, and cleanse women from their white-flux, and so stretch and establish them for conception. Also they stay or relax being by women with child, for yielding them ease in their bellies gently, without any hazard of miscarrying at all, one every night before Supper.

IV. They kill and check all worms that are bred in the Wombs of Children, big-bellied women that are bound in the belly, and of men; yea, not any body, that frequently use these Pills, can breed worms at all.

V. And if in women with child that the belly be bound, which often happeneth, you must have a special care that in the time of her birth, the great Gripes, being exercised with costiveness, do not engender her pains in travel; to avoid which, it is any counsel, that in such easie, you have already ready to your Cabinet Case of these Pills, especially seeing such that Glisters nor Suppositories are so convenient, because they trouble and importune [...]

VI. [...] They use moreover, to be given to those that are against nature, over-much pain; and who have need to be delivered of superfluous humors of the body.

VII. They hinder likewise the procreation of many diseases, and the corruption of the food: and wonderfully defend the body against the surfeit in eating or drinking, which most frequently after sleep beget corrupt and crude humors, and so are a sovereign help for the gravel, Scurvey, Chollick and Dropsie, and green-sickness and Palsie, one every day.

VIII. If the head be subject to destillations, by such intelligence with a moist and fuming Stomach, and threaten the joynts with a dead [...] these disgusted grains will so stop those Streams, that famous Physician hath promised they shall be free from the Gout, and all other diseases of the Joynts, who that use these Pils frequently and familiarly: for by them the daily cruelties and superfluities of the Meat being taken away, and carried into the sink of the belly, they cannot harm the joynts at all, nor procure diseases, which otherwise could not be avoided; whilest the more noble parts, being oppressed therewith, could not but for their own preservation send them to be quartered in the baser parts of the body.

IX. You may use of them at your pleasure, whether late or early, or at any hour of the day, before meat or after meat, or in the time of feeding; but being taken in time of Supper, they defend the body (as we have said) from those vapours and fumes that abound to it in the night. They are familiarly taken in time of meat, without trouble to the Mind or harm to the Body, and not any hindrance of your business. The Dose is, Seven, Nine or Eleven, and that three or four times a month, as necessity or the temper of the Body shall require. They give not many stools, neither do they work so violently and not only; Sometimes they open the belly twelve hours after they are taken: sometimes sooner, according to the disposition of the Stomach and Body; and they may be used without any special care of rules in your dyet, whether in Summer or Winter, in Frost or in Thaw Weather, without any inconveniency to ensue thereupon.

X. They are of so safe and innocent operation, that they may be given to children and decrepit old men, and that most securely: and to delicate persons who are not much imployed in labour, and others that cannot away with other purgatives, may easily swallow down these. They are an enemie to most diseases, and have much friendship to the noblest Intral of the bodie. And is of so wholesome and general use, and so much both known and approved in this Nation, that none who have once tryed the same, and found the good effects thereof will willingly want the same again, when they stand in need of Physick: which they may have ready for all sudden accidents, which through the neglect of these grains, if they suffer them to take rooting, will not afterward be removed so easily. But he that desires to live a long life and an healthful, take every day he use one of them at his mid-day and evening refreshment, he will soon find the benefit of them. They are exceeding good for the wind in the Stomach.

XI. We suppose there are few or none in this Kingdom, but knows of the use and excellency of Doctor *Andersons* Angelical pils, who perhaps are ignorant of the dangerous abuse and counterfeiting of them by sundry unskilful women: whereby some persons of great worth have been cast in hazard of their Lives, instead of being bettered, and because this is a business of high concernment to every nation, for prevention of such inconveniences to the people for the future, it is thought very fit to signifie, that these upright Pils are now only made by the said Doctors two Daughters, at their own dwelling houses, and no where else; and for your more security, call for a printed paper and Doctor *Andersons* own Picture at it; without that picture they are none of his Pills. And all the Boxes are sealed with her Name and Arms, K.A.

These Pils are to be sold by *Katharine Anderson*, Daughter to the late Dr. *Patrick Anderson*; at her house in *Edinburgh*, on the south-side of the street, in Sir *John Smiths* Closs, over against the head of the Land-Market: And they are to be sold by Mrs. *Reddess* at her house in *Kings-Street Westminster*, at the signe of the Cradle; and no where else at *London*.

Printed in the Year, 1677.

Handbills for quacks and patent medicines.

In the *Strand* near the Middle *Exchange* in *Salisbury* Street, at the Second House on the Right hand where a Barber's Pole hangs out, Liveth *John Butler*, An Expert Operator and Oculist.

YOu may find him there from Seven in the Morning till Twelve, And then he goes into *Sweeting's* Alley, to that which was *Joseph's* Coffee-House, now called the *Flanders* Coffee-House, next Door to the Sign of the Horse-Shoe near the *Royal Exchange*, there he stayes till Four of the Clock, who (by Gods Blessing) cureth the Distempers following, (*Viz.*)

He Cureth Blindness by Couching of Cataracts, He taketh Specks off the Eyes, and Cureth Defluxions of Rheums in the Eyes ; He hath singular good Skill and Knowledg in Curing of Deafness, when the Party comes to him, he will tell them the cause of their Deafness, whether the Deafness be Internal or External, or whether curable or no. He Cureth Noises, Singing or Buzzing in the Ears ; He cureth Bursten Bellies, he cureth Ulcerated Legs, and Itch in any part of the Body ; He hath an Excellent Art in drawing forth of Corns out of the Feet and Toes with the whole substance in length and similitude of a Clove, and drawing no blood, nor putting the Party to any pain at all : And by the Operation of a Plaister to kill them, that no other Corns will ever come again in the same places.

He is none of those which you call by that Vulgar name Corn-Cutters, could he perform it no better than such persons, he would scorn to set it forth in Print. For every Corn he draweth in his Chamber is Six pence ; if any person sends for him to their dwelling places, he expects Twelve pence. If any person doth conjecture that other Corns will come again in the same places, upon Consideration he will admit of a Years trial and take nothing for the present ; And if other Corns do come again in the same places within the Year, then he will expect nothing.

Alderman *Rugg* dwelling in St. *Albans* in *Hertfordshire*, he was very Lame with Corns, he had Five and Fifty Corns taken out 26 years ago by this Professor, and never any other Corns came again in the same places.

Capt. *Body* dwelling in *London*-Street in *Ratcliff*, had Thirty Corns taken out Three years ago, and never any came since ; he was so troubled with them, that he was forc'd to Ride up and down to do his business, but now goes very well without any pain.

Mr. *Morgan* a Herald-Painter in *Threadneedle*-Street near the *Royal Exchange*, he was much troubled with Corns, I took them out Two Years ago, And he was never troubled with any Corns since that time.

Mr. *Peck* now dwelling in *Noble*-Street, he had Fourteen Corns taken out by the Professor hereof Four and Twenty Years ago, and was never troubled with any Corns since.

He can give Testimonies of some Hundreds of Persons more that he hath Cured of the Particulars abovesaid, since his coming to *London*, which will be too Tedious to Insert here. He cureth many other Distempers not here mentioned.

This Oculist has a Large House and Shop wherein he now dwells, known by the Sign of the B E L L in *Pye-Corner* near *Smithfield*, which he is willing to Sell, Lett, or Exchange for another of the like Value in or near the City.

If any Person please to send for him, they are desired to leave a Note at his Chamber.

These handbills, preserved by Pepys, are among his papers in the Bodleian.

aspect of politics. The great Catholic question which was to play such a destructive part in Pepys's later career first forced itself on him in the person of Elizabeth. But whatever he may have feared or suspected she did not avow her Catholicism until the Diary was nearing its end; when, indeed, their marriage had been undermined by estrangement and deception.

In the early years at the Navy Office Pepys made at least spasmodic efforts to share with his wife the enchantments offered by the great fair of the world. He took her with him to the theatre. He engaged a music master for her so that she might join in his keenest pleasure. He even — advanced test of matrimony — enjoyed teaching her the mathematics. He arranged drawing lessons for her and was surprised and impressed by her pictures '. . . which now she is come to do very finely, to my great satisfaction, beyond what I could ever look for'.[10] They often read to each other; and even more often Pepys records his pleasure in his wife's conversation. From the evidence of the Diary, indeed the only source on this topic, it was not the widening of Pepys's intellectual and artistic horizons that loosened the ties between them. Elizabeth's formal education, like her antecedents, left, no doubt, much to be desired. Left to herself she would, it seems, have preferred playing blind-man's-buff with the maids to hearing about the methods of limiting population practised in East Prussia or the million other subjects on which Pepys was ready to absorb information. But she consistently shows in the Diary an attractive and unselfish readiness to enter into her husband's interests and to offer him her untutored natural abilities and tastes to shape and direct.

'What would you give, my lad, to know about the Argonauts?'
'Sir,' (said the boy) 'I would give what I have.'
Johnson was much pleased with his answer, and we gave him a double fare.

Is there an exchange in the whole of English literature that states a purer ideal of education or a more eloquent profession of the trust implied? Elizabeth was ready to make such a profession good. She was generous, her husband mean.

The benevolence that makes the letters of the ageing Pepys so delightful was, like his sobriety, not achieved without a struggle. The Pepys of the Diary is in many ways mean and even harsh. If he was generous to his own family he was stingy to his wife. Lady Sandwich, whose kindness and good sense he admired, felt at last impelled to speak to him about it:

Among other things, my Lady did mightily urge me to lay out money upon my wife, which I perceived was a little more earnest than ordinary; and so I seemed to be pleased with it and do resolve to bestow a lace upon her.[11]

Elizabeth was told to make a selection and then to leave the final choice to Lady Sandwich. Two days later:

. . . I find my Lady hath agreed upon a Lace for my wife, of £6, which I seemed much glad of that it was no more, though in my mind I think it too much, and I pray God keep me so to order myself and my wife's expenses that no inconvenience in purse or honour fallow this my prodigality.

Was it so very prodigal for a man who was making money hand-over-fist and spending it freely enough on the things that pleased or amused him? The conclusive answer may be found two years later when Pepys had been spending an evening over his accounts:

. . . and to my great sorrow, find myself £43 worse than I was the last month; which was then £760 and now is but £717. But it hath chiefly arisen from my layings-out in clothes for myself and wife — viz., for her, about £12; and for myself £55 or thereabouts . . .[12]

Lady Sandwich, least interfering of women, had evident reason for her action. Only when he was very rich — worth over £2,000 besides his Brampton estate — did he give Elizabeth a diamond ring ' — valued at about £10 — the first thing of that nature I did ever give her'.[13] 'Valued' it will be noticed: even then Pepys had not bought it for her: it was a present to him for helping a man to a purser's berth.

It would be easy to multiply instances; but there are aspects of his behaviour to her which, if not so cold-bloodedly selfish, are scarcely less repulsive. That he should nag and bully over her running of the house was to be expected. The idea that it was hers as much as his clearly never entered his mind. But the physical and psychological violence that he resorted to sometimes made him ashamed. It was cowardly to pull her nose and make her cry. It was disgraceful to black her eye in bed. But it was perhaps more odious to damage in childish spite the workbasket he had given her as a present; and unforgivable to snatch his old love-letters out of her desk and tear them up in front of her.

And yet it was not that he was not in love with her: '. . . sad for want of my wife, whom I love with all my heart, though of late she hath given me some troubled thoughts'.[14] When it seemed that a minor operation on her might be necessary he could not bear the idea of witnessing it.[15] And the jealousy that he himself recognised as making 'a very hell in my mind'[16] perhaps drew something from his love. Mainly it was nourished by his selfishness, his competitiveness, his egocentricity. And it was these as yet untamed forces that estranged him from the wife whom he loved and who loved him. As in the spring of 1660 when he went to sea with Mountagu she still had no power, no resources, no friends. Her *raison d'être* was to please him. She could make herself disagreeable, but that was all. He held all the cards; money, freedom, social opportunity, and played them for himself. Increasingly this meant that the world he lived in grew apart from hers. Sometimes the fact could soothe a qualm of conscience, if cited as evidence of her inadequacy to the position he had won: '. . . the indiscretion of a wife that brings me nothing almost (besides a comely person) but only trouble and discontent.'[17] Sometimes he recognised that the inequality was of his own making. Children, the natural corrective of his egoism and her boredom, were denied them. Signs of winter were appearing in his most intimate affection at a time when his intellectual and aesthetic responses were at their spring.

9

A very rising man

Even when every allowance is made for the inextricable confusion of
business and pleasure that was natural to the seventeenth century and seems
so odd in the twentieth, it still takes an effort to realise that while Pepys
was experiencing life with a multiplicity of consciousness that takes the
breath away he was also establishing himself as the most brilliant new
arrival in the most important department of government. 'Chance without
merit brought me in' he remarked to his friend Thomas Hill on November
1st 1665. But as early as August 1662 Coventry had described him to
Sandwich as 'the life of this office . . . So that on all hands by God's
blessing I find myself a very rising man.' Less than three years after that
Albemarle, a gruff and severe critic at the best of times, told Pepys to
his face '. . . that I was the right hand of the Navy here . . . so that he
should not know what could be done without me — at which I was [from
him] not a little proud.'[1] It was even more telling from its timing. War
had been declared on the Dutch and the first fleet action could not be
more than a few weeks, perhaps only days, away. No one knew better
than Albemarle, a professional of forty years' standing, that battles are
won by proper preparation, or at least cannot be won without it.

Had Pepys devoted himself single-mindedly to naval administration it
would still have been an astonishing achievement to have won such an
opinion from such a man at such a moment less than five years after

entering the office as a novice. But even in that part of his life which, as it whirls past us, we can plausibly identify as naval or, more broadly, concerned with Government business, it is by no means the good of the service or the interest of the state that is his sole preoccupation. The opportunities for enriching oneself in the Government service were large. Pepys was poor, extravagant and greedy. The charm and vivacity of his personality have combined with the immensity of his public service to melt the sternest judicial glare that has been turned on his early career as Clerk of the Acts. Except, perhaps, the coldly penetrating gaze of Pepys himself. 'We do nothing in this office like people able to carry on a war. We must be put out or other people put in.'[2] Yet, so rapidly do the facets of Pepys's mind spin round, in the same short entry, a bare half-dozen lines away, he justifies to himself a monumental piece of corruption over the Tangier victualling contract: ' – for which God be praised. For I can with a safe conscience say that I have therein saved the King £5,000 per annum, and yet got myself a hope of £300 per annum without the least wrong to the King.' God be praised indeed: but as the gentlest of judges has written of this very transaction in his authoritative book on Navy Board contracts, 'This, of course, is nonsense.'[3]

What makes the contemplation of Pepys, either in general or in detail, so dizzying is that the interlocking circles of his nature revolve too fast for the eye to distinguish a clear and individual movement. It is like watching an electric egg-whisk. Pepys is the life of the office, the right hand of the navy. Coventry says so, Albemarle confirms it. But Pepys is also corrupt. He is, further, a factious and disloyal colleague – witness a hundred entries in the Diary, notably those concerning Sir William Penn. But, as we shall see, he is also a tenaciously loyal colleague – witness his lifelong relationship with Hewer – and the man who time and again defends the office when it is under attack. He is a demon for efficiency and reform: yet no one watches more closely or understands more profoundly the dynastic nature of the Navy Office – witness Sir George Carteret's allying himself by marrying a son to one of Sandwich's daughters and a daughter to a (supposed) illegitimate son of Prince Rupert, that alarming, uncompromising, unpredictable figure. Sandwich and Coventry, Penn and Batten, Monck and Rupert, the King and the Duke, patrons, colleagues, politicians, admirals, princes, all these forces are constantly in a state of flux, constantly acting on each other, and yet must be severally and collectively held in equilibrium to promote the career of Samuel Pepys. So viewed, and that is how the Diary views it, this looks a full-time job. But not at all. There is the theatre, books, music, lust, social pleasures and social obligations, all the hundred and one themes already touched on whirring round at full speed without, apparently, ever getting in each other's way.

At least so full a life must surely have required a high degree of organisation. In the sense of reducing matters to order, of imposing form on chaos, of keeping records, accounts, files, minutes, even a diary, this is evidently true of Pepys. But it is far from true of the way in which he organised his day. Regularity of hours was not his habit. If he wanted to finish some major undertaking, a paper on the method of measuring masts or mustering stores, a letter to the Duke on the general administration of the navy or to Sir William Coventry on pursery and victualling, he would work from four to five o'clock in the morning till midnight for several consecutive days. On the other hand the office hours that he kept during the winter of 1662 for example sort oddly with Coventry's description, unquestionably correct, of the rising man. On November 26th a hangover kept him in bed till near midday and he did not visit the office till summoned there in the late afternoon. On the 28th it was again afternoon before he attended the office and on the next day he did not get up until his colleagues sent word that the Duke of York required their presence at Whitehall that afternoon. Apart from this brief interview the day's official labours seem to have consisted of a very fine dinner at Sir William Coventry's lodging and a visit to the theatre with Sir William Penn. This agreeable course of life persisted into December until on the 14th the diarist himself remarks on it: 'All the morning at home, lying abed with my wife till 11 a-clock – such a habitt we have got this winter of lying long abed.' Pepys was no sluggard but he was not, as so many of his successors are, a slave of the clock.

It will be remembered that one of Pepys's first concerns was to master the nuts and bolts of his job. In particular he set himself to learn his way about those commodity markets in which the navy was a large buyer. Masts, canvas, timber, iron, hemp, tar and the whole range of ships' stores were his immediate preoccupation. The artist in administration had to master his medium. It was intolerable to be ignorant of that which could be learnt by taking pains. No entry in the Diary is more characteristic than the comment on the signing and sealing of the contract for the building of the mole at Tangier: 'a thing I did with a very ill will, because a thing which I did not at all understand, nor any or few of the whole board.'[4] Muddle enraged him: and to the man of business no muddle is more exasperating than the lazy confusion of what can be known with what cannot. The mole at Tangier to which his colleagues so light-heartedly put their names that afternoon was, as Pepys's sure instinct warned him, a gigantic undertaking, demanding the closest scrutiny and assessment. Not until we reach our own age has any English government in time of peace committed so vast a proportion of the nation's expenditure to so ambitious and so fruitless a project. To construct an artificial harbour in deep tidal water exposed to the violent storms of the Atlantic and to the frequent and fierce gales from the Levant on a part of the African coast, twelve hundred miles from the nearest English port, that was dominated by a wild and warlike Moorish tribe was an amazing venture by the standards of the seventeenth century. Simply as a piece of engineering the mole was the greatest work ever undertaken by Englishmen. And the cost proved, before long, far beyond the resources of a preindustrial economy. Pepys could not have known this: but he understood at once that a decision involving huge sums and incalculable consequence was being taken casually and carelessly. And this offended him.

But the artist was, if the deepest, only one of his parts. The opportunist was another. If the government had however rashly committed itself to pouring out hundreds of thousands on Tangier, it was not in Pepys's character to watch the gold flow by without seeing what could be done to divert some of it in his own direction. He had been appointed a Commissioner in November 1662 and finding 'Tangier one of the best flowers in my garden' drove a bargain with the elegant but futile Povy to succeed him as Treasurer of the Commission in the spring of 1665. Even splitting fifty-fifty with Povy he made money hand-over-fist, much of it, as is clear from the Diary, by the corrupt practices he denounced in others.

The same easy transitions may be observed in his Navy Office negotiations. He sets out to master the commodity markets because he wants to know, he must know, he cannot bear to be at the mercy of other people when industry could make him his own master. He hob-nobs with Captain Cocke, the hemp contractor, with Sir William Warren, the great importer of masts. He knows the going rate and he investigates the possibility of alternative sources of supply. He is not too proud to go to school to shipwrights, ropemakers, boatswains and such people. His blood boils when he learns the tricks put upon the King by dishonest contractors and connived at by his colleagues. And yet when Cocke offers him a rake-off he jumps at it. When Warren provides him with arguments to convince the board of the superior value his masts offer to those of his rival, Wood, who is hand-in-glove with Sir William Batten it is difficult not to feel that best argument of all was the £100 in a bag handed over in the Sun tavern on September 16th, 1664. All through the Diary period Pepys is using the technical and commercial knowledge he has acquired to line his own pockets.

Was he then insincere in professing a desire to root out corruption and to see that the King was given value for money? Was his enthusiasm for the reforms propounded by Slyngsbie and Coventry a pretence? There seems no reason to think so. Pepys was often hypocritical, notably in his holier-than-thou headshakings over the shiftiness of his colleagues, but he is rarely cynical. On the other hand his admirers have perhaps been in more of a hurry than Pepys was to establish his reputation as a public servant of fearless probity. That was what he became; it was not the point from which he started.

The chameleon quality which made, and makes, Pepys so companionable exacts its price. The company of shrewd and thrusting dealers like Cocke and Warren teaches other lessons besides the quayside costs of Milan hemp or the different methods of sawing Eastland timber. Not that all the people Pepys did business with were city magnates. Some were country gentlemen like Colonel Bullen Reymes of Waddon in Dorset, a Royalist who had been brought up in the service of the first Duke of Buckingham. Reymes, like Cocke, was an M.P. and had connections at court: it was his brother-in-law who had sheltered Charles II at Trent when he was on the run after the battle of Worcester in 1651. A widower, he had, after the Restoration, entered into a partnership as much personal as commercial with a remarkable woman who was wife to the Puritan mayor of Weymouth. Mrs. Pley and Reymes were important suppliers both of West Country and Breton sailcloth. There were two other career women whom Pepys evidently respected for their commercial talents. Mrs. Russell, the tallow chandler, seems to have been unremarkable beyond the fact that she was a woman in business. Mrs. Bland, another sailcloth supplier, emigrated with her husband to Tangier where they quarrelled fiercely with the military governor. Their son emigrated to America and took part in one of the earliest attempts at revolution. He was captured, sentenced and executed. Mrs. Bland's last letter to Pepys, a bitter, fearless denunciation of the whole system of government brought her to the attention of the Attorney-General.[5]

In spite of Sir William Coventry's disapproval the commercial and the official worlds interpenetrated each other. Bullen Reymes, for instance, was sent out as a special emissary to report on the state of affairs at Tangier after the Governor and a large part of the forces under his command had been cut to pieces by the Moors.[6] Both he and Captain Cocke were joined with John Evelyn in the Commission for the Sick and Wounded set up just before the outbreak of the Second Dutch War. The Houblons, too, with their network of trading connections in Spain and the Western Mediterranean were invaluable sources of intelligence and could often keep a useful eye on the activities of captains who thought themselves far enough away from Admiralty surveillance to do pretty well as they liked.

Altogether these connections with the merchants who supplied the navy or who, like the Houblons, needed its protection against the Arab pirates of North Africa were among the most enjoyable as well as the most instructive aspects of life as Clerk of the Acts. The people involved were diverse; they were all experts; they were all quick-witted; they were all citizens of the world. As has already been pointed out they were often men of high civilisation. But they had yet greater charms than these. None of them was a colleague. None could ever be a rival. All were, in some degree, suitors for Pepys's favours. A rejected suitor might, of course, turn nasty and tell Batten or Penn things that were either untrue or embarrassing. Most of them had the sense not to prejudice happier relations by such proceedings. And all of them understood that an official had to live.

Besides increasing his practical knowledge Pepys also set himself to learn something of the arts and sciences material to his profession. Hydrography, navigation, naval architecture, naval history and maritime law found a place in his intellectual curriculum which they retained to the end of his life; indeed beyond, for these subjects are nobly represented in the library that is his chosen monument. The study of naval architecture led to one of the longest and most fruitful of Pepys's long and fruitful professional relationships. Anthony Deane, assistant shipwright at Woolwich, taught Pepys enough to hold his own against the experienced sea officers on the board and supplied him with drawings, still preserved in his library, that were much admired by John Evelyn, one of the greatest connoisseurs of the century. In return Pepys was a zealous promoter of Deane's career. In October 1664 when war was imminent he secured his appointment as Master Shipwright at Harwich. The ships he built there won him a European reputation. Louis XIV and Colbert courted him: at the end of the century his son went to Russia to superintend the shipyards of Peter the Great. But eminent as he might become, he was the protégé, Pepys the patron. Strong paternal admonition characterised such a relationship

. . . I will not dissemble with you because I love you. I am wholly dissatisfied in your proceedings about Mr Browne and Mr Wheeler . . . Mr Deane, I do bear you still good respect, and (though it may be you do not now think that worth keeping) I should be glad to have reason to continue it to you. But, upon my word, I have not spared to tell the Board my opinion about this business, as you will shortly see by a letter we have wrote to Commissioner Taylor. Wherein I have been very free concerning you, and shall be more so if ever I meet with the like occasion.[7]

This letter was written after Deane had established himself at Harwich and was within a few years of a knighthood and a large fortune. Perhaps the vehemence and openness of Pepys's communications with his subordinates, so very different from Sandwich's well-bred reserve, made friendship easy. Certainly Deane's attachment never weakened in fair weather or in foul.

The same is true of the closest of all Pepys's associations, that with Will Hewer. Pepys's intolerance of deviation in the matter of dress led to correction that did not always stop at words. Hewer's habit of wearing his hat in the house affronted Pepys. His wearing his cloak 'flung over his shoulder like a Ruffian' enraged him. It was Hewer's 'slight answer' on this occasion that provoked Pepys to box his ears. Worse followed two months later when Pepys who had waited up for Hewer at the office till late at night found that he had gone straight home from the job he had been doing at Deptford and was 'at ease in his study'. Pepys lost his temper and hit him. He then stayed up even later 'chiding him' and at last, after midnight, stalked off, convinced that Hewer 'hath got a taste of liberty since he came to me that he will not leave' and threatening to find a replacement for him. Hewer's mildness in the face of such treatment is the more remarkable in that he was evidently a young man of means. When in 1663 he left Pepys's house to live in lodgings of his own Pepys was much impressed by their splendour. It is characteristic of them both that Hewer should present, and Pepys send back, 'a locket of dyamonds worth about £40' to Elizabeth, 'out of his gratitude for my kindness and hers to him'. 'It becomes me more to refuse it than to let her accept it.' Of that kindness, and of the fierce loyalty that went with it, there can be no doubt. Early in 1662 Penn had advised Pepys to get rid of Hewer because Sir George Carteret believed that he was passing on confidential information to his uncle Robert Blackborne. It took some pluck to disregard such a hint from such a quarter.

Gradually Hewer took the place of the son that Pepys could not have. In his will Pepys acknowledged 'his more than filial affection and tenderness expressed to me through all the occurrences of my life for forty years past'. Other relationships were briefly contemplated and, happily, dismissed. Hewer as we have seen declined Pall's hand out of a general disinclination to matrimony. Pepys's lurid jealousy tried once or twice to imagine him carrying on an adulterous intrigue with Elizabeth but collapsed at the effort. On the contrary when Pepys's infidelities at last threatened the marriage with disaster it was Hewer who did more than anyone else to save it. How close their professional relationship was is early apparent. Pepys trusted Hewer absolutely. Hewer knew and used the system of shorthand in which minutes of confidential matters were better kept.

Pepys was not always so fortunate or so perceptive in his choice of assistants. An example of some interest because it involved a head-on collision with a sea officer of some standing comes to mind in the person of Richard Cooper, whom he employed to teach him mathematics. The two men had first met in the spring of 1660 aboard the *Naseby*; Cooper was master's mate, that is assistant navigator, junior enough to be approachable and expert enough to be worth learning from. He was serving in the same capacity aboard the *Royal James* when Pepys ran across him again in July 1662. Impressed by his ability and prudently reflecting that he was unlikely to ask much in the way of a fee Pepys promptly engaged him. The lessons were a success. By the beginning of August the syllabus had apparently been extended to include mechanics[8] and Pepys was able to reward his tutor by having him appointed master of a fourth-rate under orders for a voyage to the Straits and Tangier. By the end of September she had sailed.

But she was back before the swallows, bringing trouble with her. Early in March Pepys met her Captain fresh from sea who told him:

> strange stories of the faults of Cooper, his master, put in by me; which I do not believe but am sorry to hear, and must take some course to have him removed, though I believe that the Captain is proud and the fellow is not supple enough to him.[9]

Both these judgments were to receive abundant confirmation. Meanwhile Pepys lost no time in writing to Cooper urging him to make a clean breast at once as the only means by which his patron could defend him from injustice:

> You are said to be a Mutinere, a man ignorant in your duty that have several times endangered the shipp and very often been drunk . . . you know wherein you are justly accused, wherein not . . .[10]

To strengthen his flank with an impartial expert Pepys also wrote to the Commissioner at Chatham, where the ship was lying, asking his opinion of Cooper's fitness for his post. Commissioner Pett replied that Cooper though of a weak brain and 'sometimes disguised with drink' might be continued in his appointment provided that he chose a competent master's mate. This was hardly what was wanted to beat off an attack from so formidable a figure as Robert Holmes, the Captain who had made the complaint. Holmes's record both as a young cavalry officer in the Civil War and as Rupert's right-hand man in the semi-piratical cruise to Portugal, the Mediterranean, West Africa and the West Indies that had followed it was evidence enough that here was no tame conventional spirit. In any case Pepys already knew Holmes and had been rather frightened by his open cynicism. No wonder that his first reaction had been to accept Cooper's dismissal as a foregone conclusion, even though to save the Board's honour and his own reputation within it some show of resistance would have to be made.

In the event it was very much more than a show. At a full meeting of the Navy Board on the afternoon of Saturday, March 21st:

> Captain Holmes being called in, he began his high complaint against his Master, Cooper, and would have him forthwith discharged — which I opposed, not in his defence but for the justice of proceeding, not to condemn a man unheard. Upon [which] we fell from one word to another that we came to very high Termes, such as troubled me, though all and the worse I ever said was that was insolently and illmannerdly spoken — which he told me it was well it was here that I said it. But all the officers, Sir G. Carteret, Sir J. Mennes, Sir W. Batten and Sir W. Penn cried shame of it. At last he parted, and we resolved to bring the dispute between him and his Master to a trial next week — wherein I shall not at all concern myself in defence of anything that is unhandsome on the Maister's part, nor willingly suffer him to have any wrong. So we rose and I to my office troubled, though sensible that all the officers are of opinion that he hath carried himself very much unbecoming him.

This was an age when duelling was common: even more common, where a man of rank considered his dignity impugned by a social inferior, was naked violence. The solidarity of one's colleagues at the Navy Board was no doubt consoling but it would not be much comfort if one was set on by a gang of thugs or was to find oneself at the point of a sword with Holmes's thin-lipped face behind it. Pepys spent a thoroughly uncomfortable weekend. On the Monday duty took him, in spite of trepidation, to Whitehall and a meeting of the Tangier Committee. At last in the evening where he least expected it he ran into Holmes on Sandwich's doorstep. Holmes made as if to go away. Pepys would not have it and himself offered to go. In this exchange of civilities and the conversation that ensued Holmes 'did as good as desire excuse for the high words that did pass in his eat the other day, which I was willing enough to close with'. That is easily believed. What is interesting is that Pepys should have allowed his

strong sense of propriety, of what was owing both to the dignity of his own
position and to the conduct of official business, to overcome his prudence
not to say his timidity. And what of Holmes? Why did he not teach that
soft and self-important young Clerk of the Acts a lesson? For all his
amoral professions he never lacked loyalty or courage and may have
respected Pepys for an unlooked-for display of both. He was, too, himself
a highly efficient and professional officer, qualities again that he could
have seen reflected in Pepys. Or it may have been a simple calculation.
For a sea officer to assault or even to challenge a member of the Navy
Board might risk a scandal even in that loose and bullying age.[11]

The next day saw the end of the matter. At the board:

> . . . among other things, had Cooper's business tried against Captain
> Holmes. But I find Cooper a fudling, troublesome fellow, though a good
> artist [i.e. mathematician]; and so am content to have him turned out
> of his place. Nor did I see reason to say one word against it, though I
> know what they did against him was with great envy and pride.[12]

The proud and envious 'They' of this passage must refer to Pepys's colleagues on the board. But, as in the Great Caucus Race, everyone has won
so everyone must have prizes. Holmes has got rid of an incompetent master.
Pepys has successfully maintained the principles or at least the procedures
of elementary justice. Cooper may have been fudling and troublesome;
he may have been the object of envy and pride; but at least he was not
condemned without being heard.

But who was right, in the matter of professional judgment? Was Cooper
as Holmes maintained a drunken neurotic, unfit to be trusted with the
safety of a man of war? Or was he 'a good artist' as Pepys continued to
insist? Three years later towards the end of the Four Days Battle, one of
the fiercest of all the fierce sea-fights with the Dutch, the *Royal Prince*
flagship of the White squadron, ran aground on the Galloper sand where
the Dutch captured and burnt her, taking Sir George Ayscue, back to
Holland as a prisoner. This is the only occasion in the history of the Royal
Navy that a flagship has been captured and her admiral made prisoner.
The master responsible for the navigation and pilotage was Richard
Cooper.[13]

This conflict with Holmes foreshadows much in Pepys's own career.
And not only in Pepys's. Here in embryo is the division between the
frocks and the brass that grew to such alarming proportions in the First
World War. Pepys himself would have seen it as an early confrontation
with one of the gentlemen captains whose arrogance and indiscipline undid

all. Again it could be interpreted as an incident of political gang warfare. Cooper as well as Pepys were Sandwich's men; Holmes was Prince Rupert's. A case could be made out for all three views, none of which are mutually exclusive. But what is illuminating about the facts is that Pepys's judgment seems to have been hasty and unwise. And what a difference the affair reveals between the England of Cromwell and that of Charles II. One can hardly imagine one of the Protector's civil servants quaking about his business in the expectation of physical violence from a serving officer. The lesson was not lost on Pepys.

From his appointment to the Navy Office in the summer of 1660 to the outbreak of war with the Dutch in the spring of 1665 Pepys was laying the foundations of achievement, talking, listening, reading, learning, measuring men and mastering detail. If he had fallen a victim to the plague that made its appearance late in 1664 what would have been his record as a naval administrator? Hundreds of letters would confirm the evidence of the Diary that he had shown himself a man of system, order and business-like habits. He had realised to the full the ambition he had set before himself in his official dealings. '. . . that . . . which I labour most to merit by — I mean the easiness, civility and dispatch which I pretend to give to all that have occasion of applications to my Office.'[14] He had prepared important state papers on victualling and on the pursery; he had criticised estimates and schemes for remodelling the finances of the navy; but solid achievement, so far, had been limited to standardising the stationery in official use at Woolwich Dockyard.[15]

He had made a reputation. He was known to all the people who mattered. The King knew him.[16] The Duke of York saw him day in day out. His secretary Coventry was among his warmest admirers. Clarendon, the Lord Chancellor knew him. So did Lord Ashley, who as Earl of Shaftesbury was to do all he could to destroy him. The men behind the scenes, Sir Philip Warwick who ran the Treasury, Sir George Downing, who managed Anglo-Dutch relations and much else besides, the City men, the Royal Society men, all knew Pepys. 'How little merit doth prevail in the world, but only favour' he had argued in the conversation with his friend Hill, quoted at the beginning of this chapter. But he went on to draw confidence from his own diligence: 'living as I do among so many lazy people, that the diligent man becomes necessary, that they cannot do anything without him.'

10

The right hand of the navy

If mastery of the multiplication table was a rare achievement in seventeenth
century England, calculation of the Mystical Number in the Book of
Daniel and the Revelation of St John was commonplace. The object of
these exercises was to predict the end of the world: and the year 1666
compounded as it was of 1000, a hot favourite for Doom in its day, and the
magical number 666, was widely recommended as a solution of the problem. If it was not to prove the Time of the End, in spite of the promising
adjuncts of War, Pestilence and Fire, it was at least the year of destiny
for Samuel Pepys. By its close he had shown indisputable mastery of the
business of the Navy Office which he had often been left to manage on his
own, and this under the stress of war conducted by a government that was
neither experienced nor strong. He had also made himself a rich man. The
war with the Dutch that he had feared, opposed and bewailed had established him.

The immediate cause of the war was the attack on the West African
possessions of the Dutch East India Company mounted by a naval force
under the command of Pepys's recent adversary Robert Holmes.[1] Technically the naval vessels that fired on the Dutch forts were rented to the
Royal African Company, a body in which the King, the Duke of York,
Prince Rupert and many of their servants (but not Pepys) had some financial
interest. Thus some thin disguise could be put on what was nakedly

challenge to the Dutch. Holmes had interpreted his instructions, in themselves aggressive enough, with characteristic brio. To satisfy the decencies of international life he was sent to the Tower on his return. But the Dutch ambassador reported, quite correctly, that this was mere deception. Sir George Downing at The Hague, the thrusters among the city men, the younger politicians and courtiers who resented the power of the old Royalists and its personification in Clarendon, were all hot for war. Captain Cocke hemp merchant, Cavalier member of Parliament and a director of the Royal African Company, put the matter succinctly when he told Pepys, '. . . that the trade of the world is too little for us two, therefore one must down'.

Cocke like many of his contemporaries took it for granted that the volume of world trade was static, from which it followed that a nation could increase its share only by wresting something from someone else. This robust view of the commercial process was supported by the political wisdom of non-partisan patriots such as Monck who saw in fighting the foreigner the surest way to unify the nation and to submerge the memories of civil war. Whether the King favoured this policy is at least doubtful: but his brother, as Lord High Admiral, was naturally enthusiastic for a war that was bound to be ninety per cent naval and perhaps to offer him the chance of a place in history beside Henry V or the Black Prince. Coventry, both as his secretary and as a leader of the anti-Clarendonians, was, at this stage of the game, also in favour of the war.

Pepys's opposition was emphatic and consistent. All through the spring and summer of 1664 the Diary records nothing but dread and foreboding at the general desire for war. Largely this was the sober judgment of an expert who knew the true state of naval affairs reacting against a fatuous national conceit. But partly it derived from the fact of Sandwich's being out of things, a condition that Coventry was anxious to perpetuate. If he succeeded, Pepys's position would be difficult indeed. Sandwich's power was based on the navy. If he were to be excluded from command in a major war, he, and perhaps Pepys with him, would be left high and dry. Hence from Pepys's point of view the necessity of reinsuring with Coventry, whom in any case he liked and admired. Personally no less than professionally he found himself in a most delicate situation, especially when Coventry commissioned him to sound out Sandwich's readiness to command a squadron of twelve ships that was being fitted out in the summer of 1664. Was not so minor a post beneath the dignity of a General-at-Sea? Coventry hoped he would think so as then he would be out of play when the real game began. Sandwich told Pepys that he was ready to serve in that or any other sea command that might be offered. Coventry and the

Duke of York received this coolly. In the event of war the Duke wanted to command the fleet himself; and how, with three Generals-at-Sea, Sandwich, Penn and Albemarle, still active, not to mention Prince Rupert, was the conduct of operations against the first naval power of the world to be entrusted to a man who had seen no service at sea? The King, it seems, found the solution that satisfied everybody. His brother was to have the command of the fleet, with Penn at his elbow in the unique appointment of Great Captain Commander. Sandwich was to be Rear-Admiral of the Fleet and to command the Blue Squadron, Rupert was to have the White, and Albemarle, the elder statesman of war, was to remain ashore to give the King and Council the benefit of his advice. Pepys always admired Charles's judgment in naval affairs of which this is a good instance.

For Pepys the advantages of this arrangement were nicely counter-balanced. It removed the horrid prospect of a collision between Sandwich and Coventry. But the immense prestige acquired by Sir William Penn drove Pepys into paroxysms of jealousy. Even before the war broke out the regard paid by the Duke to Penn's experience against the Dutch could, Pepys was sure, only be explained '. . . by some strong obligations he hath laid upon Mr Coventry, for Mr Coventry must needs know that he is a man of very mean parts, but only a bred seaman.'[2] And the elevation of Prince Rupert was even worse. Pepys had seen him as a colleague on the Tangier Committee where he had not been impressed. 'Prince Robert [Rupert] doth nothing but swear and laugh a little, with an oath or two, and that's all he doth.'[3]

That the Diary alone provides good evidence of Rupert's remarkable range as scientist and artist makes no matter. Antipathy probably, fear certainly, inspire a vision of an overbearing brute of a cavalryman that is difficult to reconcile with what we know of the most intellectual of the later Stuarts. Perhaps his manner gave offence. It is clear that both Clarendon and Pepys disliked and resented him. Rupert for his part was not the man to conceal his conviction that his past services and professional talents were much superior to Sandwich's.

War was declared on February 22nd, 1665. A month later the Commander-in-Chief went aboard his flagship, accompanied by Coventry, Penn, and a host of lesser lights. Courtiers wished themselves on to captains of their acquaintance as volunteers so that the official world of London and Westminster was suddenly emptier. The size of the pond had not changed but there were noticeably fewer fish. The balance of power at the Navy Board tilted sharply in Pepys's favour. For who else could be applied to if men or stores were urgently needed at Plymouth or Dover or Chatham or Harwich? Penn and Coventry were with the fleet, Carteret, as a Privy Councillor and Vice-Chamberlain of the House-hold, was often required to attend the King. To answer questions and get things done the only people to apply to were Batten, Pepys, Mennes and Lord Brouncker. Brouncker, an eminent mathematician, was a good man of business when he could spare the time from his commitments as President of the Royal Society and from his domestic obligations to an ugly mistress in Covent Garden. Coventry had summed the matter up in his usual inimitable manner when Pepys had gone to call on him as he was packing for sea:

> He tells me the weight of despatch will lie most upon me. And told me freely his mind touching Sir W. Batten and Sir J. Mennes — the latter of whom, he most aptly said, was like a lapwing; that all he did was to keep a flutter to keep others from the nest that they would find.[4]

It was at this period that Albemarle paid Pepys the great compliment al-ready mentioned. Batten was his superior in standing and in experience but he was beginning to feel his years. At the outbreak of war he was seriously ill and not expected to live. He did in fact recover and survive till a few months after the peace but at critical moments he was often absent from the office through ill-health.

So almost before he was aware of it Pepys found himself running a naval war of unprecedented proportions. The fleet with which the Duke of York sailed from the Gunfleet in April 1665 was the largest that England had ever sent out. Penn's son who had been with his father till the landsmen were ordered ashore counted 103 men of war besides fire ships and ketches, a figure substantially confirmed by Will Hewer from Harwich a few days later. Even if we accept the slightly lower estimate of modern scholars[5] it was still by the standards of those days enormous. And manning, victualling, paying and supplying it were a challenge worthy of administrative genius. In theory not all these tasks should have fallen on the Navy Board. In practice they did. If the fleet had run out of beer, if the victualling ships were still taking on stores in the river when they should have been at sea, it was Pepys not Gauden the victualler who threatened, pestered, ordered and went in person to see that his orders were obeyed. Pepys cut through red-tape. Organisations naturally engender a prejudice in favour of obstruction. To get anything out of them the prerequisite is to find a heretic prejudiced in favour of action. Once such people have been identified the channels of business change course to-wards them. By this process Pepys soon became what Albemarle called him.

The Diary for the opening months of the war records the range and tempo of Pepys's activity. But for the sheer mass of detail, marshalled by an exact and lawyerlike intelligence, the best evidence is the Letterbook of his official correspondence now in the National Maritime Museum. A business letter from Pepys must often have sounded to the recipient like the opening speech of prosecuting counsel, recapitulating all the facts and circumstances of the case to be tried. The charge that subordinates or colleagues found themselves most frequently accused of was failure to observe the proper routine:

> I returne you the enclosed bill for Knees* (though signed) that you may certify them (as the Duke commands) to be agreed by contract. By which omission I wonder you should so often put us upon a necessity either of delaying satisfaction to merchants (as now in this case of Mr Castle's) or of passing their bills unjustifiably. Pray let it be completed as it should be and sent hither by the messenger tomorrow and at the same time let me know the reason of our not receiving the whole parcell (of which he complaines) it being a commodity which wee should unwillingly spare any at this time . . .

The two senior shipwrights at Deptford perhaps thought that they knew more about buying knee timber than Pepys did. Their answer appears to have been disrespectful; perhaps even ribald, for the very next day an even more orotund and circumstantial letter of reproof was directed at them:

> I am sorry you should thinke soe slight an answer as that I received from you this morning should satisfie me being (I thinke) not used to ask questions to so little purpose. But since you have so mistaken me let me rectify it by observing to you that I doe not think you can imagine that the Principal Officers turned over every knee but in general did very well like of their appearance . . .
>
> But let me tell you either they were very good and worth our money, or the contrary. If the former, then at a time of such use for them as this, why should we not have the whole quantity . . .? If the latter, why should we not know in what manner they are found so defective as that of 80 loades you should receive but 47 or if (as you say) you had nothing to do with the quality of them, how come you to except against any of them?[6]

---

* Crooked pieces of timber used to connect the deck-beams with the sides of a vessel.

And so, inexorably, on, referring them to an earlier letter to the merchant of which they had been sent a copy. How were unlettered shipwrights to stand against the method of argument taught at the Universities? This technique was better reserved for inferiors or perhaps equals. Employed against men like Prince Rupert or the Duke of Albemarle it could be counterproductive.

Fitting out a fleet created shortage in everything the Navy Office existed to provide — rope, masts, plank, tar, sailcloth, flags and, above all, seamen. Stockpiling against emergencies was impossible because Charles II's Government never had enough money to pay off its creditors, let alone finance forward buying. Pepys who never tired of demonstrating the obvious proves in letter after letter and memorandum after memorandum that the Government inflated the prices of all its purchases by its known inability to pay up. Shortage of ready money is the shortage most often mentioned by Pepys since it made his job more and more difficult as the war went on. But at the outset it was shortage of goods that was most serious. Demand had mopped up supply. Hence the importance he attached to the safe arrival of the Hamburg convoy with its cargo of masts, spars, pitch, tar and shiptimber. Its capture by the Dutch on May 20th was a heavy blow.

'Up betimes to the Duke of Albemarle about money to be got for the Navy, or else we must shut up shop.'[7] The war had not been going for two months when that entry was written. Always, for the rest of the war, Pepys was saying that this was the end; that things just could not go on like this; that men were starving in the dockyards for want of pay; that widows and discharged seamen were dying in the street. Always he was securing the last parcel of Milan hemp, even at an astronomical price; his dockyard commissioner was cajoling a blacksmith who had not been paid for twenty months into repairing one last anchor before dowsing the fire of his forge for good. Sometimes the reader is reminded of the early silent films in which hero or heroine is forever hanging on by the eyebrows while the cliff-top slowly crumbles. Was the abyss into which the Clerk of the Acts was gazing real, or a figure of speech employed to get results?

Pepys's reports of men unpaid, of workmen starving, of small tradesmen ruined, of widows and children thrown on the world have every appearance of truth and are supported by much other evidence. Probably, too, he was not exaggerating when he warned that certain essential stores were in dangerously short supply. But simply on the facts that the war went on, that ships did, somehow, get repaired, that the sails, masts and spars so abundantly destroyed in action were replaced, it seems that

Pepys underestimated the resilience and the sheer power of survival that so often goes with poverty. Like most of us Pepys had never known hunger and hardship, had never depended on his will to keep him alive when his reason told him that statistically he might as well lie down and die. It is this quality that constantly compels the admiration of everyone who studies the past. And again how are we to reconcile those heartfelt cries about the total absence of cash with the ecstatic reckonings of the diarist's huge personal gains? On December 31st, 1665, after only ten months of war he could write, 'I have raised my estate from £1300 in this year to £4,400'. He was not counting in cowrie shells. And what of his friends who supplied the navy on a large scale, Cocke and Warren and the rest? They seem to have commanded large funds with which to sweeten the conclusion of Navy Board contracts. There was more money about than Pepys sometimes cares to admit: and insiders like himself were well placed to catch it. The public finances of Caroline England were like some antiquated system of domestic water supply subjected to constant airlocks. A monitory gurgling and shuddering in the pipes told the initiated when the taps might be expected to emit. It is characteristic of Pepys that he used his expertise in financial plumbing not only to enrich himself but to promote efficiency and to honour public obligations. It was Batten, not Pepys, who was Treasurer of the Chatham Chest, that pioneer scheme of contributory social insurance for seamen initiated by Sir John Hawkins. But it was Pepys, not Batten, who saw to it that the administrators of the Chest were notified when a ship was to be paid. The deductions from the seamen's wages were, as things stood, the only source of its income; and consequently the only source of pensions for the disabled. Pepys was among the first to recognise the inadequacy and to press Coventry for its improvement.[8]

In the sharpening necessities of war Pepys's immediate financial concern was obtaining money. But he never forgot that public servants are accountable down to the last penny and that some day he would have to answer to some tribunal, the Treasury, the Council or a Parliamentary Committee, that might well be hostile. It was, obviously, extremely difficult to keep proper accounts in the press and confusion of war. Writing to Sir Philip Warwick, an old Royalist whose grasp of Treasury affairs Pepys wholeheartedly admired, he prefaced his accounts for the first six months of the war as follows:

> . . . But many difficulties concur to make it impracticable to state the last six months expense in the method and with the positiveness I have heretofore done it. For in the unavoidable confusion we have for

some time been in, 'tis not possible to take a right muster of ye men where Commanders are never bounded as to number nor (through the sickness [i.e. the plague], death, insufficiency and other necessities of altering their number for supplying other ships or prizes) are capable of ascertaining their complement three days together. This makes the computing of wages, victuals, wear and tear (the three great articles of our expense) noe more to be perfected than by estimate . . .[9]

A sympathetic and intelligent colleague was one thing: a Day of Reckoning was another. Yet Pepys, for all his apprehensions as to the course and outcome of the war, doubled, trebled and even tried to quadruple his administrative stake. A month after war had been declared he negotiated his appointment to the treasurership of Tangier in succession to Povy. In November he became Surveyor-General of the Victualling, in itself a vast commitment. And even before the war had started Pepys had joined the other Principal Officers in an application to be made Commissioners of Prize. On Coventry's advice (the letter giving it is endorsed in Pepys's own hand 'His advice to mee most friendlily touching the Prize Office'[10]) this was not pursued. But for a man who expected the war to end in humiliation and who knew better than anyone else how vulnerable were those charged with its administration this was boldness indeed.

> He either fears his fate too much
> Or his deserts are small
> That puts it not unto the touch
> To win or lose it all.

Again it would be misleading to represent Pepys simply as a daring administrator who had done his sums and knew his stuff. Like Winston Churchill he was often fascinated by the details of material problems and clearly enjoyed fresh challenges to his ingenuity. One of the first shortages complained of was the absence of wadding for the guns. Pepys at once consulted Mr. Myngs, the shoemaker, father of one of the bravest and most humane commanders of the Restoration navy. Pepys thought that the leather shavings might be bound up and used for this purpose, but Myngs *père* '. . . feares (the common shavings being but very small snips) wee shall finde but few fitt for our turne'. Undeterred Pepys inquires what might be thought of using tobacco stalks and follows the letter up with a consignment of them together with some twine.[11]

And besides finding men, money and supplies, besides the meeting of unexpected demands and the solving of problems that no one had foreseen, there was endless opportunity for making, or at least influencing, appointments. One of the roles in which Pepys perhaps fancied himself was that of the righteous magistrate, rewarding merit and punishing failure. To advance a promising young carpenter like Bagwell was a pleasure in itself, irrespective of others incidental to it. So, too, with an outstanding naval architect like Deane. And the provision of parsons and surgeons diversified the strictly naval aspect of the business. Already from the weeks he had spent in the fleet as Sandwich's secretary he had acquired a useful knowledge of the personal reputation of most of the leading officers. Now that he was exchanging letters almost every day with Coventry he was building up an index of sea officers that would help him to shape the profession and to frame its rules.

But as the professional tempo grew, so did the private. The different parts of his personality move at a uniform velocity, maintaining a rhythmic balance that is his triumph in the art of life. His official business increases, and vastly; his private transactions soar. Yet it is at this period that his intellectual life expands with his election to the Royal Society; that assignations with Mrs. Bagwell, musical evenings with Hill the merchant, buying books, buying clothes, sauntering, gossiping, arguing, flirting, every pleasure in the Pepysian calendar, are pursued more and more avidly. Intensified activity is matched by intensified observation and intensified self-awareness. The more he does the more there is to notice and to analyse. He observes (how few do!) that as he grows richer he grows stingier.[12] And the scenes of London in the plague and the fire are stated with the directness and the poignancy of a Breughel.

The plague elicits an unusual profession of courage in a man who knew himself to be timid and seems on the evidence of the *Diary* to have thought himself cowardly. 'You, sir, took your turn at the sword: I must not grudge to take mine at the pestilence.' These words with which Pepys answered Coventry's solicitude for his safety have a self-confident ring. But was he quite as steadfast as they suggest? Coventry, who had fought in the Civil War, and was serving afloat with his master, The Duke of York, while the London Bills of Mortality climbed from hundreds to thousands, was a man on whose intelligence and integrity Pepys set the highest value. To attempt to bluff him would be to act out of character. Yet in fact Pepys spent by far the greater part of the autumn of 1665 outside London. On August 28th, only three days after writing to Coventry, he joined his wife in the lodgings he had taken for her at Woolwich in July. In August, in response to an earlier suggestion of his, the Navy Board were assigned quarters in the magnificent but still unfinished King's Pavilion at Greenwich, the building that now forms the right-hand side of the Grand Square of the Royal Naval College viewed from the river. In October the Pepyses moved to Greenwich and stayed there till the following January.

There is no doubting Pepys's tenacity of purpose of his readiness to take risks in pursuing a course of action he believed to be right. His conduct over the Great Letter of Reproof supports this. Besides, the plague, dangerous as it was, offered him the same ghoulish pleasures as he derived from watching a public execution:

> . . . so I went forth and walked toward Moorefields to see (God forgive my presumption) whether I could see any dead Corps going to the grave; but as God would have it, did not. But Lord, how everybody's looks and discourse in the street is of death and nothing else, and few people going up and down, that the town is like a place distressed — and forsaken.[13]

A few days later in a letter to one of Sandwich's daughters he refines and extends the description:

> . . . I having stayed in the city till above 7400 died in one week, and of them above 6000 of the plague, and little noise heard day nor night but tolling of bells; till I could walk Lumber Street [Lombard Street] and not meet twenty persons from one end to the other, and not fifty upon the Exchange; till whole families (ten and twelve together) have been swept away; till my very physician, Dr Burnet, who undertook to secure me against any infection (having survived the month of his own being shut up) died himself of the plague; till the nights (though much lengthened) are grown too short to conceal the burials of those that died the day before, people being thereby constrained to borrow daylight for that service; lastly, till I could find neither meat nor drink safe, the butcheries being everywhere visited, my brewer's house shut up, and my baker with his whole family dead of the plague.[14]

Such perfection of phrasing makes one forget that Pepys was in London to run a war, not simply to write one of the greatest books in our language. In spite of his apprehensions, the first fleet action of the war resulted in an English victory. After two fruitless cruises off the Dutch coast the English fleet was at anchor in Southwold Bay — Sole Bay as it was then called — when the combined fleets of the United Provinces were reported in sight in the afternoon of May 31st. The English at once stood out towards them and for two days kept as close as they could get to the enemy who had the wind of them. On the third day the wind began to shift, enabling the English to close. Very early in the morning of June 3rd the two fleets engaged some forty miles south-east of Lowestoft, both somewhat out

of the intended formation of line ahead. Like almost every action against
the Dutch, the battle was hard-fought and bloody. Rupert's White or
Van squadron took the brunt at first, but in the later stages Sandwich's
flagship found herself knocking it out for two hours with four or five
large ships of the line including Obdam's *Eendracht*, the flagship of the
combined Dutch fleet. He was joined by the Duke of York in the *Royal
Charles* at about four in the afternoon, and almost immediately the
Eendracht blew up. The Dutch who had been getting the worst of it thereupon fled, closely pursued by their enemy. Total victory might well have
been achieved, but during the night a courtier aboard the flagship,
pretending the authority of the Duke, ordered the captain to shorten sail.
As a result the Dutch reached safety without further loss.

Not that their losses had been light; seventeen ships sunk or captured,
three admirals killed, and about five thousand casualties against the English loss of one ship, two admirals, and about eight hundred casualties.
So complete a victory ought to have been more decisive. Pepys, like
everyone else, did not learn about this scandalous misconduct until long
after the event. It was to cost him and his colleagues at the Navy Board
a high price in suspicion and mistrust. At the time however his mood seems
to have veered from detachment, verging on irresponsibility, to euphoria.
On the day on which news of the Dutch sighting reached London Pepys
had only spent the morning at the office, going on to the Exchange at
noon to do some business before returning home for his dinner. He then
put on his 'new silk Camelott sute – the best that ever I wore in my life'
and went off to a very splendid funeral in the City where the press of people
was so great that even a silk suit was too hot; unless it was a plain silk suit
which, struck by the thought, he briefly left the entertainment to order.
When the festivities were at last over he took a coach to Westminster Hall,

> where I took the fairest flower and by coach to Tothill fields for the
> ayre, till it was dark. I light, and in with the fairest flower to eat a cake,
> and there did do as much as was safe with my flower, and that was
> enough on my part.

By the time he had taken the girl back and got home himself (twice
changing coaches to prevent recognition) the hour must have been late.
Yet it is only as he goes to bed that he records the certain news that the
two fleets were in sight of each other.

The next entry opens, 'Lay, troubled in mind, abed a good while,
thinking of . . .' Of what? The impending battle on which so much lay
at stake, for the country, for the Navy Office and for Pepys himself?

Not a bit of it. It was 'my Tanger and victualling business' that pre-occupied him. It is only late in the afternoon, after a morning spent chiefly in flirtation, that the imminence of a fleet action is again mentioned. The following day the sound of the guns, heard clearly on the river and roundabout, filled Pepys with concern for the safety of 'Lord Sandwich and Mr Coventry after his Royal Highness'. The order of the names, no less than the saving clause, reveals Pepys's instinct for harmonising the natural with the formal even in so intimate a record. The next two days brought confused and uncertain reports of the Dutch in full retreat. Some thought this a tactical ruse; and Pepys himself was so sceptical of an English success that on the 6th he derided Batten's dispatch from Harwich announcing a victory for its clumsiness of expression. On the 7th there was still no news. It was so oppressively hot that the whole household, Elizabeth, the maids, the boy and even Will Hewer, rose at two o'clock in the morning 'to refresh themselves on the water to Gravesend'. Pepys had to stay behind to clear Sir George Carteret's accounts, a process that was completed by a hilarious dinner at the Dolphin tavern where Sir George was host to his colleagues. The day grew hotter; so hot indeed that Pepys abandoned his office for the river and the cool walks of Spring Garden. There was still no news, even though he waited up till midnight for the return of his wife and family. The heat persisted, matching its oppressiveness to the apprehension Pepys felt at having seen that afternoon two or three houses nailed up in Drury Lane 'marked with a red cross upon the doors, and "Lord have mercy on us" writ there'. It was the first evidence he had seen of the silent, invisible invader.

A short night was disturbed by flashes of lightning and one great shower of rain. At five in the morning Elizabeth came in and lay down on the bed, too tired to undress. Pepys spent the morning in the office and dined at home, again alone as the rest of the household were at a family party. He had an appointment that afternoon to meet some of the leading bankers at the Lord Treasurer's house with the object of wheedling a loan out of them. It was there, early on the afternoon of the 8th that '. . . I met with the great news, at last newly come . . . from the Duke of Yorke, that we have totally routed the Dutch. That the Duke himself, the Prince, my Lord Sandwich* and Mr Coventry are all well. Which did put me into such a joy, that I forgot almost all other thoughts.'

The news was confirmed by the Duke of Albemarle 'like a man out of himself with content' at the Cockpit, and, most reassuring of all, by a letter in Mr Coventry's own hand. The Diary becomes ecstatic. 'A great

* Pepys here gives the flag officers in order of squadronal command, not of personal concern.

victory, never known in the world. They are all fled . . . my heart full of
Joy.' How full may be gauged by the fact that he distributed four shillings
in largesse to the boys in the street and, after a visit of congratulation to
Lady Penn, actually brought himself to write 'and good service endeed is
said to have been done by him'. Raising money from the stoniest banker
was easier than allowing any merit to Sir William Penn. When Pepys
went to bed that night his heart was 'at great rest and quiet, saving that the
consideration of the victory is too great for me presently to comprehend'.

Even at the moment of great events Pepys is at least as much interested
in his own reactions as in the events that call them forth. This is the
inspiration of his historical sense and of his genius as a reporter. His
mind, sceptical, critical and informed, had been prepared for disaster
and had to find room for triumph. As we have seen the triumph was not,
as things turned out, proportionate to the victory. It was thus easy for
Pepys to revert to the mood in which he had originally viewed the war and
to which he remained constant. But in terms of his own personal affilia-
tions the battle of Lowestoft had achieved all and more that he could have
hoped for. Sandwich, by all accounts, had seen some of the hottest
fighting and had shown the coolness, tactical sense and will to win required
of a commander. Coventry shared in the honour won by his master the
Duke of York as Commander-in-Chief and, together with Penn, had
won for the administrators some of the glory usually reserved for the sea
officers. All Pepys's patrons, actual and potential, Sandwich, Coventry
and the Duke of York, had done more than well and, best of all, not at
each other's expense. True some of Pepys's enemies and rivals had done
well too: Sir William Penn, Prince Rupert and his formidable follower
Robert Holmes. But even here fortune was unexpectedly favourable.
Penn made no attempt to exploit the credit, so obviously his, for the
successful handling of a huge fleet largely inexperienced in fighting a formal
battle. Prince Rupert was still in bad health, was sometimes confined to
his cabin and might have to come ashore. And Holmes had thrown up his
commission in a rage at not being given, as Rupert wished, the Rear-
Admiral's flag vacant by Sansum's death in action.[15] Even the casualties
turned to the advancement of Sandwich. Lawson, his old rival from pre-
Restoration times, died of wounds he had received. And the slaughter,
by one piece of chain shot, of three court favourites standing beside the
Duke of York — 'their blood and brains flying in the Duke's face' — lent
powerful support to those, the King among them, who thought that the
succession to the throne should not be exposed to such risks. If the Duke
were to be relieved, if the Prince was unwell, Sandwich, as the senior
flag officer, would have strong claims to command in chief.

Sandwich himself was too wary to take anything for granted. He met the congratulations of his cousin by pointing out that his name was hardly mentioned in the official account of the victory in spite of the fact that he had been in action for longer than any other flag officer and had had more men killed in his ship than any other commander except Jeremy Smith in the *Mary*. Success at sea must be made good by strengthening his position at Court. He therefore proposed that Pepys should open negotiations for a marriage between his daughter, Lady Jemimah and Sir George Carteret's eldest son Philip. No commission could have given greater pleasure. To combine busybodying and amorous intrigue with innocence, indeed with a virtuous sense of doing one's duty; to play the parts of man of the world, of confidential servant, of go-between, of humorous observer all in the same aristocratic comedy — what could any actor ask more? The ineptitude of the young principals for love scenes of any kind provided Pepys with endless material for the type of joke he most enjoyed.

Fortunately for Sandwich, both Coventry and the Duke of York seem to have regarded Prince Rupert's succession to the command as the danger to be avoided at all costs. Sandwich told Pepys how they had all three joined in laughing at Rupert behind his back; and Coventry, reunited to his adoring colleague, after the first exchange of endearments was careful to report 'how my Lord Sandwich, both in his counsels and personal service, hath done most honourably and serviceably'. For one brief moment Sandwich, the champion of sea-borne empire, the prime mover in the acquisition of Tangier (had not he and Oliver aspired to the capture of Gibraltar?), the protagonist of the blue-water school, was in alliance with Coventry who had not yet found his true position as a kind of seventeenth-century forerunner of John Bright, bent on reducing military expenditure and avoiding commitments overseas. It was an alliance on which everything smiled. Coventry was knighted and made a Privy Counsellor. Sandwich was given the command of the fleet with Penn, readier to serve his country than to urge his own claims, as his Vice-Admiral. The Duke of York was sent to the north to guard against a Dutch landing, Albemarle remained in London, Rupert, who had angrily rejected proposals of a joint command, was left without employment. Their turn would come soon enough: and so would that of the Captains who had been knighted and given flags for their performance in the opening battle, Spragge, Tiddeman, Jordan, Allin, Myngs, Harman and Jeremy Smith. Meanwhile there was news of rich Dutch convoys inward bound from the Indies and the Eastern Mediterranean. Early in July Sandwich and Penn were at sea with sixty ships to intercept them.

11

Pepys, Sandwich and Coventry: the height of the War, 1666

The perfect coalition of Pepys's interests and loyalties had hardly been achieved before it began to disintegrate. Sandwich, that shrewd, wary watcher of steps, was suddenly guilty of two careless misjudgments that might easily have ruined him. The first was in a field of war and diplomacy peculiarly his own. The Dutch merchantmen that he was out to catch were returning northabout round Scotland, intending to make use of the neutral harbours of Scandinavia for shelter. Through our ambassador in Copenhagen it was proposed that Denmark should, when the ships were safe in harbour, denounce her treaty with Holland, join the English in seizing the ships and split the proceeds. The ambassador, according to Sandwich, gave him to understand that 'the king of Denmark was ready to declare his treaties broken with the Hollander but would be glad to take an advantageous time to say it'.[1] Without any written agreement, without any further intelligence that the King had communicated his intentions to his commanders on the spot, Sandwich at the end of July detached a squadron under Sir Thomas Tiddeman to attack the two convoys that were known to be sheltering in Bergen. The result was unrelieved disaster. The Danish governor had no instructions to permit this invasion of his country's neutrality. When Tiddeman attacked the Dutch ships the Danish forts opened fire on the English who after some hours were forced to retire. Damage and casualties were severe — four hundred seamen and six captains were killed—and the Dutch had hardly suffered at all. The blame lay fair and square on the Commander-in-Chief.

The fillip to Dutch recovery was angrily recognised in London. It was immediately and immensely increased by the safe return home of the great De Ruyter, commanding the small escort force that Sandwich's fleet could have eaten for breakfast if only it had come up with it. A much stronger Dutch force then put to sea to bring home the Bergen ships. Irresponsibility and ineptitude had thrown away the fruits of the great victory in June.

Action, successful action, was imperative if Sandwich and those who depended on him were not to be swept away. The fleet had had to come in again, partly to make good the damage suffered but mainly to replenish the victuals that, throughout the year, consistently fell short of both the quantity and quality contracted for. At the end of August the fleet sailed with fifteen days' supply of beer and ten weeks' dry provisions. Five days out Sandwich's frigates sighted seven or eight strange sail about 100 miles north-north-west of the Texel. The English gave chase and, in the laconic words of Sandwich's journal: 'In the evening we took them, viz. 2 great East Indiamen and 4 men of war; 1300 prisoners. The *Hector* of ours sunk by a shot or his lee ports neglected; the Captain and near 80 men drowned.'

Six days later even closer to the Dutch coast another fifteen sail were sighted and chased. Four large warships were taken with nearly a thousand prisoners and half a dozen or so smaller merchant ships including two West Indiamen. Four days afterwards on September 13th Sandwich brought his prizes into the Nore. The year's campaign was over.

In the fortnight that the fleet had been at sea Pepys's effervescence had lost some of its sparkle. The Bills of Mortality were beginning to shake his nerve. In the office there was no money and no prospect of any. Huge sums were already owing to the seamen and to the merchants who supplied the navy. There had already been a strike among the shipwrights and carpenters in Woolwich Dockyard. The Government was tired: '. . . the King is nor hath been of late very well, but quite out of humour and, as some think, in a consumption and weary of everything.'[2] The well-informed like Pepys and Evelyn and Captain Cocke were

. . . full of discourse of the neglect of our masters, the great officers of state, about all business, and especially that of money — having now some thousands prisoners kept to no purpose, at a great charge, and no money provided almost for the doing of it. We fell to talk largely of the want of some persons understanding to look after business, but

all goes to wrack. 'For', says Captain Cocke, 'My Lord Treasurer he
minds his ease and lets things go how they will; if he can have his
£8000 per annum and a game at Lombre, he is well. My Lord
Chancellor, he minds getting of money and nothing else; and my Lord
Ashly will rob the devil and the Alter but he will get money if it be to
be got.' But that that put us into this great melancholy was news
brought to-day, which Captain Cocke reports as a certain truth, that
all the Dutch fleet, men-of-war and merchant East India ships, are go
every one in from Bergen the 3rd of this month, Sunday last — which
will make us all ridiculous. The fleet came home with shame to require
great deal of money, which is not to be had — to discharge many men
that must get the plague then or continue at greater charge on shipboard
Nothing done by them to encourage the Parliament to give money —
nor the Kingdom able to spare any money if they would, at this time
of the plague. So that as things look at present, the whole state must
come to Ruine. Full of these melancholy thoughts, to bed — where
though I lay the saftest that I ever did in my life, with a down bed . .
yet I slept very ill, chiefly through the thoughts of my Lord Sandwiches
concernment in all this ill-success at sea.[3]

Pepys did not, as it happens, share Cocke's opinion of the three politicians
in question, but Cocke's words convey perfectly the mood and temper of
the moment.

The depression of the dark hour lent brilliance to the dawn. Leaving
Cocke's comfortable house at Greenwich Pepys walked over to spend
Sunday with his wife at her lodgings in Woolwich. He found her over
come at alarming news of her father's health and had to tell her that it
might be the plague as he had noticed that the house was shut up. But
just before he left to return to Greenwich an express letter arrived from
William Coventry, enclosing Sandwich's report of his first success on
September 3rd.

'This news doth so overjoy me, that I know not what to say enough to
express it.' Arriving at Cocke's he found not only Evelyn, his fellow guest of
the previous night, but his colleagues Mennes and Brouncker.

. . . the receipt of this news did put us all into such an extasy of joy
that it inspired into Sir J. Mennes and Mr Eveling such a spirit of
mirth that in all my life I never met with so merry a two hours as our
company this night was . . . it being one of the times of my life wherein
I was the fullest of true sense of joy.

Against all expectation Sandwich's colours were first past the post. Dazed with delight his backers had barely time to cheer the winner into the unsaddling enclosure before it was known that an objection had been laid. A pay-off there was to be; but not in the sense that Pepys had looked for.

The immense wealth of the Dutch prizes – Pepys estimated their value at between £350,000 and £400,000 – had proved too tempting. When a ship was taken custom allowed the seamen, but not their officers, the plunder of all goods lying between decks. They were expressly prohibited from 'breaking bulk', that is, opening the holds and rummaging the cargo. The sale of ship and cargo and the division of the proceeds among those entitled to a share was the function of the Prize Court and the Prize Commissioners. The money so obtained was, right up to Victorian times, easily the most lucrative reward to which an officer and even more a Commander-in-Chief could look forward. Pay was a mere appetiser in comparison.

Hardly had the ships come into the river before it was known that Sandwich, in collusion with some of his subordinate flag officers but in direct opposition to others, had himself broken bulk, and had even transshipped some of the goods aboard a vessel bound for King's Lynn so that they could travel easily and cheaply up the Ouse to Hinchingbrooke. So flagrant a breach of the rules was too good an opportunity for his enemies to miss. Monck had been biding his time. Coventry seized on the disrespect shown to the Duke of York as Lord High Admiral in this open defiance of instruction and precedent. In next to no time there was talk of an impeachment.

Sandwich was saved by the King. Charles was not yet ready to throw over the Clarendonians. And to throw to the wolves of the House of Commons one whom he had himself honoured and promoted would certainly bring back unfortunate memories of his father. But though he could save him, he was not going to take any chances. In a remarkably short space of time Sandwich was sent out of the country as Ambassador to Madrid. This postponed the inevitable inquiry into his conduct over the Prize Goods until his return to England three years later.

From Pepys's point of view the balance of power at the Navy Office that had been achieved at the outbreak of war was now in ruins. He immediately set to work to construct another, based this time on Coventry's improved position and his own undeniable success. But first of all he had to extricate himself from the scandal. Like his patron he had himself acted with less than his usual circumspection but he had not so far to fall – yet. And he certainly showed more agility in scrambling back to

safety when no one was looking. His involvement began on September
18th, the day that he and Cocke went aboard Sandwich's flagship at the
Nore. At Cocke's suggestion Pepys borrowed £500 from Will Howe,
Deputy Treasurer of the fleet, to buy 'above £1000 – worth of goods,
Mace, Nutmeggs, Cynamon and Cloves' on behalf of themselves and
Lord Brouncker. Ten days later Cocke arrived unannounced at Pepys's
temporary office in the King's Pavilion at Greenwich with the first wagon
load. The office seemed the obvious place to store the goods: 'but then
the thoughts of its being the King's house altered our resolution, and so
put them at his friend's'. Pepys had already scented trouble. After another
ten days two more wagons rolled up, hotly pursued by two customs officers
who attempted to seize the goods while Pepys was stowing them in the
lodgings of the office messenger. By now it was clear that unwelcome
publicity could not be avoided. Indeed the next convoy of wagons was
arrested in the street by Greenwich Church. Pepys was summoned by an
agitated servant of Cocke's; angry words were exchanged; a crowd collected; the game was up. Pepys wrote urgently to warn his master, adding:

> . . . And further, my Lord Brouncker has wrote me word that the King
> and Duke do disown their order or allowance in the case. Whence this
> arises, your Lordshipp can best tell upon the place, but I pray God there
> be no foule meaning towards your Lordshipp in it.[4]

Sandwich was apparently nettled by this solicitude. In a stiff letter Pepys
was told:

> The King hath confirmed it, and given me order to distribute these
> very proportions to the flag-officers, so that you are to own the posses-
> sion of them with confidence; and if anybody have taken security from
> them upon seizure, remand the security in my name, and return their
> answer. Carry it high; and own nothing of baseness or dishonour, but
> rather intimate that I know who have done me indignities. Thank my
> Lord Brouncker and Sir John Minnes for civilities and tell them I expect
> no less in reality, for I have befriended them; and that I shall very
> ungratefully hear of news of base examinations, upon any action of
> mine.[5]

For all his bold words Sandwich had been sufficiently perturbed to hurry
to Oxford where the King and Court had gone to avoid the plague and
where the new session of Parliament was opening. Even this venture was
unlucky since the Dutch chose the moment of his absence from his post of

duty to put to sea for a final cruise off the mouth of the Thames. Albemarle
in London threatened to take the fleet to sea himself, but as there were
barely half a dozen ships in any sort of readiness there was in fact nothing
any one could do. Nonetheless it helped the anti-Sandwich movement.
Too late, in the last week of October, the Commander-in-Chief rejoined
his ship. During the preceding days when he had been in Oxford Coventry
had been active in carrying the First Reading of a bill to make it felony
to break bulk. That the Dutch fleet should be riding in English home
waters while the English admiral was ashore defending his own dubious
transactions could hardly help his reputation.

Sandwich was technically right and Pepys's informant Brouncker wrong
on the point of the King's having granted a post-dated authority to the
division of the prize goods among the flag officers. But Pepys had read the
signs that Sandwich, strumming his guitar in the great cabin of the
James, had missed. Bluff and threats, 'Carry it high . . . tell them I expect
no less . . .' would not answer. Retreat was the only sound tactic. On
September 27th Cocke had offered Pepys £500 clear profit in exchange for
his share. Pepys stood out for £600. The ominous weeks that followed
brought down his price and on November 13th he was glad to settle for
the original offer. On November 22nd Sandwich hauled down his flag.
The bad weather that had kept the Dutch from doing any serious mischief had at last driven them back to the shelter of their home ports.
But the storm that was brewing over the prize goods looked ever blacker.
On December 6th Pepys was not less surprised than delighted to hear of
his patron's appointment as Ambassador to Spain. It was his habit on the
last day of the year to survey in his diary the general and personal course
of events in an annual stocktaking and casting up of accounts. In spite of
his personal prosperity the year had been bad. There had been the plague;
the war had not gone well. But to neither of these does Pepys give pride
of place:

> The great evil of this year and the only one endeed, is the fall of My
> Lord of Sandwich whose mistake about the Prizes hath undone him,
> I believe, as to interest at Court; though sent (for a little palliateing it)
> Imbassador into Spayne . . . and endeed, his miscarriage about the prize-
> goods is not to be excused, to suffer a company of rogues to go away with
> ten times as much as himself, and the blame of all to be deservedly laid
> upon him.

That conclusion epitomises Pepys's view of embezzlement and corruption.
Sandwich had acted wrongly, he admits: but, far worse, he had acted

stupidly and obtained no adequate *quid pro quo*. Worst of all he appeared to have forfeited his credit with the King and Duke.

Pepys by contrast had enlarged both his fortune and his reputation. Quietly disembarrassing himself of the prize goods (and making a handsome profit in the process) he had diagnosed in the malfunctions of the victualling system the main cause of England's failure at sea and, after a careful analysis of the symptoms, now proposed a remedy. There were two ways of victualling the navy, by contract or by direct supply, victualling 'on account' as it was called, in which the Government undertook the whole business through its own officials. In Cromwell's war with the Dutch, the obvious precedent to consult in any difficulty, the navy had been victualled on account. This had worked well under a strong Government but the changes and uncertainties of the eighteen months between Cromwell's death and Charles II's Restoration produced chaos and complaint. The King had therefore reverted to the earlier practice and had granted the contract to a merchant, Denis Gauden, whose brother John was the ghost-writer of the record-breaking best-seller of Royalist propaganda, *Εικων βασιλική*, the Pourtraicture of His Sacred Majestie in His Solitudes and Sufferings. This work, which purported to record the meditations of Charles I during his last days, ran into forty-seven editions and, at the Restoration, won its author in rapid succession the Bishoprics of Exeter and Worcester. He had, however, set his heart on the see of Winchester, in which diocese his brother Denis had built him a house of suitably prelatical proportions at Clapham, which Pepys visited and described in his diary on July 25th, 1663, and which, as Will Hewer's guest, was to be the home of his old age. But Bishop Gauden died in the autumn of 1662, of rage, it was believed, at not being preferred to Winchester. The ultimate rewards of authorship reaped by his brother were to consist in the profits of supplying substandard groceries to sailors.

Not that Pepys, who in any case did not have to live on purser's issue, contended that Gauden was profiteering. Indeed the first grounds on which he had criticised the system in a letter to Sir George Carteret in August[6] was that Gauden's services were too valuable for the state to expect from one man in a time of plague. Simple prudence demanded that the one responsibility that could accurately be described as vital should be shared among at least three or four competent persons. To prove that there was no personal animosity or censure implicit in this suggestion he at first proposed that Gauden should take his own sons into partnership. But as he examined the returns from the ports and compared them with the accounts and requisitions from the ships it became plainer to him that the discrepancies between what the Victualler claimed to have delivered and what the Purser, often supported by his Captain, admitted to receiving could only be cleared up by an administrator who would be, preferably, beholden to neither. In October when the prize goods scandal was at its height he wrote a long letter to Monck proposing that a surveyor of victualling should be appointed to each port, charged with the duty of sending to a Surveyor-General in London a weekly report of all victualling transactions together with a statement of what provisions were, at the time of writing, available on the spot. This would not only go far to prevent fraud. It would, much more important, let the central government know what the real position was. And that would be the first step towards a remedy for the random, unpredictable returning to port of a famished or parched fleet whose business ought to have kept it at sea. Efficient victualling was not only essential to the proper deployment of sea-power. It was, on the longer term, the master key to discipline and, above all, manning. Starvation was a standing incitement to desertion. As Pepys himself wrote towards the end of his official life in one of his most familiar aphorisms:

Englishmen, and more especially seamen, love their bellies above anything else, and therefore it must always be remembered in the management of the victualling of the Navy that to make any abatement from them in the quantity or agreeableness of the victuals is to discourage and provoke them in the tenderest point, and will sooner render them disgusted with the King's service than any one other hardship that can be put upon them.[7]

Within a week of sending the letter Pepys heard both formally and informally that it had been warmly approved by the King and the Duke and their principal advisers. On the 19th he wrote to Coventry proposing himself for the position of Surveyor-General. The letter was opened in Coventry's absence by the Duke of York who at once indicated his support. On the 27th over dinner Albemarle offered him the post and he accepted it. The salary was £300 a year but Gauden supplemented it by a further £500, thus making nonsense of one of Pepys's main arguments for instituting the arrangement.[8] The other, one might have thought, had already been knocked endways by combining the job in the person of the Clerk of the Acts and the Treasurer of Tangier.

Pepys valued the appointment the more from the terms in which, according to Albemarle Coventry had proposed him: 'the most obliging that ever I could expect from any man and more – it saying me to be the fittest man in England . . .' Gratifying as this must have been, the announcement a few weeks later that next year's fleet was to be under the joint command of Prince Rupert and the Duke of Albemarle must have taken a little gilt off the gingerbread. In spite of Albemarle's present cordiality Pepys feared, disliked and distrusted him. And Prince Rupert was never a man that Pepys would have chosen to serve. Sure enough they had the temerity to ruffle his administrative feathers.

> . . . We are not [they wrote to the King on August 29th 1666] supplied with provisions according to the necessity of your affairs, notwithstanding the repeated importunities we have used . . . and that when we send up our demands instead of having them answered, we have accounts sent us, which are prepared by Mr Pepys of what hath been supplied for the fleet, whereas that will not satisfy the needs of the ships except we could find them also here in specie.'9

Throughout the campaign of 1666 Coventry remained ashore, in ever closer collaboration with Pepys. As their admiration and value for each other increased so did their common hostility and contempt towards the joint Commanders-in-Chief. By the end of the summer correspondence was acrid. And when Rupert presented his report to the House of Commons at the end of the war he complained of:

> . . . the intolerable neglect in supplying provisions during the whole summer's expedition, notwithstanding the extraordinary and frequent importunity of our letters which were for the most part directed to Sir William Coventry . . . and to the Commissioners of the Navy . . .'10

Strong words. But by then the whole Navy Office was under heavy attack as Pepys had always known it one day would be.

The year began badly with a declaration of war from France and Denmark. If, as seemed likely, the French fleet then based on Toulon were to leave the Mediterranean and join forces with the Dutch, the English would have heavy odds against them. As it was, the Dutch fleet of 1666 was slightly superior in ships and guns to that commanded by Rupert and Monck. Any further tilting of the balance would be extremely dangerous. Consequently when the French fleet sailed out of the Strait of Gibraltar on May 8th English nerves were stretched for reports of movements in the western approaches to the channel. At the end of May just when the Dutch were ready to sail and the English were sending their fleet down to the anchorages in the mouth of the river, exactly such a report was received. Instantly the decision was taken to divide the fleet. Rupert was sent to the westward with twenty ships to pick up reinforcements at Plymouth and find the French. Monck was left with about sixty ships of the line to act as he thought best against De Ruyter with eighty-four. Almost as soon as Rupert had sailed on May 29th it was known that the Dutch fleet had put to sea. Immediate orders were sent to recall him but these did not reach him until June 1st when he was off St. Helen's. The decision to divide the fleet, hotly debated then and since, at once imposed on Albemarle another not less fiercely contested, whether to keep the fleet in safety until Rupert had rejoined or to fight the Dutch with a far inferior force.

His decision to fight was so much in character that his enemies and critics, Pepys among the bitterest and best-informed of them, have never allowed him a rational defence. Yet as Dr. Anderson has pertinently inquired[11] what would have happened to Rupert and his twenty ships if Monck had withdrawn to the safety of the Thames and left the channel to De Ruyter? Once the decision to divide the fleet had been taken the risk of fighting on disadvantageous terms had to be accepted.

The Battle of the Four Days, initiated by Monck bearing down with some fifty-five ships on De Ruyter's eighty-four on the morning of June 1st ranks with Dunkirk and the Armada Fight as one of the longest, fiercest and most desperate actions ever fought in home waters. The punishment taken by the English fleet was terrible: the damage inflicted on the Dutch comparatively slight. On the second day Monck's losses meant that he was fighting at odds of two to one and on the third he had been forced back towards the Thames when late in the afternoon Rupert's squadron was sighted coming up channel on a light south-easterly breeze. At a council of war held that evening it was agreed that Rupert's fresh force should lead the attack on the following day. The fury of the final engagement fought, at last, on more or less equal terms was unabated. But though it was the Dutch who in the end broke off the action no huzzas could disguise the fact that the English had suffered a costly defeat. Recriminations began at once and quickly grew more envenomed. Albemarle blamed the cowardice of his captains. 'I assure you I never fought with worse officers than now in my life, for not above twenty of them behaved themselves like men.' Rupert blamed Coventry for sending his recall by express post and not by special messenger. But the most powerful lobby of naval experts, Coventry, Pepys, Sir William Penn, Sir John Harman, Pearse the surgeon (who as usual was present at the battle) united in blaming Albemarle for fighting once the fleet had been divided. And as soon as it became known that the original report that the French fleet had been sighted was false a hubbub of accusation broke out whose confusion and ferocity were worthy of the battle itself.

Pepys's own reactions to a series of events that seemed, repeatedly, to graze the edge of disaster was calmer and more tranquil than the alarms recorded in the Diary for 1665. Partly this may have been because he was in better form. The entries for 1666 overflow with high spirits and conscious enjoyment. The plague if not gone was evidently going. He had brought back his wife to Seething Lane in the autumn. He was making a lot of money and winning golden opinions. His sexual partners were submissive and his wife unsuspicious. He was conscious, as perhaps never before, of power, position, independence and appetite. 'I must now stand upon my own legs' he had written in the aftermath of Sandwich's fall; and he had proved that he could do it.

The news, dated eleven o'clock on June 1st and received on June 2nd, that action was imminent 'put us at the board into a tosse'. Within a few minutes Pepys was called away from the table to organise food and transport for 200 soldiers who were to be sent as urgent reinforcements to the fleet. Finding ships to carry them took him down to Greenwich and there in the park he 'could hear the guns from the Fleete most plainly. . . . All our hope now is that Prince Rupert with his fleet is coming back and will be with the fleet this noon . . .' Subsequent cross-checking of times and narratives led him to doubt it might have been thunder. But the tension of the moment touches his reader across the centuries as does his observation of the shouts and kisses with which the soldiers, now mostly drunk, parted from their wives and sweethearts as they sailed on the afternoon tide. The next day, Whitsunday, brought a mixture of reports including a letter from Harman in the *Henry*, aboard which Balty was serving as muster-master, telling a fearful tale of fire and slaughter. Pepys sighed for the dangers his brother-in-law was undergoing, but pursued a round of pleasure that included two morning services at Westminster (St. Margaret's and the Abbey), a particularly rewarding visit to one of his Westminster Hall ladies, and a jaunt to Hyde Park by coach in the company of Creed. Creed and Pepys shook their heads over the probable outcome, spared a thought for the nation and agreed how lucky it was that Sandwich was not involved. Pepys's patriotism was never a lush, romantic growth.

On the 4th the longed-for news of Rupert's junction with Albemarle was brought by a young officer well-known to Pepys 'all muffled up and his face as black as the chimney and covered with dirt, pitch and tar, and powder, and muffled with durty clouts and his right eye stopped with Okum'. Together with other wounded he had been put ashore at Harwich at two in the morning and had ridden through the night. Relief at the avoidance of disaster for a time encouraged optimism, but as the damage and casualties became known Pepys eagerly substantiated his hostility to the two commanders. The courage and leadership that could inspire men to go out and fight a much stronger enemy who had already mauled them not once but twice and even three times seems to have passed him by. Yet he knew very well that these things mattered. Among the killed was Sir Christopher Myngs, whose funeral Pepys and Coventry attended as a mark of respect to a flag officer. The unforgettable testimony to the affection and loyalty that he had inspired in his men, recorded in the Diary on that occasion, touches the naval profession with the sublime.

> About a Dozen able, lusty, proper men came to the coach-side with tears in their eyes, and one of them, that spoke for the rest, begun and says to Sir W. Coventry — 'We are here a Dozen of us that have long known and loved and served our dead commander, Sir Chr. Mings, and have now done the last office of laying him in the ground. We would be glad we had any other to offer after him, and in revenge of him — all we have is our lives. If you will please to get his Royal Highness to give us a Fireshipp among us all, here is a Dozen of us, out of all which choose you one to be commander, and the rest of us, whoever he is, will serve him, and, if possible, do that that shall show our memory of our dead commander and our revenge.' Sir W. Coventry was herewith much moved (as well as I, who could hardly abstain from weeping) and took their names; and so parted, telling me that he would move his Royal Highness as in a thing very extraordinary.
>
> . . . .

But Pepys passes straight from admitting his emotion to the reflection that Myngs will be quite forgotten in a short time because he died before he had taken the opportunity of enriching himself. And with that he sneaks off to Mrs. Bagwell, secure in the knowledge that her husband, if not killed or wounded, must be safely aboard his ship.

Monck and Rupert might complain of the administrative system that kept them hammering the table with demands for men and beer and victuals when they should have been free to concentrate on fighting the enemy: Pepys and Coventry might sneer at the admirals as a pair of fire-eating old blockheads, ignorant of everything involved in running a navy and careless of the new science of sailing-ship tactics. But whatever may be said of the campaign of 1666 the quality of leadership and administration that could take the fleet out to fight and win a major battle six weeks after so searing a defeat proves itself beyond any need of demonstration.

From the moment that the Commanders-in-Chief had ceased to engage the Dutch they turned a brisk fire on to their subordinate officers and civilian colleagues. Almost all their ships were severely damaged and many required a complete refit. 'We desire you with all imaginable expedition to fit a whole suit of masts and yards for the *Royal James*, boltsprit excepted, and such other sails and cordage and such stores expended as Sir Tho. Allen Admiral of the White shall give you an account as wanting in the said ship.'[12] This order dated June 7th is eloquent of the shattered condition of the fleet. Every need was more pressing than every other. Apart from the damage to be made good and the stores to be replaced, the English had been at a disadvantage from a want of fireships and boats, so often the surest method of communication when signalling was still in its infancy. Above all else towered the want of men. Skilled men, carpenters and sailmakers, first to help to fit the ships: but seamen, watermen, even soldiers, to man them as soon as they were ready for sea. Monck and Rupert reckoned they needed at least 3,000 straightaway. The first ships that left dockyard hands were sent out to prey on English merchantmen homeward bound, pressing the prime seamen before they could escape ashore. In spite of constant objections from Sir William Coventry the admirals also kept up a hot press in London. They might tread on powerful and privileged toes but they did get results. Pepys, whose sympathies certainly lay with Coventry and whose humanity was outraged by the operation of so barbarous a system[13], bears them out. At midnight on July 2nd he wrote to Coventry:

> My whole time yesterday till midnight and the same time this day till now hath been spent in the businesse of Prest men. We have cleared all places and ye numbers shipped away is about 1000 little more or less. . . . More will be gotten to-morrow and sent away besides Sir Jo: Robinson's* 100 souldiers . . .[14]

Pepys was too good a Government servant and too sensible a man not to see the urgency of the requirements and to do his best to meet them. Yet his neat, orderly fastidiousness was revolted by the hugger-mugger of it all. While the admirals' letters to him are full of agonised demands for every necessity of sea warfare, his own letters to the Lord High Admiral are full of agonised recapitulations of the expense incurred by buying on credit instead of paying in cash. The administrative offence of being in a hurry is gross. Matters reached a climax at the beginning of the second week in July. Three new ships of the line, the *Cambridge*, the *Greenwich*

* Lieut-Governor of the Tower.

and the *Warspight* were all but ready to join the fleet. Monck and Rupert, knowing that the Dutch were off the mouth of the Thames, were fretting to get out. Thanks to the enormous efforts of the past few weeks the bulk of their force was with them at the Nore and could sail on the next tide. When were the new ships coming? At last on July 9th they sent Sir Robert Holmes up the river with a party of seamen from his own division with orders to bring the ships down and further orders to their captains to do what Holmes told them.[15] The reaction of the officials was predictable:

> He [Coventry] spoke contemptibly of Holmes and his Mermidons that came to take down the ships from hence, and have carried them without any necessaries or anything almost, that they will certainly be longer getting them ready than if they had stayed here.[16]

Was Coventry, and by association Pepys, right? We hear the same dispute, conducted in exactly the same tone, as that which still rages over Lord Beaverbrook's tenure of the Ministry of Aircraft Production in the summer and autumn of 1940. It is entirely appropriate that Pepys should figure as the protagonist of a professional civil service against the buccaneering, inspired or reckless who shall say, of the man who thinks that rules were made to be broken.

But the Battle of Britain was a victory and so was the battle, fought on St. James's Day, July 25th, in which these laggard vessels took part. This time numbers were equal and, in spite of Pepys's strictures on the Commanders-in-Chief, the tactics employed come closest of all the battles of that war to the scientific copybook pattern of fighting in line. Pearse the surgeon drew an elaborate plan of its three stages which Pepys preserved among his own papers.[17] The battle ended in the rout of the Dutch van and centre leaving their rear squadron with the whole English fleet to evade or fight. When darkness fell Sir Jeremy Smith commanding the English rear anchored, perhaps too prudently, well off the Dutch coast. The waters were dangerous: his pilot was apprehensive. But the Dutch saw their chance and took it. Morning showed their masts safe behind the sand bars and shoals where no English ship could follow. Once again an English victory had not paid off.

The fierce recriminations that at once broke out among the sea officers foreshadowed the Parliamentary accusations of misconduct which almost everyone involved in the direction of the war would have to face. Sir Robert Holmes who had commanded the rear division of the centre squadron flatly accused Smith of cowardice, subsequently fighting a duel with him and ultimately provoking the King in Council to pronounce on the conduct of the battle. A bad matter was made worse by the fact that Holmes was Prince Rupert's particular favourite and Smith was Monck's. But Pepys, gliding on a euphoric current of easy money and easy success, knew nothing of the rough weather blowing up towards him. He was convinced that the disorder of the Rupert–Monck regime could produce no good – 'no discipline – nothing but swearing and cursing, and everybody doing what they please; and the Generalls, understanding no better, suffer it . . .'[18] But these jeremiads are pitched in a key that Johnson identified in his remark to Boswell: 'When a butcher tells you that *his heart bleeds for his country* he has, in fact, no uneasy feeling'. On the next day Pepys was able to spend the morning 'setting money-matters and other things of mighty moment to rights, to the great content of my mind' and spent the afternoon listening to the royal architect, Hugh May, on the proper principles of laying out gardens. And the day after that is hallowed by the entry, sacred to all who know and love his library:

> . . . And then comes Simpson the Joyner, and he and I with great pains contriving presses to put my books up in, they now growing numerous, and lying one upon another on my chairs, I lose the use, to avoid the trouble of removing them when I would open a book.

The guns were heard plain at Whitehall on St. James's Day while the Court were at chapel, celebrating the patronal festival of the Lord High Admiral. But after the distant reverberations died away no news reached London for forty-eight hours, and then only the letter of a Captain who took such good care of himself and his ship that he left the battle almost before it had begun. Not till the 29th when Pepys was in church did an official dispatch addressed to Batten arrive soon after the preacher had mounted the pulpit. Pepys sent it out unopened to Batten's house, stoically sweating out the sermon. In fact the dispatch was about something else but as Pepys pushed his way out the bells were ringing for a victory. Both Pepys and Coventry correctly interpreted its value '. . . but a poor result after the fighting of two so great fleets . . .' Which, as Pepys candidly admits in summarising the months events, was exactly what he wanted:

> Mighty well and end this month in content of mind and body – the public matters looking more safe for the present than they did. And we having a victory over the Duch, just such as I could have wished, and as the Kingdom was fit to bear – enough to give us the name of conquerors and to leave us maisters of the sea. But without any such

great matters done as should give the Duke of Albemarle any honour at all, or give him cause to rise to his former insolence.

Passages such as this make it absurd to pretend that Pepys, at this period, put the interests of his country above all considerations of faction or party, let alone of crude personal gain.

12

The Dutch in the Medway

Hardly a fortnight later Pepys had news of another victorious action, executed by a handful of ships and costing less than a dozen casualties, that inflicted damage estimated at the then staggering figure of a million pounds. Sir Robert Holmes took a few light craft and fireships into the anchorage of the Vlie and burnt well over a hundred (Coventry put it at a hundred and sixty) merchantmen. The ratio of force employed to results obtained was inverse to that of the St. James's Day Fight. Holmes's bonfire, as it was called, was the last, and certainly the most brilliant, action of the campaign. In the following month Monck was recalled from his sea command to lend his strength and solidity to a government dazed and shocked by the Fire of London. The fleet came in early in October to a general feeling of opportunities missed and money thrown away, of divisions and quarrels among the commanders and the civilian administrators, of shock, of exhaustion, of a wide and deep lack of confidence in the policy and purpose and prosecution of the war.

Glummest of all were Pepys and Coventry. The mood of summer had gone with the season. It was so stale a topic of conversation with them that the gentlemen captains had undone all and ruined the discipline of the fleet that the groans of the Diary take this proposition for granted. Yet one may wonder what ideals of discipline and loyalty were cherished by a senior official of the navy who clearly encouraged captains to denigrate their admirals, and admirals to speak to the dishonour of their Commanders-in-Chief.[1] There had already been an alarming scene in cabinet when Pepys, called to attend a meeting on the state of the navy and finding his colleagues silent, gave impromptu a lucid account in the course of which he found himself admiring his own powers of exposition. He had only too good reason. The minute he had finished Prince Rupert jumped up and complained angrily to the King of the aspersions cast on the condition in which he had brought the fleet back to base. Pepys apologised for giving offence but pleaded that he was merely transmitting the reports of the dockyard authorities. Rupert muttered a repetition of his complaint. A long, embarrassed silence followed, ending in the withdrawal of Pepys and his fellow officers, Batten, Mennes and Brouncker. Coventry, as a member of the council, stayed behind and tried to smoothe things down.[2] Pepys, after a twinge of apprehension, felt sufficient confidence in the weight of his evidence and the strength of his position to dismiss the matter from his mind. The contrast between his agitation after the scene with Holmes at the Navy Board and his calmness after Rupert's attack in front of the King and the principal ministers shows how far he had travelled in three and a half years.

The disgust that Pepys and Coventry felt for the indiscipline and favouritism of the courtiers and gentlemen captains, the contempt in which they held the late Commanders-in-Chief, and the galloping financial deficit of the navy all distracted them from bothering about the Dutch and turned their attention more and more to the in-fighting of domestic politics. No one believed in the war any more: diplomatic negotiations were opened in Paris in December. It became increasingly clear that no provision would be made to fit out a fleet for the summer of 1667.

Yet the Government was perfectly well aware that the Dutch were by no means running down their war machine. Intermittently it even initiated defensive measures based on this intelligence, as for instance when a new fort was planned at Sheerness to strengthen the defences of the fleet anchorage in the Medway. The Elizabethans had recognised how vulnerable a position this was and had protected it by a chain across the river at Upnor. In Charles I's time Sir William Monson recommended the strengthening of Upnor Castle and urged that the ships themselves should never be without at least some of their guns and ammunition even when out of commission.[3] All this was half remembered. The King and the Duke went down to inspect the site for the new fort at Sheerness in February 1667. Four weeks later Penn, Spragge, the flag officer in charge and Pett, the Commissioner at Chatham, took a host of officials down to do the same. A month after that an officer was sent down to superintend

the construction and no doubt given a few months more something might
actually have been done. But the Government had not got its mind on the
job. It was thinking about the peace negotiations, about the threatening
noises Parliament was already making at being asked to pay the debts of
a stupid and unnecessary war, about the possible fall of Clarendon, the
personification of traditional Royalism. Even Pepys, recording in the
Diary entry for March 23rd Penn's plans for defending the ships laid
up in the Medway, notes the necessity with somnolent approval. Indeed,
the King and the Duke and Sir William Penn seem to have had the
clearest grasp of how serious and urgent the matter was. Coventry and
Pepys, for all their self-congratulation and mutual compliments, did in
fact little or nothing to forestall the greatest disaster of the war. Coventry
had entered the John Bright phase of his career and was bent on cutting
down military expenditure. As early as mid-December he and Pepys were
sneering at the pride and perversity of Sir Robert Holmes who had
objected to the discharge of the officers and men under his command at
Chatham.[4] But Holmes knew that bonfires was a game that two could
play.

The servants of the Restoration Government, civil and military, were
so often obsessed with faction that it was all too easy for them to see the
national interest entirely in its light. A course of action became good or
bad, wise or foolish, according as it was championed or opposed by particular people. Every subsequent writer has endorsed Pepys's condemna-
tion of the indiscipline of the Gentlemen officers, but his own standards
have generally escaped criticism. Largely this may be explained by the
brilliance of his record as an administrator and by the profusion of documents that support it. But we should not be blind to the fact that
Pepys was every inch as factious as Monck, Rupert, Holmes and the rest
of them; nor to the fact that their judgment, acquired in a lifetime devoted to the profession of arms, was sometimes superior to his own.
Holmes and the others who had opposed paying off the ships were right:
Penn who had pressed for the strengthening of the Medway defences was
right: Pepys and Coventry in opposing the one and lending insufficient
support to the other had mistaken their priorities. It was to prove an
expensive error.

In March negotiations with the Dutch had fixed on Breda as the seat
of the Peace Conference. In May the delegates arrived there and at once
embarked on the wrangles over precedence and procedure that took up so
much of the time and energy devoted to diplomacy in the seventeenth
century. In what order were the ambassadors of the powers to enter the
room? In what order were their names to be appended to any agreement

that they might reach? On such points were careers blasted and treaties brought to nothing. But while the English Government and its representatives gave these matters their best attention they were kept fully informed of the alarming activity in the Dutch naval bases and arsenals. The failure of the King and his ministers to act on the overwhelming intelligence available to them is indefensible. But though Pepys and Coventry constantly deplored the idleness and irresponsibility of their masters they show no sign of having grasped the real danger. Coventry indeed was pressing for the reduction of the already undermanned complements of the fireships in the Thames and Medway as late as May 29th. And on June 3rd, when the Dutch fleet was known to be at sea, he wrote to the Navy Board:

> We heare by the letters from Holland that the Dutch fleete are certainly abroad, consisting of about 80 men of warre and neare 20 fireshipps, and although I do not thinke they will make any attempt here in the River, yet it will be fitting that ye command^{rs} of the frigatts that are in the Hope be on board to provide against anything may happen.[5]

The Hope is the first great loop made by the river before it straightens out into Gravesend reach. Four days after that letter was written the Dutch fleet was to be anchored in the King's Channel at the mouth of the Thames: forty-eight hours later a squadron had been sent up to deal with the frigates in the Hope. Only a lucky change in wind and tide saved them. Coventry's misjudgment was total.

Pepys, for all the vehemence of his strictures on others, did no better. He had a long talk with Coventry on the morning of June 3rd but their topics were chiefly the preparation of naval accounts and the shortcomings of Sir George Carteret in this particular. As it was Trinity Monday Pepys attended the Trinity House dinner where he found his friend John Evelyn. Evelyn seems to have impressed him for a moment with the gravity of the situation. But the next day the Dutch have faded into the background: the question that presses is whether Pepys can afford to keep a coach. The following day brings another long and delightful conference with Sir William Coventry 'he being a most excellent man, and indeed, with all his business, hath more of his employed upon the good of the service of the Navy than all of us, that makes me ashamed of it'. Coventry provided 'a very good and neat dinner, after the French manner, and good discourse', but no one seems to have touched on the subject of defending the fleet and its principal bases from imminent attack. Nor is it so much as mentioned for the rest of the week until on Saturday Pepys received reliable reports of a Dutch fleet of eighty sail off Harwich and of gunfire heard to the north-east of London on Friday night. But even this was not allowed to disturb the characteristically Pepysian round of Sunday pleasures: a long chat with Coventry, sermon-tasting in Whitehall and Southwark, a visit to the submissive Mrs. Martin of Westminster, rounded off by a long and beautiful evening on the river, alone with an excellent translation of an amusing Spanish book. The Diary communicates no sense of emergency. Pepys went 'as high as Barne Elms, and there took a turn'. The situation of the kingdom might have been as calm and still as the evening itself. When he got home he found his colleagues Penn and Batten returned from their country houses dealing with demands for the immediate provision of fireships for use against the Dutch, now known to be in the King's Channel and hourly expected up higher.

By the morning of Monday the 10th even Coventry's complacency was shaken. The Dutch had reached the Nore. Fireships were now the only hope of defence. The danger signals had been repeatedly disregarded: humiliation was now certain and disaster probable. Batten, Penn and Pepys rushed to St. James's but found the Lord High Admiral already gone from his lodging to hurry reinforcements down to Chatham. Pursuing him across the park to Whitehall they met Coventry, 'who presses all that is possible for fireships'. So back they all tore to Seething Lane where they found Sir Frescheville Holles, a gentleman captain, a friend of Sir Robert Holmes, a courtier, everything that in the ordinary course of life Pepys most feared and detested. Normally too Pepys took great exception at his profanity and deplored the debauchery that his men acquired from the example of their commanding officer. But men like this had their uses in a desperate situation. Holles was ready to command the fireships 'in some exploits he is to do with them on the enemy in the River' and not even Pepys doubted his courage, his dash and his leadership. So down they all went to Deptford to choose the ships and to set men to work. Six ships were quickly chosen, one of them, a Dutch prize, ironically bearing the name *De Ruyter*, the admiral who at that very moment held England's lifeline in his hand. This vessel lay down the river at Grays, so Pepys was sent down to Woolwich to see about fitting her out while Holles went up to the Ordnance Office to obtain materials for fire-raising.[6] The enemy were reported to be already in the lower end of the Hope and to have fired the villages on the Essex side. Pepys, who seems to have regarded his mission as a pretext for a general reconnaissance, broke his journey at Greenwich and extended it beyond Grays to Gravesend where he found the Duke of Albemarle, attended by 'a great many idle lords and gentlemen with their pistols and fooleries'.7 The place, in Pepys's view, could not have maintained its defence for half an hour. Most of the inhabitants had left in a panic, taking their valuables with them but Pepys found no difficulty in being served with a meal. Fortunately the Dutch had withdrawn down to Sheerness where Albemarle intended to go next day, having first ordered such warships as were at Gravesend to be moored in line with the two blockhouses. 'Which I took then to be a ridiculous thing.' The word 'then' is a rare tribute, paid in writing up the Diary entry, to Albemarle's superior judgment. When it had come to praising Monck and recognising the merits of Sir Frescheville Holles things must have looked black. However Pepys could still appreciate the beauty of the evening. In the boat that bore him up to London he read Boyle's *Hydrostatics* as long as the light lasted and then took a nap. It was one in the morning when he got home and at once sat down to write a report to Coventry.

On the 11th it became clear that the crisis was imminent. Letters from Commissioner Pett at Chatham 'who is in a very fearful stink for fear of the Dutch, and desires help for God and the King and the kingdom's sake' brought news that Sheerness was already in Dutch hands. The Commissioner's state of mind communicated itself to his colleagues who hurried down to Deptford to 'consider of several matters relating to the dispatch of the fireships'. The phrase hardly answers to the urgency of the occasion. Pepys and Batten then went back to the office

and there to our business, hiring some fire-ships, and receiving every hour almost letters from Sir W. Coventry, calling for more fire-ships; and an order from Council to enable us to take any man's ships; and Sir W. Coventry . . . says he do not doubt but that at this time, under an invasion, as he owns it to be, the King may, by law, take any man's goods.'8

Pepys was determined, even at so grave an hour in his country's fortunes, to minimise this threat to his own. Acting on a timely tip from Hewer that the paymaster to the navy had some cash in hand he secured £400 in respect of his own salary. And that evening he discussed with Elizabeth the possibility that the Government might abandon the city to its fate. Not that he had any more intention of deserting his post than he had had in the plague or the fire. But a prudent man had to look to his own, especially when the Government was thinking of making free of every man's property.

Wee have been considering of the yet further number of fireshipps which you demand [he wrote to Coventry] . . . but wee thought it convenient to tell you that to take them up by treaty will aske soe much time and the taking of them by violence never a whitt lesse (because of the owners determyning theyr furniture and many other obstructions they will give us) that considering that and the difficulty of manning them wee doe dispayr of having them in any reasonable time, at least soone enough, by many days, to accompany these.[9]

Pepys's cool realism brings Coventry's excited proposal for invoking emergency powers firmly but courteously down to earth. What good will it do? And what use are ships without the means of damaging the enemy, above all without men?

This was the constant, enraged cry of Monck as he ranged tirelessly up and down the estuaries of the Thames and the Medway, trying every expedient, gathering every scrap of material to make some show of defence against a daring and powerful enemy. But where were the men? The ships had been paid off, or the sailors, starved and cheated in the King's service, had deserted. The dockyards had been unpaid so long that at Chatham he found, '. . . scarce twelve of eight hundred men which were then in the king's pay, in his Majesty's yards; and these so distracted with fear that I could have little or no service from them.'[10] The tale of incompetence, corruption, neglect and cowardice culminated in the most humiliating defeat ever suffered by the Royal Navy when the Dutch broke through the chain in Gillingham reach, defied the shore defences, burnt the newest and most powerful units of the fleet and towed away the flagship.

Even before the full extent of the disaster was known Pepys realised that anyone at all responsible for naval policy and administration was in hideous danger. The office might be attacked by an infuriated mob and he and his colleagues lynched. There was no police in seventeenth-century London: he had several times been pursued and threatened with violence by angry sailors demanding their pay: only two years earlier the populace of Amsterdam had reacted to the far less disgraceful defeat off Lowestoft by throwing the Commander-in-Chief into the sea. The precedents for mob vengeance were many and suggestive. Still more probable was the prospect of being made a scapegoat by a Government anxious to save its own skin. The certainty of Parliamentary inquiry receded into the background before these lively terrors.

Pepys faced them with the rational, stoic calm that he kept in reserve for the moments of real danger. His father was staying in the house, a useful circumstance to be framed into the plan of action. On the evening of the 12th, the day that Pepys knew that the Dutch had broken the chain at Gillingham and burned the ships, he called his father and Elizabeth up to her room,

> and shut the door; and told them the sad state of the times how we are like to be all undone; that I do fear some violence will be offered to this office, where all I have in the world is; and resolved upon sending it away—sometimes into the country—sometimes my father to lie in town and have the gold with him . . .

The next day brought confirmation of the disaster and added the alarming news that the King and the Duke of York had been personally supervising the sinking of ships by Barking Creek since four in the morning. A Dutch attack on the city seemed imminent. Pepys at once decided on sending his wife and father into the country. Within two hours they were in a coach with £1,300 in gold in their night-bag. All the money standing to his credit with the various Government departments, notably the Tangier Commission, might be written off but both Pepys and Hewer showed, as might be expected, a superior turn of speed in the run on the banks that had almost exhausted their liquidity. This produced considerable sums which still required safe disposal. About midday Pepys sent away one of his clerks to Huntingdon with a thousand guineas, under the pretext of his carrying an express letter to Sir Jeremy Smith,

> . . . who is, as I hear, with some ships at Newcastle; which I did really send to him, and may, possibly, prove of good use to the King; for it is possible, in the hurry of business, they may not think of it at Court, and the charge of an express is not considerable to the King. So though I intend Gibson no further than to Huntingdon I direct him to send the packet forward.

Even in so pressing an emergency there is time for self-justification. Gibson's mission broke the back of the problem. For the rest Pepys endured the discomfort of wearing a specially made girdle with £300 in gold 'in case I should be surprised'. His two silver flagons were sent to one cousin; his most important private papers 'and my journals which I value much' to another, '. . . that so, being scattered what I have, something might be saved'. Two hundred pounds' worth of silver coin still presented a difficulty. It was impossible to change it for gold: it was too bulky to carry about. Pepys thought of flinging it into the earth closet but was understandably deterred by the problem of retrieval.

All these dispositions had to be made under the cover of an industrious official constant to his duty. 'My business the most of the afternoon is listening to everybody that comes to the office, what news?' There was grave unrest in the city; talk of being betrayed by the Papists and others about the King, reports of attacks on the Lord Chancellor, rumours of French troops massing at Dunkirk for an invasion. The Papists were sure to be at the bottom of it, as, no doubt, they had been the year before in the Fire. The point was at least half established by the recent slighting of Upnor, 'the good old castle built by Queen Elizabeth' and thus an edifice conspicuous for its Protestantism, and clinched by the assertion (untrue, as it happened) that Legge, a protégé of Spragge's recently promoted to command the *Pembroke*, was a Papist.

In these lurid vapourings the silhouette of a scapegoat became gradually discernible. Pett, the Commissioner at Chatham, had got black marks from everybody. He had failed to carry out the Navy Board's repeated instructions to take the *Royal Charles* higher up the river 'and deserves, therefore, to be hanged for not doing it'.[11] He had antagonised Spragge, the senior naval officer in the river, by assuring Albemarle, against Spragge's advice, that the Dutch could be confined to the lower reaches of the Medway by sinking three ships at the Mussel Bank. And he had exasperated Albemarle by proving wrong in this particular and ineffective in every other task assigned him. To the innumerable professional delinquencies of which he was accused was added the report that he had employed scarce dockyard labour in carrying his own possessions to safety when the ships and yards entrusted to his care cried out for every pair of hands. To some of these charges Pett could, in time, produce a convincing answer; and from others he could find shelter in the sheer volume of allegations made against him. No doubt he was very much to blame, but it would be absurd to attribute so vast a failure to the derelictions of one man. Pepys was quick to notice the turn affairs were taking and to see how he might profit by it. On the 14th he comments on the dullness of the letter from Chatham giving the official account composed by Pett and Lord Brouncker of the events of the week and concludes darkly, 'I doubt they will be found to have been but slow men in this business.' On the 15th he hears of 'horrible miscarriages' and of the use of men and boats to carry away private possessions: 'and I hear that Commissioner Pett will be found the first man that began to remove; he is much spoken against, and Brouncker is complained of and reproached for discharging the men of the great ships heretofore.' If Brouncker could be carted for Coventry's policy of paying off the fleet before the war was over and if Pett could be made the scapegoat for everyone else, things were looking up. In any case the clerk Gibson had returned with news of the safe arrival of all the money, except for one or two pieces that fell out of a broken bag. The next day a warrant was issued for committing Pett to the Tower.

Pepys, when he heard of this on the 18th, was for a moment shaken: '. . . which puts me into a fright, lest they may do the same with us as they do with him. This puts me upon hastening what I am doing with my people [i.e. his clerks] and collecting out of my papers our defence.' The historian's insistence on documentation, instinctive to Pepys, provided ammunition for the beleaguered defenders of the Navy Office. The very next afternoon he was ordered to attend the Council bringing with him all his books and papers relating to the Medway. Although the probable reason for this summons was the examination of Pett, there was an unpleasant possibility that the door would open to the dock and not the witness-box. At the preliminary examination before a large and formidable committee of the Council — Albemarle was there, and all the rising stars of the Cabal, Arlington, Ashley, Clifford and Lauderdale — Pett cut a very poor figure. 'He is in his old clothes, and looked most sillily', an impression confirmed by his answers. Hostility slid into derision. Arlington had spiced his questions with the candid aside that if Pett was not guilty the world would think the Council was. Pepys, when called on, gratefully adopted this policy of *sauve qui peut*:

> I all this while showing him no respect, but rather against him for which God forgive me! for I mean no hurt to him, but only find that these Lords are upon their own purgation and it is necessary I should be so in behalf of the office.

The Committee then adjourned briefly, ordering, on Arlington's suggestion, that the minutes of Pett's examination should be given to Pepys, the acknowledged expert, to knock into shape. On his return with his books and papers he still felt apprehensive:

> . . . I thought myself obliged to salute people and to smile, lest they should think I was a prisoner too . . . but my fear was such . . . that at my going in I did think fit to give T. Hater, whom I took with me to wait the event, my closet-key and directions where to find £500 and more in silver and gold . . . in case of any misfortune to me.

Pepys's instinct was sure. He and everyone else who had had a hand in the running of the war might count themselves lucky that the storm of resentment should break on the unhappy Pett. But the weather would not clear for many days thereafter. There were too many scandals to be smoked out, too many old scores to pay, too many trumps left undrawn. It was naïve to imagine that there was enough flesh on Pett to satisfy the robust appetites of faction or that public opinion would accept him as responsible for everything that had gone wrong. Marvell's lines on the subject are among the supreme achievements of English political satire

> Whose counsel first did this mad war beget?
> Who all commands sold through the Navy? *Pett*.
> Who would not follow when the Dutch were beat?
> Who treated out the time at Bergen? *Pett*.
> Who the Dutch fleet with storms disabled met,
> And, rifling prizes, them neglected? *Pett*.
> Who with false news prevented the Gazette,
> The fleet divided, writ for *Rupert? Pett*.
> Who all our seamen cheated of their debt?
> And all our prizes who did swallow? *Pett*.
> Who did advise no navy out to set?
> And who the forts left unprepared? *Pett*
> Who to supply with powder did forget
> *Languard, Sheerness, Gravesend and Upnor? Pett*
> Who all our ships exposed in Chatham net?
> Who should it be but the fanatick *Pett*?
> *Pett*, the sea-architect, in making ships
> Was the first cause of all these naval slips.
> Had he not built, none of these faults had been;
> If no creation, there had been no sin.

Pepys, when he read them noted how sharply they reflected on Sandwich. Satire by its nature must be selective in its targets. Marvell, whose authorship of the poem was a well-kept secret, had a strong partisan interest in naval affairs. Sir Jeremy Smith, Monck's protégé who was given his flag in 1666, was a close personal and political friend. Marvell was to act as executor of his will and Smith exerted considerable local influence in the borough that returned Marvell to Parliament and paid his wages.[12] The wit, the force, the mastery of his poem have dominated the general historiography of the Second Dutch War, have cast the heroes and villains of the piece, just as Dryden's *Absalom and Achitophel* has for the Exclusion Crisis a decade later. The hero of Marvell's interpretation is Smith's patron, Monck. Full credit is given for his activity in the moment of national paralysis when the Dutch were in the river; but nothing is said of what many contemporaries thought the worst mistake of the war, his decision to fight after the fleet had been divided in June 1666. Similarly James, Duke of York's victory off Lowestoft is lost behind criticism of the misconduct that followed; and of Smith's arch-enemy, Holmes, who had inflicted more damage on the enemy at less cost than any other commander, there is no mention. Piercing and brilliant as Marvell's analysis is Pepys was entirely justified in scouting its impartiality.

But at the high tide of danger it was Pett over whom the flood waters surged. Pepys and the others trembled for their defences and listened for the cracking and rending of the dykes. Each day was a day gained and soon it began to appear that the worst was over. The Dutch were still blockading the river and threatening the East Anglian and Northern Channel ports — what was there to stop them? But the peace negotiations were going forward; the populace had not rioted; no other Navy Commissioner had joined Pett in the Tower. By June 19th Elizabeth had returned from Brampton and there was even leisure for speechless rage at her folly in permitting his father to bury the gold in the garden in broad daylight during churchtime on Sunday instead of after dark. There was leisure too for an orgy of theatre-going and for river-parties and excursions to the country. So urbanised has Pepys become that a shepherd met on Epsom Downs appears in the Diary as a romantic even a picturesque figure, half from pastoral poetry, half from the Bible.

In August the Peace Treaty was signed at Breda. All through July it had grown clearer that the Dutch, having strengthened their position by their brilliant raid, had no further interest in prolonging the war, indeed by exposing their returning East India Fleet might lose by doing so. For Pepys, relief that the whole futile business was at last over was balanced by disgust, contempt and anger at the frivolity and incompetence of his masters. He had made so much money and so much reputation that he knew now that he could not be easily overset. The long and intimate association with Sir William Coventry had brought him as close to that detachment and fearless honesty of mind, so very different from the shrewd realism of Sandwich, as it was possible for a man dependent on his service to Charles II's Government to go. On the day that news of the ratification reached London Pepys and Coventry were discussing what had to be done in the navy and agreeing how cordially they had long detested the war. In the course of their talk Pepys suddenly realised that Coventry really believed in and acted on the disinterested impartiality that he preached: 'I perceive he do really make no difference between any man.'[13] It was a recognition that echoed the profoundest quality of Pepys's own mind, instanced in his freedom from national prejudice in comparing the enemy's performance with our own.[14] Nowhere in the Diary is the scorn for Charles II's levity more repeatedly expressed. It was the son of an old Royalist actually imprisoned by the Protector who prompted Pepys's famous observation, 'It is strange how he and everybody do now-a-days reflect upon Oliver, and commend him, what brave things he did and made all the neighbour princes fear him.' And the same man, a courtier and Pepys's colleague on the Tangier commission went on to declare 'that he expects that of necessity this kingdom will fall back again to a commonwealth, and other wise men are of the same mind'.[15] No longer the client of Lord Sandwich or the jealous rival of Sir William Penn, Pepys, for the moment, withdraws to the heights from which in our day the Treasury and the Cabinet secretariat survey the crimes and follies of mankind. He is not a whit dismayed at the ending of his profitable appointment as Surveyor of the Victualling. He even contemplates (though not seriously or for very long) a premature retirement.

The carelessness and mismanagement that had humiliated the nation left the professional administrative interest represented by Pepys and Coventry for the moment in a strong position *vis-à-vis* the courtiers and favourites. But the Quaker whom Pepys saw pass through Westminster Hall, 'naked . . . only very civilly tied about the privities to avoid scandal, and with a chafing-dish of fire and brimstone burning upon his head . . . crying "Repent, Repent"', was only translating into more scriptural language the message that his co-religionist Billing had put with his customary pithiness a week earlier:

'Well,' says he, 'now you will all be called to an account;' meaning the Parliament is drawing near.[16]

13

Fire and brimstone

The last year of the war marks a turn in Pepys's private as in his professional life. Perhaps for all his pleasure at bringing his wife home after the plague he had in her absence acquired or developed tastes and connections that, somehow, excluded her. Business brought him into ever more interesting and sophisticated circles. His infidelities increased and Elizabeth herself, it seems, no longer excited his desire. On August 2nd, 1667, he recalls that he has not lain with her for a whole half-year and thinks it possible she may have noticed this. The old simplicities and shared amusements of the marriage are neither so spontaneous nor so frequent. The world of the Diary was changing.

By far the most dramatic transformation was effected by the Fire of London in September 1666. In a few hours the great medieval city that Pepys had known from earliest childhood, his father's house, the school where he had gone as a boy, the physical background of every memory and every impression of his formative years had been effaced. Like Johnson, like Dickens, Pepys was a Londoner to the roots of his being. The pages in which he describes the fire, besides being among the best reporting in our language, are more eloquent of deep emotion than any passage in the Diary except for one or two inspired by music. Every faculty, every sensibility, every power of observation is at once heightened and their perceptions articulated into the wholeness craved by the spirit of the artist. Everything is freshly, sharply, distinctly seen, and yet

perfectly, mysteriously, related. Design is imposed on chaos. Compre
hension inspires action. The artist and the administrator are at one
The opening passages bring details and individuals to instant life:

> Everybody endeavouring to remove their goods, and flinging int
> the River or bringing them into lighters that lay off. Poor peopl
> staying in their houses as long as till the very fire touched them, an
> then running into boats or clambering from one pair of stair by th
> water-side to another. And among other things, the poor pigeons
> perceive were loath to leave their houses, but hovered about the win
> dows and balconies till they were some of them burned, their wings
> and fell down.[1]

After watching the fire rage from about half-past eight to half-past nin
in a boat just above London Bridge, Pepys noticed that no steps wer
being taken to put it out. He went straight up the river to Whitehal
where, as it was a Sunday, he found the King and Duke in chapel. Hi
was the first news the Court had had, so word was sent in to the Kin
who at once came out with his brother to hear what Pepys had to say
They listened with some anxiety and the King accepted Pepys's urgen
recommendation of creating fire-breaks by destroying houses that lay i
the path of the fire. Armed with royal commands to this effect Pepy
sped back to the city in search of the Lord Mayor:

> At last met my Lord Mayor in Canning Streete, like a man spent
> with a hankercher about his neck. To the King's message, he cried lik
> a fainting woman, 'Lord, what can I do? I am spent. People will not obey
> me. I have been pulling down houses. But the fire overtakes us faster
> than we can do it.' That he needed no more soldiers; and that for
> himself, he must go and refresh himself having been up all night. So
> he left me, and I him and walked home – seeing people all almost dis
> tracted and no manner of means used to quench the fire.

It was still hardly midday, and warm, brilliant weather. Faced with such
obstructive futility, Pepys enjoyed the last cooked meal he was to have
for some days and entertained the guests invited to Sunday dinner as wel
as he could. By the afternoon the King and the Duke had come down in
their barge to give personal orders for the pulling down of houses. But
now the fire had got a real hold both above and below the bridge and the
chance of stopping it had been lost. In the early evening Pepys crossed for
coolness to an alehouse at Bankside:

. . . and there stayed until it was dark almost and saw the fire grow; and as it grow darker, appeared more and more, and in Corners and upon steeples and between churches and houses, as far as we could see up the hill of the City, in a most horrid malicious bloody flame, not like the fine flame of an ordinary fire. . . . We stayed till, it being darkish, we saw the fire as only one entire arch of fire from this to the other side the bridge, and in a bow up the hill, for an arch of above a mile long. It made me weep to see it. The churches, houses, and all on fire and flaming at once, and a horrid noise the flames made, and the cracking of houses at their ruine . . .

So far Pepys had done nothing to save his own possessions. Coming home that night he found his clerk, Hayter, with a few of his things salvaged from his house in Fish Street Hill, one of the first places to be engulfed. Pepys gladly gave him shelter but nobody got much sleep as the night was spent in shifting furniture out into the garden, money and strong-boxes down to the cellar, and collecting papers, bags of gold and Exchequer tallies into the office ready for a hurried departure. Pepys's neighbours the Battens had brought in carts from the country. About four in the morning Lady Batten sent over to offer him one. Up came the strong-boxes from the cellar and Pepys accompanied by his plate, the Diary and all his most treasured possessions (the gold only excepted) jolted off to Sir William Rider's house in Bethnal Green. Pushing his way back on foot he joined Elizabeth in transferring everything that was movable on to a lighter lying at the quay above the Tower dock. Such an upheaval provided rich material for the social observer. Looking at other people's goods piled into lighters Pepys noticed that almost one household in three possessed a pair of virginals.

Anxiety for his own goods, anxiety over preserving official papers, snatched meals, snatched sleep, did not blunt his perception or diminish his industry in noting down what he saw. On the Tuesday, when the fire had reached Tower Street he joined Batten in digging a pit in the garden to accommodate Batten's wine (his vineyard at Walthamstow produced, we are told, some notable bottles) and his own papers and Parmesan cheese. Early the next morning he was roused by Elizabeth to find the fire had reached All Hallows' church at the bottom of Seething Lane. It was time to be gone. Taking his bags of gold (£2,350 worth) he embarked for Wool-wich with Elizabeth, Will Hewer and Jane the cook. He never expected to see his house again.

But when he came back about seven in the morning he was astonished and delighted to find that the fire had at last suffered a check. The wind had fallen in the night but the real improvement came from Pepys's own suggestion, made to Penn the previous afternoon, that the dockyard hands from Woolwich and Deptford should be sent for to help blow up houses. Penn had acted and the Navy Office had saved itself by its own exertions. From this point Pepys resigns his executive obligations in favour of his descriptive genius. Anyone who wants to know what it was like to be in London during the closing stages of the fire has only to read the Diary. The hot ash burning through the soles of one's shoes, the pathetic groups of people clutching a few fragments of what had been home, jealously kept separate as though their identity depended on it, the melted, buckled, stained glass from a church window, the cellars full of oil still burning after the fire had receded, the desolation of a lunar landscape – how faithfully all this was observed could be confirmed by the many survivors of the Blitz. It was widely believed that so enormous a disaster could not have come about (as in fact it did) simply by accident. The French probably, the Papists certainly, must be at the back of it. Riots were feared and feeling ran high but its eruption was postponed a dozen years to the Popish Plot.

On the Saturday there was leisure to exchange anecdotes of the meanness shown by the rich in rewarding people such as the dockyard men who had often risked life and limb to save their property. In the afternoon Pepys retrieved his Journal from Bethnal Green and much of the Sunday was devoted to writing up the entries for the past week. The next few days saw the gradual return of furniture, valuables, wife, gold and the rest and their re-installation in their proper places. There was so much to do that the unexpected arrival from sea of Brother Balty was greeted with positive pleasure instead of the usual wary apprehension. He apparently made himself useful and returned two days later bringing his own wife to stay. Balty's somewhat shaky career was at this point promising a degree of robustness. As a Muster Master, an officer appointed at Pepys's instigation to check the grosser frauds of captains and pursers, Balty had got on well with his shipmates and, far rarer achievement, had won golden opinions from his brother-in-law. 'I do much wish,' Pepys had written to Prince Rupert's secretary only ten days earlier, 'that the Muster Masters were quickned for we owe to their negligence our Ignorance in the manning of the fleet, having not to this day received Bookes (as we ought) from more than one or two of all the Muster Masters in the fleet.'[2] That Balty was the shining exception is made plain in a Table of Muster Books returned which Pepys constructed at the end of the year.[3] By September 20th, a fortnight after the fire, the house was almost back to normal. Even the books were in their places, except for five particularly valuable ones whose mislaying nagged at their owner (they turned up in the end). Both Balty and his wife were commended for their usefulness, but Elizabeth soon counterbalanced this with tales, all too characteristic, of their selfish and improper behaviour to her father and mother.

Pepys himself was not best placed to cast the first stone, if selfishness or impropriety were in question. The Bagwell affair had now reached a degree of squalor at which even he felt repulsion. Mrs. Martin and the Westminster Hall troupe went regularly through the motions required of them; the servants at Seething Lane were the frequent recipients of their master's attentions. Elizabeth's suspicions and jealousies, so long evaded or repressed, began to break out with disturbing frequency. At first it was the actresses such as Mrs. Knepp or her friend Mrs. Pearse, the surgeon's wife, both long and openly admired by Pepys, that excited accusations and quarrels. In both cases Elizabeth's bitterness was intensified by being left at home, bored and kept short of money, while her husband was not stinting himself or these ladies in pursuit of the gay life. The balance of power within the marriage was beginning to shift. On September 22nd, 1667, Pepys records his annoyance at being obliged to accept his wife's domestic accounts and not being in a position to find fault. 'The truth is I have indulged myself more in pleasure for these last two months than ever I did in my life before, since I come to be a person concerned in business.' Elizabeth had got the better of him at his own game.

It was an unfortunate moment at which to lose ground. Two days later a catspaw of wind ruffling the surface of the Diary presages its fiercest emotional storm.

> This evening my wife tells me that W. Batelier [brother to Mary, the linen draper, whom Pepys considered one of the finest women he ever saw] hath been here to-day, and brought with him the pretty girl he speaks of, to come to serve my wife as a woman, out of the school at Bow. My wife says she is extraordinary handsome, and inclines to have her, and I am glad of it — at least, that if we must have one, she should be handsome.

Deb Willett's entrance is characteristic: graceful, unobtrusive, touching the imagination with the serious innocence so irresistible in children. It was this quality that captivated Pepys from the moment he set eyes on her.

> While I was busy at the Office, my wife sends for me to come home, and what was it but to see the pretty girl which she is taking to wait

upon her: and though she seems not altogether so great a beauty as she had before told me, yet indeed she is mighty pretty: and so pretty, that I find I shall be too much pleased with it, and therefore could be contented as to my judgment, though not to my passion, that she might not come, lest I may be found too much minding her, to the discontent of my wife . . . she seems by her discourse, to be grave beyond her bigness and age, and exceeding well bred as to her deportment, having been a scholar in a school at Bow these seven or eight years. To the office again, my head running on this pretty girl . . .[4]

Deb had hardly been in the house a fortnight before Elizabeth was showing signs of jealousy. Pepys seems to have lacked the energy to control a situation whose dangers he had recognised from the start. For once the multiplicity of his consciousness weakened instead of strengthening him. On the professional side of his life the menacing steps of the Committee of Inquiry into the miscarriages of the war were drawing closer. On the family side the problem of marrying off Pall if not solved soon would lead to others yet more intractable. On the personal side there was his failure of will in not enforcing self-discipline in matters of money and pleasure; and worse, far worse and worst of all was the fear of failing eyesight that runs through the Diary from the end of the war to the poignancy of its closing entry. Pepys felt, for once, self-doubt and loss of nerve. 'I do plainly see my weakness that I am not a man able to go through trouble, as other men, but that I should be a miserable man if I should meet with adversity, which God keep me from.'[5] He underrated himself.

But his original estimate of the risk he was running in falling in love with Deb was only too accurate. In spite of Elizabeth's acute perception, or perhaps because of it, he seems to have achieved an unusual restraint over his passion; and passion it was, tender, strong, at times harrowing, as unlike the computerised lechery of the Bagwell affair as could be. It was nearly Christmas before he first kissed her. And he had in the meantime made notable efforts to resuscitate his marriage.

> . . . I bought some Scotch cakes at Wilkinson's in King Street, and called my wife, and home, and there to supper, talk, and to bed. Supped upon these cakes, of which I have eat none since we lived at Westminster.

This affectionate revival of the old days in Axe Yard took place early in December. A little later another entry remarks on the interruption of conjugal relations caused by Elizabeth's being ill for two or three days.

And just before Christmas the Diary is full of affectionate distress at the pain she suffers from an abscess on a tooth. But there was too long a tale of selfishness and neglect for the old ease and security to be so easily restored. At the end of December she made a dreadful scene, 'mad as a devil, and nothing but ill words between us all the evening while we sat at cards – W. Hewer and the girl by – even to gross ill words, which I was troubled for . . .', when she heard that her husband had been to the theatre with Mrs. Knepp and Mrs. Pearse. They went to bed without speaking to each other. Next day they made it up. But less than a fortnight later on January 12th there was another searing score-raking row, this time over the question of Pepys *père* coming to live with them after Pall's marriage, an event that against all the odds was now about to take place. Elizabeth could not abide her father-in-law, as her husband was at last forced to recognise. Yet only the day before she had pleased him by offering to have Pall married from their house. There is a ding-dong, over-excited quality about their married life at this time. Hardly a month goes by without Elizabeth turning on Deb or picking a quarrel with her husband. She had, as the Diary shows, better reason than she knew. Beside the liaison with Deb that she yet only suspected, beside the junketings with Mrs. Knepp and Mrs. Pearse that especially enraged her, Pepys still employed the frequent services of Mrs. Martin, had even re-opened the affair with Mrs. Bagwell, and yet prowled the streets eager for fresh adventures. No doubt her suspicions deepened as her tight-fisted husband dangled a coach before her, thought better of it and offered the redecoration of her room in lieu, finally settling on an even more splendid equipage than he had first proposed. Pepys, too, knew that he was playing with fire. He seems to have hoped, not without reason, that the flames would spread to his old passion for Elizabeth. There were expeditions of pleasure, to Oxford, Salisbury, Bath and Bristol. Elizabeth's beauty was, again, much admired. Samuel Cooper, perhaps the greatest artist of the age, took her portrait in miniature.

But returning from their jaunt to the West in the middle of June Pepys was glumly forced to the conclusion that 'my wife hath something in her gizzard, that only waits an opportunity of being provoked to bring up'. Two nights later it came up with a vengeance. In the small hours Elizabeth became hysterical. In the morning she asked for a separation so that she could go and live in France by herself; 'and then all come out, that I loved pleasure and denied her any, and a deal of do; and I find that there have been great fallings out between my father and her, whom, for ever hereafter, I must keep asunder for they cannot possibly agree.' Pepys was mild, pacific, conciliatory. She quietened down. They went to the theatre together with great pleasure. Only two days after these disturbances Pepys could write contentedly '. . . dined with my wife and Deb alone, but merry and in good humour, which is, when all is done, the greatest felicity of all . . .' But his passion for Deb grew overmastering. On October 25th Elizabeth, whose irritability must have revealed her suspicions, found them embracing. The fury and recrimination that followed may easily be imagined and are vividly sketched in the Diary. Elizabeth certainly showed signs of hysteria, perhaps of mental instability: but it is difficult to criticise the rationality of her refusal to trust her husband. Pepys longed above all things for domestic peace and good temper (enhanced to a psychological necessity by the dangerous mood of politics and the threat to his sight). Yet he could not bear to part with Deb. Leave the house she must: abjure her he must: but never to see her again, so young, so tender, so trusting, was this endurable? To stop Elizabeth's shrill stormings he would agree to anything: but if he broke his agreement would he be found out?

There is abundant evidence in the Diary that Pepys was a kind-hearted man, that he had a strong sense of justice, that he had the rare courage to face his own shortcomings and the rarer resolve to make them good. But he had not yet taught himself magnanimity. Thus although he could sympathise with, or at any rate admit, the justice of Elizabeth's anger and distress, although he could pity Deb and lament the trouble he had brought on her, although (in different ways) he really loved both women, his inveterate egocentricity was the force that told. How unconscious this was is suggested by Pepys's words after a secret assignation, in direct breach of his repeated promises: 'I did give her the best council I could, to have a care of her honour, and to fear God, and suffer no man para haber to do con her as yo have done.' Deb passes from the Diary and thus from history[6] with the same well-bred refusal to draw attention to herself with which she entered it. Unlike Elizabeth, Deb hardly speaks. She looks, she lowers her eyes to hide a tear, she smiles; at our last glimpse of her she even winks. Lashed by Elizabeth's tongue she does not answer back; and Pepys records no word of reproach for the embarrassment and disgrace he had caused her.

Next to Deb the most attractive role is that of Will Hewer. So transparent was his affection and loyalty that Elizabeth, overwrought as she was, had no hesitation in trusting him where she could not trust her husband. Hewer was charged with the delicate task of preventing his master from pursuing Deb 'like a jaylour, but yet with great love and to my great good liking, it being my desire above all things to please my wife therein.'

With so much good will the marriage would surely have mended. But the male supremacy on which Pepys had traded had gone for good. Elizabeth had seen him abject before her fury and neither would be likely to forget it. And a new danger had been revealed in the terrible flow of emotional lava: Elizabeth had returned to the Roman Catholicism of her upbringing. All this required most careful handling. A month after the great eruption Pepys could write:

> Lay long in bed with pleasure (with my wife), with whom I have now a great deal of content, and my mind is in other things also mightily more at ease, and I do mind my business better than ever and am more at peace, and trust in God I shall ever be so, though I cannot yet get my mind off from thinking now and then of Deb, but I do ever since my promise a while since to my wife pray to God by myself in my chamber every night, and will endeavour to get my wife to do the like with me ere long, but am in much fear of what she lately frighted me with about her being a Catholique . . .

Meanwhile both her and his attention had been thrillingly distracted by the purchase of a coach and all its attendant magnificences: horses, harness, livery for the coachman, painted panels and heaven knows what. Pepys had chosen the vehicle and agreed its price the day before his domestic downfall. But even in the week that followed he found time to think of taking Povy, the supreme arbiter of the elegances of life, to run his eye over it. Povy was aghast. It was badly designed: it was much too heavy: it was out of fashion. Pepys accepted his criticism humbly and gratefully (but does the memory of it help to explain his uncharacteristic bitterness towards Povy in later life?)* and commissioned a new one to be built to his specifications. It was delivered in time, but only just in time, for an outing on May Day 1669, the apotheosis of the married splendour that had taken its rise, also in a coach, when Pepys showed Elizabeth his patent as Clerk of the Acts in the summer of 1660.

> At noon home to dinner and there find my wife extraordinary fine, with her flowered tabby gown that she made two years ago, now laced exceeding pretty: and indeed was fine all over; and mighty earnest to go, though the day was lowering; and she would have me put on my fine suit, which I did. And so anon we went alone through the town with our new liveries of serge, and the horses' manes and tails tied with red ribbons, and the standards there gilt with varnish, and all clean, and

* See p. 34b, Chapter VIII, note 3.

green reines that people did look mightily upon us; and, the truth is, I did not see any coach more pretty, though more gay, than ours, all the day.

So, in the last month of the Diary, in the last few months of Elizabeth's life, the Pepyses sweep past our dazzled eyes at a spanking trot. If the diarist himself had been able to fix a single impression on posterity that would stand as the symbol of how he wished his married life to appear, this would surely have been his choice. But the reality he records was naturally less decorous, less imposing. Deb's banishment by no means soothed Elizabeth's agitation and Pepys himself could not unlearn his old ways all at once. Summing up the position on New Year's Eve he recognises that his domestic tranquillity is precarious and admits his own responsibility:

> . . . the year ends, after some late very great sorrow with my wife by my folly, yet ends, I say, with great mutual peace and content, and likely to last so by my care, who am resolved to enjoy the sweet of it . . .

Yet three days later he annoyed her by haggling over her dress allowance. Next day he not only gave way, but gave her more than she had expected. A week passed, heavy with Elizabeth's unspoken suspicions. She was snappish, he was sulky. On the night of January 12th she refused all entreaties to come to bed, stoking the fire and lighting fresh candles. After some hours Pepys, alarmed, tried again to persuade her, only to be met with furious (but vague) accusations about secret trysts with Deb. 'At last, about one o'clock, she come to my side of the bed, and drew my curtaine open and with the tongs red hot at the ends, made as if she did design to pinch me with them.' Pepys leapt up, and with a few words easily induced her to lay down her arms. But it took another hour of listening and reasoning before she could be got to bed. The even tenor of life for which Pepys yearned seemed to have been broken. Even when he took her to the play his roving eye gave grounds for offence. At last on January 21st when Elizabeth had been 'mighty dogged' and he had been 'mightily troubled' he left her sulking and silent and went to bed 'weeping to myself for grief, which she discerning, come to bed and mighty kind and so with great joy on both sides to sleep'. There were fallings-out after that — and only too good grounds for them on Pepys's own evidence — but the era of red-hot tongs was over.

The marriage was both strained and strengthened by the threat of Parliamentary inquiry that hung over the heads of Pepys and all his colleagues. Strained, because coming home worried, apprehensive and exhausted he was easily irritated by Elizabeth and the more inclined to seek the company of women who would distract and amuse instead of nagging: strengthened, because Elizabeth really did share his joys and sorrows as no one else; and the dangers and triumphs of the post-war period in Pepys's career seemed at the time immense.

The scale and the thoroughness with which the House of Commons was preparing its investigation into the whole conduct of the war could only be alarming to men like Pepys and Coventry. They knew that they had acted in good faith and had set high standards of efficiency and order. But they had had a hand in many pies, some of which hardly did credit to the administrative cuisine. How could it be otherwise? They had to act with colleagues, some of whom were in varying degrees incompetent, dishonest or lazy. They had to carry out orders whether they thought them sensible or no. In either of these broad contexts it would be impossible for any man to appear blameless. And they had made enemies, known and unknown. The courtiers, the gentleman-captains who undid all, would certainly take the opportunity of making mischief. The merchants who had not succeeded in landing profitable contracts, the men who had applied for jobs and had been sent away without them, the officials who had been dismissed for misconduct, the jealous, the resentful, the malicious, all these persons could mount attacks that not even the most agile tactician could forestall. And in Pepys's case, if not in Coventry's, there was a great deal that simply could not be explained away. The huge bribes from Sir William Warren and Captain Cocke, the large sums paid by the Houblons to secure passes for their ships trading to the Mediterranean, the frequent use of naval property for private purposes, the cutting of corners and the breaking of rules that Pepys knew himself to be guilty of cannot have made for ease of mind.

The Committee to inquire into the miscarriages of the war was appointed in October 1667. Signs of a political upheaval had been evident some time before. A month earlier Coventry had astonished Pepys by the news that he was leaving the Duke of York's service. But Pepys, who had been taken by surprise at the King's dismissal of Clarendon a week earlier quickly recognised the connection between the two events. Clarendon was the Duke of York's father-in-law: and Coventry had worked tirelessly for the great minister's downfall. Coventry, who still remained a Navy Commissioner and a member of the Privy Council, insisted to Pepys that he had long been seeking an opportunity of resigning his secretaryship to the Duke. He may well have been speaking the truth; Pepys, always impressed by his open dealing, clearly thought so; in any case the two explanations do not exclude each other. What is certain is that Clarendon's fall opened a breach between the King and his brother the Lord High Admiral at a moment when the Royal Navy needed every hand to work her out of range of the Parliament's batteries.

Pepys was pleased and flattered to hear that he had been considered as Coventry's successor. But he was not, as in the filling of a later vacancy in the same post, in the least hurt or disappointed. He had more than enough to do in fighting the Navy Office's corner without undertaking to defend the strategic conduct of the war. In this as much as ever Coventry was the only ally on whom he could wholly depend. Coventry's advice given on December 3rd, 1667, is the timeless directive for a civil servant charged with drafting a Parliamentary answer:

> He advises me . . . to be as short as I can, and obscure, saving in things fully plain; and that the greatest wisdom in dealing with Parliament in the world is to say little, and let them get out what they can by force.

Coventry turned the same clear, penetrating gaze on the King his master and, on occasion, told him unpalatable truths. No wonder he did not last long: but no wonder that Pepys exclaimed after one of their wide-ranging talks, 'the ability and integrity of Sir William Coventry in all the King's concernments I do and must admire'. As early as December 1667, within a week of Clarendon's exile, Captain Cocke reported that Coventry's impeachment was imminent. The detail and the timing were both far out, but the point was true, as Coventry himself knew well enough when he told Pepys at this very time:

> that the serving a Prince that minds not his business is most unhappy for them that serve him well, and an unhappiness so great that he declares he will never have more to do with a war, under him.

This insight was echoed by the comments in the Diary two days later, December 9th, on the King's carefree disloyalty to the men who had served him and were now under attack.

It was an attack mounted on two Parliamentary fronts: the Committee for Miscarriages already referred to, and the Committee for Accounts, later called the Brooke House Committee from the place assigned for it to sit. The Brooke House Committee was not nominated until December 1667 and did not get into its stride for another two years. Pepys at first approved the expert knowledge and intellectual calibre of its membership but lived, as we shall see, to revise these opinions when he found himself the principal object of its investigations. His Homeric exchanges with it must be postponed to another chapter. But to understand the strain he was under, it is important not to forget its existence. He knew that if and when he escaped with a whole skin from the Committee bent on knowing why the war had gone so badly he would have to face another determined to find out what the Navy Office had done with the unheard-of sums of money that had been voted it.

The Committee for Miscarriages lost no time in getting down to business. Within four days of its appointment Pepys heard that he was to be summoned before it to answer questions about the Medway disaster. But by then it had already ripped off the coverings beneath which one of the most celebrated scandals of the war had been concealed. The fatal order to shorten sail that had allowed the Dutch to escape annihilation after the great victory off Lowestoft in 1665 had been nailed on Henry Brouncker, the courtier brother of Pepys's colleague. Since Pepys himself with all his personal sources of information had not previously established this fact, the Committee had shown an alarming grip. Pepys slept badly, spent a harassing morning preparing the Board's case and hurried straight to the Commons without time for any dinner. As he drove there in Lord Brouncker's coach he and his colleagues anxiously tried to co-ordinate their defence in the immensely complicated business of discharging of seamen by ticket about which they had been severally and collectively accused of malpractices. With a body like a House of Commons Committee one could never be sure that they would stick to one thing at a time. After a short period of waiting Pepys found himself facing his examiners. In the heat of exposition there was no time for nerves; and no need either, since his habitual lucidity and his methodical documentation at once brought every neutral to his side. A chair was brought for his books and papers, and the sun went down and candles were called for before he had finished. He knew he had dominated his audience and watched scornfully while Commissioner Pett and Lord Brouncker mumbled and bumbled. Congratulations flowed in. Cousin Roger, the member for Cambridge, was among the first to tell him how well he had done. He returned to a hearty supper and a contented night's rest.

His colleagues knew that their best hope lay in keeping quiet and letting him do the talking. Walking in the Matted Gallery at Whitehall a few weeks later he and Coventry agreed 'that we that have taken the most pains are called upon to answer for all crimes, while those that, like Sir W. Batten and Sir J. Minnes, did sit and do nothing, do lie still without any trouble.' This last statement was incontestably true of Batten who had died eight weeks earlier. Towards the end of January 1668 the Committee for Accounts began to show unwelcome signs of life. Here again Pepys was to answer for the office. But what really agitated him was the knowledge that they were going to question him about that unfortunate business of the prize goods. Worse still they examined him on oath. If they did not get under his guard, he still felt only a modest satisfaction at his performance. By the middle of February the double pressure was beginning to tell:

> All the morning till noon getting some things more ready against the afternoon for the Committee of Accounts, which did give me great trouble, to see how I am forced to dance after them in one place, and to answer Committees of Parliament in another.

At any moment cats might leap out of a number of ill-secured bags. Sir William Warren hinted that the Navy Board's failure to place any recent orders with him might lead him into unfortunate — and uncharacteristic — candour about past transactions when these were scrutinised by the Committee. Pepys concluded that he was bluffing: but he noted uneasily a day or two later

> . . . I do perceive by Sir W. Warren's discourse, that they [the House] do all they can possibly to get out of him and others, what presents they have made to the Officers of the Navy;* but he tells me that he hath denied all, though he knows that he is forsworn as to what relates to me.[7]

Even Coventry, whom Pepys met next day, was apprehensive of the trouble he would find himself in through taking the customary fees for appointments until his own suggestion of a fixed salary in lieu had at last been adopted. If Coventry, the most scrupulous public servant of Pepys's acquaintance, felt cause for alarm, the chances for anyone else must have looked slender. Coventry identified Sir Frescheville Holles as the man who was stirring the pot. He had recently been elected to the House of Commons and had thus found wider scope for the profanity and mischief that so scandalised Pepys. And yet was he quite so thorough-paced a villain as he appears on the occasions when he was so impertinent as to question the wisdom and efficiency of the Navy Board? Only a month later he entertained Pepys and Lord Brouncker in the officer of the guard's room at Whitehall in the most friendly manner and performed

---

* 'Officer of the Navy' meant member of the Navy Board. What we call a naval officer Pepys and his contemporaries called a sea officer.

with great skill on the bagpipes. And a week after that he went out of his way to warn Pepys, whom he met by chance at a play, of an impending move in the Committee for Miscarriages. In any case Holles, high-spirited, dashing, indisciplined, ought, on Pepys's principles, to be no match for the steady systematic professionals like Coventry and himself. More was to be feared from malicious and disgruntled insiders.

Two of these soon disclosed themselves. James Carcasse, a protégé of Lord Brouncker's, had been dismissed from his post in the Ticket Office through Pepys's exposure of his corrupt practices. Seeing a chance of getting his own back he charged Pepys and his colleagues with paying the crew of a privateer which they jointly owned in preference to the sailors of the Royal Navy. The charge appears to have been well-founded. But much more serious mischief was to be feared from the activities of an old Cromwellian sea officer, Valentine Tatnell. Tatnell's career in the Commonwealth navy had not been spectacular. At the Restoration he had been in command of a hired merchantman and, ambitious of better things, had sent Pepys a barrel of oysters. But promotion did not come his way. Instead he was reduced to service with the Press Gang, in which connection there was an ugly story of cheating the widow of a brother officer out of some money due to her. Before that, too, he had been involved in a case of fraud over seamen's tickets, for which he was kept in prison for several months.[8] Tatnell was now reported to be active in promoting charges against both Coventry and Pepys. In late seventeenth-century England once the wound of an accusation had been inflicted it was sure to swarm with maggots of this kind. A decade later in the heyday of the Popish Plot men were to be sent to a horrible death on the evidence of men with an unbroken record of utter rascality.

The crisis was to come early in March. The Commons had appointed Thursday, March 5th, as the day on which the Navy Board was to answer the allegations of sharp practice over the seamen's tickets. As the date drew nearer Pepys became more and more anxious and despondent, relieving his fear and despair by raging at his colleagues for being so little use in their common danger and, surest solvent of all, by immersing himself in the detailed preparation of their defence. The tempo increased. The last Sunday Pepys spent in prolonged conferences with Coventry and Will Hewer, apart from the usual intermission with one of his Westminster women. On the Monday he and his clerks worked till after midnight 'preparing my great answer'. Hewer reported the latest rumour that all the Officers were to be sacked except 'honest Sir John Minnes, who, God knows, is fitter to have been turned out himself than any of us, doing the King more hurt by his dotage and folly than all the rest can do by their knavery, if they have a mind to it.' On the Tuesday he was infuriated by finding that Lord Brouncker was trying to save his own skin at the expense of everyone else and, particularly, of Pepys. Wednesday was cold and wet: even the rich binding of a newly acquired book could give no pleasure. There was nothing for it but to close the doors of the office and work with the clerks until the mind ground to a standstill. Too ill and exhausted to eat any supper, sleep did not come easily: nor, when it came, was it deep or long: 'but then waked, and never in so much trouble in all my life of mind, thinking of the task I have upon me, and upon what dissatisfactory grounds, and what the issue of it may be to me.'

At six o'clock he could stand it no longer and sought comfort from Elizabeth. She soothed him at last by convincing him that a career that involved so much worry was not worth pursuing, once he had cleared himself of the charges now laid against him. The recognition that life was not bounded by the Board on the one side and the Committee on the other was a glimpse of daylight after nightmare. Pepys returned refreshed for a final tussle with his notes. Then at nine o'clock he took a boat up to Westminster with his faithful assistants, Hayter and Hewer. It was the moment of calm before the curtain goes up, before the light goes on, before the trolley squeaks down the corridor to the operating theatre. The adrenal glands took over. Pepys reinforced them with half-a-pint of mulled sack at the Dog and a dram of brandy at Westminster Hall. Between eleven and twelve they were called in, Pepys, Brouncker, Mennes and their newest colleague, Sir Thomas Harvey. Penn as a member of the House was sitting in his place. Pepys saw that 'the whole House was full and full of expectation'. They were not to be disappointed.

Exposition was Pepys's forte. Clarity of mind, method of analysis, organisation of matter: the reasonableness of the civil servant, the authority of the lawyer, more than a touch of the schoolmaster. There are few among the hundreds of official papers that Pepys has left behind which do not show most, if not all, of these his most characteristic attributes. This speech, it is clear, exhibited them in their highest degree. Never again, certainly not when he was a Member of Parliament, was he to dominate the House of Commons with such intoxicating success:

After the Speaker had . . . read the Report of the Committee, I began our defence most acceptably and smoothly, and continued at it without any hesitation or losse, but with full scope, and all my reason free about me, as if it had been at my own table, from that time till past three in the afternoon; and so ended, without any interruption from the Speaker; but we withdrew. And there all my Fellow-Officers, and all the world that was within hearing, did congratulate me, and cry up my speech as the best thing they ever heard; and my Fellow-Officers overjoyed in it.

The salutes of praise reverberated for several days. 'Good-morrow, Mr Pepys, that must be Speaker of the Parliament-house,' was Coventry's greeting when they met next morning. The Solicitor-General thought Pepys 'spoke the best of any man in England'. In the Park the King and the Duke of York came up and congratulated him. Men whose Parliamentary memories went back to Charles I's time were emphatic that it was the best speech that they had ever heard. By common consent it transformed the position of the Navy Board and it confirmed beyond a doubt Pepys's own standing as by far the ablest man in his field. Neither he nor his colleagues were safe yet, but the betting was now on their being so.

14

Recriminations: the Brooke House Committee

The threats to marriage and career had been met, if not mastered: there remained the threat of going blind. Pepys first found his eyes troublesome in the days when he was drinking too much. With sobriety these symptoms disappeared. But the long hours of close work, much of it by candlelight, which the war and his increased commitments imposed soon produced fresh complaints of strain and soreness. By the autumn of 1667 he was seriously alarmed: 'My eyes so bad since last night's straining of them that I am hardly able to see, beside the pain which I have in them.' That winter he went to the leading spectacle-maker of the day, whose advice has been described by a modern authority as 'superlatively bad'.[1] The spring and summer that followed the triumph before the Committee for Miscarriages brought some relief, no doubt because the jaunts to Cambridge and Brampton, to Oxford and the West took him away from his books and papers. But at the end of June, with an answer to prepare for the Brooke House Committee in July, the pain and incapacity were causing him acute anxiety. '. . . I very melancholy under the fear of my eyes being spoiled and not to be recovered: for I am come that I am not able to read out a small letter . . .' Recourse to the spectacle-maker again proved useless. In the middle of July bleeding, the first and last shot in the medical locker of the seventeenth century, was tried. At last in August, in the middle of drafting a 'great letter' to the Duke of York which would (he hoped) reform the administration of the navy at the cost (he feared) of mortally antagonising all his colleagues, he heard of an expedient that really had some effect. This was the paper tube spectacles, to which the addition of a glass — pooh-poohed by Pepys's expert adviser — brought a marked improvement of vision. But it was still summer with enough hours of daylight for even so busy a man as Pepys. The winter brought the glitter of candles and the glare of snow. Both hurt him cruelly. By the spring even strong daylight brought pain and watering of the eyes. On May 8th, 1669, 'now I am not able to bear the light of the windows in my eyes', he changed the place he had occupied during the eight years and more that he had sat at the Navy Board for one on the other side of the table. A week later he applied to the Duke of York for three or four months' leave of absence, 'his sole aim being the relieving of his eyes by such a respite from his present labour'.[2] At the end of the month he wrote his final entry in the Diary, closing it with the coda that echoes in the mind of every reader:

> And thus ends all that I doubt I shall ever be able to do with my own eyes in the keeping of my Journal, I being not able to do it any longer, having done now so long as to undo my eyes almost every time that I take a pen in my hand; and, therefore, whatever comes of it, I must forbear: and, therefore, resolve from this time forward, to have it kept by my people in long-hand, and must therefore be contented to set down no more than is fit for them and all the world to know; or, if there be any thing, which cannot be much, now my amours to Deb. are past, and my eyes hindering me in almost all other pleasures, I must endeavour to keep a margin in my book open, to add, here and there, a note in short-hand with my own hand.

> And so I betake myself to that course, which is almost as much as to see myself go into my grave: for which, and all the discomforts that will accompany my being blind, the good God prepare me!

The truth of the heart is so poignant and so solemn that it seems almost trivial to remind oneself that Pepys did not go blind: that great as his achievements had been, still greater were to come; that he was to survive into a long and cultivated retirement, corresponding with the leading scholars and scientists of his day and reading, shortly before his death, the opening Books of Clarendon's great *History of the Rebellion*, first given to the world in the reign of the author's granddaughter. The liability to eyestrain remained a nuisance. In the memorandum on the state of his health already referred to, which Pepys drew up in 1677, the limits that it set are precisely defined. Most of them could be overcome by secretarial assistance. To quote his own words:

> But when I came to leave off working with my own eyes and fell to the employing clerks, my eyes shortly grew well, and from that time to this never knew any of that pain till [by] the necessity of my employment, which is often indispensable, I am driven often to write and read with my own hand and eyes when pain immediately ensues (as I have already said) and continues longer or shorter as I continue working with them.[3]

In the spring of 1669 Pepys could not know that, any more than he could know that he was suffering from 'hypermetropia with some degree of astigmatism' (the latter a condition that was not identified until the early nineteenth century). There was in fact no danger of his going blind. But this fact by no means disposes of the counter fact that he, after taking the best advice available, thought that there was.

Such an interruption to a man's career must always appear disastrous. In this case it must have been the more bitter (though Pepys does not say so) because he had, quite suddenly, arrived at the summit. The end of the war had left him as one of the leading men, and certainly the best hope, in naval affairs. Then within a few weeks Batten had died, Carteret had exchanged his place with Lord Anglesey, the Deputy Treasurer of Ireland, and Penn was (most unjustly) under a cloud over the Medway disaster. But Sir William Coventry even though no longer (after 1667) a Commissioner of the Navy, no longer (after 1668) Secretary to the Lord High Admiral, was still a Commissioner of the Treasury, still a member of the Privy Council, still, in Pepys's view, the most effective man in the Government. On certain points of naval policy and finance, in particular his contention that the navy could be maintained acceptably on a budget of £200,000 a year, Pepys ventured to differ, even to criticise. But in doing so he showed an unaffected deference, an anxiety to win approval rather than to win an argument, that leaves no room for doubt that he thought of Coventry as his superior not only in age and in rank but in professional knowledge and capacity. And besides Coventry, the noonday sun of Pepys's career, Sandwich, its morning star, was again visible in the heavens. Late in October 1668 Pepys went to call on his old patron who had concluded his mission to Madrid.

With Sandwich and Coventry both in play Pepys could hardly feel himself a principal. And yet in spite of himself he was forced to recognise that he was. Both men had lost the self-confidence, the assurance of their position, which Pepys, for his part, would never have questioned. Rumours that Coventry was on the way out disturbed him late in September, though he could hardly credit them. Yet by December 7th when he walked over to see him, enjoying the first frosty weather of the winter, to both men his dismissal had become far from unthinkable, Pepys 'telling him that, with all these doings, he, I thanked God, stood yet' and Coventry telling Pepys that 'he is represented to the King by his enemies as a melancholy man, and one that is still prophesying ill events, so as the King called him Visionaire . . . whereas others that would please the King do make him believe that all is safe'. Under fire Pepys's loyalty redoubled. Coventry was (on November 27th) 'the man of all the world that I am resolved to preserve an interest in'. When, in the spring of 1669, Coventry, at Buckingham's instigation, is disgraced and sent to the Tower, Pepys visits him every day. Even after his release when he judges, regretfully, that it would be impolitic to be seen with him walking in St. James's Park he still qualifies the decision with words that show his true feeling 'though to serve him I should, I think, stick at nothing'.[4]

The contrast between these feelings and those evoked by Sandwich is conspicuous. At their first meeting on his return from Madrid both men seem to have felt a certain reserve. This hardened at what should have been an intimate discussion on November 9th, when Pepys was in the throes of Elizabeth's first fury over Deb and Sandwich was to appear before the Tangier Committee to give an account of his mission and justify his expenses. Creed and Pepys agreed that he made a poor fist of it 'I fearing that either his mind and judgment are depressed, or that he do it out of his great neglect'. Was Sandwich a depressive? He was certainly not the singleminded, unemotional player of the power game such as the bare outline of his career might suggest. The depths that mystified Pepys open wider as their association lengthens. A fortnight later he found him now so reserved, or moped rather, I think, with his own business, that he bids welcome to no man, I think, to his satisfaction.' The patron he had known best and longest had become a stranger.

On personal grounds this was a matter for regret but professionally it had its advantages. When Sandwich proposed the creation of a local paymastership at Tangier and nominated one of his followers for it, the Duke of York at a formal meeting of the Tangier Board deferred the decision until Pepys's views were known. Pepys's description of Sandwich recounting the story to him fixes the last phase of their relationship and opens the chapter of direct royal patronage that was to close only with the Revolution of 1688:

This my Lord Sandwich in great confidence tells me, that he (
take very ill from the Duke of York, though nobody knew the meani
of these words but him; and that he did take no notice of them, b
bit his lip, being satisfied that the Duke's care of me was as desirab
to him as it could be to have Sir Charles Harbord [the man Sandwi
had proposed]: and did seem industrious to let me see that he was gl
that the Duke of York and he might come to contend who shall be t
kindest to me, which I owned as his great love, and so I hope and belie
it is, though my Lord did go a little too far in this business to move
so far without consulting me.[5]

Pepys ended this crucial conversation by inviting him to the splend
collation mentioned on page 89, 'he having never yet eat a bit of n
bread'. Sandwich's unhesitating acceptance confirmed to the world in t
plainest terms what Pepys records more subtly in his Diary. He had dipp
his ensign to his ex-servant: and the salute had been gracefully, but no
the less confidently, acknowledged.

The head of the department, shrewd, authoritative, self-important,
beginning to cast his shadow over the pages, so near their end, that rev
the devices and desires of a much merer mortal. After the spring of 16
we can see Pepys only as his contemporaries saw him, as indeed everyc
else sees each one of us, from the front he chose to turn to the wor
Sometimes, as in letters to old and intimate friends, he is open, easy a
communicative. Sometimes in the mass of official correspondence th
is a flash of the Cambridge undergraduate, a wink from the *vie
boulevardier* of Restoration London. There is always — how could there n
be? — wit, clarity, zest, punch. There is abundant material for portraitu
but there is not the gift of systematic self-revelation. Before the lights
the Diary have dropped behind in the darkness a last look at that inco
parable self-portrait in motion may sharpen the blunter perceptions o
biographer.

No man, says Johnson, is a hypocrite in his pleasures. What, at
end of the Diary period, was Pepys's idea of pure enjoyment? On Ma
2nd, 1669, he records '. . . extraordinary pleasure, as being one of the d
and nights of my life spent with the greatest content; and that which I
but hope to repeat again a few times in my whole life.' To anatom
these delights is to see how little Pepys has changed in spite of wealth
success, in spite of the Royal Society and Mr Povy, of the world of
City and the Court. The interesting part of the day began with
coming back from the office at noon, to a family dinner party of ei
guests at which the women much outnumbered the men. Socially t

ranged from the Roger Pepyses (M.P. for Cambridge and a successful lawyer) down to an ex-barrister's clerk. The dinner itself was 'noble' but no hushed gastronomic awe prevented the party from going with a swing: 'mighty merry, and particularly myself pleased with looking on Betty Turner [one of his young cousins], who is mighty pretty.' After the meal people were free to talk to each other tête-à-tête, and the host indulged the pleasure of showing off his books, his furniture, his pictures, the setting in which he took such pride. This was followed by a paper game, something on the lines of Consequences, in which Betty's elder sister, The. (short for Theophila) was praised for her wit, though Pepys would have traded some of it for more of Betty's gaiety and good-nature. By now it was beginning to get dark. Musicians arrived — carefully chosen like every other item of the entertainment: two excellent violins and the best theorbo in London. The office had been made ready, candles were lit, the party was strengthened by half a dozen more guests, including two strangers introduced by Will Howe as dancing partners for the young ladies. The fiddles struck up and they danced till two in the morning, breaking off only for a good supper. It was the jigs and country dances that Pepys remembered in writing up the entry. The laughter and high spirits are captured in the Diary as nowhere else. The junketings of Mr. Wardle and the Pickwick Club have the same flavour but the exuberance has got into the description instead of staying in the scene described.

Pleasure had not been displaced by business from its primacy in the Pepysian view of life. Rather business had been subsumed as an important source of active enjoyment. Few men explored a wider range or developed a more conscious and explicit philosophy of the subject. Innocent pleasure has, to twentieth-century ears, a faintly mocking, patronising overtone. There is an implication of naivety, inexperience, lack of self-awareness. Not, one would have thought, the first ideas that come to mind in connection with Pepys. Yet from the rich and varied catalogue of hedonism that could be extracted from the Diary simplicity and innocence easily outshine all other qualities. Weather, music, good-tempered domesticity, a family party such as that just described, are at the end as they were in the beginning the inspiration of its lyricism. Here is the key to Pepys's mind and personality, or if we adopt the bold intellectualism of his own motto Mens cujusque is est quisque,* to the man himself.

Tributary pleasures were continually added or extended. The books and prints, the fine bindings and the portraits of himself and his wife, pleased not only in and for themselves but as a collection that could be shown to visitors and guests. Pepys had the instincts and gradually

* For a translation of this phrase and Pepys's own commentary on it see below, p. 326-7.

acquired the knowledge of a connoisseur. He was feeling too the first tug of an interest that was to grow in strength until it became, in his eyes, a vocation: the urge to write history, or at least, to collect and criticise the materials for so doing. As long ago as June 13th, 1664, Coventry had suggested to Pepys that he should write the history of the First Dutch War, 'which I am glad to hear, it being a thing I much desire, and sorts mightily with my genius, and, if well done, may recommend me much'. The Second Dutch War was upon him before he had gone far in his researches, but he put them to immediate use by drawing comparisons between the performance and expenditure of the navy in the two wars wherever it suited his argument to do so. Soon after the war had ended he was entertaining his clerks to dinner, an occasion he always enjoyed, when he discovered to his great delight that one of them, Richard Gibson, shared his historical enthusiasm: 'he telling me so many good stories relating to the warr and practices of commanders, which I will find a time to recollect: and he will be an admirable help to my writing a history of the Navy, if ever I do.' The saving clause was, sadly, justified in the event. But manuscripts both in his own library at Magdalene and in the Rawlinson collection at the Bodleian bear substantial evidence to the zeal with which he pursued the material for such a study. A year later, on March 12th, 1669, he found, after several attempts, a rich haul of Navy Accounts and Treasurer's patents in the office of Auditor Beale: and three days later he bestows a rare accolade of praise on the Rolls Office for the excellent order in which they kept their records.

In historical research, and even more in forming his collection of engravings, he was later to profit from the guidance of a man whom he already knew and respected, his fellow diarist John Evelyn. Their earliest connections were official. Evelyn had married into the hierarchy of naval officeholders. His father-in-law was the grandson and great-grandson of successive Treasurers of the Navy under Queen Elizabeth. Evelyn himself had been a Commissioner for the Sick and Wounded in the war; and his house and estate at Deptford adjoined the navy yard. As a leading Fellow of the Royal Society he would have been familiar to Pepys even before their occasions brought them together. He was to be the evening star, as Sandwich had been the morning and Coventry the sun at noon. In the spring of 1669 all these luminaries are clearly visible in the Pepysian heavens.

Steadily growing in intimacy was Pepys's friendship with the Houblons, that remarkable family of Flemish origin who combined a cultivated and affectionate domestic life with a business reputation for honesty, judgment and valuable connections overseas. On February 14th, 1668, Pepys records seeing 'old Mr Houblon, whom I never saw before, and all his sons about him, all good merchants'. This was old James Houblon, the father of the London Exchange, whose epitaph Pepys was to compose, commemorating the facts that on his death at the age of ninety his five sons were all flourishing City merchants and that out of a hundred grandchildren seventy survived him. James Houblon the younger was Pepys's closest friend among the brothers. As has been pointed out earlier they represent much that he most valued in the civilisation of his time. Rich, high-minded, liberal, owing nothing to aristocratic or territorial influences, repudiating religious bigotry and the vulgar prejudices of nationalism, making straight in the wilderness of the seventeenth century the pathway for Free Trade and the Idea of Progress, the Houblons, like Pepys himself, seem to

> Show what Everybody might
> Become by simply doing Right.

When at the end of his life Pepys sent his nephew John Jackson on a tour of Europe he drew heavily on Evelyn for advice in the planning of it and on the Houblons for introductions, letters of credit and practical help of every kind. That he consulted Evelyn for his own much less ambitious expedition with Elizabeth in the early autumn of 1669 is, unfortunately, about all we know of a journey which this passionate traveller recalled in old age as one of the most valuable experiences of his life. Evelyn gave him some introductions in Paris, recommended some names to look out for on his visits to the printsellers and, anxious not to overburden his friend — 'Yours is a Running voyage and desultory' — left it at that. Since Pepys was still, even on holiday, the Government's leading naval expert, the tour began with a visit to the principal Dutch naval bases. From the coast Pepys and Elizabeth, accompanied by her brother Balty, made their way through Holland and Flanders to Paris. On their way back they broke the journey at Brussels. The whole expedition lasted, as Pepys himself emphasised thirty years afterwards, 'a bare two months'. Two months for the Holland of Rembrandt, whose etchings are among the glories of the Pepys library, for the Flanders still aglow with the colours of Rubens and Van Dyck, for the Paris where the *Institut* was rising on the left bank, was a thin ration for such an artistic and intellectual appetite. But the rarer talent for enjoyment triumphed over every limitation, up to the tragedy with which this last great party ended. Coming back through Flanders Elizabeth caught a fever. By the time they had got back to London she was very ill. On November 10th, only three weeks after they had landed, she was dead.

Of the distress and of the unselfpitying courage with which it was met, Pepys's silence is eloquent. Fortunately for him there was work, more work, and more work yet that would leave him no leisure for the foreseeable future. The Brooke House Committee had called in the Navy Board to answer the charges of misconduct and corruption that had been so freely bandied about in the humiliation with which the war had ended: and Pepys was, obviously, the only man who could confront so formidable a prosecution. He had in fact already done so by letter before leaving for his holiday in August as far as concerned his own irregularities. But on his return he found waiting for him a paper containing eighteen separate and highly detailed accusations, among which the very charges he had angrily rebutted were once again set out. One of them concerned his own grossly improper conduct in selling flag-material to the Board of which he was a member. As it was certainly true, the challenge could not be refused. Even while Elizabeth was still on her deathbed, he was checking his references, collating his materials and applying to the Brooke House Commissioners themselves for access to the Navy Office Contract Books on which they had founded their charges.[6] The lawyer, the historian and the rhetorician in Pepys all had their work cut out. After Elizabeth's death he must have worked almost without interruption, for by November 25th he had prepared an answer that in length, argumentative force and above all command of intricate detail showed the Commissioners that they would have to fight every inch of the way against an enemy who knew the country blindfold. But before the letter could have achieved its full effect of strengthening the faint-hearted in the administration and cooling the ardour of its critics, the Parliamentary situation suddenly got out of hand. A demand for the report of the Brooke House Commissioners resolved itself into a vote of censure on Sir George Carteret. The Commons suspended him from the House, on which the King at once prorogued them and announced that he himself would hear the charges against Carteret and the Navy Board in the presence of his Council.

This meant in effect that Pepys had to prepare all over again a defence brief for virtually the whole financial and administrative conduct of the war. The original charges would form the spearhead of the attack he would have to meet. But the power of the Commissioners to argue, to question, to raise new topics, to switch the hunt made the whole undertaking more perilous. It was one thing to refute a case stated in black and white with an answer which had itself been pondered, tested in the undisturbed stronghold of a Government office with its superb (because Pepysian) filing system and its posse of clever young clerks. It was another to think on one's feet. Pepys, fortunately and exceptionally, enjoyed both forms of intellectual exercise. But he was too old a hand to rely simply on the quickness of his wits and the readiness of his tongue, much as he valued himself on both. He knew that his real power to annihilate his enemies lay in his unique mastery of the relevant records and statistics: they were his creation, his instrument, on which, given time, he could pick out any tune he chose. The rights and wrongs of any single question could soon lose their sharpness of outline once it could be lured into the forests of administrative detail where he alone knew the paths. The preparation of so gigantic a brief, the organisation of such unwieldy materials into a form in which everything that might be wanted would lie ready to hand turns the imagination faint. It stimulated Pepys to the height of his powers. This time it was all or nothing.

So crucial seemed this official inquiry, in its procedure something like a modern Special Tribunal, that Pepys kept a journal of its proceedings as they affected himself. Although written in the first person it has little else in common with the great Diary so lately closed. It is in long-hand (not his own) and the style, like the matter, is much closer to that of the civil service panjandrum, sure of a respectful and patient audience, so familiar in his letterbooks. It records – unsurprisingly – a series of exchanges in which Pepys invariably gets the better of his opponents: its tone towards the King shows, predictably, none of the freedom and candour of the Diary; and the Commissioners are treated with a weary irritability that perfectly suggests to the reader the amateurishness and malice that may safely be ascribed to all who presume to criticise officials. In all this, as in some of its direct statements, the document is intentionally misleading. Pepys did not think that Charles II had deserved well of his country by his conduct of the war. He did not think, as Sir Arthur Bryant appears to suggest, that Lord Brereton, the Chairman of the Commissioners, was a pompous booby of a country squire. On the contrary he knew him as a founder member of the Council of the Royal Society and a man whose breadth of learning was admired by John Evelyn.[7] Indeed he had greeted the news of his appointment to the Commission with particular approval.[8] On the incapacity of Colonel Thomson, a wooden-legged Cromwellian who played a leading role on the Commission, Sir Arthur enriches the Brooke House Journal with sallies of his own. But what Pepys had written in the Diary on February 14th, 1668, was '. . . Colonel Thomson, one of the Committee of Accounts, who, among the rest, is mighty kind to me, and is likely to mind our business more than any; and I would be glad to have a good understanding with him.' Yet the clear and vivid account given in the first chapter of *Years of Peril* is faithful both to the letter and to the spirit of the Brooke House

Journal, particularly in the half-pitying, half-sneering representation of
Thomson as a bumbling old bore intent on proving how much better the
First Dutch War had been run when he was a Commissioner of the
Admiralty and Navy and Cromwell was in Whitehall.

This goes far to explain why Pepys both at the Committee and in the
Journal did all he could to ridicule and discredit him. His real opinion of
Thomson has already been cited. He was in Pepys's eyes exceptionally
qualified to drive home the question everyone was asking: why did the
First Dutch War, fought a dozen years earlier, result in a resounding
victory and the Second, in spite of unparalleled Parliamentary votes of
money, in defeat? This was saying in public what Pepys and Coventry
had been deploring to each other for the past two years. What was on
trial at Brooke House was not simply the conduct of Sir George Carteret
and his colleagues but the performance of Charles II's government, even
the whole Restoration regime. Pepys in his Diary has shown how largely
he sympathised with the critics. But the Brooke House Journal is, as he
had envisaged, '. . . kept by my people in long-hand, and [I] must be
contented to set down no more than is fit for them and all the world to
know.'

At Brooke House Pepys is defending himself, and that left him, as we
have seen, some awkward corners to turn. He is defending his colleagues,
complaining even in this semi-public journal loud and long at how much
he does for them and how little they do for him, but he stands or falls
with the office. He is the champion, directly and without any intermediary,
of the King and the Duke, and carries the Stuart colours. Sandwich and
Coventry have been left behind, though not abandoned or even abated in
personal loyalty or affection. Like a medieval tenant-in-chief he holds
directly of the King. He was to maintain this position unchanged
though not uninterrupted for the rest of his public career. To fulfil it a
seat in Parliament was almost a necessity. Pepys had expended a good deal
of time and ink that summer in an unsuccessful attempt to secure election
at Aldeburgh. But that is a trivial and temporary setback. At Brooke
House Pepys has established himself as a bulwark of the regime.

Powerful as all these motives were to vindicate himself and to out-
argue the opposition there was a yet deeper spring of action. Be the rights
and wrongs of the matter what they may, Colonel Thomson by the very
nature of his case was advancing himself and the Government he had
served in the first war as rivals to Pepys and his masters in the second. A
rival was not to be treated with civility; a successful rival was not to be
endured.

Pepys's historical collections gave him valuable material for a counterattack. Any reader of the Journal might conclude that he felt nothing but professional contempt for the administration of the navy under the Protectorate. He certainly felt at all stages of his career that he could do better. But except when playing the role of advocate he listened to its survivors with a respect that is the best evidence of his real opinion.

Above all Pepys clearly enjoyed himself at Brooke House. He allowed himself an exuberance, sometimes a loquacity, that tested everybody's patience. He began in fine style by twitting Lord Brereton for not having made in the Commons the full and civil acknowledgment now offered that Pepys had, by his letter, cleared himself of one matter alleged against Sir George Carteret. Pressing the attack briskly he charged the Commissioners with the same economy of truth concerning £514,000 voted by Parliament '. . . to have given occasion to the World's believing that it had been to uses of Pleasure or other Private respects of his Ma^{ty}'s wch it will be very hard now by any meanes to undeceive them in. Of which the King largely expressed his resentment.'9 To represent Charles in a posture of injured virtue was a bold *coup*.

The hearings lasted from the beginning of January 1670 to the last week in February. The only anxieties that Pepys records are at those moments at which his colleagues took the floor. '. . . soe much trouble as I of long done and must still look for, while yoak'd with persons who every day make worke for futer censure while I am upon ye tenters in their preservation from ye blame done to their failures past.'10 Watching them swear to their papers on oath he observes 'Sir John Mennes did ye like, though poor man to that day he had not seen one word of it.'11

The charges themselves and the arguments they gave rise to covered every major and many minor aspects of naval administration. Pay, victualling, stores: the purchase of masts, plank, timber, sailcloth, flags, and iron for anchors: even on occasion, operational matters such as the provision of convoy. The councillors stifled their yawns while Pepys and Thomson argued long and learnedly as to whether it had or had not been the practice of the navy at any time to measure masts at the butt end instead of at the partners, the point at which mast and deck meet. Thomson accused Pepys of insufficient eagerness in the purchase of English plank: Pepys rhapsodised over English plank, only deploring its absence from the market at the height of the war. Besides plank and timber it had been the King's policy to encourage domestic production of sailcloth, most of which now came from Brittany, and iron, hitherto largely bought in Sweden or Spain. Only masts could not be found in English forests in anything like sufficient size and quantity.

Masts was an embarrassing subject. Commissioner Pett had given sworn evidence of a cheap offer that the Board had rejected. And how did it come about, in the general scarcity of money, that Sir William Warren seemed to have received so much cash on the nail? 'Imprests' was the term used for such payments, nowadays called advances. The Commissioners, by Pepys's account, '. . . proceeded . . . pressing very earnestly ye great value of ye Imprests granted to Sir William Warren and that in a particular beyond what wee were obliged to do by any Contract appearing.'[12] They were getting warm. But Pepys threw them off the scent by defining with elaborate pedantry the different occasions on which Imprests were, or should be, granted, a masterly and successful switch of the argument from the particular to the general. By the time they struggled back to masts Pepys had moved on to the sellers market created by the Swedish king's edict prohibiting felling for the next seven years. Against the fierce competition from Dutch and French buyers England should think herself lucky to have any supplies at all.

Through the pages of the Brooke House Journal Pepys and Colonel Thomson circle the ring, waiting for an opening, clinching, breaking, planting a quick punch. Why was the fleet in the Channel put on short allowance — the lighter diet on which ships were victualled for the Mediterranean and the Indies? First, replies Pepys, there is no evidence that the efficient conduct of the war was in any way impaired on the occasion cited: second that no ship's company complained more than that of the Commanders-in-Chief who were in the best position to judge such questions: third there were such a number of supernumeraries on board: fourth

that ye shipps happned in both yeares to fight presently after there taking on their victualls soe as to be forced to fling over much Provisions to make roome for Wounded men . . . After all wch I appealed to them . . . what service or designe . . . during the whole warr has suffered any miscarriage by this want of provisions or ye badness thereof; takeing upon mee the makeing some comparison between the management of ye victualling between this and ye former warr wherein soe many Thousands of Tuns and Provisions were Flung overboard, Fleets come in for want, Men Mutinying and ye Contractors, but for ye friendshipp wch ye interest of some of them found, had probably been hanged for it . . . Thomson answered that Gauden [Pepys's colleague in the victualling] was then one of them. I replied that Pride was another . . .[13]

It was a brilliant touch to rake up the hated associations of Pride's Purge; and it was characteristically bold to challenge comparison with the first war. By the speed of his footwork as much as by his professional assurance Pepys forestalled his opponents 'by letting the world see that . . . matters in ye Navy have been at least as well or rather much better than in ye time of usurpation'.[14] On the historical evidence he had collected it was a perfectly tenable view; certainly it has gained ground from the most recent publications of modern scholarship. But the proof of the pudding is in the eating, and Cromwell had won his war outright.

The burden of the charges against the Navy Board was that they had not obtained value for the country's money. The burden of Pepys's answer is contained in his own epigrammatic phrase 'the costliness of poverty'. The necessities of war had to be met at their own pace and pressure, not at the irregular tempo of the Treasury's disbursements. Credit cost money. Pepys and Coventry had been saying this to each other from the first day of the war to the last; and the observation gains nothing from repetition. But Pepys like Burke,

> . . . too deep for his hearers, still went on refining
> And thought of convincing, while they thought of dining.

The Journal gives us instances of material that Pepys thought too good to throw away even though by an uncovenanted mercy his audience had escaped it.

> . . . Thomson replyd that method might be as easily observed in a great Action as in a little one and instanced that a defect in Architecture might be sooner observed in Pauls as Pancrace.* At which position and Instance ye King and ye Board seeming to make mirth of it I thought it unnecessary for mee to returne any answer to it though I had an Instance in my mind which my Lord Brereton as an Understander of musick would have allowed mee for good. viz. if a theorbo is neither soe soon putt nor so easily and cheaply kept in tune as a violin or a Trump-marine; nor a harp as a Jew's trump . . .[15]

A man who could be so easily pleased with his own ingenuity was over the sharpness of bereavement.

What Pepys was like when he got the bit between his teeth is perfectly hit off by Sir Arthur Bryant when he describes his 'interminable oration on the complicated business of balancing Storekeepers' Accounts'.[16] Like the Victorian artists Pepys valued detail for its own sake. He fingers it lovingly and can hardly bear to let it go. To it he even sacrifices the passion for order that puts his mind in tune. One of the thorniest of questions on

---

* St Pancras: not the present church which dates from the early nineteenth century.

which the Board collectively and Pepys individually had to acquit themselves was Payment by Ticket. In an age when few seamen were literate
and none had bank accounts any system of deferred payment was certain
to produce injustice and confusion on a large scale and to offer easy opportunities of fraud and corruption. Here Pepys drew a telling comparison
with the practice of the Cromwellian administration which had not even
felt able to introduce printed tickets and counterfoils until after the war
had ended in 1654. He had tried to maintain peacetime standards but
could not feel guilty at falling short of '. . . the preservation of ye nicety of
a new Forme in ye Hurry of a warr, in ye management of an infinite
number of loose single papers, each conteyning for every single man as
many several circumstances to be attended to, if not more, in a warrant
for a six months Victuall for a whole shipp.'[17] In expounding the insanities
of a system under which most of the men to be paid off were scattered on
shore or serving in different ships his style loses its structure as detail after
detail, each too important to be omitted, presents itself to his mind:

> . . . Nay, and frequently ships newly fitted forth could not be mann'd
> but by inviting men on Board with promise of paying them their
> wages due to them for other shipps, then I say it was impossible for
> either counterparts to be lookt into or sea books and muster books
> compar'd whilst nobody could either foresee what shipps these men
> should belong to, and so neither what counterparts or books should
> be sent to the pay.[18]

The only remedy yet discovered for these ills was to compound them.
As Pepys shrewdly pointed out:

> Great summes of money are yet due to Seamen for service before ye
> 14 March 1658 w[ch] might have in part been satisfyed if ye shipps kept
> long uselessly in pay by ye Commissioners of Parliament had been
> discharged by Tickett . . .[19]

As concerned himself, Pepys was accused of a misdemeanour, of which
he was probably guilty, and of a crime which seems in the highest degree
improbable. The misdemeanour consisted in diverting money to pay the
crew of the *Flying Greyhound*, a privateer leased to himself, Penn and
Batten, in preference to honouring the tickets of men serving in the
King's ships.[20] The crime was ticket-broking: buying a man's ticket at a
discount and cashing it in full at the Ticket Office. To steal from the
starving was not in Pepys's character. Both his Diary and his corres-

pondence throughout the war provide abundant evidence of his detestation
of ticket-broking, of attempts to prevent it by administrative reform,
and even of action against individuals involved in it.[21] The charge rested
on the deposition of James Carcasse, who had been dismissed from the
Ticket Office, at Pepys's instigation, for improper conduct. Lauderdale,
a powerful member of the Council, remembered the name and 'askt what
Carkes this was . . . whether the same that . . . had beene turned out of the
office and that it was a pretious youth.'[22] Pepys denied the charge in the
most vehement and absolute terms, challenging the Commission to produce evidence of a single such case.

> 'How, Mr Pepys [said Lord Brereton], do you defy the whole world
> in this matter?'
> I replied, 'Yes, that I do defy the whole world and my Lord Brereton
> in particular if he would be thought one if it.'[23]

According to Pepys his antagonist was 'strook dumb'. But repeated warn-
ings that the Commissioners had a card up their sleeve seemed to be justified when, just over a week later, Lord Brereton produced a ticket for
£7. 10s. made out to one of the *Lion*'s ships company but inscribed in the
hand of Sir George Carteret's clerk 'Paid to Mr Pepys'. Pepys stuck to his
guns. Whatever the explanation he knew nothing of it. The King publicly endorsed his denial by asking whether it was likely that an official
who had had the handling of such vast sums for so long a period would
have chosen to betray his trust for £7. 10s. The matter was never officially
cleared up. But after the Brooke House hearings had ended Pepys took
it up with Carteret's clerk in a firm, candid letter that could never have
been written by a man with anything to hide. No answer survives, but the
sad history of Carcasse, who ultimately went off his head, suggests an
obvious solution.

By this time both the Council and the Brooke House Commissioners
had had enough of each other; enough, too, even his admirers may dare to
conjecture, of Pepys on the proper method of mustering carpenter's stores
or whether the Treasurer of the Navy had been allowed Exchequer fees in
the reign of Queen Elizabeth. The attack, formidably mounted, had been
beaten off. With the King as judge it could hardly have been a fair fight.
But would the House of Commons have been any fairer? Certainly Pepys
was helped over some exposed ground by the King's covering fire. Still,
the defence had stood up because the Navy Board had, on the whole,
discharged its duties honestly and efficiently and because Pepys knew his
job well enough to demonstrate this convincingly. The core of all the

trouble, and thus the core of the defence, was inadequate public finance. As Pepys put it at one of the last hearings 'the observation itself answers itself when want of money is considered'.[24]

What was becoming daily clearer was that if once the Committee were allowed to adduce further charges beyond those already laid there was no logical stopping-place. Or as Pepys at his most orotund expresses the same point:

> . . . Besides that I observed . . . that they did now not only suppress ye old instances they are satisfy'd in, but bring upon us new ones by surprize contrary not only to all faire proceedings but to our repeated desires by letter . . . and my Lord Brereton's and Colonel Thomson's repeated promises before His Majesty and this Board . . .
>
> W^ch method of theirs I showed would more over perpetuate ye dispute without any end to be foreseen of it while answers being given to satisfaction shall never be owned, but in lieu thereof a new race of objections shall be started, soe as I plainly told His Majesty my work must bee to get a son and bring him up only to understand this controversy between brook-house and us and that H.M. too should provide for successors to be instructed on his part in ye state of this case, which otherwise would never likely bee understood either as to what thereof had allready been adjusted or what remained further to bee looked after in it.[25]

That Pepys could joke in public about fathering a son shows, if the Brooke House Journal has not already shown, how far he had recovered from the shock of Elizabeth's death. With his sentiments about Brooke House the King heartily agreed. No more hearings were called and the Committee lapsed when Parliament was adjourned. At last Pepys was free from the recriminations of the Second Dutch War.

15

Secretary to the Admiralty

For the ten years between the dismissal of Sir William Coventry in the spring of 1669 and the terrorism of the Popish Plot, Pepys was always in fact and latterly in name the man in charge of the navy. Sir William Penn, cleared of the unjust imputations put on him over the Medway disaster, might have challenged his supremacy. But his health had long been failing. In the summer of 1670 he knew that he was dying. His son's conversion to Quakerism and his committal to Newgate for street preaching in defiance of the Conventicle Act agitated his last few weeks. But suddenly the sea fell smooth: his son, against all the evidence and against the pressure of the bench, was acquitted: the King and the Duke who had wished to raise the Great Captain Commander to the peerage with the title of Baron Weymouth exchanged an honour that the son would have disclaimed for the even greater one of naming the American state of Sylvania after the family in whom its governorship was made hereditary. Penn, to quote his monument in St. Mary Redcliffe, 'with a Gentle and Even Gale, In much peace, Arrived and Anchored In his Last and best Port'.

To what transports of rage Pepys would have been moved if Penn had been ennobled is, fortunately, a matter for speculation. Certainly he never forgave him the trust and admiration that Coventry and the Duke of York felt for him as a great public servant and a great admiral. This vindictive-

ness reveals itself in the notes he continued to make of gossip alleging
Penn's cowardice or incompetence in action. It reveals itself too in the
hostility with which he pursued those sea officers who had been connections
or protégés of Penn. Luckily for them the Duke of York did not forget his
own loyalties and understood, as Pepys whole-heartedly confirms, the business of a Lord High Admiral. The service career of Sir William Poole
offers the best example of these powerful cross-currents.[1]

In this clean sweep of experienced administrators it seems strange that
Pepys was not promoted either to a higher position at the Navy Board or
to the personal staff of the Lord High Admiral. That Pepys himself felt
this is shown by his efforts to secure the appointment of secretary to the
Duke of York when the post fell vacant in the summer of 1672. He
applied at once to Coventry, who had himself filled the position with such
distinction, for his backing. This would gladly have been forthcoming
had not a nephew of Coventry's been nominated before there was even
time to write a letter. What could an uncle do? Pepys understood his
difficulty and simply asked his good offices with his successful rival. He
was rewarded by a letter which described him in such terms that he
copied a part of it in his own hand.

> How long [wrote Coventry to his agreeable but scapegrace nephew]
> your relation to the Navy is like to continue I will not take upon me to
> prognosticke, but I will with confidence say that while it doth continue
> you may receive more help and learn more of the Navy affairs from
> him than from any man living.[2]

This apparently humiliating defeat at the hands of a young courtier
who knew nothing of the job soon proved itself a fortunate deliverance.
The Third Dutch War, engineered by Charles II in collusion with
Louis XIV as the first fruits of their secret treaty, recoiled on its maker.
At sea the United Provinces ought to have been easy meat for the combined navies of England and France. Yet the cold-blooded act of villainy
with which England opened the war, an unprovoked attack on the Dutch
Smyrna convoy as it made its way up channel in the spring of 1672, only
achieved disgrace at a bitter cost in casualties. Two months later the
great De Ruyter caught the allied fleet napping at Solebay and forced the
stronger side into a desperate and bloody battle in which Sandwich, among
many, lost his life. Even more disastrous for this experiment in *Realpolitik*
was the effect of allied success on land. The French army swept all before
them: the Dutch, faced with the subjugation offered as terms of peace,
overthrew the great leaders of the Republic and turned to the House

Orange to lead the nation once again in a struggle for national existence
against the dominant power in Europe. These events awoke swelling
echoes in the hearts of God's Englishmen. Once again a small Protestant
nation was confronting the Popish Goliath. Once again the Low Countries,
that dagger pointed at the heart of England, felt Goliath's fingers closing
round them. The fact that the French squadron had not taken the same
hammering as the English at Solebay had already provoked a revulsion of
feeling against the alliance. With Charles II's Declaration of Indulgence
relaxing the penal laws against Roman Catholics and Dissenters in the
spring of 1673, the anti-Catholic, anti-French reaction grew more menacing. Not only was the King forced to withdraw the Declaration but the
famous Test Act was passed, excluding all but members of the Church
of England from civil or military employment. James as Lord High
Admiral was the first and most eminent victim of this law. The Admiralty
was put into commission and Pepys was appointed Secretary. Had he
retained the post of James's secretary the year before he might have
prejudiced his chances. As events were soon to show he was already tarred
with the Papist brush. Had not his wife, hardly the discreetest of women,
disclosed dangerous leanings? Was not the man always buying foreign
books and pictures, some of which to be sure offended Protestant susceptibility? Had not his curiosity and his love of music taken him more
than once to hear mass in the Queen's chapel? The age of the Royal Society
was also the age of the Popish Plot.

The promotion was of more external than intrinsic importance.
Coventry had, as so often, put the matter in a nutshell in the letter just
quoted. Wherever Pepys was, be it Navy Board or Admiralty, there was
the nerve centre of naval planning and administration. The division of
responsibilities between an Admiralty that supplied and controlled commissioned officers and a Navy Board that supplied and controlled everything else was perfectly sensible in an age when the navy was thought of as
something one did not need every day, or even every year. But once the
idea of a permanent force had been reluctantly accepted the division
became ever more pointless until it was finally abolished in the early
nineteenth century. What counted was where business was transacted
and where decisions were made. To do the one effectively and to base the
other on rational grounds bureaucracy is indispensable. Pepys's animating
principle bureaucratised his surroundings just as culture put into a glass
of milk transforms it into yogurt. During the five years between the wars
when he was still at the Navy Office the Lord High Admiral consulted
him or, more exactly, was prodded into action by him on matters well
beyond his strict province as Clerk of Acts. Pepys reported on the

competence of his colleagues, suggested appointments and re-allocation o
duties, drew up estimates, planned new construction, was courted b
captains and even admirals. He recruited and trained the men who wer
to run the navy well into the next century. Some, like Hewer, were to
closely identified with him to survive his fall. Others like Sotherne an
Burchett did not enjoy an untroubled relationship with him. But they al
served their administrative apprenticeship under a great master. Creative
omniscient, efficient and formidable Pepys did not need position and title
much as he might desire them. The plain fact was that there was no doin
anything in the navy without him.

The change to the Admiralty in 1673 perhaps did more for that insti
tution than it did for Pepys. The Navy Board had had, as we have seer
snug quarters in the city that had survived not only the overturnings o
the Commonwealth and the Restoration but the Great Fire. The Admiralt
on the other hand inhered in the person of the Lord High Admiral an
one or two secretaries. It had no postal address. Pepys's elevation change
all that. Wherever he was, his files, his clerks, his porters and messenger
must be too. His fondness for his home in Seething Lane and the tim
and money he had spent in its embellishment might have led him to brin
the business of the Admiralty there. But there had been a fire early i
1673 that had destroyed most of the old Navy Office and had forced hir
to take lodgings near by. It is possible that this coincidence had some par
in determining the place and the manner in which the control of Englis
sea-power was institutionalised. Certainly the active interest of the Kin
in even the minutiae of maritime affairs, so much deplored by Bisho
Burnet, exerted a pull up the Thames and away from the City. Officia
accommodation was ultimately found at Derby House, on the rive
between Whitehall Palace and Westminster. Pepys began to date hi
letters from there in January 1674. In the following year Will Hewe
established himself at York Buildings just by Inigo Jones's Watergate (stil
standing) on the other side of Whitehall Palace. It was into these comfort
able mansions that Pepys was received when he was hounded from office
When he came into his own again he stayed on with Hewer and transacte
a good deal of Admiralty business from the house, even giving it officia
status by adorning it with the Royal Arms in the pediment and a carve
shield containing the anchor of the Lord High Admiral. This in its tur
led to an acrimonious correspondence with his successors under William I
who claimed that the house was now a Government office and that Pepy
must clear out. He didn't, at least not until it suited him to do so. Bu
the point that the Admiralty was now a great Government departmen
that had its own local habitation next door to the King was established

The King was now Pepys's immediate superior. He did not openly resume the office of Lord High Admiral, of which his brother's tenure had been circumscribed and sometimes overshadowed by his own proprietary interest, but presided in person at the Commission to whom he had in theory delegated his functions. As Michael Lewis has well written:

'Charles was now not only his own First Lord of the Admiralty. He was much more: he was really his own Lord High Admiral, with all that official's powers and perquisites . . . he had gone back through the centuries and reassumed the Crown's original control.'³ Thus, although Pepys suffered no sea-change in his translation from Navy Board to Admiralty, he did find the potentialities much greater. He was, as he had been before, in the driver's seat: but the car was a new and improved model.

Following his sovereign's example of centralising control he ordered the Navy Board to report weekly to the Admiralty at eight o'clock each Saturday morning. This to us ungodly hour was that at which the Board of Admiralty itself sat on Mondays, Wednesdays and Fridays.⁴ The vast bulk of business was routine, often of a minute and sometimes a homely kind, and whatever was decided took executive shape in a letter from Pepys. September 25th, 1673 offers a good representative example of his day-to-day work at the Board. His first letter was to the Navy Board telling them to discharge two smacks that had been commandeered for intelligence purposes. He then writes to encourage the captain of a fireship and to warn the captain of a privateer against expecting the Admiralty to subsidise him without a clear agreement as to the use of the vessel. The captain of a pink is told that the Navy Board will honour his bill for stores taken in at Yarmouth and that he is to lose no time in getting to sea. The captain of an escort vessel for a convoy bound to the Straits hears that his reasons for coming into port without orders have provisionally been accepted but he is to take care to obey the orders of the Commander-in-Chief of the western squadron. The Governor of Plymouth receives the sympathy of the Board at having the returning Virginia fleet driven back and damaged by storms but he will have to wait till the Straits fleet are in before he can have a convoy for Havre. The senior officer of the escort is told that the King will examine his allegations of cowardice against Captain Cotterell when the Dutch attacked the convoy off the coast of Virginia. Another escort captain has his excuse for delay accepted but is urged to return to his station as soon as possible to protect the expected convoy from the Straits. Anthony Deane, the great naval architect now Commissioner at Portsmouth, is warned that the Captains due to form the Court-Martial on the Captain and officers of the *Reserve* have been wind-bound in the Downs. Deane's opinion is therefore requested as to whether the ship is, under these personal tensions, an efficient fighting unit and whether the Captain is an alcoholic. Pepys rounds off the day by telling the master of one dogger that his ship seems to be doing too much of her sea-time in the Downs, and ordering another to discharge two men he has pressed out of a ship that had the Duke of York's protection for bringing stone from Portland for the public buildings of London.

Some of these raps on the knuckle evidently originate from Pepys himself, without benefit of the Board's assistance. But then as now it is perennially astonishing to what humble and insignificant detail the most august authority will descend. Can the King really have been interested in the choice of a cook or a carpenter for a fifth-rate? Yet Pepys insists that the warrant must have his approval. When Captain Roome Coyle's wife complained to the Board of her husband's ill-treatment and asked for an allotment out of his pay he was ordered to appear before them and answer to the King in person. The Royal Navy had, in those days, some of the characteristics of a family firm. Too many in Pepys's view. The King's control over commissions and appointments often, through a lazy pretence to good nature, favoured the incompetent and the fashionable. His frivolous use of warships, equipped and manned at great expense, to fetch home a present of wine instead of paying the freight charges infuriated Pepys both as an administrator and as an accountant.[5] All this was the more exasperating since Pepys very soon realised and for the rest of his life freely acknowledged that Charles 'best understands the business of the sea of any prince the world ever had'.[6] Why then was he ready to stand with his arms folded, imperturbably watching fools make a hash of naval affairs even to the extent of putting England's sea-power at risk? Pepys could not have kept quiet in his place for any consideration. His itch to regulate and to teach, above all the creative ordering instinct of the artist, would have been too strong. He could diagnose the strange passivity of the King so well hit off in Halifax's character: 'It was resolved generally by others, whom he should have in his Arms, as well as whom he should have in his Councils. Of a Man who was so capable of choosing, he chose as seldom as any Man that ever lived.'[7] But, unlike Halifax, he could not understand it.

The tone of his Admiralty letters, preserved in fourteen folio volumes in the Pepys Library, is sharp and shrewd but not unkindly. He inquires, he reproves, he raps out orders, but he also commends and sympathises. No one understood better the timely use of what he calls 'a letter of civility'. Tact, mastery of detail, energy, promptitude, all the virtues of

a great manager are much in evidence. But beyond and behind this scin-
tillating display of executive talent was a searching, generalising, codifying
intelligence: the omnivorous reader, the Fellow of the Royal Society, the
historian and the aesthete. What was the function of the navy? Did its
organisation correspond to its purposes? Could it do its job better or
cheaper? Who ought to ask these questions and who was qualified to
answer them? Pepys approached the large problems with the same intellectual fearlessness, the same confidence that they would yield to rational
analysis, that he had brought in his early days at the Navy Board to matters
hitherto considered as belonging to the mystery of the shipwright or the
seaman. But even when immersed in the calculations of the commodity
market he had never slipped into a technocrat's view of the service. It
was men first and last that he was judging and assessing.

The navy as it was and the ideas Pepys had of remodelling it demand a
separate chapter. Before embarking on it something must be said of his own
altered circumstances as a rich widower, eminent in the public service and
in the friendship of the most distinguished men of his time. Circumstances is often genteel long-hand for money. Pepys's translation to the
Admiralty put him well above the sordid shifts to which he had resorted
in his earlier days at the Navy Office. His salary rose from £350 to £500,
but that was a trivial improvement. What really brought in the cash – and
hard cash too since it did not come from the public revenue – was the
customary payment of twenty-five shillings for each pass granted to a ship
trading with the Mediterranean. Since the number in any year ran well
into four figures this was a handsome income in itself. Pepys whose estimates of his own financial affairs are conceived in the pessimistic spirit
of a man preparing a valuation for probate admits to a thousand which
would bring in £1,250. The real figure was probably three or four times
as much. And Tangier if no longer the best flower in so thriving a garden
was still blooming. Promotion enabled a man to provide for his connections. Pepys's surviving brother John, the unbeneficed parson whose
spiteful letters had given such offence, was made joint Clerk of the Acts
with Thomas Hayter one of the best and most faithful of Pepys's assistants. Elizabeth's brother Balty, appointed Muster-Master at Deal on the
strength of his performance in the earlier Dutch War added the responsibility of Deputy Commissioner for the Sick and Wounded during the
third one. There is no more eloquent testimony to the effect of knowing
that Pepys had his eye on one than the fact that these two dubious figures
discharged their duties at least satisfactorily. The rest of the family were
settled on the small estate at Brampton.

What of Pepys's domestic arrangements? The comfort and order of his new quarters may be easily imagined. Although the fire at the Navy Office had destroyed part of his collection of prints the bulk of his library survived as did the famous presses that the joiner had built to his own specification. The lady who presided over the household was the young daughter of a city neighbour, Mary Skinner. That their relationship was close, tender and enduring is evident from the rest of his life. Why they did not marry is still a mystery and was, at first, a cause of bitter exchanges with her family. Had it something to do with the long-standing family friendship with that dangerous figure John Milton? The sonnet addressed to Mr. Cyriack Skinner, Mary's uncle, was first published in the 1673 edition of the *Poems* and one of her brothers, Daniel, was the poet's last amanuensis. Towards the end of 1676 Pepys was horrified to hear that the young man whom he had recommended to the English ambassador at Nimwegen was making arrangements with the great Dutch publishing house of Elzevier to bring out a posthumous edition of some political and theological writings that Milton had entrusted to him. Sir Joseph Williamson, a don turned civil servant who was now Secretary of State, gobbled with fury at the news. Skinner abandoned the project with the same airy insouciance he had shown in initiating it, cheerfully handing over the last manifestoes of the great Republican to the King's agents.

> . . . invocato Deo never had I the least thought of prejudicing either King or State, being infinitely loyall to one and mighty zealous for the other, all the concerns that ever I had with Milton or his works being risen from a foolish yet plausible ambition to learning.[8]

Milton is one of the two contemporary writers of genius — Bunyan is the other — on whom Pepys expresses no judgment. His name is not so much as mentioned in the Diary. Some have seized on this as confirming the shallowness of taste they find in his judgments of books and plays. 'Il restera à la porte du seul poème epique de l'Angleterre; Milton jouait de l'orgue dans une cathédrale inaccessible.'[9] To those who do not find it necessary to pity Pepys's sensibility a more obvious explanation suggests itself: that he found Milton's doctrines pernicious and subversive. To admire or to possess his books might, to a servant of Charles II's Government, seem rash or improper. Pepys had passed his formative years in an age of revolution; he was to prove entirely right if he thought that the nasty political habits then acquired, denunciation, witch-hunts, judicial murder, were likely to reappear.

To marry into the Milton circle might be imprudent. But was it not, by Pepys's standards, sluttish to live openly with a woman? Lord Brouncker, his colleague and neighbour at the Navy Office, is constantly censured in the Diary for this very reason. This is one of the puzzles of Pepys's life — another is why he was never knighted. Certainly Mary Skinner was accepted by close friends like Evelyn as though she were his wife: and Robert Hooke, the brilliant scientist and architect, who was only a slight acquaintance, actually refers to her as Mrs. Pepys in his Diary.[10] The disparity in age made it natural for Pepys to call her as she comforted his deathbed his 'dear child': some of the letters of his last years are written in her hand and her none too literate spelling. She was not, in his eyes or her own, his equal. Perhaps that was one reason why the relationship was so tranquil. In any case Pepys was ripening and mellowing. The course of his life was less combative and more sedate. No man was ever more punctilious in matching his style to his stage in life. Perhaps the bust of Elizabeth, her head turned in laughter towards the Navy Office pew in St. Olave's, offers the best comment on his decision not to marry again.

Her death freed his social life from the embarrassments so often recorded in the Diary. His remaining years at the Navy Office and his establishment at Derby House saw the widening and deepening of friendships begun at Whitehall or at the Royal Society with men like Evelyn, Sir Robert Southwell, Sir William Petty or Sir Christopher Wren, and with the *haute bourgeoisie* of the City. He was a liveryman of the Clothworkers' Company (Master in 1677); he was elected an Elder Brother of Trinity House in 1672.

His social, professional and intellectual life interpenetrated each other. Evelyn was not only the greatest connoisseur of his time but a man whose political judgment and executive abilities were highly valued. His performance as Commissioner for the Sick and Wounded earned Pepys's respect. The King encouraged him to write the history of the Dutch Wars 'enjoying me to make it a little keene, for that the *Hollanders* had very unhandsomely abused him, in their pictures, books & libells etc'.[11] On February 19th, 1671, he records 'this day dined with me Mr Surveyor Dr. Chr: Wren, Mr Pepys, Clerk of the Acts, two extraordinary ingenious, and knowing persons, and other friends; I carried them to see the piece of Carving which I had recommended to the King'.[12] This was by Grinling Gibbons whom Evelyn had discovered copying a Crucifix from a Tintoretto cartoon in a country cottage. Here, surely, is the genesis of Gibbons' magnificent carving of the Eye in Glory, the showpiece of the famous Boardroom at the Admiralty, a room known to Nelson and to Churchill but to which Pepys can have been present only in spirit. There is no telling where Evelyn will crop up. His expert knowledge of dendrology was extremely useful to Pepys in his efforts to plan the future timber supplies of the navy.

Sir William Petty's versatility has already been mentioned. He had begun life as a ship's boy but was forced to abandon the sea because his short-sight made him dangerous as a look-out. His skill as an economist and statistician made his conversation especially valuable to the administration of the largest spending department in government. His plans for building a double-bottom boat, though ultimately unproductive, received much practical encouragement from Pepys. Similarly Sir Robert Southwell, Petty's great friend, mixed the speculative life of the Royal Society with a successful career as a diplomat and civil servant. Both men were the kind of people one met dining at the Houblons. And such men profited in one way and another from their association with Pepys. Southwell for instance found a valuable ally to protect his family's interest in the victualling contract at Kinsale, said to be the most lucrative of the home stations.[13] The Houblons in their turn provided foreign and commercial intelligence besides letting the Secretary of the Admiralty know more about the activities of H.M. ships in the Mediterranean than he could glean from the dispatches and journals of their captains. The real task of the navy as Pepys saw it was to promote and protect English seaborne trade. Claims to the sovereignty of the sea and the right of salute to the flag were doctrines of which he became increasingly sceptical. City merchants, not courtiers, lawyers or politicians, were the people with whom he preferred to discuss naval policy.

The Third Dutch War, during which he attained the Secretaryship, was, by these standards, a misuse of sea-power. Its pretext was an assertion of the sovereignty of the sea so grotesque as to have embarrassed anyone except Charles II who put it forward or Sir George Downing who was sent to The Hague to make sure it became a *casus belli*. John Evelyn condemned it in scathing terms and is one of the many witnesses to Sandwich's double conviction that the war was a disaster and that it would cost him his life. His flagship was burnt to the waterline at Solebay and his body was afterwards found at sea. Pepys was one of the six who attended the coffin carrying the Mountagu bannerols at the state funeral in Westminster Abbey. Solebay was the end of an era in the Restoration navy. It was the last battle at which James, Duke of York commanded in chief 'most pleasant when the great shot are thundering about his ears'.

The old flagmen of the earlier war had had their day. Rupert, Harman, Spragge, Kempthorne and Jordan were to serve, some to lose their lives in the murderous battles of 1673 when so little was achieved at so high a cost. But the admirals with whom Pepys was to deal were for the most part men he had first known as Captains and Lieutenants. In the case of Rupert it was perhaps as well. He had growled at Pepys's remarks about the condition of his fleet in 1666. How long would he have been content to be addressed in such firm no-nonsense tones as this?

> . . . And further we do expect to receive from you advice of your haveing sent away the ships for the westerne squadron or others in their roome, the necessity of secureing that coast calling for their dispatch thither, the Virginia fleete being dayly lookt for home.[14]

Pepys knew that he had the whip hand. Charles had never forgiven Rupert for his tiresome insistence on honouring debts instead of relieving his penniless exile with the money he had realised on winding up the affairs of the Royalist navy in 1653.

In November 1673 Pepys was elected M.P. for Castle Rising. The support of the King and the Duke turned the scale with the borough's patron, Lord Howard, later Earl of Norwich and Duke of Norfolk, whom Pepys had already solicited unsuccessfully for an earlier vacancy. Even so the election was contested and the defeated candidate carried the war into the House of Commons, challenging the validity of Pepys's right to sit on the grounds that he was a Papist and that Lord Howard, a known Papist, had used improper influence. The petition was supported by the partisans of Lord Shaftesbury, dismissed from office in the same month as Pepys entered Parliament. Shaftesbury himself, whom Pepys had known as a connection of Sandwich's for twenty years and as a Prize Commissioner in the Second Dutch War, was quoted as having seen an altar and a crucifix in Pepys's house in Seething Lane. Pepys, as might be expected, furiously denied these and similar allegations. A Committee was appointed to investigate. In the strong tide of anti-Catholic emotion then running Pepys was lucky that his old and fearless friend Sir William Coventry was one of its three members. The charges crumbled. Most witnesses flatly denied having laid the information alleged: and even Shaftesbury, turning and twisting with well-bred effrontery, left nothing but a smear. In such times a smear is all that is asked or desired. It was the prorogation of the House, not the demolition of the evidence, that saved Pepys from expulsion.

In spite of the brilliant début defending the Navy Office before a committee of the whole House six years before he entered it as a member, Pepys was not a conspicuous success in Parliament. In his first encounter he had been lucky to get away without serious damage. As it was the taint of Catholicism was already successfully planted on him. And in spite of Lord Howard's noble patronage the bill he had to foot was immense. £700. Even that, as it turned out at the next election, did not buy security of tenure. He had wanted to enter the house as he said in a letter to Henry Savile, Coventry's nephew who had obtained the secretaryship Pepys had coveted the year before:

> . . . not so much, I do assure you, out of any ambition, as the just consideration of those opportunities it might give me of doing His Majesty and Royal Highness better service in the station I am now in: having too many instances before me of the prejudices and disadvantages the affairs of the Admiralty and Navy, and the King's service in both, have fallen into and with difficulty been afterwards delivered from, for want of timely remedy, which a few hands in Parliament thoroughly conversant in these affairs, might with ease enough have administered.[15]

Give or take a parenthesis, this is to say that a great spending department ought to have an expert to represent it in the Commons. In this respect Pepys achieved a good deal, notably in driving through his great naval construction programme of 1677 'the thirty new ships'. But he was not by temperament a House of Commons man. He preferred hierarchy to equality, order to rough-and-tumble, the conversation of learned men to the upper-cuts of debate. He could triumph as a virtuoso but he had not always at command the steady nerve and even temper that made a man like Coventry so effective in the Long Parliament of the Restoration. Indeed on the negative side his fellow-members were often irritated by his punditry.

In spite of this Pepys had many of the requirements for success in Parliamentary politics, a ready tongue, a quick mind, astuteness in judging people and tact in handling them. What he had not, in any form, was the instinct of the games player. He despised gambling and was revolted by the cruel sports of his contemporaries. Politics is a game, however deadly, however earnest, and perhaps in each age takes some of its colour from the prevailing idiom of play. The man who would rather prove himself right than win a point is at a disadvantage. Such, certainly, was Pepys.

He knew that he knew more about the navy than anyone else. He had a programme of action and an administrative machine of his own design and building with which to carry it out. In the prime of life, at the height of his powers, he had been given somewhere to stand and he would move the world.

16

Pepys and the sea officers

For posterity Pepys's literary fame rests on a book that none of his contemporaries knew that he had written. For his friends, ironically, it grew
on a book he never wrote: but which, according to Evelyn, 'he had for
divers years under his hand the History of the Navy, or, *Navalia* (as he
call'd it).'[1] Like Lord Acton's *History of Freedom* it remains one of the
unexecuted masterpieces of English historiography. The site was laid out,
the materials bought (they still form the most important single part of
the Pepys Library) but the book was not written. Had it been we should,
for a certainty, have had a lucid analysis and an exact definition of what its
author conceived the functions of the navy to be. In its absence a clumsier
hand must do what it can with the edged tools of his letters, journals,
notes and memoranda.

Pepys saw the navy, as he saw many things, in two lights. First in its
immediate application, a national force to defend national interests at
sea, and second as part of the general scheme of civilisation, that higher
and nobler concept that has in different ages been invoked under such
different names as Christendom, Reason, Progress or Humanity. The
priority of the first, defence against invasion, protection of trade, was of
course absolute; but that does not mean that the second was negligible.
Exploration and hydrography are two of the most obvious ways in which
a navy can serve the general good of mankind. In both of these fields

Pepys was energetic in promoting enterprise and in publishing the results to the world at large. He was aware of the arguments and the mentality that were in the fullness of time to produce the Official Secrets Act and jealous of their encroachment. He noted with approval the self-confidence of the French in publishing the *Neptune François*, a magnificent collection of charts of their own coast, at the very height of a war against the English and the Dutch.[2] The charts of the Straits of Magellan that Sir John Narbrough drew on his voyage to the South Sea in 1669–70 are dedicated to Pepys, whose name was at the same time given to an island in the South Atlantic. Alas for the mutability of things: the island is no longer there; probably it never was; an error in navigation may have invested one of the Falkland Islands with undeserved dignity. As master's mate Narbrough had with him John Wood, assisted by Greenville Collins, both as Captains to leave their names in the history of exploration and hydrography. In 1676 Wood commanded the *Speedwell* in an attempt to discover the North-East passage. Collins sailed with him as master and preserved his notes and observations when she was lost on the coast of Novaya Zemlya. Pepys had devoted much care and time to the preparations for this expedition in which the Royal Society was as much interested as the Royal Navy. There were other considerations too. The *Speedwell*, fortunately for her company who would otherwise have frozen or starved to death, was accompanied by the *Prosperous* pink, freighted with a cargo for trading on the coast of Tartary or Japan. Pepys was one of the eight adventurers, headed by the Duke of York, who had a share in her.

Narbrough's and Wood's voyages are the earliest examples of exploration directly commissioned by the Admiralty and conducted by naval officers in naval ships. Pepys had been instrumental in opening the line that leads to Cook and Scott. Greenville Collins left as his monument the magnificent folio *Great Britain's Coasting Pilot* (1693) that went into edition after edition for a century after its first publication.[3] All three men found Pepys a steady friend to their careers.

It would certainly be in character, with his love of order and his concern for justice, to credit him with a vision of the navy as the upholder of *Pax Britannica*, 'a security for such as pass on the seas upon their lawful occasions'. But the navy with which he had to do was too puny to undertake so vast a responsibility. It could be argued that the Mediterranean policy which he and his patron Sandwich had always championed led in this direction, since it involved maintaining a base and a permanent force to keep the North African pirates from having things all their own way. This was the *raison d'être* of Tangier. After Tangier had been abandoned

Pepys turned to Gibraltar, the original choice of Cromwell and Sandwich. Early in 1686 Jonathan Gauden, the Victualler's son, was sent out there with instructions from Pepys to obtain what base facilities he could, if necessary by bribing the Spanish Governor.[4]

The Barbary ports of North Africa, Algiers and Tripoli within the Straits and Sallee outside them, were the wasps that stung England into sea-power. It had been their intolerable intrusions into the channel, not only seizing ships but dragging off terrified Devon villagers into slavery, that had brought the ship-money fleets of Charles I into being. From there the line to the Commonwealth navy runs straight and true. Cromwell's use of this instrument, 'the brave things he did and made all the neighbour princes fear him', let the genie out of the bottle. A permanent, professional navy, inherently probable since the emergence of the gunned warship in the sixteenth century, had come to stay. In Pepys's words:

What could the naval strength of this nation be when the Crown had no other force at sea in the case of invasion than the command of what ships and stores it could find from the merchants? And what would that do at this day, whatever it did then? And therein is our policy quite altered, our neighbours being so much stronger than before, and there being quite a different use and service for men-of-war now than there was then, when merchants' vessels and those of war were the same.[5]

The behaviour of the European powers, Spain, France and Holland, rapidly became more reasonable when it was clear that England was able to defend her growing share of sea-borne trade, into the Mediterranean, down the African coast and across the Atlantic, by a professional navy. The Barbary ports had nothing to gain from being reasonable: they lived by piracy and holding poor sailors to ransom. An occasional punitive expedition such as Blake's in 1655 or Narbrough's in 1677 might induce a brief spell of law-abiding conduct, but, like the tribesmen on the North-West Frontier, they did not wish to enter the comity of nations. Thus all through Pepys's time even when England was not at war some naval force, often a sizeable fleet, was usually present in the western Mediterranean.

To maintain a squadron on a foreign station presented problems of finance, supply and manning. But these, to Pepys, were child's play compared with the problem of discipline. What was the use of keeping ships out there if the Captains did not do what they were told and if the Admiralty did not know even where its ships would be? If one had to sum up the difference between Pepys's time at the Navy Office and his years at the Admiralty, in a phrase, one could say that at the first he was always complaining that there was no money and at the second that there was no discipline. And by that he meant the Captains. 'I dread not the men: it is the indiscreet, licentious conversation of the officers which produces all our ills'. St. Vincent's words after the great mutinies of 1797 express Pepys's apprehensions of a century and a quarter earlier. All that the men needed was to be properly fed and paid. The only difficulty there was getting hold of the money. But the officers – there were problems there to occupy Pepys for the whole of his professional life and to reflect on during a long retirement.

The heart of the matter lay in the distinction so often drawn by Pepys himself between the Gentlemen and the Tarpaulins. The Gentlemen, as we have seen, get the rough edge of his tongue: 'the gentlemen captains who undid all . . .' is a theme that approaches monotony. Yet in his *Naval Minutes*, those pithy, darting sentences that condense a lifetime's reflection, it transpires that Pepys's considered criticism of the officer structure is not that it is too aristocratic but that it is not aristocratic enough. Socially the sea is a despised profession:

Have any of our Heralds allowed in express words the seamen for a gentleman? Observe the maliciousness of our English proverb towards the service of the sea, viz. that the sea and the gallows refused nobody. Which is verified too much in our practice of sending none thither but the vicious or poor. And where a merchant or seaman gets an estate, he either out of pride or some other less satisfactory reason seldom brings up a son to his own trade, but advances him in the Law, the Court, the University, or disposes of him some otherwise than to the sea; whereas you shall have lawyers and gownmen of all sorts, soldiers and courtiers, continue their trades from father to son for many generations, seldom assigning any to the sea but in the cases above mentioned. And it was the Rebellion and necessity that made seamen of the King and Duke.[6]

In a comparison of genius he cites the reinforcement of the already formidable battery of game laws 'while how few and imperfect are all that I can find towards the obtaining any discipline or even securing our ordinary trade at sea.'[7] Once the aristocracy could be induced to identify themselves with the navy they would exert their influence and power on its behalf. Pepys was anxious to welcome them in, provided they were serious about their profession. Recommending a Reformado, or supernumerary officer serving as ship's company, to the Captain of the *Reserve* he wrote:

He is ye first that I have interested myself so far for, and I am apt to believe may be ye only one for whom I shall concern myself in that kind: nor should I have done it for him but for ye assurance I have from himself and his friends of his resolucon to betake himself most strictly to ye Duty and labor of a Seaman . . .'[8]

What he did not want and all too often got was '. . . land-commanders . . . pestering and annoying the ships with their hen-coops etc.'[9]

That Pepys himself was without social prejudice seems clear from the impartiality with which he was attacked. He records with amusement that in the Parliamentary furore of the Popish Plot, Colonel Birch, an old Commonwealthsman attacked him for favouring gentlemen and cavaliers at the expense of the old salts who had learned their trade under Blake and Penn.[10] The preference that he and Coventry repeatedly expressed for the old Cromwellian commanders had nothing to do with their social origins: it was a rational, unbiased recognition of their superiority in seamanship, experience and discipline. The same critical eye discerned the limitations of the Tarpaulin considered as a type. Admirable as private captains or as junior flag officers, stout fellows who would knock it out yardarm to yardarm as long as their ships would swim, punctual, obedient and faithful to their duty, were not their very virtues inimical to the intellectual detachment, the originality, the flair that distinguishes the *grand chef* from the *bon ordinaire*? It was this perhaps that Pepys had in mind when he wrote of Sandwich, 'The King, Duke and he the most mathematick Admirals England ever had.'[11] What is quite certain is that Pepys believed that a trained mind could master the lore and the skills of the Tarpaulin and the shipwright;[12] like Drake he would have the gentleman to haul and draw with the mariner and the mariner with the gentleman. A professional himself, he did not want to settle for anything less than professionalism in the sea officers.

In his second tenure of the Secretaryship he had in James II a master who was, for all his crudity and want of judgment, straightforward and loyal to his subordinates. Charles II was none of these things. Intelligent, devious, charming, amused at the jokes his courtiers made to his face about his untrustworthiness, he was the last man to stiffen the disciplinary backbone of the service. Pepys in attempting a course that was certain to make him powerful enemies and might at any time be disowned showed courage of a high order. Again, though he makes no parade of it, he knew and prided himself on the risk he was taking. Like Danby he refused to take out the normal political life insurance of a Royal pardon which could be pleaded as a bar to Parliamentary vengeance.[13] Danby had been Joint

Treasurer of the Navy from 1668, subsequently holding the office alone from 1671 till his elevation to the Lord Treasureship in 1673. Pepys respected him as a colleague. There are, particularly at this stage, similarities in their careers and their objectives and both were to be struck down in the Popish Plot. Both men disdained an easy popularity. The language in which Pepys recalled an errant captain to his duty was not that in which the gentry were used to being addressed by the son of a tailor. Indeed given the conventions of military and naval service hitherto prevailing it was inevitable that they should feel resentful and insulted. But it was precisely the conventions that Pepys wanted to change.

The indiscipline of the Captains took many forms. Absence without leave was the speciality of Captain Preistman whom Pepys 'spied . . . at a distance sauntering up and down Covent Garden', when he and his ship ought to have been in Portsmouth. That was on July 9th, 1675. Pepys, double-shotting his guns, found that he had brought his ship into the river without orders, no doubt to facilitate access to the bright lights. On July 19th he fired his broadside. But Captain Preistman was unsinkable. In spite of repeated indiscipline he was given command after command. Although a favourite of both Charles and James he survived the Revolution. Pepys's last sardonic reference to him shows him for five weeks in the company of his own successor as Secretary of the Admiralty taking the waters at Tunbridge Wells, at the height of King William's war.[14]

Loitering in port was even more common, particularly when the port was an agreeable one (Leghorn was a great favourite on the Mediterranean station: and the ships in the West Indies sometimes passed several months without putting to sea). With what glee Pepys must have seized on the dereliction of Penn's kinsman, Sir Richard Rooth, in the *Adventure*. '. . . Of the whole 21 months which he was abroad [May 1675–Jan. 1677] beeing sent particularly to attend to the services of Sally . . . he spent only 4 months on that service, 13 months in port and the rest on other service . . . 43 days in Cadiz when ordered not to spend above 6' etc. etc.[15] The practice variously known as 'freight' or 'good voyages' was, in Pepys's eyes, the most pernicious of all. This was a constructive and highly profitable abuse of a practice permitted, even discreetly encouraged, by the Admiralty down to the beginning of the twentieth century. If a warship was under orders for a particular voyage her captain was entitled to take on board such freight or more often bullion as he thought consistent with maintaining the sea-worthiness and efficiency of his ship. In an age when the sea teemed with pirates and privateers this was a limited form of commerce protection that yielded a useful return:

officially the captain was allowed to charge one per cent of the value of
the cargo but the rate was often much higher since this kind of regulation
was very difficult to enforce. In the Mediterranean and on more distant
stations captains grew adept at concocting excuses for taking their ships
on voyages that offered this traffic. 'Good voyages' as they were called
were a red rag to Pepys; perhaps it was the use of the word 'good' about
which he can hardly control his sarcasm. Their danger lay in dissolving
a fleet into so many floating strongrooms plying for private charter. As
he found when he went out to Tangier in 1683 it was often impossible to
tell where any ship was going to be when.

Indiscipline worked upwards and downwards. Captains disobeyed the
orders of their flag officers, sometimes to the extent of refusing action or
even shamefully surrendering without a fight. In return the lieutenants
either disputed their captain's authority or the officers were split into
factions. The patient investigation of these collisions of personality took
up an infinity of time. What sort of a service do they reveal? In July 1678
Pepys ordered the convening of a court-martial to 'examine matters in
difference' between Captain Roydon of the *Sweepstakes* (a fourth-rate) and
his Lieutenant, George Aylmer, 'the said Lieutenant haveing (either
with or without cause) absented himself for several months from his
shippe'.[16] The proceedings suggest how richly eccentricity could luxuriate
aboard a seventeenth-century man of war.

At the end of October 1677 the *Sweepstakes* was at anchor off Kinsale.
At one o'clock in the morning her Captain came aboard 'crying a huge
storme, calling for the Master, bidding I should be Caled and if I did not
Com I should be dragued out. A Rogue! What! Not come and save ye
King's ship?' The calmness of the weather contrasted with the excitement
of the commanding officer. He continued in this state for several days
abusing his Lieutenant and striking him with his cane. Aylmer therefore
applied to the Duke of Ormonde the Lord-Lieutenant at Dublin Castle for
permission to come ashore 'by reason of his Captain's usage'. This was
granted pending further directions from England. Roydon countered
this version of events by asserting that Aylmer was constantly absent
from his duty and that he boasted that he had come up from being
footman.

The spiritual state of the vessel appears to have been no happier than
the temporal. When the ship had been in Portsmouth the chaplain George
Bradford had a run ashore with the Corporal of Marines. While they were
drinking and playing cards 'my Corporall found that my Chaplin put the
bent on him'. Taxed with this the enraged cleric exploded with, 'God
Damn him and sinck him: soe upon that the said Corp. went to leave

him, the Chaplin ketching hold of him and called for six canns of beer
more and swore by God that he should take part of that beer and pay
sheere of the reckning . . .'

In Ireland his conduct was even less edifying:

At Dublin the said Chaplin being drinking and ranting with the
Collegeants and having dranck soe much that he took off his clothes and
swearing God Damn Him he was a man of warr: soe that the people
had much adoe to gett him into the house and afterward did gett from
them and leapt over the wall and tore his shirt almost from his back . . .

At Carrickfergus the minister complained to the Captain:

. . . that he could not be at peace for my Chaplin being there a-
catterwoolding till twelve or one o'clock in the morning with his wife
. . . they coming both together dressing and undressing one another in
an Antick manner . . .

Mr. Bradford was dismissed the service and Captain Roydon relieved
of his command. Next year when Pepys was a victim of the Popish
mania Roydon did his best to get his own back by claiming that he had
been dismissed for saying that his Lieutenant was a Papist. It seems most
improbable that he was, as he was continuously employed throughout the
high tide of anti-Catholic hysteria. And the allegation that he had been a
footman* was perhaps Roydon's way of expressing his resentment at
Aylmer's having enjoyed the favour of aristocratic patronage.

Out of material such as this Pepys set about constructing a profession.
It is perhaps possible to detect in the account given of life aboard the
Sweepstakes the 'us' and 'them' division in the form characteristic of the
late seventeenth century both in Parliament — Court versus Country —
and on the stage — the sophisticates of London against the rural booby
squires. Captain Roydon, one feels sure, would not have applied to the
Duke of Ormonde in Dublin Castle: and if he had the butler would have
shown him the door. Divisions in any society outlive their original causes
and nourish themselves on fresh issues. At the Restoration a gentleman
officer was by definition a cavalier. Thus by an easy progression the Tarpaulins become to some extent identified with the Country party, and
the faction fights of politics are domesticated in the navy. The Revolution
of 1688 by changing the parties round only strengthened a tradition that
was not entirely extinguished until the two world wars of our own century.

* See p. 282.

The same pattern can be discerned in another row that took up the best part of James II's reign (October 1685–January 1688) and has left seventy-six folio pages of documentation among Pepys's papers in the Bodleian.[17] In an altercation with Mr. Trevor, the purser of the *Suffolk*, Captain Vittells, the Master Attendant at Chatham broke a boat-hook over his head. There are sworn statements before magistrates, doctors' certificates, and every conceivable kind of written evidence relevant and irrelevant. But once again there is the smell of faction, social, political and religious. All the standing officers of the yard – Tarpaulins by definition – swear in Vittells's defence that Trevor was always ashore and never did his job, while Trevor throws into the scale certificates of his religious orthodoxy attested by the Dean of Rochester. The fact of the assault was not denied so Pepys and Lord Dartmouth closed the matter by ordering Vittells to pay the purser £50 in five quarterly instalments.

Pepys was no friend to doctrinal inquisitions. He had noted as a young man how easily the fellows of his college conformed to the ideology required of them and he carried out the injunctions of the Test Act without enthusiasm.[18] Neither personal honour nor professional competence, the two things that mattered in a sea officer, could be guaranteed by such methods. If there were to be examinations, let them be professional ones. As to character, aspiring officers should be made to serve a proper apprenticeship and to produce their captain's reports on their behaviour. Above all to encourage literate and orderly habits every officer should be required to keep a journal. This was the three-pronged strategy by which Pepys hoped to eliminate the stubborn inarticulacy of the Tarpaulin and the go-as-you-please dilettantism of the Gentleman, infusing both of them, for good measure, with a tincture of the Royal Society. The great triumph of this policy, the cornerstone, ever since, of the officer structure of the Royal Navy, was the introduction of the examination for the rank of Lieutenant in 1677. Like the introduction of a driving test on the roads or the abolition of purchase in the army this was the kind of measure that people may resist but which they will never dare to rescind. Had Pepys died of a heart attack on the day after it had been accepted he would still tower above any rival as the radical reformer, the remodeller of the naval profession. He had introduced a principle that must sooner or later carry all before it. No newcomer to the service after December 1677 was going to be allowed to hold a Lieutenant's commission, much less a Captain's, who had not satisfied the stringent requirements which Pepys had, at the Admiralty's invitation, defined. A candidate presenting himself for 'a solemn examination' at the Navy Board of 'his ability to judge of and perform the duty of an able seaman and a midshipman and his having attained to a sufficient degree of knowledge in the theory of navigation capacitating him thereto' by three senior officers including a flag officer and a commander of a first- or second-rate had first of all to produce evidence of three years' service at sea, of which one year at least must have been as a midshipman. He had to produce certificates from his commanding officers as to his 'sobriety, diligence, obedience to order and application to the study and practice of the art of navigation' and he must be at least twenty years of age. This last provision was often bent in the next century: Nelson was a captain at the age of twenty and no one thought this anything out of the way: but the rest of this rigorous code was generally observed. In Pepys's time it certainly was: only a few months after its adoption he was rubbing his hands:

. . . I thank God we have not half the throng of those of the bastard breed pressing for employments which we heretofore used to be troubled with, they being conscious of their inability to pass this examination, and know it to be to no purpose now to solicit for employments till they have done it.[19]

The smoothness and speed with which this major reform was carried through illustrates both Pepys's opportunism and his ability to bide his time. The initiation of the policy, so skilfully camouflaged as to conceal its real outlines, can be traced to November 1674. On the 14th of that month Pepys at a Board meeting drew attention to a dangerous anomaly. By custom sixth-rates did not, like larger vessels, carry a master. Since the captain was expected to discharge this function it seemed sensible to lay it down that before a man could be appointed to command a sixth-rate he must produce a certificate of competence from Trinity House. The agenda was huge: Pepys raised the point after they had already been sitting for some time and still had a lot of business to get through. In any case it seemed obvious common sense. Everyone agreed and they sped on to discuss the generous offer of the Genoese Republic to present the King with a galley for Tangier. There the matter rested for close on three years when Pepys raised another dangerous anomaly arising out of the first. What was the form when a man who had previously commanded one of the higher rates (and there enjoyed the services of a master) found himself appointed to a sixth-rate, which did not carry one? In logic should not such an officer submit himself to an examination in seamanship and navigation by the Brethren of Trinity House? The point was not merely academic since Captain Preistman, that ornament to the service, finding himself in this situation had employed a master and had left the Admiralty to pay his wages. The Duke of York was present at this meeting of the Board from membership of which he was disabled by his Catholicism and clearly added his voice to the general support for Pepys's view. Indeed he went further and deplored the inadequate standards in these matters among the 'young gentlemen with pretensions to lieutenancies'. Could not Trinity House examine them while they were about it? Or the Navy Board? Or both? It is hard to believe that Pepys had not planted these questions. Sir John Narbrough's complaints from the Mediterranean of the deficiencies of his lieutenants certainly reinforced them.

Pepys was invited to prepare a draft of the duties of a lieutenant and to propose a suitable method of examination. On December 1st he produced his scheme which was approved except that Rupert and Lord Ossory argued that the duty of an ordinary midshipman was 'a service beneath the quality of a gentleman to go through'. This particular was referred to a special committee consisting of the Principal Officers of the Navy Board and a distinguished list of senior commanders, both Tarpaulins and Gentlemen. A week later they all turned up at the Board meeting and were so emphatic in their repudiation of the social slur detected by Rupert that they delegated Legge, the future Lord Dartmouth, a gentleman of the gentlemen, to digest their reasons. These the Board found

> . . . so convincing that not one word was afterwards urged in the opposition . . . saving this question — whether he [Legge] did ever perform one year's midshipmanship before he pretended to the office of lieutenant? To which he answering *No*, but that it had cost him many an aching head and heart since to make up the want of it, that point was unanimously RESOLVED on . . .[20]

Describing the scene Pepys alludes to the attendance of 'several commanders, both gentlemen and others, which distinction I am both ashamed and afflicted to mention, and should be more, but that among other good ends of what I am now doing the removing of that distinction will be one'.[21] This is the note of integrity, not simply in the sense of honesty but in the sense of concerting moral, intellectual and practical concern, that sounds so insistently through Pepys's later life. He has outgrown the sleaziness of the deals with Captain Cocke and Sir William Warren. The standards of Sir William Coventry and John Evelyn have become natural to him.

To those rash enough to offer a bribe for place or promotion the answer was stunned and stunning.[22] Even more strait-laced by the accepted notions of the time was his attitude towards nepotism. To appoint a relation, a friend's son, even a friend's nominee, to a vacancy was perfectly proper. He had brought his brother John into the Navy Office, Balty into his place at Deal, and was ready to do the same kindness for others. All this was common form. What was unusual was his regulation of this practice by the requirements of the service and the idea of justice. His ghost was looking over the shoulder of Lord Fisher when he wrote in the log at Dartmouth, 'Favouritism is the secret of efficiency.'

In October 1676 the Purser of the *Royal Sovereign*, a first-rate, died suddenly. A pursery, in effect a privileged monopoly selling to a captive market, was a plum. Pepys was besieged by applications, including some from his oldest most respected friends. On the 19th Sir William Coventry wrote applying on behalf of his landlord's brother.[23] Living at Minster Lovell he had not been as quick off the mark as everyone else. Only the day before Pepys had written to Elizabeth Pearse, the good-looking wife of his close friend the Surgeon-General to the Navy, declining with tact and gentleness to put forward the claims of their son. His position, he explains, would be impossible since he has at last induced the King and Duke to encourage honesty and good service among the pursers by reserving the top jobs for men who have proved themselves in lesser ones. He has had

applications from commanders, old clerks of ye Navy and ancient Pursers from whom I have a whole bundle of petitions and recommendations to present H.M. with at his return and such as I must confesse were it for my brother or son I could not justify to myself overbearing in behalf of one that had never knowne any part of ye service abroad which he is pretending to (and which I could wish you would think fit to let Mr James have) and this upon ye first Ship Royal of England where ye Charge of a Purser calls for little less experience than any one office in a Fleet.

'This Madam, for your satisfaction and for ye doing right to my owne friendship I thought fit for me to observe to you . . .[24].'

The next day he saw the King and the place went to the purser of the *London* who was himself succeeded by a senior clerk in the Navy Office.[25]

The respect paid to truth and propriety as well as to the feelings of others, above all the care taken by an eminent and busy man to make sure that his correspondent who has asked a favour shall understand completely why it must be refused, stand comparison with Dr. Johnson. Neither Coventry nor the Pearses stopped asking him favours. Indeed hardly six months later Pearse tried, unsuccessfully, to obtain the pursery of the *Royal James* for his son. Pepys's interest in the boy and readiness to help were steady and unaffected. They were, by the same token, realistic as the following letter[26] shows:

To Mr James Pearse.

Derby House, 27 September 1677

His Majesty's service beginning now to call for the employment of a muster-master to his ships in the Straits, I have out of my confidence of your having so improved the time you have already spent in the Navy, and now at sea, as to have qualified yourself for the well executing thereof, obtained and herewith send you His Majesty's commission and instructions for that employment, as one instance of the remembrance I have of and the care I shall always have for you so long as the respect which I truly bear to my worthy friends your father and mother shall be accompanied with a just endeavour of sobriety and diligence on your part to deserve it. For so long as you give me that encouragement, I shall not only continue your benefit and advancement but take delight in doing so; but must, on the other hand, be as plain with you in telling of you that I shall be inquisitive after you, as having heard of some of your past liberties, though from my willingness to impute them to your youth I never took notice of them till now; that having provided you a commission that entitles you to the trust and business of a man, my kindness to you, as well as justice to myself, will not let me longer withhold my giving you the same cautions which I would with more severity give a child of my own (and did to my only brother in the last day he lived in the Navy)* namely that you do never entertain one thought of any indulgence from me under any neglects of business, and much less under any misdoings therein, for I am one that will never be guilty of contributing to the advancement of any man that will not be contented to rise by the same steps of diligence and faithfulness which have (by God's blessing) raised me to this capacity of doing good offices. And this I the rather choose to observe to you out of the hopes I have that what my example may want my friend your father will supply to you, of the fruits of whose cares and labours in the world you have so largely tasted in your liberal education . . .

To a twentieth-century reader the formality of language gives, at first, a flavour of pomposity just as the characteristically Pepysian length of the opening sentence, like a morning mist, hangs for an instant over the clarity

* John Pepys had died in that year.

revealed by the brightness of his irrepressible intelligence. He could not be obscure because he had always used his mind before he began to speak or write. Like Sir Winston Churchill he felt the structure of an English sentence to be a noble thing and used his architectural sense to relieve his central theme with features suggested by the multiplicity of a mind that was never still or empty. Yet, as with Johnson, it is the grand and simple virtues, justice, uprightness, warmth of heart, that this style, at a superficial view so elaborate, expresses so compellingly. The cold folksiness of our now fashionable informality is shown up as a sham.

Patronage, nepotism, influence, 'interest' to use the word most comprehensively employed to denote these things, was bound to affect the career of an officer in a service which did not yet offer continuous employment. As Pepys, and Lord Fisher two and a half centuries later, understood, this could be used to give the outstanding man a great deal more than his fair share of the jobs that were going. Sir John Narbrough and Sir Clowdisley Shovell are often cited with approval as examples of officers who got to the top of the late-seventeenth-century navy through their own unaided merit. Unaided? Both came into the service as the protégés of Myngs, to whom it seems likely they were related. Both came from the same parish in Norfolk. After Myngs' death Narbrough looked after Shovell and gave him his first great opportunity as his lieutenant in the attack on Tripoli. This, as Pepys is at pains to emphasise in his letter to young Pearse, is the proper and intelligent use, indeed one of the obligations, of executive power. Narbrough who perhaps came closest to Pepys's idea of what a sea officer should be was an old and trusted friend of the Pearses and gave James passage in his own ship when he took up his appointment in the Mediterranean.

Until the navy was given enough money to provide its officers with a continuous career there could be no automatic system of seniority. Its absence vexed Pepys with petty personal jockeyings that could yet have serious consequences in the conduct of operations. Suppose a squadron contained a second-rate, commanded by some young sprig of nobility, and a third-rate whose captain knew every part of his job from twenty or thirty years' experience. Which, in the absence or incapacity of their flag officer, should take his place, the 'eldest captain' or 'the greater ship'? Pepys had no doubt that it was right to go for the man. He argued the case one afternoon late in 1683 when, together with Lord Dartmouth and some other captains, he had been dining aboard the *English Tiger* off Tangier as the guest of Captain Preistman. The conversation had already acquired a note of asperity. Preistman and others had been critical to the point of disrespect about the drafting of their instructions. Pepys had countered with some pointed remarks about commanding officers lying ashore without leave:

> But all ended with his observing that there was wanting in the Navy a certain settlement about commands at sea . . . whether the greater ship or the older commander. . . . I did tell him that in this we might learn of the French, for they were under a rule in it and it was according to the seniority of the commander, to which like a fool he found fault that we should be thought to learn anything of the French (though I showed him we did much and might more) and yet he agreed that method was the true rule to go by.

The French had already, as Pepys pointed out to the Duke at Newmarket in 1680, cut the Gordian knot by keeping 'their commanders and lieutenants constantly in pay'. This is, after all, the fundamental criterion by which the professional is distinguished from the amateur.

Pepys did not live to see the completion of the officer structure he spent his best energies in building. To the creative mind such a loss may be of only minor importance. Certainly Pepys saw deeply enough into what he was fashioning to apprehend the realities that he could only know in imagination. He was, for instance, alert to the new dangers of the *esprit de corps* he was seeking to create:

> Observe the impropriety of a court-martial of commanders to judge of the ignorance or negligence of a master or pilot, who do not pretend or dare take upon them any answerableness for the safe navigating of their ships, but are continually putting the King to the charge of pilotage, even of the 5th-rates, in or out of the River of Thames or over to the coasts of Holland or France, and in case of any miscarrying lay all upon their master; and yet at other times take it ill not to be thought great seamen, and presume at a court-martial to censure a master or pilot as if themselves were the only judges of navigation.[27]

He notes with approval his old clerk Gibson's observation:

> . . . how certainly partial our courts-martial ever are to commanders in any matters of difference between them and their under-officers, or in cases of miscarriage where it is possible to lay it upon any under-officer, instancing at present in Captain Greydon's case for the loss, I think, of the *St David*, where the court laid it upon the carpenter, and

after the rising thereof one of the captains were heard to say to Greydon: 'God damme, Jack, we have made shift to bring you off, but by God you must remember to do the like by any of us when it comes to our turn.'[28]

Here expressed in the idiom of the quarter-deck these sentiments are nothing if not professional.

Although the creation (give or take a decade or two) of the regular naval officer was Pepys's most lasting contribution to the service and to the social ethos of England at the height of her power, it was by no means the only or most obvious one. He himself clearly considered the condition and power of the King's ships and the regularity of naval finances during the periods at which he was responsible for them to be his best claims on the gratitude of his country. There was no aspect of naval affairs that he did not in some measure improve or rationalise. In the next chapter something must be said of them.

17

Men and ships

It is a paradox that Pepys, least military of men, should have won his place in history as the architect of a great fighting service. But it is sometimes forgotten that to most civilised men participation in war is a duty not a choice. Pepys hated from the heart cruelty and killing, destructiveness and waste. Where he accepted them, as in watching a public execution, he did so because they seemed the only means of serving a yet higher purpose; justice, order, the preservation of society. He would not have felt anything but horror at witnessing an underworld execution. Similarly although the navy existed to exert armed force Pepys conceived that function as defensive – 'our neighbours being so much stronger than before' – and disapproved of aggression. The reader of the Diary can see how wholeheartedly he detested not only the policy that produced the Dutch Wars but the mentality that underlay it. Anyone who reads through the *Naval Minutes* or the *Tangier Papers*, those distillations of a mind glancing, reflecting, grappling with every aspect of naval theory and practice, will search in vain for traces of jingoism.

His most characteristic and congenial achievements for the navy are thus not necessarily the most conspicuous. The officers who were charged with the maintenance of ships and men in soundness and health, the master, the surgeon, the purser, the parson (though he was not, and is not now, an officer) all felt their professional standing and qualification scrutinised and improved. The victualling was regulated by a scale that was at least generous in aspiration, if even Pepys could not extirpate the inveterate corruption of this easiest of fields for the swindler. The terms under which men served and the punctuality with which they were paid challenged his sense of justice. A delight in good craftsmanship and proper materials naturally attracted him to the world of the shipwrights and the dockyards. Artist, scientist, administrator and jurist, Pepys found scope for his constructive talents in the non-combatant side of the service.

For the master Pepys won higher esteem by his insistence on a certificate from Trinity House. No doubt this contributed to the steady rise in his pay. But the most characteristic expression of his heightened value was the foundation of the Mathematical School at Christ's Hospital. This was designed specifically as a nursery for navigators. Pepys was the moving spirit in putting forward the idea, in obtaining Government money, in choosing the mathematics master and in making sure that he did what he was paid to do. Not the least part of this achievement was that commemorated in Verrio's painting in the hall of Christ's Hospital, the dignifying of a hitherto base mechanic trade with the panoply of royal patronage. This is the quintessence of Pepys. He knows how to use the political machinery of his time, the social prejudices of his age, the needs of an expanding merchant marine to forward the aims he has at heart: the diffusion of useful knowledge, the opening of a career to the talents, and the provision of a pool of navigators from whom the navy can draw in an emergency. He was appointed a Governor on February 1st, 1676, and the seriousness with which he took his duties is attested by the mass of correspondence still preserved in the Pepys Library.

Pepys's great interest in questions of health and his (rare) experience of successful surgery would have doubtless led him to reconstruct the ramshackle medical services of the navy if he had not, for once, had as colleagues in this department two men whom he admired and trusted, two, indeed, of his closest friends, John Evelyn and James Pearse. For once Pepys seems to have been entirely content to play second fiddle: to Evelyn and his fellow-commissioners for the Sick and Wounded during the wars; to Pearse in providing such medicines, doctors and other services as the poverty, both of the navy and of medical knowledge could supply. Pearse was a professional of Pepysian quality. In the earlier of Charles II's two Dutch Wars it was he who pressed for the commissioning of a hospital ship and, powerfully seconded by William Coventry at sea and John Evelyn ashore, obtained one in 1665 and two in 1666.[1] This is the first time in English naval history that such a vessel is even mentioned, barring one obscure reference in the disastrous expedition against

Hispaniola in 1654 when the troops from General Venables downwards seem to have been in such a miserable state that the description would have fitted almost every vessel in the fleet. Pearse, who throughout the war was styled Surgeon-General of the Fleet, a title that, incredibly, carried no salary or fees, was brought ashore in the summer of 1666 and made Warden of the Company of Barber-Surgeons who maintained such medical services as the fleet enjoyed. He went back to sea for the St. James's Day Fight, following the action in a yacht which left him leisure to observe and record its developments.* His account is in a class by itself. But his energy and administrative skill were even more fruitful ashore. Although he returned to private practice at the end of the war (because his appointment as a naval surgeon was at once terminated) he was at last, in April 1670, established at a retainer of £100 a year in the post of 'Chyrurgeon Generall of H.M. Navy'.

By the time the Third Dutch War broke out in 1672 Pearse had made his preparations. His draught of equipment for a hospital ship includes for the first time the supply of soap at the public charge. Most akin to Pepys was his introduction of a system of printed forms to control and record the medical treatment of the seamen, particularly in securing accommodation and attendance for men discharged to shore, and to prevent embezzlement and fraud. Once again on the outbreak of war the Commission for the Sick and Wounded and Prisoners was reconstituted with John Evelyn as its moving spirit. When it was dissolved in 1674 Pearse as Surgeon-General was specifically directed to take over its duties. He held his appointment until after the Revolution, inspiring in Pepys's great building programme of 1677 the bold requirement of three hospital ships, two for the Channel and one for the Mediterranean. The disasters that overtook Pepys in 1679 might easily have destroyed Pearse, since as personal surgeon to the Duke of York his connection was even more dangerous. He survived but it was not until Pepys came back to the Admiralty in 1684, and most notably when he set up the Special Commission of 1686† that Pearse was able to take his reforming programme a stage further. In the report on his department that he submitted in September 1687 he claimed in words reminiscent of his friend the Secretary to have 'reduced it into such a method that it is not possible for me (or whoever shall succeed me) to wrong his Majesty or injure his subjects'. He was denied the chance of putting it to the test: in 1689 his close personal attachment to both the Stuart brothers cost him his post. His great contribution to an efficient medical service, the raising of the surgeon's rate of pay, a truly Pepysian criterion of professionalism, did not

* See p. 348, note 17.   † See pp. 287–291.

save him from dying in poverty. In 1696 his widow whose beauty had
excited Pepys in the days of the Diary asked him to act as trustee in the
sale of her house.

But the best provision that could be made to keep men in health was
to see that they were properly clothed and fed. Under the captain this
responsibility fell upon the purser. This officer was to the old sailing-
ship navy what the mother-in-law was to the music-hall. Jokes about his
dishonest practices easily outweigh all other types of humour. As so
often in government service he was put in a position where he was invited
if not actually commanded to make money by sharp practice. 'A purser
without professed cheating is a professed loser' Pepys wrote in his Navy
Office days. His experience at the Admiralty confirmed this judgment.
As the licensed supplier of victuals paid for by the Government and the
monopolist of everything else the ship's company might want he was well
placed to swindle both of them. Who, except the captain, could tell if he
gave the sailors less than the Government had contracted for, or if, still
more common, he charged the Government for victualling men who had
died, or, perhaps, had never existed? Collusion, between captain and purser,
was common. One captain was alleged to have borne his dog on the ship's
books under the name of Mr. Bromley.[2] But most of these frauds lacked
this touch of bravura: and a very large number were perpetrated against
the seamen. It was to remedy this state of affairs that Pepys insisted on the
appointment of Muster-Masters. But the only real solution was to raise the
standards and the self-respect of pursers and captains by rewarding merit,
enforcing discipline and paying the rate for the job.

No one can read far in lower deck autobiography without being disgusted by details of biscuits alive with weevils, mouldy bread, rotten
cheese, beer that stank, wine that turned the stomach and water too foul
for human consumption. How different it sounds from the Victualling
Contract of 1677 for which Pepys was responsible and in which he took
such pride:

. . . Viz. every man to have for his allowance by the day, one pound
avoirdupois, of good, cleane, sweet, sound, well bolted with a house[3]
cloth, well-baked and well-conditioned wheaten Bisquet, of w^ch
samples are to be brought unto and approved of by the Principall
Officers and Commissioner of H.M. Navy . . . once every three months;
one Gallon, wine measure, of Beer of such a standard. [Here follows
a sentence on the quantity and quality of malt and hops and on the
arrangements for judging them, so exact, so specific and so parenthe-
tically qualified that even Pepys could hardly have taken it at a canter]

> . . . Two pounds, avoirdupois of Beef, killed and made up with salt
> in England, of a well-fed Ox not weighing lesse than 5 cwt. . . .

Enough is enough. The wholesome plenty of Pepys's Victualling
Contract leaves one feeling that the calorie intake needs watching. Even
the lighter diet prescribed for vessels sailing to the warmer climates
south of 39°N — figs, currants, rice, olive oil and wine — sounds appetising
and abundant. Yet, as Pepys's own Admiralty letters show, reality fell
far short. Thorough, resourceful, vigilant, he was all, perhaps rather more
than all, that an administrator could be. But he could not, like Moses
striking the rock, produce money by rapping people's knuckles. Unpunc-
tual payment meant bad provisions. The contractors had to make a profit
to stay in business. When Pepys fell from office in 1679 his successors
reversed the system of victualling by contract and returned to the practice
of the Commonwealth which had run its own state victualling department.
Alone of the changes they introduced this seems to have been an improvement. Pepys himself retained it when he returned to the Admiralty in
1684.

If money dictated what could or could not be done in the matter of
food, still more obviously was this the case with pay. Apart from keeping
a sharp eye on the Ticket Office and punishing ticket brokers when evidence could be produced against them Pepys could do little. 'The King's
wages better than merchantmen's yet his service shunned by reason of
bad pay.' As usual it is impossible to better his own summary. The affront
to his sense of justice as well as to his passion for good order did not
diminish with the passage of time. It led him, as a modern scholar[4] has
shown, into disingenuousness in the famous passage so often quoted from
his *Memoires*, the *pièce justificative* that he published in 1690.

> . . . not a *Penny* left unpaid to any *Officer, Seaman, Workman, Artificer* or
> *Merchant*, for any *service* come in, or *commodity* delivered to the use of the
> *Navy*, either at sea or on shore, within the whole time of this *Commis-
> sion* where the Party claiming the same was in the way to receive it . . .

The statement is, strictly, true thanks to the qualifying phrase. The
Commission to which Pepys refers had been set up in March 1686.
During the two and a half years that he had subsequently spent at the
Admiralty the arrears of wages due to the seamen had risen to the enormous
sum of £85,244, while the arrears due to the merchants and dockyard
workmen were in comparison trivial. Safe aboard a man-of-war, especially
if bound for the West Indies or the Mediterranean, the Party claiming the

same was not indeed in much of a way to receive it. The best of a bad job was all that Pepys could make of paying the seaman; he carried the habit on in arguing his own case.

Unsatisfactory as both naval pay and victualling were there is good ground for thinking that both were, on the whole, better than those prevailing in merchant ships. Pepys certainly believed that they were. His views are powerfully supported by the direct statement of Edward Barlow, whose journal gives the fullest picture we have of the life of a Restoration seaman: 'Their Majesties ships are better victualled than most merchant ships are, and their pay surer . . .'[5] Why, if this were true, were sailors so unwilling to serve in the navy?

One answer is, no doubt, that it is quite impossible to generalise about conditions either in the navy or the merchant service. Barlow's contemporary, Edward Coxere, gives a charming account of transferring from a state ship to a merchantman in the Mediterranean simply because the pay was higher. The captain raised no objection; indeed the only solicitude he felt was for Coxere's safety. 'When I was in the boat the captain called "Edward, have a care!"'[6] Even in the navy itself conditions varied so widely from ship to ship and captain to captain that a clear-cut statement such as Barlow's has to be taken as the evidence of one man's experience, indicative, suggestive, but not definitive.

But on another point, itself almost a sufficient explanation of the navy's unpopularity, there is complete unanimity, and that is impressment. To the modern reader the press gang means grinning sailors armed with clubs and cutlasses dragging poor wretches from the streets and taverns. To men like Barlow and Coxere it meant something more callously unjust and more desperately resented, the boarding of ships inward bound after a voyage of perhaps two or three years and the pressing of men without allowing them to see their wives and children or to collect their wages. Men like Coxere who had actually been imprisoned by the Turks were not exaggerating when they compared, as they sometimes did, the humanity of their countrymen unfavourably with that of the infidel.

Pepys sympathised. Where he could, he secured the release of individuals. When he could, he resisted pressure from captains to be allowed to make up deficient complements by pressing. Seamen, unlike carpenters and sawyers for the dockyard, were in theory only liable to impressment in time of war. Money, of course, would have disposed of the whole problem. But society had established a prescriptive right to claim the seaman's services without paying him and it would take more than Pepys's sense of justice to induce the rich and powerful to abandon so profitable a form of exploitation. Disgraceful as it was, it was not practical politics to abolish it. Pepys therefore tried to contain it by observing such limitations as the law had put upon it and to work for its supersession by campaigning for a navy that would be properly paid and adequately financed. When at the very end of his career his old friend James Pearse 'putt a precedent into my hand' for the pressing of surgeons for the fleet that was going out to meet the Dutch invasion of 1688, Pepys even in that dark hour would not grant a press-warrant until he had examined the matter more thoroughly and discussed it with his friend.[7] Exceptionally in the summer of 1675 when England was at peace in Europe he allowed the ships sent to reinforce Narbrough in the Mediterranean to press after all else had failed.[8] Since the country was in a state of war with Tripoli this was perfectly legal. But much more characteristic is his intervention on behalf of four carpenters and a bricklayer engaged in building a new house for his friend Sir John Bankes at Aylesford, dangerously accessible to the pressing parties from the Medway Towns.[9] Watching from a disgruntled retirement the naval conduct of King William's war Pepys observed that

> more complaints arise, and justly, every day of the irregularities and violences committed in that one particular of the pressing of men, than would by many degrees be consequential to all the power of coercion that needed to be asked of a Parliament for securing the government of the service of the seamen it hath, and making their number more.[10]

Injustice, irregularity and violence are the despised marks of amateurism in administration.

It was perhaps Pepys's sense of the injustice suffered by the seamen that led so hearty an anticlerical to champion the cause and raise the status of the naval chaplain. Like the surgeon the chaplain was subsidised by compulsory deductions from the men's wages — twopence a month for the doctor, fourpence for the parson. All that the Government paid was the wage of an ordinary seaman. In Charles I's time there had been so few takers for employment offered on such wretched terms that the seamen's groats — their monthly fourpences — accumulated into a pile over which courtiers and placemen squabbled at the trough. Even after the Restoration two flag officers, Sir Thomas Allin and Sir William Berkeley, secured grants of £1,000 apiece from this source.[11] Under the Commonwealth the chaplain had risen high. One of them had even challenged the dubious practices of the Pett dynasty in Chatham dockyard and had come off equal. The importance of preaching in the Puritan Revolution raised them, in some cases, almost to the position of a political commissar. This was going too far for Pepys: but he meant to see that the men got value for the money that was spent in their name and that Divine service should, at least, be conducted without indecency.

It was a tall order. That the pranks of the chaplain of H.M.S. *Sweepstakes* did not seem as extraordinary then as they would now is suggested by the terse comment of the Dean of Rochester recommending one of his brethren for a vacant living: 'He has been a sea chaplain for some years and unlike most of them is a sober well-tempered man.'[12] To proceed to Holy Orders was still the obvious step for a young man who had taken a university degree but had no particular prospect of employment. Poverty might drive them to serve as a chaplain, as was the case with the most famous of them, Henry Teonge. His Diary gives perhaps the most vivid picture we have of life aboard a Restoration man-of-war; certainly, reflecting the personality of its author, one of the most cheerful and good-natured. Teonge was a country clergyman with a wife and family to support. He went to sea in 1675 because he could hold his benefice in plurality with a chaplaincy. His naval pay, modest though it was, thus increased his total income. Sensible, kindly, mature and responsible he stands at the opposite end of the parsonical spectrum from Mr. Bradford of the *Sweepstakes*. No sot, he enjoyed to the full the hospitality and sociability of ward-room life and as a man who had often gone hungry he relished the huge quantity and excellent quality of the food provided at the captain's table or ashore by the English consuls and merchants at the ports at which they called. Teonge took his ministry too much for granted to say much about it. He was conscientious in preaching, although it appears that he delivered the same sermon, or at least preached on the same text, for four Sundays out of five (on the fifth there were prayers but no sermon) in the summer of 1676. None the less when, confined to bed with an attack of influenza, he heard that Lord Mordaunt, a rich young volunteer, had persuaded the captain to let him preach at Sunday prayers he struggled to his feet and prevented it. For an obscure, penniless parson to antagonise a courtier and an aristocrat was a bold act. Teonge may safely be taken as the highest type of man likely to have served as a chaplain in the navy of Charles II. Yet his mental culture, for all that he was a Cambridge graduate and a man of lively mind, would have left Pepys politely pitying. He believed that the marabouts of Tripoli could make fogs to cover their fleet's putting to sea. He thought that Prester John regulated the flooding of the Nile Delta by an elaborate series of sluices and dams for which the Egyptians paid him a kind of water rate.

Pepys was too much of a realist to expect a learned ministry. And his own theological leanings were still vestigially Presbyterian. Were episcopally ordained ministers essential to the service? For his own part he thought not.[13] Still, on grounds of supporting the established order in church and state, he accepted them. And having accepted them he naturally wished to regulate their appointment 'with respect both to the honour of God Almighty and the preservation of sobriety and good discipline in His Majesty's Fleet'.[14] In 1677, that *annus mirabilis* of the Lieutenants' examination and the Thirty New Ships, he established procedures for notifying requirements to the Bishop of London who would then propose suitable candidates. No chaplain was to be admitted on board who had not produced a certificate from the Bishop as to his piety, learning, conformity and other qualifications. The success of the scheme was limited. Compton, the Bishop of London, was touchy and difficult. Hewer, he said, had been rude to him — an accusation that Pepys politely but firmly declined to credit. The list of ships requiring chaplains had reached him at insufficient notice, and he was riled at Captain Langstone preferring his old chaplain to the candidate suggested. Pepys defended the captain. The King and their Lordships had found the style and orthography of a paper delivered by Compton's candidate 'not over-Clerk-like'.* Courteous up to this point Pepys cannot resist the chance to cut the proud prelate down to size:

> . . . And for what concernes myself in ye point wherein yr. Lp. is pleased (in yr. owne right) to observe yr. getting nothing by this employment I beseech you to believe that I who have not in near 20 years service once descended to ye taking of a Fee (though my knowne right) for a Comm[n] or warrant to any-one Lay-Officer in ye Navy neither have nor will ever blemish that costly self-denial of mine by beginning an Imposture on ye Church, towards whose prosperity I shall ever acquit myself as becomes a Dutifull sonn . . .'[15]

A further sign that the right men did not come forward in sufficient numbers may be discerned in Pepys's praiseworthy efforts to make sure that the surplus of seaman's groats should go to the Chatham Chest, not to some greedy official.[16] No doubt if the money had run to it Pepys would himself have devised and conducted a chaplain's examination of his own. How he would have set about it may be seen from the methods he employed in judging the candidates for a chaplaincy at Bridewell. He drew up a table under the following headings and recorded his assessments.[17]

---

* That this was probably not an isolated instance is suggested by the fact that Mr Bradford of the *Sweepstakes* had been approved by Compton. Rawl. A 181, f. 383.

Prayer: (set or ex tempore)
Text
Appositeness: mostly 'none'
Action, voice, tone and stile: 'Presbyterian' 'ordinary'
                              'stiff and schoolboylike'
Age:
Countenance: 'Tolerable' 'Grave' 'Very Good'
            (this applied to nearly all)
Length: 'Convenient' '5 Quarters' 'An hour'
Within-book (i.e. read): about half the candidates.
Learning: 'Little' 'Much latine' 'none'
Orthodoxness: All were good except two: the first 'Good, saving much
            freewill' and the second 'Not conformable to himselfe,
            inferring from Humane history, ye truth of ye Scripture.'

Statistical analysis is still a fascinating instrument: what must it have
been to a man of Pepys's intellectual appetite when it was brand-new?

But it was the material side of his naval achievement in which Pepys
took the greatest pride and felt the keenest pleasure. The Thirty Ships of
1677 represented the largest building programme England had ever
carried through. The size of them – they were all second- or third-rates –
except the *Britannia* a first – increased the power of the Royal Navy in
relation to its rivals, the French and the Dutch, beyond the mere increase
in units. Into their design and their armament had gone, not only Pepys's
comprehensive knowledge, long experience and power of rationalising
and standardising, but the skill of the marine architects, notable among
them Sir Anthony Deane, whose friend and patron he was. Deane, perhaps,
was the only man who could match his combination of technical knowledge
(in which indeed he far surpassed him), managerial skill and varied experience of naval affairs. He had been a master mariner before he turned to
shipbuilding and was at different times in charge of dockyards, victualling
and storekeeping. An artist whose draughts were admired by Evelyn he
was an extremely capable man of business. Above all he could argue and
discuss, unlike the older type of craftsman so perfectly caught in Pepys's
phrase 'their knowledge lying in their hands confusedly'.

At the same time as Pepys, almost single-handed, won the approval of
a by no means docile House of Commons for the Thirty Ships he secured
the acceptance at the Admiralty Board for his establishment of men and
guns. From that point on a commander would be able to calculate with
exactitude the weight of a broadside that a ship of any given rate could
throw. He would know, too, exactly what type of ordnance each ship

would carry and in what numbers. The scientific or as Pepys would have put it 'Mathematick' approach to naval warfare was gaining ground. In all the achievements of this wonderful year the debt to the example of the French and the Dutch and to the active and informed support of the King is evident and freely acknowledged. Pepys was never too proud to learn.

It was much easier to maintain good discipline and efficient service in the dockyards than in the fleet, partly because they were more directly under the hand and eye of the Admiralty and the Navy Board but most because they offered continuity of service. Although they were not troubled with the pretensions of courtiers they had an entrenched aristocracy of their own which Pepys could neither overawe nor afford to disregard. The great dynasty of Pett at Chatham has already been mentioned. The family of Shish, about whom Pepys generally had some waspish things to say, had established similar but less extensive bailiwicks at Woolwich and Deptford and Sheerness. Deane himself was an important figure in his native town of Harwich, for which he and Pepys were elected to Parliament in the spring of 1679. But the general run of resident commissioners were appointed by Pepys in consultation with the King and Duke strictly on merit. Men such as Colonel Thomas Middleton, who served successively as Commissioner at Portsmouth, and Chatham before becoming Comptroller of the Navy exemplify the standards that Pepys demanded. His correspondence with them is not so much taken up with reproving their delinquencies as with palliating the symptoms of incurable financial paralysis – strikes, absenteeism, desertion arising from unpaid wages, press warrants to obtain the necessary labour – the old, old tale of accounts unsettled and supplies refused familiar from earliest days at the Navy Office. Theft and corruption were still common, unsurprisingly; but they certainly did not run riot.

18

Prisoner of State

———

To Pepys the strengthening of the fleet that resulted from his efforts was obviously defensive. It would protect our trade: it would preserve a balance of power against the Dutch and the French. To those who distrusted the good faith, the Protestant sympathies and the constitutional intentions of Charles II any accretion of military power under the direct control of the King was deeply disturbing. A lot had happened since those scenes of intoxicated enthusiasm with which the Diary chronicles the Restoration. To a Catholic Queen Mother had been added a Catholic Queen Consort. The year of 1672 had witnessed the disclosure of the alliance with the militantly Catholic Louis XIV and the Declaration of Indulgence which everyone saw as a transparent disguise for suspending the good old penal laws against the Catholics. And then, in the uproar of enraged Protestant reaction, James, Duke of York, heir to the throne, had publicly avowed his conversion to Catholicism. In the very year in which Pepys had pressed through his naval programme the King had been up to his tricks again in Europe, raising troops nominally to assist the Dutch against the French but bringing them back with unwelcome suddenness and failing to disband them with yet more unwelcome delay. From the distance of three centuries we can see that Charles II was too clever a man to attempt a military imposition of Catholic absolutism *à la Française* on the England he knew. But perhaps we forget that to contemporaries he had shown himself too clever by half. We know that the explanation of this last action lies in a bungled diplomatic *coup*: his contemporaries may be forgiven for not perceiving this. Its effect, anyway, was catastrophic.[1] The anti-Catholic hysteria that ran so deep yet lay so near the surface of English political consciousness in the seventeenth century was ready for its most violent eruption. The popular conviction that the Great Fire had been a piece of Catholic sabotage, the smouldering resentment over the French alliance and the Declaration of Indulgence, all the pent-up hatreds and fears of a society that had known revolution and preferred conspiracy to all other theories of politics, formed one vast pile of psychological tinder. Titus Oates was ready with his flame.

In the hideous light of such a conflagration what shadows would be cast by the figure of Pepys? Pepys, who had married a Catholic wife, whose house was known to be full of altars and images and suchlike superstitious bric-à-brac, who had worked in the closest intimacy with the Duke of York, who had devoted his life to increasing the military power of the Crown and in doing so had shown his resentment of Parliamentary control and scrutiny. He had left only a touch or two to be added by the artist in political denunciation.

The attack, when it came, was launched obliquely. Doubly so, for Pepys, who was struck at through a subordinate, was himself to be the means of striking at the Duke of York. It was a classic example of what is now called the Domino Theory: knock over the front rank and the others will collapse in series. From the energy with which Pepys reacted it seems that he thought this tactical appreciation of the situation dangerously sound.

The mass hysteria of the Popish Plot was unleashed by a murder which has remained one of the most famous of unsolved mysteries. The body of Sir Edmund Berry Godfrey, a London magistrate, was found several days after his disappearance in a place and in circumstances that clearly bore no relation to the manner of his death. The sword that transfixed him had been run through his body when it was already cold and stiff; and the evidence of bruising, like the planting of the corpse, suggests in itself the underworld killing that Professor Kenyon in the most recent and authoritative study of the subject accepts as the most probable explanation. What makes further pursuit of the topic futile is, as Professor Kenyon emphasises, our virtually entire ignorance of a seventeenth-century criminal world that was, to say the least, complex and sophisticated. Isolated incidents such as the Popish Plot or Colonel Blood's attempts to kidnap the ex-Lord-Lieutenant of Ireland or to steal the Crown Jewels present a sudden view of a society and a way of life that we can never see steadily or investigate with any system. That the underworld afforded a number of people a long and various career; that its ramifications extended across frontiers and that it was used and sometimes protected by governments and eminent persons could be demonstrated from the history of the plot alone. But beyond that lies darkness, and the endless, pointless gabble of mendacious hearsay. Criminals do not keep records and if they did they would be worthless. Then as now vanity, egocentricity and the hope of easy money were powerful inducements to talk, but are less compelling as credentials.

How Oates, the psychopath who had been bundled out of a naval chaplaincy for homosexuality, exploited Godfrey's murder belongs to the general story of the plot. The flanking attack on Pepys that developed directly from it, so directly as to suggest a co-ordinating intelligence, was led by a straight professional rascal from a milieu to which Pepys was soon to devote his energetic curiosity and talent for research. William Bedloe, sharper, forger and confidence trickster, had swindled his way across Europe before the happy chance of being in his native land at the time of Godfrey's murder put him in the way of the rich rewards open to the informer. Among the innocent men whom he either sold or did his best to sell to the barbarities of execution on a charge of treason were several who had employed or befriended him. The accusation brought against Pepys's clerk, Samuel Atkins, by so cold-blooded a villain was no random lie. He claimed to have seen Atkins by the light of a dark lantern standing over the corpse of Sir Edmund Berry Godfrey in Somerset House two nights after the murder had been committed by a gang in Jesuit pay. The melodramatic irrelevancies bear the hallmark of perjured testimony. People who deal in lies take the bigger the better for their first axiom. The original allegations against Atkins had been made, much less daringly, by a disgraced gentleman captain who had surrendered his ship* to the Algerines without firing a shot. He deposed that Atkins had asked him to recommend a seaman of his acquaintance who would stick at nothing as Pepys had a grudge against Godfrey and wanted some assistance in murdering him. It was on this absurd story that Atkins was arrested.

Pepys at once set to work organising his defence. By the time the trial came on in February 1679 — Godfrey's body had been discovered in

---

* The *Quaker* ketch. This vessel's name, a strange choice for a man-of-war, proved uncomfortably apt. Her next captain was court-martialled and sentenced to death for striking his top-sails to a Spanish ship in the Bay of Biscay. Since the officer, an old tarpaulin of proven courage, was thought to be unhinged by reason of head wounds, he was to be pardoned after being brought before the firing party. Pepys seems to have found nothing objectionable in this cat-and-mouse cruelty.

mid-October and Atkins had been imprisoned at the beginning of November — he had put together an armour-plated alibi for his young assistant covering the whole of the material weekend during which Godfrey was alleged to have been murdered and Atkins had been, so Bedloe asserted, keeping vigil over his body. The total demolition of the prosecution case marked the first check to the mad, evil hunt on which the nation was hallooing. Even so shameless a liar as Bedloe was discomfited and made to mumble that he might have made a mistake. The key witness was Captain Vittells, whose hot temper was to bring him before the judgment of Pepys and Lord Dartmouth in the next reign. At this point Vittells was captain of a small dispatch vessel on which, that Saturday afternoon, Atkins and two young ladies had been his guests. Such was the hospitality that Atkins when rowed home at midnight by two of Vittells's seamen was in no state to keep vigil over anyone with or without a dark lantern. Lord Chief Justice Scroggs, dismissing the case, seized with relief on its convivial aspect. But it had been no laughing matter for Pepys: still less for young Atkins who had been alternately coaxed and threatened to perjure himself and incriminate his employer by men, Shaftesbury and Buckingham in particular, of whom he must have been terrified. Pepys was amazed and heartened by his courage and staunchness: 'For certainly no youth of his wit and straightness of fortune ever withstood such temptations to have been a villain.'[2]

The grotesque case against Atkins suggests very strongly that he was hurriedly brought in as a last-minute substitute for Pepys himself. On the eve of the weekend during which Bedloe claimed to have witnessed Godfrey's murder Pepys had been unexpectedly summoned to Newmarket by the King. So complete and so public an alibi was too much for the most dedicated perjurer to swear away. But no one, certainly not Pepys himself, thought that he was out of danger: or even that if Atkins got off he would be safe. Friends such as Sir Robert Southwell shook their heads and watched for the fatal stroke: '. . . And Mr Pepys, however prepared, must certainly be destroyed.' This was written two months after Atkins' acquittal, when the Parliamentary attack on Pepys and Deane was swelling in fury and when the King was giving ground to an opposition he could not master. What everyone, friend and foe, seems to have left out of account was Pepys's skill and courage in fighting back. Considering how often this had been demonstrated it was a surprising oversight.

The principal agent of the men compassing his destruction was a figure whose universal shadiness beggars description, a certain Colonel John Scott. The military title, mandatory for ruffians with social pretensions in every age of English history, had perhaps a slender technical validity. Scott *may* have talked the Dutch into giving him command of a regiment but the story that says he did ends with his ignominious dismissal at the first whiff of grapeshot. Killing and firearms, even cannon, certainly feature in his *curriculum vitae* but he took great care never to expose himself to the unpleasant risks attendant on the military profession.

Scott entered Pepys's life under one of his many disguised identities. At the height of the hue and cry after Godfrey's murder he had left London for France in a most suspicious and circuitous manner, riding first to Gravesend, doubling on his tracks by disembarking at Margate and then hurrying to Folkestone where he took passage in a fishing smack. All this cloak-and-dagger activity roused the local officials. Pepys was informed and issued immediate orders to the commander in the channel. But by then Scott was safe in Paris. Not, indeed, that he had much to fear from the police work of a century that knew nothing of fingerprints or photographs, had no system of criminal records and no force specifically charged with keeping an eye on professional criminals. Throughout his long career which included murder, rape, bigamy, fraud, theft, desertion and suchlike Scott rarely seems to have encountered the difficulties on crossing a frontier which beset even the most innocent traveller in the twentieth century. He had begun active life in New England, returned to his native Kent, found his way back to New York and from there to the West Indies where he appears actually to have got as far as the scaffold before his gift of the gab came to his rescue. Next it was England again, then Holland (and his alleged Colonelcy) then Flanders and, at the time of the plot, a regular alternation between London and Paris, selling his services to a number of important people in both capitals. Long after the plot he was apparently in London again and one of Pepys's correspondents records a somewhat inconclusive conversation with him in a Norwegian port in 1683. How much of all this is true no one can tell because almost all of it comes either from Scott's own associates, *ipso facto* untrustworthy, or else from sources whose reliability we cannot evaluate. Pepys collected all the material to which Sir Arthur Bryant has faithfully adhered in his full and vigorous portrait of this entirely odious man.[3] Extraordinary it may sound, but there is nothing incredible in the story: In history as in life it seems that Scott's gift is to render improbability no barrier to belief.

His function in the plot was to establish a treasonable connection between Pepys and the French, thus reinforcing the allegations of secret Catholicism for which there was such a dangerous abundance of circumstantial evidence. Pepys had not been to Paris since his one short visit with Elizabeth just before her death, but his closest colleagues Anthony Deane and Will Hewer had been received at the French court and had met the

principal naval ministers and officials in 1675 when Deane took over two
yachts that he had built for the lake at Versailles. Scott claimed to have
conclusive evidence of Deane's having sold the French secret charts of
English coasts and harbours for the furtherance of a Popish invasion, a
conspiracy of which Pepys had been the mainspring.

Who paid Scott to concoct these stories? A connection with the Duke
of Buckingham, whose morality was never fastidious, seems well established. Pepys himself was satisfied that Shaftesbury was deeply involved:
certainly his lieutenants in the Commons were, notably William Harbord,
brother of Sandwich's young friend and companion in arms who had
lost his life at Sole Bay. And it was Harbord who produced the much more
damaging evidence of Pepys's ex-butler John James who testified to his
old master's secret Romanism. James had been dismissed after he had
been found in bed with the housekeeper by Pepys's domestic musician,
Cesare Morelli. Morelli had been recommended to Pepys in April 1673
by his friend Thomas Hill, the Lisbon merchant, as having 'a most
admirable voyce, and sings rarely to his Theorba, and with great skill'.
To his gifts as an executant he added, as his correspondence shows,
considerable musicianship. But he neither concealed nor paraded his
Roman Catholicism. In Lisbon the Inquisition had apparently found him
too lax, perhaps because of his readiness to associate with foreign Protestants. In London Pepys had, in the early stages of the anti-Catholic
witch-hunt, attempted to convince him of the errors of the Church of Rome
through the agency of his friend James Houblon. Morelli remained un-
shaken. In obedience to the proclamation banishing all Papists from
London he left Derby House for lodgings in Brentford and prepared to go
abroad. James was not behindhand in seizing the opportunity for revenging
himself at one stroke on both his ex-employer and the foreigner who had
cost him his job. The usual rubbish about images, pistols, daggers, cruci-
fixes and the rest was heightened with musical touches of Pepys and
Morelli singing mass together (Titus Oates swore that Morelli was a
Jesuit) and, later, sauced with allusions to Pepys's wind colic.

The importance of James's evidence lies in its extremely full and circumstantial retractation, recorded on his death-bed in March 1680.
Here in a document that cannot be impugned are the names of the men
who paid him, Harbord among them, and here are clearly established the
links that join feeble creatures like James with real villains like Scott.
James had also on his own confession helped to fabricate the third charge
with which Pepys was to be brought down if Popery and Paris failed,
the piracy of the *Hunter* sloop. During the Third Dutch War Balty,
characteristically, and Sir Anthony Deane, who ought to have known better,

embarked on the risky speculation of leasing a king's ship, the *Hunter*, and fitting her out as a privateer. The inherent disadvantage of such a venture was that its success depended on an altogether improbable combination of honesty, discretion, legal punctilio and piratical dash in the captain. Pepys had burnt his fingers in the earlier war over his partnership with Batten and Penn in the *Flying Greyhound*. Where two such knowing old hands had found themselves in some awkward situations it was hardly to be expected that Balty would escape embarrassment. The *Hunter's* captain, obtaining French letters of marque, did his hunting against English ships which were no doubt easier prey than those of the enemy. Even at the time Pepys was alarmed:

> . . . where (as in your Case) the nearness of relation suffices to make me a partaker in the blame, though never so much a stranger to the guilt or matter of it, as you know to how much trouble to me it did in the late case of the Privateer.[4]

Raked up five years later and spiced with a charge of treason against Sir Anthony Deane brought by one of the *Hunter's* captains it gave harmony and elegance to a case that needed something to disguise the total lack of respectable evidence.

In the state of passion and hysteria induced by the anti-Catholic mania (as it seems to us) of the nation and the patent duplicity of the King it was enough, more than enough, to send Pepys and Deane to the Tower. That was on May 22nd, 1679. After the crescendo of the preceding six months the Tower for all its grim associations perhaps afforded a certain tranquillity. Throughout the autumn the storm that had burst on Godfrey's murder had raged unchecked. Danby, the King's first minister, was only saved from impeachment by the Lords: the Duke of York escaped exclusion from the succession by a hair's breadth: the Queen's banishment was voted by the Commons: the Catholic peers were disabled from taking their seats in the Upper House and six of them were sent to the Tower on a charge of High Treason. The King, in a tight corner, showed a boldness, a skill, even a certain tenacity of principle that might if displayed earlier in a more modest degree have prevented the situation from running away with him. He faced the Commons as long as he dared, steadily refusing to throw over his brother or his Queen or even his minister. When he could hold the line no longer he prorogued Parliament on December 30th and dissolved it by proclamation early in February 1679.

At the General Election of the following month – the first since 1661 –

Pepys was busier in securing the return of other members favourable to
the Court than in managing his own campaign. His own constituency of
Castle Rising had shown ungrateful signs of listening to the accusations
of Popery that had, naturally, been revived against him at so propitious
a moment. He thought it wise to reinsure by standing at Portsmouth
(where he was infuriated by the failure of Legge, the future Lord
Dartmouth, the Governor of the town, to unite the Crown interest
behind the candidacy of the Chancellor of the Exchequer) and at Harwich,
where, thanks to the local influence of his fellow-candidate Sir Anthony
Deane they were elected '. . . with an unanimity and excess of courtesy
hardly to be equalled in the case of two (both of Court dependence)
within the whole kingdom'. He was not less surprised than touched by the
generosity of his old enemy, Sir Robert Holmes, in offering to provide
him with a seat in the Isle of Wight. Considering the venom with which
he and Coventry had been used to speak of him in the old days of the
Diary he had good reason. The Revolution of 1688 and Pepys's exile from
public life cast their shadows in the letter he wrote to Legge, reproving
him and contrasting his conduct with that of Holmes. Things might have
turned out very differently for the Dutch task force in 1688 if Holmes
had had command of the fleet and Legge the Governorship of the Isle of
Wight.

In spite of being elected almost without expenditure and with only the
most fleeting visit to the constituency Pepys's electioneering was a disappointment. Castle Rising did turn on its benefactor as a Papist. Sea
officers who ought to have remembered whose bread they ate had supported
opposition candidates. Sir John Berry had even applied for leave to go and
make mischief of this kind at Dover.[5] Pepys spent an unconscionable
amount of time in bringing the full weight of the dockyard interest
behind his friend Sir John Bankes at Chatham. He was returned. It
would indeed have been a bad day for the political stability on whose
growth Professor Plumb has recently concentrated attention if the dockyard towns had turned against the ministerialists. But the results as a
whole left the King even weaker than before. Oates and the plot-
merchants were riding high in spite of Atkins's acquittal. Danby fell,
his life at least saved by Charles's issue of a pardon that he had disdained
to ensure for himself. Shaftesbury took his place once more at the Council
table. At the beginning of March James, the heir-apparent to the throne,
was forced into ignominious exile in the Low Countries.

If Charles could not even protect his own brother, he was powerless
to defend Pepys. On April 21st the old Admiralty Commission was
dissolved. It had included men like Prince Rupert, by no means friendly

to Pepys, who knew enough about the navy to put a spoke in his wheel when they wanted to. But compared to the new Commission which soon asked for and obtained wider powers it had been Paradise. The new Commission's most active members were Pepys's declared enemies and none of them knew anything about naval business. Yet, allegedly to repair this deficiency, he was retained as Secretary. Office on such terms was not worth having. On May 6th in a long and eloquent letter to his old master now in exile he urged the Duke to support his request to the King that he might be relieved of the Secretaryship and appointed, if his expert opinion was thought indispensable, a member of the Commission. He opened his plea by arguing the enfeebled state of his health, particularly of his eyesight 'after almost 20 years continued drudgery in the Navy', but disclosed, unanswerably, its real base in these words:

. . . charged with a new piece of duty, and that not a little one, of informing those who should informe and are to command me, and I remain accountable for all the ill success that should attend my obeying those commands, though possibly differing from my own advice.[6]

James answered with the warmth and loyalty that make him so much more likeable than his more talented brother. But release from an impossible situation was to come too swiftly for any help that he could afford. On April 28th the Commons had appointed a committee under the chairmanship of William Harbord to investigate the miscarriages of the navy. This was the tribunal before which Pepys and Deane were to answer the absurd accusations already described. It was on the strength of them that on May 22nd he was committed to the Tower. But before that the whole of his conduct as a naval official had been attacked with the usual recklessness of political controversy. Every appointment had been corrupt, every contract a swindle, every sympathiser with popery had been favoured. Captain Roydon, late of H.M.S. *Sweepstakes*, took the opportunity of explaining that he had been dismissed for calling his Lieutenant a Papist rather than for the state of his ship disclosed by the Court-Martial. Pepys, although his case needed no such extravagance, answered in kind. Among the papers he prepared for submission to the Committee was a list of the names, salaries and wages of all naval office holders. Prince Rupert, as Vice-Admiral of England and Lieutenant-Admiral of the Narrow Seas, leads off with £469. 5s. 9d. Below him comes the Secretary of the Admiralty, Samuel Pepys esq. The clerk drawing up the schedule had left the salary blank. Pepys in his own hand inserted the word 'Nothing'.[7] In the atmosphere of 1679 objectivity was at a discount.

Yet even then there were men who would not go with wind and tide. Sir William Coventry, not the least formidable Parliamentarian among the critics of the court, spoke up for his old colleague, and cast doubts on the trustworthiness of James the butler. Colonel Norwood, the ex-Deputy Governor of Tangier, whose discussion of gastronomic questions Pepys once thought ill-bred, wrote to him in the Tower with the most heart-warming denunciation of Scott. John Evelyn and James Houblon were among the first and most frequent of his visitors. His friends, his relations, his subordinates all stood by him and, even more gratifyingly, senior sea officers such as Narbrough and Sir John Holmes, brother to Sir Robert, wrote to record their solicitude. After the nightmare of the past few weeks he knew where he was and could begin to plan a counter-offensive.

The core of the enemy position was Paris. So far as it is possible to prove a negative Pepys had already ample evidence that he was *not* a Papist, that Morelli was *not* a Jesuit, or even a priest, that he was not and had not ever been in any way involved in whatever mischief the *Hunter* had got up to during the last Dutch War. But Colonel Scott's allegations might unless they were shown to be false open a short way to the scaffold. Pepys's own direct contacts in Paris were few. But there were friends, close friends, with the best of relations there in every department of life: Houblon with the world of commerce and finance: Southwell with that of government and diplomacy: Evelyn and the Royal Society with the great international world of learning and the arts, a passport sometimes more valuable in highly civilised countries than those issued by politicians. Coventry's nephew, Harry Savile, then serving in the English embassy, was a highly intelligent and valuable source. As an official and an aristocrat with a marked taste for conviviality, a sense of humour and not much use for protocol he was better placed than anyone to initiate inquiries about Scott. Savile at once established that he was a criminal of a particularly unpleasant kind. Pepys pressed the embassy to approach the Marquis de Seignelay, to whom he and Deane were alleged to have sold charts and other information prejudicial to England's security but found it reluctant.* Inquiries such as this could not be prosecuted with the necessary rigour through third parties, however well disposed. Pepys needed a man of his own in Paris.

The obvious choice was Balty. '. . . He being', as Pepys wrote two

---

* Sir Arthur Bryant (*Years of Peril*, 273) seems to attribute this to the deference proper to years and lineage: 'But Pepys was insistent and continued to urge that a direct approach should be made to the old aristocrat.' The Marquis was in fact aged twenty-eight and his father, the great Colbert, was himself the son of a draper.

years later, 'the only person (whome from his relation to me together
with his knowledge in the place and Language, his knowne dilligence
and perticular affection toward me) I could at that tyme and in soe greate
a cause pitch on . . .'[8] Balty was on the point of embarking for Tangier
where he had been appointed Muster-Master and surveyor of the victualling.
The King granted a double request that the Tangier squadron might sail
without him and that he might have leave to go to France. Balty's delight
at exchanging a long and uncomfortable voyage to a subordinate position
in a dismal colonial outpost for independence and an expense account in
Paris may easily be imagined. 'Be also as good a Husband as you can,'
wrote Pepys apprehensively from the Tower on June the 19th in the letter
of instructions he sent him enclosed in a note to Mr. Brisbane, the
Secretary of the Paris embassy, under whose wing Balty was to operate.
But Brisbane was soon afterwards recalled and Balty for six glorious
months was on his own in Paris. For the last three he even had an assistant,
characteristically demanded to support pretensions of Herculean labour,
characteristically resented as implying a slur on what had been achieved
single-handed. This was Balty's finest hour. Absurd, posturing, melodramatic egotist that he was, there is no denying his energy or his anxiety
to maintain his brother-in-law's good opinion. Even his absurdities for
once could be turned to account: posturing and melodrama are highly
congenial to the criminal mind. Balty, it seems probable, got on much
better with the con. men and shysters to whom Scott's trail led than abler
men like Hewer or James Houblon would have done. They recognised him
as a kindred spirit. Certainly he got results. He found the man at whose
house Scott lodged when in Paris, a shady English watchmaker called
John Joyne, and succeeded in persuading him to come over to London
(expenses paid, naturally) to give evidence about Scott's movements and
general character that would have been most unwelcome to the prosecution.
Through Joyne he met other and even shiftier members of Scott's circle,
Sherwin and Foster. Sherwin, like Joyne, had been associated with Scott
in an experimental gun-foundry at Nevers in which both Shaftesbury and
Prince Rupert had been involved. Foster had known Scott well in Paris.
Both were evidently prepared to reminisce in whatever vein their audience
required. But both expected a handsome advance on their memoirs
(Foster had, apparently, written a Life of Scott): and both turned coy at
the idea of appearing in a court of law. From these, and other such sources,
Pepys built up that lurid dossier on Scott's career which is contained in
'my two volumes of Mornamont', still in his Library. Their name is that
of an imaginary castle which Scott at one time claimed to possess.

It was Balty's other great virtue that he would do what he was told.

Pepys, first from the Tower, then from the Marshalsea, latterly on bail at Hewer's house in York Buildings, kept up a steady stream of instructions. All Scott's allegations were to be pursued by checking them with the French naval officers or courtiers with whom Pepys and Deane were said to have done business. If they were dead, their widows or secretaries must be traced and statements taken. Since the great proportion of them were bound to be Roman Catholics they would hardly at the height of the Plot be much use in the witness box. But the gradual accumulation of truth might provide new vantage-points from which Scott might be exposed. Information properly authenticated, widely collected and systematically co-ordinated must in the end triumph over error and deceit. If it were not so, the faith of the Royal Society would be in vain.

How strong that faith was Pepys's own calm confidence best shows. Even at the worst of times the tone of his letters is cheerful, rational and humane. He jokes ruefully with the exiled Duke of York at the attempts to make him out a Papist. He quietens the agitation felt by Mary Skinner and his old father at Brampton. He remembers that other people have their troubles and where he can he tries to relieve them. Almost the last letter in the vast book that contains file copies of his private correspondence over the seventeen years up to his imprisonment is one soliciting a place at Christ's Hospital for a boy whose widowed mother has three other children to support.[9] When he wrote it he was already embattled in his last forlorn Parliamentary stand. From the Tower he sent money to Morelli at Brentwood and courteously explained to another friend why he was in no position to lend him £100.[10] The wisdom and tact with which, from afar, he handled Balty whose zeal might so easily and so disastrously have outrun discretion show a steadiness of nerve not to be found in a man of weak convictions. Once again he was fighting a battle whose nature gave full scope to his deepest instincts and highest powers, the lawyer's passion for justice and skill in argument, the historian's concern for fact and curiosity as to motive, the scientific urge to amass evidence and to criticise it, the artist's search for order and meaning. He was fighting not only for his life but for everything that made it worth living. His talents were volunteers in the service.

That the case never came to a trial was in some ways a relief, but it was undoubtedly a disappointment. Forced into a war not of his own choosing Pepys had thrown all he had into a campaign whose brilliant success surely deserved to be crowned with a great victory. But this was denied him. On June 20th when the law term opened the prosecution were not ready to proceed. Pepys and Deane applied successfully to be removed from the Tower, an exclusively political prison, and recommitted to the

Marshalsea where they would be under the rules of the King's Bench. On July 9th they were admitted to bail in £30,000, a huge sum in the seventeenth century. At the end of the vacation Pepys pressed for a hearing. Joyne the watchmaker had come over from Paris to give evidence: Balty had garnered a neat sheaf of attestations from the French officers named by Scott: even the Marquis de Seignelay in response to a direct approach from Pepys confounded the Embassy's scruples and wrote a letter disposing of Scott's nonsense.[11] Sherwin, too, had come over, uninvited and unexpected. A doubtful asset in the witness box, supposing that his repugnance to it could be overcome, he introduced Pepys to other associates of Scott from whose conversation it transpired that Balty's airy claim to have discredited his allegations in an important particular was itself ill-founded. The Pepys who gently chided his brother-in-law's dangerous mistake was very different from the man who had bullied Elizabeth for far less serious delinquencies only ten years earlier:

> And therefore by the way pray learne of mee this one Lesson, which on this occasion I have Observed not onely you but others of Our Friends, not to have yet met with, vizt to bee most Slow to beleeve what we most wish should bee true . . .'[12]

But in spite of everything the best that Pepys could obtain was a renewal of bail. When term ended in February 1680 he and Deane were released from bail and on June 30th, in face of the continued silence of the prosecution, they were at last discharged. No doubt he owed his freedom to his own exertions. His enemies had found him a tougher nut to crack than the man they had written off as one 'who had known softness and the pleasures of life'. Next to himself he owed most to the affectionate steadfastness of his closest friends: James Houblon, to whom he wrote at once with the first news of his discharge, and Will Hewer, from whose house he was writing. Immediately he had been bailed from the Marshalsea in July 1679 Pepys had written to Balty:

> I am now with Will Hewer at his house, and have receiv'd from him all the care, kindness and faithfulness of a son, on this occasion, for which God reward him, if I cann't.'[13]

Such loyalty cost something to give. Hewer did not then or later share Pepys's imprisonment; not having so far to fall he did not experience the humiliation of sudden, violent and public ejection from power and importance to disgrace and nothingness. He even succeeded in the spring of 1680 to the Treasurership of Tangier which both prudence and necessity prompted Pepys to relinquish. Prudence, both because a rich office is a dangerous possession in a time of political gang warfare and because Tangier by draining public money and providing a billet for Catholic officers might easily have found itself in the eye of the storm: necessity, because a prisoner of state is in no position to discharge public business. None the less Hewer did in his quiet way expose himself to danger in that wild and whirling time. The two most witty and damaging of the pamphlets attacking Pepys specifically couple Hewer's name with that of his master: the first, *Plain Truth or Closet Discourse Betwixt P. and H.*, the second *A Hue and Cry after P. and H.* Both make great play with the high standard of living enjoyed by the two, listing with the lip-smacking gusto of a hungry age the delicacies which James the butler had been accustomed to set out for one of his master's nobler entertainments. They hit, too, at a point where Pepys in the days of the Diary had himself felt misgivings: the magnificence of his coach. It was not so long since the Tudor Parliaments had occupied themselves with sumptuary legislation. How strong was the social prejudice it enshrined a century after Pepys can be seen from Johnson's *obiter dictum* about Garrick's style of life:

> You despise a man for avarice, but do not hate him. Garrick might have been much better attacked for living with more splendour than is suitable to a player.

Both pamphlets employ social jealousy to envenom general and specific charges of corruption. As Sir Arthur Bryant has pointed out[14] *Plain Truth* in particular shows a skill in misrepresenting Pepys's administrative reforms that any propagandist must envy. To take but one example, the line that he had taken (and so carefully explained to Mrs. Pearse) over the vacant pursery of a first-rate is brilliantly traduced into a dodge – attributed to Hewer – for multiplying a single vacancy into five or six and collecting a fee on each. Both men certainly accumulated a great deal more money than could have been saved out of their official salaries but it would be as unfair to deny Pepys's passion for justice, as it would be guileless to accept his 'Nothing' as a true return of his salary. That Hewer accepted Pepys's standards in such matters seems certain from the intimate collaboration of a lifetime. Why did he in fact escape so lightly both at the Plot and at the Revolution? It seems probable that his uncle, Robert Blackborne, who had run the Navy Office under the Protectorate and was now Secretary of the East India Company was a useful relation to have.

To James Houblon Pepys acknowledged in the letter already alluded to '... obligations to you and your family, which nothing but the grave shall, or can, or ought to put an end to'. Later he sent him his picture,

> ... in hopes that, when he sees that, it will be out of his power not to recollect his errands on my score to Westminster Hall, his visit to the lions,* his passings over the bridge to the Patten in Southwark, and a thousand other things which, by his good will, he would never come within the hearing of

and goes on to imagine the Houblon children asking 'was Mr Pepys in these clothes, father, when you used to go to the Tower to him?' It is one of the most charming of Pepys's many charming letters, written from Brampton in November 1680.

He had been brought there by the death of his father, whose last months had been cheered by the knowledge that his kind, brilliant son had eluded the malice of his enemies. Some virulent infection had visited the place, carrying off Pall's husband in the summer and her father at the beginning of October. Pall herself had caught it and only narrowly survived. As on an earlier visit Pepys found affairs — and his sister — in a most horrid pickle. But clearing up the estate offered in little the satisfaction now denied him in official activity.

Not that he was now capable of being idle. He had passed the summer supervising his French Protestant clerk, Paul Lorrain, in the great work of copying and arranging the materials that form the two volumes of Mornamont and in pursuing the literary, historical and scientific studies that had been pushed to one side by his indictment. He saw a good deal of John Evelyn; he resumed his attendance at the Royal Society; he collected material for his great history of the sea. He renewed his contacts with Cambridge and, in September, was commanded to attend the King at Newmarket. Here, fresh from his own experience of playing fox to the Parliamentary hounds, he took down in shorthand (later transcribing it into longhand) the King's famous, some yawning courtiers thought too famous, account of his escape after the battle of Worcester in 1651. He was at Newmarket when the news of his father's death called him to Brampton early in October.

Was the King, as he reminisced, contemplating, weighing the chances of another civil war? There was always, as Professor Plumb has recently pointed out, an air of carpet-bagging about Charles II's Court. The great political fever of the Plot was unmistakably moving to its climax. For

* The Tower served, among its many purposes, as London's zoo.

more than a year Charles had parried, sidestepped, given ground with a
steadiness of nerve that everyone must admire and a coolness perhaps
impossible to a generous nature. When Pepys had been sent to the Tower,
Richard Hampden, son of the great John, was moving the introduction of
a bill to exclude James Duke of York from the succession. Charles had
countered by prorogation and in July, when Pepys was admitted to bail,
by dissolution. In the same month Chief Justice Scroggs had dared to
doubt the truthfulness of Oates and Bedloe in the trial of Sir George
Wakeman, the royal physician, on a charge of attempting to poison the
sovereign. The exposure of this seventeenth-century Doctor's Plot might
have given pause. But in August the King fell dangerously ill without
benefit of medical assistance. James had to be recalled from exile. On
his brother's recovery he was sent abroad again but almost at once appointed
High Commissioner in Edinburgh. A new Parliament, summoned in
October 1679 was immediately prorogued. The King was inching back
but he was not yet ready.

For twelve months he went on proroguing, waiting for an opening in
foreign affairs, waiting for the tide of the plot to ebb. It was only a shift
in the diplomatic scene that, at last, enabled the King to face his Parliament in October 1680. Of the alarming turn that affairs then took Pepys
was informed at Brampton through the correspondence of Hewer and
James Houblon. The possibility of anti-French coalition that Charles
dangled before the Commons was brushed aside. In November the Exclusion Bill passed the Commons who then began to turn their attention to
Tangier, that nest of Papists. But on November 15th William Coventry's
nephew, Halifax, saved the day for the King and Duke in a Lords' debate
that changed our history and enriched our literature. The Exclusion Bill
was thrown out. The rage of the Commons inspired one last set piece of
vindictive wickedness, the impeachment and execution of the old and
harmless Catholic, Lord Stafford. Declining Halifax's compromise
schemes of limiting James's powers, they tried direct bargaining. No
supplies would be voted for Tangier unless Exclusion were granted. In
mid-December Charles, predictably, turned them down: on January 7th
the Commons raised their terms: no supplies at all. On January 10th, as
they were frenziedly voting that the Fire of London was the work of the
Papists, Charles prorogued them. Dissolution followed a few days later.

Pepys was back in London by November 20th. Returning, he had been
robbed by highwaymen near Highgate but what was that with the country
on the edge of civil war? 'Forty-one is come again' was a terrible refrain
to the ears of his generation. The King, however, could see light at the
end of the tunnel. Another twist to the European kaleidoscope had opened

the probability of fresh subsidies from France. With a light heart he summoned his last Parliament to meet at Oxford in March: with a light heart he dissolved them. The French subsidy was secure. By July Shaftesbury was in the Tower. The Stuart counterattack was to be pressed hard and savagely.

In all this Pepys stood on the sidelines. He was not in office: he had not sat in either of the two Parliaments that had been elected since his fall. His sympathies could not for a moment be in doubt, but his talents were not called on until the reign was nearing its end. The power of the Whigs, as Shaftesbury's party had come to be called, was effectively broken by the summer of 1681, yet Pepys was not re-employed until the summer of 1683. He had plenty to do on his own account and there were plenty of public bodies, Christ's Hospital, Trinity House, the Royal Society, his old college, to whom he could be of service. But admirable and useful as these institutions were, they could manage without him. The navy, it seems, could not. Evidence superabounds that the commissioners of 1679 were wholly incompetent. Pepys had seen and said as much in the few weeks he had worked with them. The Dutch and the French intelligence services rapidly confirmed his judgment to their Governments. Above all, Charles II, one of the foremost naval experts in Europe, in charge of the Government and in day-to-day contact with these amateurs certainly knew. Why, once he was master in his house, did he not replace them? Even Pepys confessed himself amazed.

No king ever did so unaccountable a thing to oblige his people by, as to dissolve a commission of the Admiralty then in his own hand, who best understands the business of the sea of any prince the world ever had, and things never better done, and put it into hands which he knew were wholly ignorant thereof, sporting himself with their ignorance . . .[15]

The final phrase perhaps glimpses the depths of frivolity in a nature otherwise shallow. If there is a better explanation it has yet to be provided.

19

Tangier

The autumn of 1680 took off more than old John Pepys and Pall's husband: it took off Balty, at long last, to assume his deferred appointment in Tangier. By the time he had got as far as the Downs he was already complaining bitterly of the weather, the food, the unfairness of life, the insulting treatment he received from those he considered his inferiors at the Navy Office and of Pepys's failure to make the King sufficiently sensible of his past services. The present appointment was '. . . to my misfortune and ruine . . . (for which ware I not more then comon man I shoold Runn to dispaire).' He had been

> . . . towrne from the Bowells of my sweet litill famely; and from my five small babes whoe cryed after their owne father, at my departure from them, and that to, after all my youth Spent in his Majesty's service in Ever and all dangers and trubles . . . to have at last noe other recompence than to be sent to the Divill for a New yeares gift.

Balty's devotion to family life had not been so touchingly apparent during his time in Paris, except for a suggestion, outrageous to the prudent Pepys, that he should bring home a French tutor for his children. As he recounted the misadventures of his journey, he reflected 'how full of thornes my life hath bine, and that I, and only I of My age Ever had the like measure in this world, from my first Essay in Bloody fights, both at home and a broad, to all the dangerous imployments on shore . . .' This was pitching it a bit strong for his years as Muster-Master at Deal. '. . . (Lord why was I borne) shall I never have rest from fightgs and stormes . . .' Apparently not, if he were to judge from '. . . the slights the world . . . show me dayley at the Navey office &c: beleeving me, most Ignorent in imployments and of less sowle then any other.' 'Sowle' was so obviously Balty's long suit that their imperceptiveness is unforgivable. His brother-in-law could have easily put them right about that. And it was with appeals to his brother-in-law, greased with a fulsomeness and a flattery that would offend a much grosser taste, that this very long letter[1] ends.

Pepys, who had no job himself, who had had his work cut out to secure Balty's reversion to the Tangier post, saw things very differently. At least the man was provided for, out of harm's way and without much opportunity of spending or borrowing money. His wife was under no such inhibitions. Pepys soon settled matters by packing her and the children off to Brampton to live rent-free. But even that did not answer. Ester St. Michel was no Elizabeth. Bombarded with furious injunctions to live within the twenty shillings a week that he reluctantly allowed her, exhorted with the example of Elizabeth's household accounts 'even to a bunch of carrot and a ball of whiteing which I have under her own hand to show you at this day',[2] she won in the end through her invincible incompetence. Still, Brampton, like Tangier, did form an obstacle to extravagance.

Pall had fallen ill again, or perhaps she had never properly recovered, about the time that Balty was arriving in Tangier. She came to London, vacating Brampton for the St. Michels, but was not well enough to look after her children, Samuel and John. The two boys were boarded with a schoolmaster in Huntingdon; Pepys, who was to make each in turn his heir, paid for their maintenance in a cheese-paring style. The bargain price for victualling and clothing people one did not see had become a reflex. Finally Mary Skinner's scapegrace brother Daniel had been sent to the Barbados with a letter of introduction to Will Howe, Sandwich's old steward, now married and settled there. Will Howe found him 'something soft in his Disposition' and disinclined, like so many of Pepys's young protégés, to regular employment. But the letter bearing this news did not begin its homeward journey until June 1681 so that for most of the year Pepys was freer than usual from family concerns.

He made the most of his liberty. His two charming and lively young cousins, Lady Mordaunt and Mrs. Steward, enjoyed the chief share of his gallantries. For ten years past they with his friend Thomas Hill, the Lisbon merchant, had formed a quartet expert in all the sighings and teasings of an *amitié amoureuse*. And the music, which had been by his own account the only relaxation of the days when he was new-modelling the navy, took its proper place again as the true passion of his life. Morelli on Easter Monday 1681 sent him the score of some operas he had transscribed for him and promised the immediate delivery of 'them songs wich You intend to sing with Mrs Houblon'. There were occasional commands to attend the court at Newmarket or Windsor. There were even faint echoes of his past, as when Hewer eagerly told his master that when something had been 'moved in Counsill relating to salutes, ye King was pleased to respite the doeing anything therein till they had discoursed you: this Mr Blathwaite* acquainted me with and desired me to signify the same to you . . .'³ Was there a chance of a come-back or was Hewer whistling to keep his master's spirits up? Pepys, whatever his secret hopes, acted on the principle he had impressed on Balty of being most slow to believe what he would most wish true. He threw his energies into reviving the mathematical school at Christ's Hospital which had drifted into torpor through the appointment of a man who was far too learned to bother himself with elementary teaching. He set out to win prestige for the foundation by arranging that Verrio should be commissioned to paint a grand scene of the mathematical scholars being received by the King. In the picture Pepys himself appears in a furred aldermanic gown borrowed from Sir Thomas Beckford, the great navy contractor. Although it was not finished until 1685 (and the King is therefore James and not Charles) Pepys borrowed Beckford's gown in February 1682.⁴ The heavy, rolling figure, curiously foreshadowing Reynolds's magnificent portrait of Johnson, the wide eyes and strong face so much more eloquent than the more measured statements of other likenesses taken in middle age, may therefore express the frustrations of an uncertain retirement.

To complete retirement Pepys could, no doubt, have reconciled himself. He had interests enough to fill ten lives: his power of adapting himself to circumstance was his most marked characteristic. That he should talk on his visits to Cambridge of the happiness to be found in breaking away from affairs and devoting the rest of his life to learning was true of his nature. On August 8th, 1681, at nine o'clock at night one of his friends there sent off a special messenger to tell him of the sudden death of the Provost of King's.

* William Blathwayt, soon to be Secretary-at-War, like Pepys a prototype of the professional administrator.

. . . the preferment is 7 hundred pounds per annum and I am sure you would be as acceptable a man as the King could present unto it so that if no time be lost I should with all the joy imaginable salute you Provost . . .

Pepys was attracted: he thought his academic qualifications inadequate but owned the '. . . possibility of supplying, by some other way of usefulness to the College, what I should fall short in of knowledge.' But what determined him against standing was his desire not to intrude. He had heard that there was a Fellow of the College already recommended to the King by George Legge, an old pupil.[5] Once again, this time inadvertently, Legge had got in the way.

The loss, if any, was to Cambridge. Pepys's friends there, to judge from his correspondence, were either cranks like Dr. Vincent of Clare Hall or amiable fuddlers like Dr. Peachell, the Master of Magdalene. Dr. Vincent's magpie mind recommended itself to Pepys by a collection of Conjectura Nautica. He valued himself most however on inventions such as

. . . a way of writing which can never be deciphered. It beares the reading, but a very few Minutes, and then its characters vanish . . . by which meanes the writer is secured . . . against Curiosity, sawciness or Accidental discoveries.

Dr. Vincent wondered whether the King or the Duke of York would think it worth a thousand pounds. 'I reckon it to be much more worth to a foreign Prince engaged in wars.' Pepys in a long and courteous letter demonstrated its entire worthlessness.[6] Undeterred Dr. Vincent communicated to him his experiment '. . . of relieving and interrupting the noctilucal flame . . . to find by it ye hour of the night upon a watch'.[7] He had resolved to leave Cambridge.

That happy place has been my abode from seven years of age: & whether my spirits are overcharged or insufficiently nourished by . . . ye *occultus vitae cibus* [the hidden food of life] of ye place I know not: but this I know I must transplant if I will grow any longer . . .

He thought of moving to London or Bury St. Edmunds and there 'setting to work on those two great questions Resistance to a Lawful Prince and Passive Obedience.'[8] None the less Pepys set a real value on his learning and years later granted his request for £25 to buy a rare historical work that was coming up for auction.[9]

The true centre of Pepys's intellectual life was that group of Fellows of the Royal Society, Evelyn, Southwell, Petty, with whom, when they were out of London, he maintained a voluminous correspondence. Even in the depths of the country they retain an urbanity that makes the likes of Dr. Vincent sound provincial:

I am here among my children which is at least an innocent scene of life, & endeavour to explain to them the difference between right & wrong. My next care is to contend for that health which I lost by sitting many years at ye sackbottle soe that to keepe my selfe in idleness and in motion is a great part of my discipline . . .[10]

Thus Sir Robert Southwell from his country house near Bristol. It is the tone of Pepys's proper circle. People who write like that are too grown-up to play with invisible ink or to occupy themselves with the stale arguments for the Divine Right of Kings. But they are not too superior to enjoy the little things of life. Among the letters of these eminent men Pepys has preserved a quack advertisement ('My Rupture is Cured!') and a letter to Charles II from the King of Bantam 'perfum'd with the musky odoure of sincerity' requesting 'of your love that you would send us by every ship sailing to Bantam Gunpowder and Great Guns and Match and Bullets and wherein to put the powder and match . . .' A well-conditioned mind requires diversion.

The main preoccupation of these years, the use to which the Provostship would have been put, was the research and the assembling of materials for the great history of the sea. Evelyn with characteristic generosity put the treasures of his library and the fruits of his own labours on the Third Dutch War at the disposal of his friend (the books and manuscripts are still in the Pepys Library but Evelyn's own work has, alas, vanished). He warned him eloquently of the hazards of the undertaking:

. . . 'tis not easily to be imagined the sea and ocean of *papers*, *treaties*, *declarations*, *relations*, *letters* and other pieces, that I have ben faine to saile through, reade over, note, and digest, before I set pen to paper; I confesse to you the fatigue was unsufferable, and for the most part did rather oppresse and confound me than inlighten, so much trash there was to sieft and lay by, and I was obliged to peruse all that came to hand . . .'[11]

And his heart-cry, uttered four months later, echoes in the mind of every practitioner of the craft.

It is not imaginable to such as have not tried, what labour an historian (that would be exact) is condemned to. He must reade all, good and bad, and remove a world of rubbish before he can lay the foundation.[12]

Pepys, apparently, was not a whit discouraged. But the first gleams of return to public life broke, for a moment, through the historical cloudbank. In May 1682 he was invited to accompany the Duke of York on a voyage to Edinburgh and himself to receive the freedom of Newcastle-upon-Tyne. It was not much, but it was something. Unfortunately the expedition was marred by disgrace and disaster. The *Gloucester* in which the Duke was sailing was wrecked in calm clear weather close inshore through the carelessness of the pilot. Inexcusably, nearly all the ship's company were lost though the Duke, his footman, and even his dog, were taken off with an observance of ceremony disgusting even to that age of excessive formality.* The public horror was in many hearts compounded by private grief for the loss of Pepys who was assumed to have accepted the Duke's pressing invitation to join him in the *Gloucester*. Happily he had preferred an ampler berth in one of the escorting yachts. All this agitation supplanted the excitement of travel: his letters tell us little about his only visit to Scotland: like almost every visitor he was nauseated by the abysmal standards of personal hygiene; like almost every visitor for the next hundred years he was much taken with the beauty of Glasgow and, by contrast, says nothing of Edinburgh. He stayed at Berwick, made an expedition to Holy Island, was entertained at Seaton Delaval (the pre-Vanbrugh house), fêted at Newcastle and shocked by the princely state kept by the Bishops of Durham.

Back in London he was rapturously received by the Houblons and the ladies of Winchester Street, Lady Mordaunt and Mrs. Steward. Once the excitement was over the rest of the year passed uneventfully. He was defeated over the appointment of a mathematical master at Christ's Hospital. One learned man simply made way for another learned man. What Pepys had intended as a polytechnic was taken over for a research fellowship. He resigned from the School's Committee. On the domestic front a tolerable quiet reigned. Balty had popped up again in January, returning from Tangier unannounced and without first obtaining leave. His excuse was the non-payment of his salary. Pepys quickly smoothed things over with the officers of the Navy Board, enlisted the good offices of Lord Brouncker and succeeded in getting Balty, lachrymose and loquacious as ever, aboard a vessel bound for Tangier early in March. A silence of

* For this the ubiquitous Legge seems to have been largely responsible. See Pepys's long and circumstantial letter to Hewer, printed in Howarth, 133–6.

fifteen months ensues in the surviving documents broken at the end of June 1683 with fresh mewlings 'to [his] Deare Though most cruell Benifactor to clearly thus forg[et] and leave in afflictions, in a hellish Torred-zone, a Creatur of your Owne makeing, who never yett Dishonoured you . . .'13 By the time this letter reached England Pepys was on his way to answer in person and at once its somewhat theatrical plea for '. . . Redemption from this hell, this hell of Brimston and fire, and Egipts plaugues.'

Not that Balty's *cri du cœur* had supplied the initiative. The enormous expense of the Tangier garrison and the vast capital investment of constructing the mole were probably beyond the resources of any English government of the seventeenth century. They certainly were for a King who had to rely on French subsidies. The decision, long overdue, was, at last, taken to liquidate the commitment: to slight the fortifications, blow up the mole and evacuate the population. It was fitting that Pepys who had entered public life as the protégé of Mountagu, the champion of the Tangier policy, who had lined his pockets out of its Treasurership ('one of the best flowers in my garden'), should assist at its obsequies. Will Hewer, who had succeeded him in this rewarding horticulture, was also of the party. It was completed by Henry Sheeres, a versatile military engineer, the chief constructor of the mole, whom Pepys had once suspected of designs on Elizabeth's virtue, William Trumbull, a clever young barrister and Fellow of All Souls with whom Pepys had corresponded on learned questions, Dr. Thomas Ken, the Canon of Winchester who had won Charles II's amused respect by refusing to put up Nell Gwynn, and, in command of the whole expedition, the ever-recurrent George Legge, now raised to the peerage as Baron Dartmouth.

Tangier was Pepys's second spring. At two days' notice he left London to join the *Grafton* in Portsmouth harbour. What he was to do was still hidden from him. But that he was to act once again as a senior (and highly paid) Government executive in naval business of high importance was plain beyond doubt. The winter of unemployment was over. For his biographer too the earth brings forth her increase: Pepys kept a journal of the whole episode from his setting out from Lambeth on July 30th to his going on board the *Mountagu* in Tangier Bay on December 1st to take passage for Spain and thence to England. And one other member of the party, Sir William Trumbull as he had then become, wrote down his own recollections in the Autobiography he composed some thirty years later. The *Journal Towards Tangier* is not to be compared either for quality or extent with the Diary: but it *is* a later work from the same hand. Sir William Trumbull *was* writing a long time after the events he describes

but he was a highly intelligent and well-informed observer. His autobiography[14] is unsafe in details (e.g. he claims to have embarked on May
9th when the real date was August) but there is an astringency about his
impressions that commands respect. '. . . Sir H. Sheares had written a
book in commendation of Tangier and so was sent with us to confute
every article he had so industriously praised.' French authorities confirm
his assertion that Charles II had done his best to sell Tangier to Louis XIV.
He had, unknown apparently to Trumbull, as a last resort even tried to
raise a bid from the Portuguese. The secrecy that surrounded the whole
affair is indeed understandable. According to Trumbull it was not until
they were off Cape St. Vincent that Dartmouth opened his commission:

> . . . and when he had acquainted Mr Pepys, Sheers and myself with this
> secret we lookt upon one another as those do (at a foolish sport) who
> are equally smutted. But especially ye former [Pepys] who from ye value
> he put upon himself, made him luke upon this as a distrust of him,
> & so an offence equall to sacriledg: However there was no Remedy:
> & so necessity made us (as it does other men) pretty good philosophers.[15]

The picture of Pepys's discomfiture probably owes much to Trumbull's
annoyance three years later when he asked for a man-of-war to carry him
as ambassador to Constantinople. This traditional privilege '. . . of late
yeares upon frivolous reasons (too long to be here mentioned) had been
left off and was deny'd now by positive Mr Pepys.'[16] Certainly Pepys's
Journal shows that Dartmouth had confided in him the whole purpose of
the expedition before they sailed down channel. Trumbull was not let into
the secret for another three weeks. Both men were joined, Trumbull as a
professional lawyer, Pepys as a lay assessor, in a commission to estimate
the value of the property for which compensation might be claimed by the
citizens and to advise Dartmouth on this point in his capacity as
arbitrator. In fact Dartmouth relied on Pepys's judgment and advice over
a far wider range of issues. Perhaps the King foresaw and intended this.

When Pepys received the summons to start at forty-eight hours'
notice, he tidied his desk of correspondence and bought an outfit that suggests a Victorian nanny equipping herself for a visit to an east-coast
watering-place. Galoshes and a sea-gown, plenty of warm underwear
and flannel next to the skin. Nor, as Sir Arthur Bryant points out, did he
neglect the opportunities for reading offered by a long sea-voyage. The
regular intercourse with sea officers would form an ideal background for
serious naval studies: Tangier, the object of the expedition, dictated the
choice of several works on fortification: the proximity of Spain and the

probability of making an expedition there caused him to include a number of the Spanish books in which his library was so rich:[17] for entertainment there was his favourite author Fuller, represented this time by his history of the Crusades, and Butler's *Hudibras*, enjoyed at last: there were, of course, music books and some works of religion. Pepys had been charged with finding a chaplain for Lord Dartmouth and on the advice of his learned cousin by marriage, Dr. Gale, High Master of St. Paul's, selected Dr. Ken, the author of the two beautiful hymns in the Manual for Winchester Scholars which are known to generations of Anglicans as the Morning and the Evening hymn. His fearless moral courage has already been alluded to: besides refusing to countenance Charles II's open infidelities he had earlier, when chaplain at The Hague, reproved the future William III for bullying his wife.

To meet and escort him to Portsmouth Pepys spent the second night of his journey at Winchester, dining next day in hall with Ken who was a Fellow of the College as well as a prebendary of the Cathedral. They reached Portsmouth the same evening. A week later, on Thursday August 9th, they slept for the first time aboard the *Grafton*. Dartmouth came on board next morning and the expedition sailed out of harbour to anchor in St. Helen's. The prevailing westerlies kept them there for nearly ten days, during which Dartmouth revealed the purpose of the voyage to Pepys. The surprise was complete. Most of the time that they were wind-bound Pepys spent writing letters or being entertained either ashore or aboard by their companions. The valetudinarian middle-aged widower ate and drank more discreetly than the young man who had delighted in the naval conviviality of twenty years before. For the rest the only events of interest were the arrival of Colonel Wyndham's yacht, notable as being the only gentleman known to Pepys who sailed purely for pleasure, and seeing a Turk severely whipped and his beard singed for attempting unnatural vice.

When the wind at last came round to the east of south two days' pleasant sailing brought them to anchor in Plymouth Sound. Hewer went ashore to visit relations so Pepys took Trumbull with him to pay two calls on the past. The first to Mount Edgcumbe whose châtelaine was one of his old charges, Lady Anne Mountagu, now wife to Sir Richard Edgcumbe: the second to St. Nicholas island[18] to see Lambert, the last great survivor of the Cromwellian régime. Pepys, perhaps from the force of earlier habit, refers to him as 'my lord Lambert', thus acknowledging the peerage granted by Oliver. The interview, it seems, was unproductive. Lambert was within a few months of his death and had long been ga-ga (fortunately, if such a condition may ever be termed fortunate: it had protected him from Oates's accusations of complicity in the Popish Plot). Trumbull says nothing of it in his autobiography. But the visit is characteristic of Pepys; he could not anchor in sight of the prison that held a great historical figure and not try to see him.

Next day after great comings and goings from shore they sailed for Tangier. For most of the first week the weather was very rough. Pepys was seasick and Hewer prostrated. But on the last day of August both wind and weather came fair. At dinner in the cabin (which Hewer was still too unwell to attend) there was 'a good deal of music and good humour'. In the afternoon Pepys walked the deck with Dartmouth and in the evening he read and discussed a book on the jurisdiction of the Admiralty with Trumbull alone in their cabin. He found him agreeable company though he had been peevish during the rough weather. Life went on in this agreeable manner, enlivened by a good deal of naval gossip when they entertained or were entertained by the captains sailing in company. By September 7th, when they were in the latitude of Finisterre it was warm as well as sunny. Awnings were rigged. At a party to celebrate the anniversary of the King's recovery from illness the gunner got so drunk that he had to be put in the bilboes all night. As they sailed past the mouth of the Tagus Dartmouth formally communicated his instructions to both Pepys and Trumbull. Off Cape St. Vincent Pepys and Ken argued hotly about the existence of spirits. Pepys's attitude, maintained through a long and careful accumulation of evidence for psychical phenomena, was what one might expect of a Fellow of the Royal Society. Ken based his position, interestingly, on the authority of the ancient authors rather than the Bible. On September 13th they opened the straits and came to an anchor in the Bay of Tangier at ten o'clock the following morning.

Relief at being safely arrived was tempered by the discovery that the place was closely besieged by the Moors. This was not at all the kind of thing that Trumbull had bargained for when he weighed up the loss of his vacation business against his fee for service at Tangier. Pepys too was not one of those who instinctively march to the sound of the guns. But his tenacity, as in the days of the plague, easily mastered his qualms. He had come to do a job and he was going to do it. His first reaction to the place and to the sight of the enemy camp is thus neither aesthetic nor self-regarding but professional: 'But Lord! how could ever anybody think this place fit to be kept at this charge, that by its being overlooked by so many hills can never be secured against an enemy.'

Old Tangier hands like Sheeres and some of the captains who had often served on the station looked on this state of affairs as natural. England never came near attaining local superiority during the whole of her tenure

of Tangier. On the contrary total disaster was always a possibility, sometimes advancing but never receding out of sight. The day that Fuzzy
Wuzzy broke a British square had dawned at Tangier two centuries before
Kipling and the Mahdi. In 1664 Lord Teviot, the Governor and
Commander-in-Chief, had been ambushed in a wood near the town and
annihilated with nearly all the officers and the best troops of the garrison.
In the great siege of 1680 only the magnificent leadership of the army
officers under Sir Palmes Fairborne and the presence of a powerful naval
squadron under Admiral Herbert had preserved the town after the outer
forts had fallen. How precarious a toehold Tangier was may be gauged
by the fact that the bones of Teviot's men were still left bleaching in the
wood a few miles outside the walls.

Fairborne had been mortally wounded in the closing stages of the action
in which he had shown the highest military qualities, living just long
enough to hear of the great victory in which the Moors had been driven
back. Sheeres who had served with him throughout the siege and for many
years earlier wrote of him:

> He was a very worthy, able and brave officer, who had made it his
> speciall study to qualify himselfe for his Majesty's service here where
> he had been an officer for neare 18 yeares and I am oblig'd in Justice to
> his memory to avow that (I believe at least) his Majesty hath not a
> subject in his three kingdoms of more proper qualification for this
> post.[19]

His successor who came aboard the *Grafton* shortly after she dropped
anchor was a man of a very different type. Colonel Percy Kirke, immortalised in the name 'Kirke's Lambs' given to his regiment in ironical
tribute to the atrocities with which they were credited after the defeat
of Monmouth's rebellion, was a coarse, drunken brute who commanded a
drunken regiment. Pepys was no prude but the deepest impression he
leaves on the reader of his Journal is disgust at the gross indecency and
lurching sottishness of Kirke and his men. The endless dirty stories of
the Governor's table-talk passed from the distasteful to the unendurable:
and before long Pepys and Ken withdrew from the Government Mess to
dine in each other's company. In Pepys's view Kirke's manners and morals
were reflected in the cruelty and corruption of his administration. There
were ugly stories of soldiers beaten to death with no pretence of legality:
of Jewish refugees returned to the tortures of the Spanish Inquisition
because they could not raise the bribes that Kirke demanded: of rape and
robbery and bullying of the citizens and their wives. Kirke personified

what Pepys called 'the bestiality of this place'. 'Everything,' he wrote, 'runs to corruption here.'

The effect was intensified by the enclosed nature of Tangier society. As an earlier Governor had written '. . . [we] see nothing but Moores and the four ellements and are deprived of all civill and State conversation.'[20] It certainly made itself felt even in the work that Pepys and Trumbull had come to do:

> From Wednesday morning to Thursday morning continually busy till 8 or 9 at night without an interval but only to dinner, and then presently again to receive the claims of people to propriety. But in one word so silly and supine from all of them even the people of most understanding among them, that it is plain there was a habit of disorder and forgetfulness of all method and discipline in [all] they did, even in their own private concernments, taking such evidence for their security as would not be worth sixpence in Westminster Hall . . . So that I think it is impossible for us to give any tolerable report of them, to do either the King right or them, in which Dr Trumbull and I do greatly agree and discourse of it.[21]

Pepys, it is plain, did not like Tangier. Quite apart from the vile tone set by Kirke, the life did not agree with him. The mosquitoes were terrible: the weather, often cold and wet: the women a dowdy lot, except for Lady Mary Kirke, and even she had suffered from living in Tangier. He caught a fearful cold that kept him indoors for most of November. Hardly was he over that before he was 'mightily frightened this morning with my old swimming in my head at my rising'. Perhaps as a prophylactic he adopted the curious specific of washing his feet and thighs in brandy. His health was by no means the only cause for alarm. He much disliked riding outside the walls with Kirke and Lord Dartmouth: the Moors were uncomfortably close, totally unscrupulous and rode like lightning. What if they took it into their heads to seize the Commander-in-Chief and his party? What indeed! And Kirke who had himself once led an embassy to the Emperor of Morocco seems to have encouraged Dartmouth to consider sending Pepys and Trumbull to Fez to negotiate a treaty covering the withdrawal. Dartmouth toyed with the idea for some days but at last, much to Pepys's relief, discarded it. Since he had also been proposing to cheat the Emperor over the amount of gunpowder to be left as the price of an unopposed evacuation it seems probable that had Pepys found himself charged with so unenviable a mission, his biography would have ended at this point.

After the detestable Kirke one of the first people Pepys met before going ashore was Balty 'who is mightily altered in his looks, with hard usage as he tells me'. To a degree the alteration must have extended to character since there is no further mention of him, good or bad, during the three months of Pepys's stay. Business and ill-health no doubt restricted the opportunities of social life but the stratification of an imperial outpost perhaps made it difficult for the confidential adviser to the Governor and Commander-in-Chief to hob-nob with the Agent General and Surveyor of the Victualling. The business, unsatisfactory as it was, was soon settled. By October 17th Pepys had estimated the net total payable by the King at £11,243. 17s. 4d. of which only about £7,000 was due to freeholders, the remaining £4,000 odd being in respect of leasehold properties granted by five landlords who had all been either Governors or Deputy Governors. This had, in the inextricable confusion of public and private expenditure, posed the real problem. As Pepys wrote to the local assessor joined with Trumbull and himself, the great bulk of the Commissioner's work was to assess 'stores and workmanship expended upon private Properties att his Majesty's charge'.[22] Even before the work was finished Trumbull was agitating to be sent home, complaining that each day of term lost him ten guineas in fees. Pepys and Dartmouth agreed that his true motive was cowardice. Both were contemptuously glad to see the last of him as he climbed eagerly into the boat of a ship bound for England with letters on October 20th.

In the following two months Pepys's official duties took little of his time. He pursued his general reading and his studies of naval matters with unflagging application: he saw more of the day-to-day life of a fleet than he had done since the Restoration: he talked with an interesting group of senior captains at dinner in the great cabins, admiring unwillingly the neatness of those ships whose commanders kept the best table. He saw a great deal of Ken and came to know Dartmouth intimately. The days at Tangier, at first sight so remote, constitute an intensive rehearsal for the last act of his official life. Reading his Journal it is difficult to escape the conclusion that this is no effect of historical hindsight. Pepys was amassing detailed, up-to-the-minute information, scrutinising, weighing, planning, with a view to a complete administrative overhaul of the navy: his historical inquiries, serious and deep as they were, were in parenthesis to this immediate purpose. Everything, even his conversations with Ken, was to lead somewhere, to mean something more, in the years that lay ahead. The great second Secretaryship, the Special Commission of the Navy, the Revolution of 1688, the Non-juring circle in which the sturdy anti-clerical of the Diary was to end his days, all cast their shadow over the Journal Towards Tangier.

If we are sometimes reminded of the young Clerk of the Acts eagerly questioning, sifting, drawing conclusions, we ought to remember how different a man it was with whom Dartmouth and the rest had to deal. He knew what success was and how little it could count for against personal sorrow or political intrigue. The higher value he put on honesty, courage and independence of judgment is reflected in his attitude to Ken. Not content with having refused to toady to William of Orange and Charles II, who were at least too shrewd not to recognise moral courage when they saw it, Ken had reproved the vices of Tangier and its officers in a sermon that Pepys describes as 'very fine and seasonable but most unsuccessful'. The young Pepys would have been more concerned to be on the winning side: the old Pepys respected and liked Ken the better. Four weeks later he even joined him in 'very high discourse' with Kirke 'about the excessive liberty of swearing and blaspheming we observe here'.

The contrast with Dartmouth is extreme. Although he certainly shared their views and was, after all, Commander-in-Chief he was too frightened of making enemies at home and too sceptical of Charles II's reliability to act on his own judgment. Of that judgment Pepys formed an ever higher opinion. Early in October Dartmouth showed Pepys and Trumbull a draft of his public announcement to the citizens of the intended destruction of Tangier: '. . . wholly taken out [of] my notes that I gave him, but with many good improvements that were really very good and wise and shows him to me to [be] a man of very good understanding and consideration.' Turning, as they often did, from the sterile question of Tangier to the state of the navy, they found a remarkable unanimity as to symptoms, cause and cure. The root of the trouble was indiscipline (Pepys linked this with corruption in one of those self-renewing movements so dear to historical theorists) and the root of that was the Stuart brothers themselves, especially the King. As Pepys himself noted:

> The King's familiarity with commanders and under-officers makes them insolent, presuming upon their access to the King, and frights poor commanders or others their superiors from using their just authority (especially poor tarpaulins) considering what they say of the King's familiarity with those that offend.

Dartmouth, specifically charged by the King to take the opportunity offered by the Tangier voyage of restoring discipline in at least part of the fleet, did not dare: '. . . such is the power of interest and fear of making enemies at home that there is not any one thing that he has durst to rectify . . .' Dartmouth 'notes very soberly that these princes are so much fonder of a penitent sinner than a constant friend, that he prays to God that they may not live to see their friends repent'. Rivalry and political intrigue are foremost in his mind. Will the King back him against his predecessor on the station, Admiral Herbert? He declared to Pepys that there was not room for them both in the service, comparing their case to that of Sir Robert Holmes and Sir Edward Spragge 'when the latter speaking then, as himself do now, said that he was willing to leave it to the King which he would choose, Holmes or him, and that it would spoil his whole service to make use of both'. That was the point, surely. Spragge had gone to the King and spoken out at the risk of his whole career. It was a step of which Dartmouth was temperamentally incapable.

Much as Pepys commended Dartmouth's grasp of naval problems, heartily as he concurred in his pessimistic view of the King's steadfastness, it is doubtful on the very full evidence of the Journal whether he would ever have chosen him to command in chief. For the moment they were allies, united on a common programme of naval reform, each anxious to protect or promote the interest of the other. Dartmouth opened his mind to Pepys to an extent that sometimes recalls the *tête-à-têtes* with Sandwich or Coventry. But it was not the same relationship. Dartmouth, essentially, was the client, hoping that Pepys would give him a good report when they got back to England. It is here, in the winter of 1683–4, that one can find the best evidence for what Pepys must have felt in that crucial winter five years later. The urgency of that crisis left him no time for recording his thoughts and anxieties: the swift and total ruin of his cause made any such retrospect bitter and unprofitable.

Besides the generous rate — £4 a day — at which Pepys was paid, the great attraction of his employment at Tangier was the opportunity of going to Spain. At last in December he and Hewer arrived in Cadiz to stay with Mr. Hodges, a close friend and commercial associate of James Houblon. Pepys had prepared for Spain with the excitement of the born tourist and the system that he brought to everything he did. He knew what he wanted to see and whom he wanted to meet: best of all he brought with him an appetite for new impressions and a delight in observing local peculiarities. No English traveller ever deserved better luck or had worse. His first, his only, continental holiday since Elizabeth's death was ruined by the weather. At Tangier the wind had howled and the rain had beaten down. In Cadiz and Seville it was even fouler. Floods made travel impossible, or nearly so. None the less Pepys forced his way through the elements to some, at least, of his objectives and garnered a small store of those notes on behaviour and appearances that give the Diary its fresh and idiosyncratic quality. Of more particular interest are the notes he took on the Spanish arrangements for training navigators.

The weather was not the only depressing part of his stay in Spain. The drunkenness and indiscipline of English naval officers was especially mortifying in a foreign port. Pepys was eager to be back where he could put his hand to the work he knew. Remorselessly the weather and Dartmouth's indecisiveness combined to prevent his sailing before the beginning of March. After a rough and slow passage Pepys landed at Portsmouth on April 3rd. It had been a longer absence than he had bargained for: 248 days: but at £4 a day that earned him nearly £1,000. He went straight to Whitehall to make his report to the King. Six weeks later, on May 19th, 1684, the incompetent Admiralty Commission was dissolved and Pepys was appointed Secretary for the Affairs of the Admiralty of England at a salary of £2,000 a year. No professional administrator had ever reached so powerful a position in naval affairs; there was no board to deal with — only the King and his brother. No professional administrator, and only a few of the great officers of state, received so enormous a salary. Pepys had done more than make a comeback. He had reached the top.

20

The Second Secretaryship

―――――

The Second Secretaryship from May 1684 to February 1689 is the crown and the epitome of Pepys's official career. He ranged over the whole field of naval administration from finance to shipbuilding, from the training and promotion of officers to dockyards and contracts and timber and food. He drew on the earliest lessons he had learnt as Clerk of the Acts: he acted on the up-to-date and comprehensive information accumulated during the past months at Tangier and Cadiz. He allowed his mind to play on the perspectives of naval policy without relaxing his grip on the detailed and the day-to-day. It was the administrative masterpiece for which everything else, even his immense achievements in the two Dutch wars, had been preliminary sketches. It was to form the subject of his only published work, his *Memoires of the Royal Navy*.

As in the past the multiplicity, the scope and pace of his official life stimulated the other sides of his personality. He cultivated the improvement of his library, selling as well as buying. He befriended scholars. He became President of the Royal Society, lending his name to its imprimatur on Newton's *Principia*, the most famous of all books published under its auspices. He became, for a second time, Master of Trinity House. He pursued his studies of naval history. He abated no whit of his interest in psychical research. He obtained from his learned cousin Dr. Gale a transcript of the passage in Tertullian 'touching Tiberius's proposal to the

Roman senate the admitting of Christ for a God'.[1] He corresponded widely on theology (mostly with those, like Petty, who claimed no professional status in the subject) and preserved among his papers a host of notes from his own reading of which this example breathes the *anima Pepysiana*:

He that makes Reason his guide goes by a Law of God's makeing subject to noe falsifications and misconstructions wch all other guides whether written or others are and must necessarily be.[2]

Are not these the very accents of the Cambridge of his youth? Pepys never let go his past, never lost the curiosity and sense of wonder. A few pages beyond Sir William Petty's paper on liberty of conscience 'written by my desire and given me by himselfe a little before his death' we find a jagged, scorched bit of paper with which the Gunner of the *Coronation* had plugged a hole in his cabin window. It had been struck by lightning. A careful endorsement preserves this circumstance for posterity. The same volume contains information from the happily-named Captain Mudd about dumping rubbish into the Thames at Ratcliff for the purpose of making a causeway.[3] Such universality of appetite in a man who was carrying out a virtual reconstruction of the fleet and reforming, sometimes against dangerous opposition, the rules and customs of the naval profession is amazing.

No cocoon protected the great man from the ordinary rubs of life. The years that he filled with achievement and zest had their share of personal and family troubles. His health was never rude and by the standards of his world he was getting old. At the end of 1686 he suffered severe and prolonged pain from a recurrence of the stone, aggravated by an ulcer and other alarming symptoms. He warned Balty, now making up for the extravagance denied him in Tangier, not to depend on his being well enough to stay in office. Soon afterwards Balty's own wife died in childbirth: 'commissioner St Michell is drowned in tears, and his spirrit sinking under the sence of so heavy a Loss' wrote his assistant in a prose style perhaps influenced by his superior. That meant more nephews and nieces to be settled or, at least, to keep an eye on. Of Pall's boys Samuel was sent out to the West Indies under Narbrough while John went up to Magdalene. Mary Skinner's brother Peter, as plausible as his intellectual brother Daniel, was sent on a Mediterranean cruise under an old and steady Captain. Domestic arrangements too took up time. There was a fire at York Buildings soon after Pepys returned to office. The house escaped, narrowly: but books and papers were so disordered in last-minute attempts at salvage that it took weeks to straighten them out.

Finally Pepys arranged in September 1684 to move the Admiralty Office from Derby House to York Buildings.*

The Secretaryship to which all this bustle was parenthetic is divided into two periods by the Special Commission of 1686, Pepys's last great administrative creation. Much of the first two years was occupied in taking the measure of the problems left by five years mismanagement and in establishing the priorities and the means of dealing with them. The process was interrupted by the death of Charles II early in 1685, at the very moment when Pepys had prepared one of those set-pieces with which he liked to impress his masters at Christmas or New Year. In this case it consisted of a report on the condition of the ships: 'The state of the Royal Navy of England at the Dissolution of the late Commission of the Admiralty, May 1684.' Beautifully bound in black morocco with elaborate tooling, it still graces his library at Cambridge. The tale of neglect, incompetence and decay that it recites is too well known and too well authenticated to detain us. All the terrible rumours that had reached Pepys as a private citizen of how the thirty new ships had been allowed to rot and warp and moulder at their moorings proved exactly true. Within a short time of his return to office the enraged Secretary was gathering 'toad-stools as big as my fists' in the damp, unventilated 'tweendecks of what should have been the most powerful warships afloat. Wooden ships need constant and expert care to counteract the effects of sun and water. The money voted for the great construction programme of 1677 had been thrown away. Already his predecessors, more seasoned in the arts of propaganda than of preserving timber, were putting it about that the fault lay in the original purchases of Eastland plank. It was thus an act of self-defence as well as of methodical administration to assemble all the relevant evidence as to what the state of the fleet was and how it had come about.

The condition revealed in Pepys's report was not merely scandalous: it was alarming. English sea-power was wholly inadequate to the demands of a sudden war with a European power. It could not even teach the Algerines a lesson without cautious weighing of the balance of forces. Once again Barbary pirates were active in the channel. As late as June 1687 two regular packets going over to Holland were captured, one of them with a hundred passengers aboard.[4] The physical reconstruction of the fleet would have to be planned and financed. It was this necessity that issued in the Special Commission of 1686 to which we shall soon return. But there were other necessities in Pepys's view yet more pressing than a lack of ships: the need to re-establish discipline and to restore

* See above, p. 208.

without a moment's delay the professional foundations of the service. Tangier had shown him all too clearly how quickly the jungle of corruption and courtierism surged back over the paths and clearings he had made with so much labour.

What had shocked Pepys most during his spell with Dartmouth's squadron, more even than the dirty stories of the senior officers and the profanities reported of Admiral Herbert, was the lawlessness of a service whose *raison d'être* was law. All the rules that he had instituted were cheerfully flouted: even some of the conventions on which he had built were losing clarity and shape. Of the first the most obvious example was the failure to enforce the regulations laid down for the granting of commissions:

> Capt. Dering . . . was not thought fit upon examination to take another voyage. Nevertheless he was soon after made a lieutenant and presently after a captain which he is now.[5]

Of the second the readiest instance was seniority. In the absence of the admiral, who should command? The captain whose commission bore the earliest date or the captain whose ship was rated highest – in Pepysian language, the eldest captain or the greatest ship?* What was quite certain was that it must be one or the other. Yet at Tangier he had found that matters had slipped back towards the general free-for-all that he spent his life in resisting. Admiral Herbert had claimed the right to nominate whom he pleased, even going so far as to leave his own flag flying and his lieutenant as senior officer of the fleet when he himself was ashore.[6] Dartmouth had ruled in favour of the eldest commander:

> But here is to be noted the shame that this should be to be looked upon at this time of day a new regulation or rule to set matters right. In this matter that ever was the practice of the Navy in all times.[7]

Pepys exaggerates, as his own notes show, both the certainty and the continuity of the tradition.[8] Its importance in securing professionalism from the encroachments of courtiers and favourites is central.

What happened when these rules and conventions were disregarded, Pepys argues, was that the officer corps degenerated into a greedy and immoral rabble. The Gentlemen versus Tarpaulins issue became even more envenomed when gentility was allowed to consist in mere incompetence, unmitigated by honour or good breeding:

* See above, pp. 231–2.

Sir W. Booth telling me that there are four or five captains which he knows to have been footmen, companions of his own footman, who now reckon themselves among the fine fellows and gentlemen captains of the fleet, it makes me reflect upon it that by the meaning of gentlemen captains, is understood everybody that is not a bred and understanding seaman, and so set up for gentlemen.[9]

The promotion of these 'mean rogues . . . taken out of the streets' Pepys imputes to Herbert's alleged homosexuality. How 'mean' they, in fact, were, how lurid was the love-life of the late Commander-in-Chief of the Mediterranean Fleet are points which would require closer investigation before it would be safe to rest much weight on them. It was then, and long remained, a convenient way of disparaging an officer's social origins to say that he entered the navy as a footman or, by contrast, to heighten his success in his profession by saying that he entered it as a cabin boy. Both, usually, mean exactly the same thing. In almost every walk of life the young man who hoped to rise in the world attached himself in some loose and undefined manner to an already established figure. Pepys himself had done so. Doubtless the courtiers sneered at him for having started life as Lord Sandwich's footman. Captain Roydon of the *Sweepstakes* in the fearful broils with his lieutenant, George Aylmer, already alluded to accused him of having been Lord Arlington's footman. In fact, he had been his page[10] — a very different thing. Sir Clowdisley Shovell has, on the other hand, been admired by successive historians for rising to the top of the service that he had entered as a cabin boy. In fact, as we have seen, he had entered it under the protection of Myngs and Narbrough. The terms used to describe status often tell us more about the prejudice of the writer than about the condition of the man he is writing about. It is perhaps further worth noting that both these officers were on the Tangier station during Pepys's time there: that both were to serve for the rest of their lives, in Shovell's case a long and outstanding career: and that both are severely criticised in the Tangier journal for their frivolity and dereliction of duty. Pepys in office did not permit himself the luxury of the waspishness so often revealed in his private papers. Besides, he had gone out to the Mediterranean to find evidence of the corruption into which the navy had sunk while he was not there to run it. In such cases men are apt to find what they are looking for.

That the service was factious, ill-disciplined and thus inefficient does not admit of a doubt. Behind all the symptoms that Pepys recorded, neglect, amateurism, insubordination, drunkenness and misconduct, lay two conditions that he could treat but which only a miracle could cure:

the system that penalised good discipline and the Stuart brothers who liked it that way. The huge rewards a captain could earn from what Pepys, with furious scorn, called 'Good Voyages' put the service rate of pay into the shade. And it was these, as has been pointed out, that were altogether subversive of good order. Except where a commander was governed by a high sense of duty (and such would almost by definition be 'bred seamen', not court favourites), ships on a foreign station would put to sea or stay in harbour according to the prospect of private gain. For years Pepys, in his earlier tenure of the Secretaryship, had dinned it into the royal heads that they would get better value for money if they raised the officers' wages and forbade 'Good Voyages'. But this serious, prudent approach to the problem was uncongenial to Charles II: and James, though more sympathetic, was too infirm of purpose. Charles, indeed, frankly despised officers who were too scrupulous to make easy money by breaking regulations and told Sir John Berry so to his face.[11]

Charles II quitted the world in that style, so uniquely compounded of panache and obliqueness, that he had lived in it. His deathbed reception into the Roman Catholic Church by the priest who had befriended him when he was on the run after the battle of Worcester thirty-three years earlier was the last and one of the best-kept secrets of a reign in which the right hand rarely knew what the left was doing. Pepys's excitement when the new King confided the story to him and even lent him documents proving his brother's Papist tendencies exceeded anything hitherto stimulated by his historical researches. His two closest friends, John Evelyn and James Houblon, were summoned to dine with him the following Sunday with the irresistible bait: 'I have something to shew you that I may not have againe another time.' After the meal in the privacy of his own room he told them everything and showed them the papers. Evelyn, who had known the late King as well as Pepys and was far better versed in Catholic apologetic, thought them (Charles II's hand was familiar to both), 'so well penn'd as to the discourse, as did by no means seeme to me, to have ben put together by the Late King.'[12] As a political observer no less than as a historian the guest showed a critical power superior to that of his host. Pepys was beside himself with pleasure at being let into so high a secret: Evelyn was saddened by further evidence that the new King was set on a collision course.

Pepys's elation at the beginning of the new reign is indeed understandable. Whatever James II's shortcomings as a king, he was, to a far greater extent than his brother, knowable, predictable and loyal. He and Pepys had shared misfortune and recovery. Both were now riding high. At the coronation Pepys walked in the procession as one of the Barons of the Cinque Ports, a medieval corporation for which he had neither veneration nor respect, deriding, in his historical notes, their supposed contribution to English sea-power. At the General Election that followed in May he was returned for both Harwich and Sandwich, choosing to sit for his old constituency. The complexion of the new House of Commons was very different from the last Parliament of Charles II. The Court, it seemed, had everything its own way.

Monmouth's rebellion in the following month provided clinching evidence. Apart from a few simpletons in the West Country no one rallied to the Whig banner. In spite of the naval weakness exposed by this landing of an invading force the Government were never in trouble. It was only the vindictiveness of Pepys's friend Judge Jeffreys and the brutality of his old enemy Colonel Kirke after everything was over that roused sympathy for the defeated. Both men certainly expressed the spirit of their master, who was not, judged by the standards of his day, a humane man. Even Pepys, who was, clearly approved. Writing to Sir William Poole, recalled from a lucrative retirement in the Customs at Bristol to command an armed merchantman during the rebellion, he urges him to drive a hard bargain with the prisoners sentenced to transportation to Virginia and the West Indies 'whether to be sold entirely, as blacks are to slavery for their whole lives, or how long . . .'13

Such mercilessness towards the poor, illiterate dupes of political gamblers is repellent. Some have seen in it merely the reflection of a hard age or of the horror felt by those who have experienced revolution. It runs too deep in Pepys's nature for such an explanation to be wholly satisfactory. There is no transaction in his life more disgusting than his sending his Negro servant out to be sold abroad in 1679. Sir Arthur Bryant's account solicits the reader's sympathy for Pepys, obliged through loss of office to cut down his standard of living: 'He was no longer a housekeeper now; even his black boy had been sold for him by kind Captain Wyborne, who had taken him off to the Mediterranean in the previous autumn and brought back instead twenty-five pistoles, transmuted at Cadiz into chocolate and sherry for Pepys's drinking.'14 One thinks of the care taken by Johnson to provide for his Negro servant, Francis Barber. That was a century later. But it is impossible to imagine Evelyn or Ken or Dr. Gale, to name but a few of Pepys's friends, behaving with such barbarity. There was a hardness in his nature with which the fineness of his perceptions was perpetually at war. Unlike James II, when he saw poverty, hunger, suffering he was moved to compassion. The poor sailors and their wives besieging the Navy Office, real people present to a consciousness amounting to genius, really touch his heart and his conscience: the lucrative deals by

which money to feed them went into his own pocket could be intellec-
tualised and made abstract. So it is with the victims of Monmouth's
rebellion. So it is, thanks to Captain Wyborne and the remoteness of the
nearest slave-market, with the black servant. So it is in a minor key with
the clerks, James Sotherne, Josiah Burchett and others, who, dismissed
after years of working for him, found repeated apologies and appeals
unanswered. Had he seen them in person, as they and he seem to have
suspected, he might have found inflexibility more difficult. So it is with
his meanness to his Jackson nephews out of sight at Huntingdon and his
generosity once they had entered his circle. If they fell from grace, as the
elder subsequently did by marrying a girl Pepys thought unsuitable,
banishment was the key to punitive action.

James II was altogether without this quickness and intensity of response.
He allowed his nephew, demoralised by failure and exhaustion, to grovel
for mercy before him and then refused it. He expressed his regret at not
being able to be present in person when the Earl of Argyle, the leader of
another unsuccessful rebellion in Scotland, was put to the torture. Yet such
behaviour, hateful as it is, did not spring from a merciless or even an
unkind nature. James's readiness to spare the feelings of a friend, the
warmth and generosity of his loyalty, are too well attested both by his
own actions and by the evidence of men like Bishop Burnet who were
anything but well disposed towards his politics or his religion. It was
his terrible obtuseness, the most unPepysian of all qualities, that undid
him.

How, in three years, the King managed to reverse the popularity and
to alienate the loyalty which he had enjoyed on his accession is only too
well known. What part, if any, did Pepys play in setting the course to
ruin? Essentially, none. Pepys was only a politician to the extent that he
had to be if he were to administer the navy. He would thus support the
Government he served up to and beyond what he might privately think
either wise or expedient. Outside his own department he was not consulted
in the framing of policy: his job was to provide the sea-power necessary
to defence and to diplomacy. He was one of the greatest civil servants that
England has ever had, but he had the misfortune to live before the civil
service had been invented. Thus by adducing his speeches in the Parliaments of Charles and James invariably toeing the Government line, by
citing his approval of James's repressive policy so savagely executed by
Jeffreys and Colonel Kirke, finally by pointing to him in the witness box
at the trial of the Seven Bishops, giving evidence for the Crown in the
most famous of all legal assaults on the liberties of Protestant Englishmen,
it is possible to depict Pepys as an ultra-Tory, perhaps a crypto-Catholic.

Such a view is great nonsense. The only sense in which Pepys, whose whole cast of mind was sceptical and eclectic, could be claimed as a Tory is that in which almost all his contemporaries and every preceding generation were or had been, that is in accepting the authority of government as axiomatic and in looking on opposition, still more on revolution, as wicked. There is nothing in Pepys's life or writings to suggest that he would not have served the dynasty of Oliver Cromwell, once effectively established, with the same loyalty that he gave to the Stuarts. In the case of religion the matter is clearer still. Pepys was a cool, Erastian Protestant, thinking hot-gospellers on the whole ridiculous and priests generally parasitical. His own theology, if that is not too pretentious a term for an attitude of mind rather than a system of ideas, was liberal. Towards the end of his life he came into closer personal sympathy with High Churchmen both of the Non-juring and the Established variety, but whatever the effects of this (and there seem to have been some) the cause would appear to have been the extraordinary learning of these divines (most notably Dr. Hickes) rather than a desire on his part for a more sacramental religion. Of any predilection for Roman Catholicism there is no trace.

How could there be? Pepys for all his long service to the House of Stuart was a born cross-bencher. The battle between Whigs and Tories had cost him severe wounds, but to a mind of his type the whole thing was laughable. In March 1682, when he had been kept for nearly three years powerless at the height of his powers, he wrote to James Houblon from Newmarket:

Sir,
That I am well got hither and well here, will (I assure myself) give you no disquiet. But how your Whigship will bear my telling you that the Duke of York is so too, and not only so, but plumper, fatter, and all over in better liking than ever I knew him, is a thing that I cannot answer for.
. . . the King (God be blessed) seems in no point less fortified against mortality than the Duke, but in one particular more; namely that (as much as that signifies) he hath the prayers of the very Whigs for his health, while we Tories are fain to pray, by ourselves, for his brother's . . .[15]

He never wrote in this bantering spirit about anything he took seriously, such as Right and Wrong, scientific evidence, money, or the state of the navy.

It was to this last question that he addressed his full powers. The story of the Special Commission of 1686 has been so well told elsewhere that there is little to add. Pepys himself was the first to tell it in his *Memoires of the Royal Navy*: J. R. Tanner, in his introduction to the *Catalogue of the Pepysian MSS*, was the first scholar to criticise the documents in the Pepys Library of which that book is an extract: Sir Arthur Bryant printed or summarised a great deal more of this material in his *Pepys: The Saviour of the Navy* (1938): more recently Mr. John Ehrman has examined the evidence from a different standpoint in his *The Navy in the War of William III* (1953). All three modern writers agree in accepting the substance of the claims Pepys made in the *Memoires*: indeed in the all-important matter of rebuilding the fleet, without reserve:

The outstanding work of the Commission, however, lay in this programme of repair. Its success rested upon three distinct achievements. First, the repairs were fully and efficiently carried out; secondly, they did not exceed the original estimate of their cost; and thirdly, they were completed in less than the original estimate of the time required. All these facts were later questioned, but all were finally established by the Parliamentary inquiry of 1691–2, in its elicitation of a defence of their work from Deane and Hewer, the two men principally concerned, and in the detailed acknowledgment of its validity by the Parliamentary Commissioners themselves.

Altogether the Special Commission repaired 69 ships and rebuilt twenty. It also built the three fourth-rates promised, and a hoy and two lighters. By the time it came to a close, only four ships still remained with their repairs not completed, and four more with their repairs not begun. In addition to the work on these 96 ships, a further 29 were repaired which had been at sea when the Commission was inaugurated, and had not been included in the original programme. Pepys's intentions were therefore more than fulfilled in the number of vessels which were tackled.[16]

Pepys's career was crowned by the refashioning of England's sea-power just in time for his patron to lose it. The great war with Louis XIV that followed was often the subject of sardonic comment from Pepys who felt, justly, aggrieved at his treatment: it was the more ironical to know that without his work it could hardly have been fought.

In conception, execution and style the Special Commission was Pepysian through and through. He drafted its terms, he chose its members, he kept, as he said himself, 'my daily eye and hand upon them'. The key appointment was that of Sir Anthony Deane, then at the height of his fame (and fees) as a naval architect. His salary (he had fifteen children to support and wanted £1,000 a year) was the only real difficulty. Neither the King nor the Lord Treasurer wanted to go so high. Pepys outflanked their opposition by producing a list of all the possible alternative candidates that showed all his old fondness for the sharp and cutting phrase. 'A low-spirited, slow and gouty man . . . illiterate and supine to the last degree.' The master-shipwright at Woolwich might stand for all, or almost all. Most, according to Pepys, were drunken, incompetent or senile: the few young men lacked either experience or application. Can they really have been so useless? If so, why had not the veterans been replaced during Pepys's earlier secretaryship? Would they have received the same character if it had been a question of obtaining a pension for them or a grant for one of their widows? When Pepys had set his mind upon some particular end he had no compunction in making free with other people's reputations.

Next to Deane, Will Hewer was the Commissioner on whom Pepys relied most. A strong contingent of sea officers, notable among them Sir John Narbrough and Sir John Berry, combined expert knowledge with personal friendship, both of long standing. The Commission also embraced Resident Commissioners at Portsmouth, Chatham and Deptford, the last of which appointments was bestowed upon Balty. It was a closely knit body.

Its second source of strength was that it combined financial and executive control. The frustration of the Second Dutch War had left its mark. At last Pepys had got his hands on the levers and he was not going to make any mistake. The Commission's terms of reference included its own budget, carefully costed and rigidly adhered to. Very skilfully Pepys retained the Comptroller and Surveyor of the Navy Board that had been responsible for the deplorable state of affairs he was to remedy and charged them with the dire task of presenting their own accounts for the locust years. They were, naturally, outside the Commission. Pepys had spent enough of his administrative life clearing up other people's mess. The Commission was to be positive, executive, in the most literal sense constructive.

In effect it temporarily superseded the Navy Board: the commissioners moved into the houses of the Principal Officers (who were given a house allowance in lieu) and occupied the Board's offices, even adding to them. Its functions were primarily those that the Board had hitherto discharged but it was given a disciplinary brief that derived more from the office of the Lord High Admiral. It was, in a word, to be Pepys put into commission: inquiring, enforcing, reproving, watching, reporting, minuting, buzzing like a gnat in the ears of drowsy officials. From its constitution in April 1686 to its dissolution, its work done, on October 12th, 1688, it provided new, swift channels for the day-to-day administration of the navy as well as giving the service a refit from truck to keel.

Why if the Commission performed such prodigies was it dissolved? Should it not rather have been institutionalised and decent interment given to the old Navy Board? Pepys, highly as he valued its achievement and admired the triumph of his own administrative workmanship, does not seem to have thought so. Historical study and reflection had induced in him, as it does in others, a scepticism towards simple solutions. On April 6th, 1688, in an informal discussion of the navy in general attended only by himself, the King and Godolphin he noted in his own hand

Its science ye most extensive of any.

	viz.	Comoditys
		Trades
Climates		Provisions
Accounts		Shipbuilding
Thrift		Discipline
Seamanship		Winds
Navigation		Tides
Sea-Laws		Seas

Noe one Man qualify'd for all
    Nor fitt to bee trusted alone
Therefore ye old Constitution provided for all,
    by a Plurality properly qualify'd . . .'[17]

The Special Commission had succeeded brilliantly because it was special, with a limited task, a clear brief, and means proportionate to its ends. It was also a highly personal success, the performance of a lifetime by the maestro conducting players, themselves masters, who had been rehearsing under his baton for a quarter of a century. The magic was in the ingredients, not in the formula. The only long-term solution to the perennial problems of naval mismanagement was, as Pepys constantly reiterates in his *Naval Minutes*, to build up an informed body of opinion among the aristocrats and landed gentry who dominated Parliament. Once they could be induced to send their sons into the service as serious professionals not as dilettanti the old cycle of ignorance and corruption might be broken or, at least, its gyrations become less wild. All this would take time. And a man in his middle fifties with a chronic kidney complaint could not reckon on much of that.

June 10th 1684.

His Maᵗⁱᵉˢ Letters Patents for yᵉ Erect-
=ing the Office of Secry of yᵉ Admiralty
of England, & Creating Samuel Pepys Esqʳ
first Secretary therein.

Charles the Second

by the grace of God of England, Scotland, France & Ireland
King: Defender of the Faith &cᵃ, To all to whome these Presents
shall come Greeting, Know yee that wee haue thought fitt to
Erect, and hereby doe Erect an Office of Secretary to and
for the Affaires and Businesse of and Concerning Our
Admiralty of England, and wee reposeing especiall Trust
and Confidence in yᵉ Experience, Ability, Care and Fidelity of
Our Trusty & Welbeloved Samuel Pepys Esqʳ, haue given and grant-
=ed, and by these Presents doe give and Grant unto the said Samuel
Pepys the Office of Secretary of and for the Affaires and
Businesse of and Concerning Our Admiralty of England,
and him the sayd Samuel Pepys Secretary, of and for
the Affaires and Businesse of and concerning, Our
Admiralty of England Wee doe Create, Make, Ordaine &
Constitute by these Presents, to haue, hold, exercise and En-
=joy the sayd Office unto the sayd Samuel Pepys during,
Our Pleasure, Giveing alloe, and by these Presents granting
unto the sayd Samuel Pepys full Power and Authority

to

Patent of Pepys's Secretaryship in the Admiralty from his Day Collection (see page 291).
The pen and ink head that embellishes the patent is of Charles II.

At the distance of three centuries the rounding off of a great career with its greatest achievement has an aesthetic rightness doubtless imperceptible to Pepys himself, resentful at his ill-usage and embittered by the preferment of men he thought unworthy. Yet even Pepys may have had, for personal not political reasons, a sense that things were drawing towards their close. We have seen that he warned Balty not to count on his being able to sustain the physical demands of office much longer. Was not the urgency that drove through the Special Commission's three-year programme in two and a half private as much as public? At all costs the machinery of naval administration was to be put into full working order at the earliest possible moment. Expedients that depended on the presence of the master-mechanic must be rejected. It was, surely, Pepys's voice that spoke when Hewer turned down James II's suggestion that the Special Commission might be carried on indefinitely by retaining himself and Sir Anthony Deane as 'Inspectors Marine', 'on the ground that the methods of the navy in accounting are now so clear that only industry and knowledge are needed.'[18] When that answer was given the Glorious Revolution was a bare three weeks away.

The sunset of Pepys's official life displays the whole spectrum of his abilities at their fullest brilliancy. York Buildings combined elegance with efficiency as only an establishment of which Pepys was unchallenged master could do. There was no Elizabeth now to introduce the principle of romantic disorder: no colleagues to obstruct, no patron to be conciliated. A lifetime's love of method and neatness was consummated in the arrangements for transacting business. On his desk lay his Day Collection, exquisitely bound in dark green morocco, containing ready to his hand the regulations and precedents governing pay, pensions, salutes, flags, the rating of ships as to officers and guns together with a complete list of the fleet and its disposition on the day he resumed office. In his pocket he carried a sheet of paper (see the example reproduced on p. 292) neatly folded with notes on each fold of matters to be raised with the King, the Ordnance Board, the Victualling Office, or whoever he might be seeing during the course of that particular day. At longer range and lower priority were his 'Momentalls' (p. 292) and 'Memorandums' a sheet of which endorsed 'Pocket Memorandums to goe before those in my pocket Memorandum Book' may be seen on the next page. The division and arrangement of the matter is a paradigm of his efficiency, of his success, above all of his cast of mind. The left-hand column methodically groups what has to be done under the name of the relevant person or place. But he is never the prisoner of his own system. The right-hand column tumbles out pell-mell all the multifarious pleasures, interests and duties

June 10: 1601

Admiralty.

   List of Books
   Bonds
S:r Nich: Armorer
   Books of fortification
   Mathem: paper book 4:o
   Milers Callender
   Lady Mordant something

Mr Houblon
   His Bond returne
   Dr De Moulins
   Burelle ---   2:2:6

Brampton
   Mr Jessife
Katherine
   Mourning --- 3:0:0
   Advance --- 5:0:0

Trinity-House
   Brother Title --- 4:0:0
   Old Pattent & ord: to Copy ---

My Self wanting
   Prospective
   Reading Desk
   A Pincer

Books & Booksell:r
   Mathem Paper
   Paid Pitts too little
   Paid Richard too much

Portsm:t Mr Hayter May 27: &c
Dr Phil: Warwick thank
A. Rob:t Howard --- 200:0:0
Mr Gregory answere
Mr Rich:d Reeve &c for Rich: R.
W:t my Gavel Cupp
Mr Ethick of Christ Colledge
Moseley Jan: 4 at Burntwood --- 15:0
Tower Hill servant
Hamper of old Books
D:o so diem in the E. King Chas 120
Dr Bradley by 2s at least 30
a Day now.
Cole: Norwood at Leek Hampton
Cholsey Debt
Mr Hollier Marg: lodex R:o 675
Dr Allen
Woodhall Guillim
Recale S:r Ph: Medows Books
Mr Sandison at ye Golden Ball
   in Hatten Garden
Cole: S:o Phillipp & Hulstone
Pay Mr Boxwich hertshire
Mr Smyth Savile
Send back to Cr
S:r D:r Mr Corbee
2 H: Crowns &c 07
Mr Peter Jones Merch:t in S:t Mary
Mr Bovery Merch:t in Minchin lane

Memorandum, Momentalls and Pocket Memorandum.

Lord Dartmouth.   Mr. Blathwayt.   King:

Greenwich House & H.   Richard E.   Sr Jn Worden's Adm: Papers
Portugale Quarys.   Navale Officer Jamaica. Navall Papers laid up.
Capt Guillim ___ Jersey.   Rec:ds Navy Comer &c
ye 2d wth Ston   Sand: C Adm semistmd &c
to be reconomd to ____ instr:con   Capt: Clear old, before new Voyage
Sewen Billy dray ones.   i Navale Guise
                                                   Greenwich House
80s slack   Vice: Com:tee of
Cont: Phillips's purpos:con   River of Thames
Portsm ___ Comptr of ye   Adm: Chudge, & Ofiicars
                                                   do: ___ but it so be
J:V:r Bridgeman   NB ___ Proportions of Prize
                                                        New York Portsmouth.
E India Compts:on   Mr Legg & Beaumont
List of Instructions for Convoys   Navy Guardshipp
Gen Ware to see Powers   Victualling ___ Office. NO.
Ale House unlicenced   Sr Go Wyborn's case
Paper Office particular ___   F must br Mr Gen
                                                   Sr Ro: Holmes ___ Election

                                                   Chapples & Liberty

                    Dr Ro: Murray.

Sea _____   Cabinet   Treasury.
To Chatham in fort   Ld Godolphin Victuals. Paymt
To House Permon   French Corts   Wm Bristol's Complemts
60 ___ boat ye land every   Algire ___ Slave Rice Ebbell. Regularly chage of Mony for
          where   ye Extra 1000 & month.
Visiting the Shipps ____   Legorne Slave ___ Mr Gard.
    weekly   Gr:t Admiralty ___   Comt:rs Care Report.
I must defire ye ____ her ____ here D: of Albemarle   Magazme.
                             Spanish Memoralle   Victualing ___ Officer. NO Depts
                             Sr E Andros ag: Sr W Phipps   Sr Jn Berry ___ 290. Dodd
                                 Sr A Perien ag: him
                             Coni: Loddington's Compt:
                                 Dr Sr Raine's Widow.
                             Capt ___ prize.
                             Sally ___ Treaty.

                             Horn Writs.

These are described on the preceding page.

of a life in which inertia had no place. Reason, method, exploited to the full, do not for an instant obstruct or inhibit the irrational. It is the hare's foot and the Royal Society transposed to another key. These were but the skirmishers of the great paper army marshalled in his vast filing system ready at a word to spring into action against irregularity or neglect. Whole brigades in full battle order still survive in his own library and among the Rawlinson manuscripts in the Bodleian.

His official correspondence shows that he could still be sharp when the occasion called for it. But the mellowing so long evident has become more pronounced. Sir Robert Holmes, once feared and hated, has become a trusted ally. Sir William Poole, not once but many times the recipient of sulphurous rebukes for idling in port or engaging in 'good' voyages, is told that the Secretary hears excellent reports of his son, now a captain. The letters, always spacious, seem to admit more light and air.

Time was thinning out the friends and associates of early life. Cambridge stood up well with Richard Cumberland, a friendship kept in good repair, and the indestructible Sir Samuel Morland for ever in some scrape over money or matrimony. The period of service with Mountagu had almost faded: Will Howe was in the West Indies, Creed, once Pepys's most formidable rival, seems to have retired into the life of a country gentleman to which his fortunate marriage probably contributed. Of Sandwich's immediate family only his third son, John, Master of Trinity, Cambridge and subsequently Dean of Durham, kept in touch. The years at the Navy Office, too, contribute little. Sir William Warren, fallen at last on hard times, makes one final appearance, 'Majestick though in ruin.' Sir William Coventry, long out of public life though never out of Pepys's admiring affection, died in June 1686 while taking the waters at Tunbridge Wells. In the spring of 1687 a Mr. Dilks was recommended for a lieutenancy: he had been examined by Sir John Narbrough but his sponsor clinches his argument, 'I have nothing more to add on behalfe of this Gentleman but that hee is a relation of Sir William Coventry and then refuse him if you can.' The commission was granted the following month.[19]

At this the peak of his career, powerful, rich, respected, a grave and reverend signior, Pepys was still subject to the capricious influence of favourites and to the pressures and presuppositions of an aristocratic society. To take but a trivial example, when the Duchess of Norfolk (whom Pepys did not know) wanted 'a parcell of pladd' safely transported from Scotland she did not hesitate to ask his good offices.[20] More seriously, in spite of his efforts to ensure that officers should be properly qualified, he hears from Sir John Berry of the Duke of Grafton's proposing to make a lieutenant of a man whom '. . . I was hardly to be brought to signe a Certificatt of his being fitly qualified to be Boatswain of a fourth rate ship: and I am of the same opinion still.'[21] This seems to have been blocked: but in spite of James II's disposition to enforce discipline in general and to support his Admiralty Secretary in particular Pepys could not count on his rules being upheld. What he could do was to make them crystal clear and to fence in, where possible, more of the waste of the manor for others to till when he had gone. The regulations restricting the carriage of freight and bullion dated July 15th, 1686 were framed in stark terms: instant dismissal and incapacitation for future service, all profits to be confiscated to the Chatham Chest. New rates of pay were established and the captain's table allowances codified according to the rate of his ship. Guns, medical stores, prize money, pensions, relief for widows and orphans, the appointment of surgeons, above all the confirmation on April 13th, 1686, of the rules for the admission of volunteers and midshipmen by which Pepys hoped to encourage the gentry to breed their sons to the sea are among the subjects for which he laid down or strengthened an establishment during James's brief reign. In the century that followed these rules were often broken, or lost sight of. But in every case reform or innovation built on his foundations or began where he left off.

To judge from his letters his closest confidant in this last and most creative phase of his administrative life was his great friend James Houblon. It was Houblon who beat down the tapestry man to 25s. 6d. per ell for the walls of York House, a reduction of ten per cent.[22] Houblon who advised on naval intelligence, on the impact of war in the Mediterranean on English trade, on the motives of the Consul at Lisbon in asking for powers to prevent English captains discharging their men there. What the Consul was really after, says Houblon, was the power to compel 'runaways, rebellious and debauched rascals' who 'lye sotting themselves there with all sortes of vice'. The captains would then have to pay off their debts and the Consul would get a rake-off.[23] How sure his understanding and how sound his information may be gauged from this quotation from a letter written to Pepys eighteen months before the Dutch fleet left on the voyage whose landfall opened the Revolution of 1688:

We have from Dutch Land such a clutter of Arming both by sea and Land that makes us poore merchants looke carefully at what may be ye end of it. Glad are we in the meantime to see heer a Disposition for peace and that we shall bee happy in a profitable neutralitie wch wee traders think best for England. I wish ye zelous R. Priesthood & Swordmen thought soe too.[24]

21

James II and the Revolution

James Houblon was not alone among Pepys's friends in taking alarm at James II's policies. Anxiety as to the internal stability of England, still more as to French domination over Europe, was perhaps to be expected from a leading member of a Protestant refugee family: but it was shared to the full by John Evelyn, whose connections and origins were purely Royalist and Tory, and even by the High Churchmen, Hickes and Ken, who became after the Revolution the leaders of the Non-jurors. All these men were close to Pepys. Hickes had been chosen to preach the sermon at his second installation as Master of Trinity House in July 1685; he was to attend him on his deathbed and to conduct his funeral. Evelyn, after Houblon, was his most intimate friend. No one, certainly not Pepys himself, can have had higher expectations of James than he: '. . . there could nothing be more desired, to accomplish our prosperity, but that he were of the national Religion: for certainly such a Prince never had this Nation since it was one.'[1] He took the King's candid profession of Roman Catholicism as evidence of good faith in his solemn promises not to undermine the Church of England. But less than nine months later he was convinced of his mistake: 'All engines being now at worke to bring in popery amaine.'[2]

The immediate provocation of this reflection was James's assault on the Universities. Evelyn, as one of the Commissioners of the Privy Seal, had already refused to seal a patent licensing the King's printer to print Mass Books in defiance of many Acts of Parliament. He was anxious lest the King might again attempt the same short-circuit in order to allow the Master of University College, Oxford, a crypto-Papist who had at last declared himself, to continue to hold his office in spite of the law. He was relieved, personally, that James chose another expedient but his disapproval and his misgivings were no less profound. Flushed with his easy success at University College James moved down the High to Magdalen. In the spring of 1687 the old President of the College died. As soon as the news reached London the King sent his mandate to the Fellows ordering them to elect a young and totally unsuitable Roman Catholic who, even if he had been a member of the established Church, was disqualified for the post under the College statutes. The Fellows however had got wind of this plan and hurriedly elected one of their own number. In the confrontation that followed the King was worsted. Rather than admit defeat he then nominated the Bishop of Oxford, but again the Fellows stood firm. They had elected their President, the Visitor of the College, the Bishop of Winchester, had confirmed him and that was that. On September 5th Pepys's friend and colleague William Blathwayt, who was accompanying the King on his Royal Progress to the West, wrote from Oxford to describe how

    ... His Majesty being informed that the Fellows of Magdalen College had refused to admitt the Bishop of Oxford to be their President ... sent for them yesterday after dinner to His Antichamber in Christ Church Colledge where H.M. chid them very much for their disobedience and with much greater appearance of Anger than ever I perceiv'd in H.M. ...'[3]

The chiding failed of its effect. Either on this or a further occasion James became incoherent with rage and the Fellows were subsequently ejected.[*]

As a servant of the King Pepys would have felt bound, in public at any rate, to defend his actions. We may doubt if he did so to intimate friends. Evelyn records an earlier instance of Pepys's remaining silent when the King was descanting on the miracles performed in Spain by the *Saludadors*,[†] one of whom, questioned by Pepys:

---

[*] An excellent account of the whole affair is to be found in John Carswell, *The Descent on England* (1969).

[†] Spanish religious enthusiasts who claimed miraculous powers of healing, etc.

. . . ingenuously told him, that, finding he was a more than ordinary curious person, he would not deceive him, & so acknowledg'd that he could do none of those feates, realy; but that what they pretended, was all a cheate. . . . This Mr *Pepys* affirm'd to me; but said he, I did not conceive it fit, to interrupt his Majestie, who told what they pretended to do so solemnly.[4]

We have, none the less, to proceed by inference. Pepys was no longer confiding his private opinions to a diary.

When, however, the King turned his attention from Oxford to Cambridge Pepys was caught in a conflict of loyalties. Dr. Peachell, his old friend, had long been Master of Magdalene and was now Vice-Chancellor. To him fell the dilemma of James's direction, 'to admit one Alban Francis, a Benedictine Monk, Master of Arts without administering any oath or oaths to him'.[5] Peachell's first reaction must have been to consult the College's most distinguished member, who was also his own friend from undergraduate days and, finally, one of the King's oldest and most valued advisers. Had the telephone existed this, it may be suspected, is what Peachell would have done. But *littera scripta manet*: a letter once written stays written: and if it ask guidance or intervention the answer accepting or refusing the invitation stays written too. It says much for Peachell and something for Pepys that he did not take the easy way out of his difficulties at the expense of involving a friend:

> I could not tell what to do, decline his Majestie's Letter, or his Lawes; I could but pray to God to direct, sanctifie, and governe me in the wayes of his Lawes; that so through his most mighty Protection, both here and ever, I may be preserved in body and soule; then by our Chancellor, I indeavoured to obteine his Majestie's release, which could not be obteined; I thought it unmannerly to importune his Sacred Majestie; and was afraid to straine friends against the graine; and so could onely betake myselfe to my owne conscience, and the advice of Loyall and prudent men my friends, and after all I was perswaded that my Oath as Vice-chancellor founded on the Statutes was against it . . .[6]

Peachell's letter to Pepys from which these quotations are taken opens with the announcement that his nephew John Jackson has just arrived to take up residence in the College.

Up to this point Dr. Peachell could hardly have been described as an impressive figure. Only the redness of his nose and the convivial habits that caused it have won him a minor immortality in the Diary. Yet forced to a decision involving at once the painful breach of a lifelong political allegiance and the loss of two much prized positions (he was suspended as Master and deprived of the Vice-Chancellorship) he showed courage and style. A regime that could drive its natural friends into such agonised opposition could not long avoid an explosion.

In the summer of 1688 the fuse was ignited at three points: James's Queen, Mary of Modena, bore him a son who would obviously be brought up in the religion of both his parents; the Seven Bishops, headed by the Primate of all England, were tried (after a brief but electrifying imprisonment) on a charge of seditious libel; and abroad the election of a new archbishop of Cologne was used by Louis XIV to force a confrontation on the rest of Europe. Suddenly the lines were drawn for another gigantic struggle such as had culminated a century earlier in Armada year, with France substituted for Spain, and, unthinkably, England in plausible danger of finding herself on the side of a militant Catholic despotism. James II, naturally, did not see it like this. His own relations with Louis XIV were cool: his nephew and son-in-law William of Orange was Louis's most implacable opponent: and the Pope, whom James was supposed to be reintroducing, was hardly less violent in his determination to resist French aggression. But the King had no one to blame but himself if his subjects were incapable of appreciating these piquant diplomatic paradoxes. And even his own dull political senses told him that something was burning. Peachell was reinstated in his Mastership: President Hough and the ejected Fellows were restored to Magdalen: but by the time these concessions were made full-scale war had broken out on the Continent and William of Orange had staked everything on the great gamble of invading England.

One of the neglected consequences of the Whig interpretation of history so brilliantly defined by Sir Herbert Butterfield is that it has lent a spurious inevitability to the Revolution of 1688, or, more precisely, to the bloodless military success of its achievement. It is hardly possible to exaggerate the daring (to use the most modest and polite term) of William's operational planning. Even in the Second World War, when ships were built of steel and powered by engines, when they could be protected from attack and warned of danger by air-power, radar and a hundred other devices, when the development of meteorology made some sort of weather forecast possible, an assault on the defended coast of a country with a formidable navy and a by no means negligible army at a time of year when daylight was short and rough weather all but certain would have been thought crazy. When ships were built of wood and propelled by wind the risks were far greater. Even if the invasion fleet reached its destination (a far from foregone conclusion) it could be pounded to matchwood in a few hours if a gale were to blow up while the troops were disembarking. And all this takes no account of James's popularity with his soldiers and sailors, of his own record as a courageous and successful commander, of his general aptitude for war. What, too, might be expected of the local population? Public opinion might be distrustful of James, some politicians and some senior officers might have chanced their arm by inviting the Prince of Orange to come over, but violent hostility to a foreign invader is the instinct of ordinary people in every age, particularly in an age that knew from experience that troops lived off the country. It is the measure of William's nerve that none of these daunting elements had been left out of his calculations. One of his most brilliant and original touches was to provide his invading force with plenty of money to pay its way.

That he should have succeeded so completely in so desperate an undertaking may be held to reflect on James as a strategist and tactician and on Pepys as his chief naval executive. Such a judgment owes much to hindsight, and something to Macaulay's indelible picture of James as an infatuated incompetent. Both the King and Pepys had first-hand experience of directing a naval war against the Dutch such as has been available to few men in our history. Both had reflected upon, argued, analysed and examined the whole subject from a number of different standpoints. One feature of these wars can hardly have escaped them: the battle season in the Channel ran from May to July. It was possible for a fleet to keep the sea in August, but even by then the danger of the elements was more to be feared than the violence of the enemy. By September the fleets ought to be in their bases. By October everyone except the standing officers, the ships' caretakers, should have been paid off. The idea of a Channel campaign in November was as unthinkable as a hay-harvest in January.

It was no part of Pepys's business to supply the Government with political and diplomatic intelligence. Sunderland remained Secretary of State and chief architect of James's foreign and domestic policy until the Revolution was open and palpable. Pepys, of course, had his own sources. Apart from the Houblons, his connections as President of the Royal Society with the world of European science furnished him with well-informed correspondents abroad. It was one such, Abraham Hill, Treasurer of the Royal Society, who wrote from Rotterdam on August 19th 'touching ye difficulty of understanding Mr Newton's Booke — & sends with ye Marques de Albevill ye first surpriseing News of ye Dutch Marine preparations'.[7] What was 'surpriseing' was not so much the news of the conspicuous activity in the Dutch bases — this could hardly be concealed and had been common knowledge for months — as the sudden realisation that a major threat, dwarfing the domestic difficulties in which the Government was floundering, had to be met in a matter of weeks, perhaps of days.[8] Both James II and Pepys had been aware that the Dutch were up to no good. A squadron somewhat larger than a normal summer guard but hardly deserving the name of a fleet had been concentrated in the Channel from the end of May, under the command of Sir Roger Strickland, a tactless officer whose exceptional experience and fine fighting record were offset by recusant antecedents and a too close personal link with the King's immediate circle. From the middle of June he was ordered to maintain two frigates cruising off the Goodwin. By the beginning of August Pepys was confident that the number of ships at sea could be reduced 'in one, two or three months at furthest'.[9]

A fortnight later such optimism was no longer possible. On August 16th the 'fleet' was ordered to remain in the Downs and not to proceed to the westward; on the 20th all leave was stopped; on the 21st one of the royal yachts was ordered to reconnoitre the coast of Holland and to report all warship movements. In the week that followed (the week in which Hill's letter arrived) Pepys turned on the heat. Complements were to be brought up to war strength: seven more warships and six fireships were to be fitted out at once and measures taken to prepare eight more fireships and six scouts. At this point James began either to lose interest or to regain confidence: foreign ambassadors reported his daily vacillations: but these did not affect Pepys. Whatever he may privately have thought about the probability of a Dutch invasion in the autumn, he had been given a clear brief to mobilise the fleet. Indeed whatever the Dutch intentions it would be most unwise to allow the balance of effective naval power to tilt any further to their side.

Thanks to the work of the Special Commission the ships were readily available and fit for sea: but storing, victualling and manning were no easier than they had ever been. Rather, with a weak, unpopular and uncertain Government, they were even more difficult. Merchants were reluctant to give credit: seamen decidedly more reluctant to come forward. Strickland's squadron had consisted of seventeen ships of the line (one third-rate, the rest fourths) and nine smaller vessels: to this were to be added in all twenty-one of the line (ten thirds, eleven fourths) and fourteen fireships. In spite of the prodigies performed by Deane and Hewer and even Balty, hardly a ship had joined the fleet before the end of September. October witnessed a steady stream of reinforcements: by the last week of the month, all the ships, except three or four stragglers, had joined.

By that time Strickland was no longer Commander-in-Chief. An

angry exchange with Pepys at the beginning of August over his entitle-
ment to Vice-Admiral's pay during his recent voyage to Portugal hardly
suggests that he was equal to the responsibilities of his present appointment.[10] His subsequent attempt to have mass celebrated aboard his flagship showed even less sense of occasion. The sailors mutinied. On
September 24th he was replaced by Lord Dartmouth, whose experience,
efficiency and popularity with the fleet made him, despite Macaulay's
jibes, a reassuring change. Personally Pepys found him a much better
man to deal with. But would he have chosen him to command at such a
pinch? The news of Narbrough's death in the West Indies, received in
London that July, was a heavy blow, 'not for private friendship's sake
only (tho' that be very great) but for the sake of the King and his Service
in which (without wrong to anybody) I do not think there does survive
one superior, if any one equal (all qualifications considered), to Sir John
Narbrough.'[11] Sir Robert Holmes, a fire-eater feared and hated in the days
of the Diary but now a trusted ally, was gouty and arthritic. Yet only a
year earlier he had actually been appointed to the West Indies command.
His infirmities had proved too much for him and Narbrough had gone in
his stead. None the less he put up a stout-hearted performance as
Governor of the Isle of Wight during the Revolution.

> . . . I am doing all I can to give a stop at Yarmouth and Hurst Castell,
> if I have any helpe from the King they shall not have this island soe
> easily as they may expect. I am in the feild every day, this I write
> before a drumhead, to-morrow I muster 2 hondered dragones that I
> macke out of the mallitia the choice of them . . .[12]

More perhaps than in the frequent and fluent letters of Lord Dartmouth
one catches the ring of a man who means business.

The critical condition of affairs did not deflect Pepys from the ampli-
tude of his high official style. When a sprig of the aristocracy saw fit to be
jocose about so serious a subject as boatswain's stores, the traffic of naval
preparation was held up while a proper rebuke was administered.

> You tell me [wrote Lord Berkeley, commanding the *Mountague*, to
> the Navy Board] you have not power to add to my allowance of junck.*
> This for your honors sake I ought to keep to myself, for should some
> sarcastical people know it, I fear it would be made a mighty jest . . .
> surely you do not think I should eat or sell ye junk, no; but he will
> suffer his boatswain to bobble him.

* Old rope suitable for use in making fenders, gaskets and such.

The Navy Board's answer, dated two days later, signed by three commissioners of whom Pepys was not one, exists in both rough and fair copies among his papers. Not for much longer would serving officers see the great Secretary coming so characteristically into action, opening up with his secondary armament before letting his big guns speak:

We have received your Lordships answer of the 17th . . . the stile of which we know how to observe, tho' not to imitate, intending to submit it with all humility to the King to judge of the difference . . . But, my Lord, the King has thought fitt in this and numberless other particulars to limitt us in the dispensing of his stores, and those limitts grounded upon measures not left to us to contrevart, he having paid too deare for the liberty heretofore allowed or taken in that particular. Nor has your Lordship (we feare) computed either the charge or difficulty that would attend the Extraordinary allowance you demand in this so contemptably [word omitted] a Commodity as Junke, should every ship of your rank (and the rest proportionately) have an Extraordinary allowance made it above the proportion established by His Majesty in the adjustment not long since solemnly made . . .[13]

The sentence, still far from its terminal point, uncoils its parentheses, as Pepys for a long moment forgets the Dutch and expounds the theory of efficient and orderly administration, making intellectual mincemeat of his opponent with an orotund gravity proper to a great officer of state and that sharp, no-nonsense tang so natural to himself. It is easy to make fun of Pepys's pomposity. But he lived in an age in which formality and punctilio, in public affairs at least, were carried to great lengths. And how else was a man of humble origins to assert authority against the insolent pretensions of courtiers and aristocrats?

Little enough of that autumn was spent in such congenial activity. James's vacillation and inertia checked the initial spirit of confidence and enterprise in which Dartmouth, most uncharacteristically, had proposed an offensive sweep along the Dutch coast. At the time of his appointment the station of the fleet had been shifted from the Downs to the Nore. Admirable as this sheltered anchorage was for taking on stores and reinforcements it had two grave disadvantages, one psychological the other physical. Its safe riding and its easy accessibility gave captains and officers dangerous opportunities of 'caballing' as their Admiral reported to Pepys with growing uneasiness. And, physically, the east wind that would bring the Dutch out would keep the English in. Towards the end of October, in the face of urgent suggestions from both Pepys and the King to take advantage of the westerly wind and get the fleet clear of the Thames,

Dartmouth moved across to the northern side of the estuary towards Harwich, taking up his station behind the Gunfleet shoal. James, who had fought in these labyrinthine waters, clearly felt the response inadequate but supported his Admiral with a loyalty that cannot have been easy. Dartmouth in a brief phase of euphoria claimed mastery of the situation: 'We are now at sea before the Dutch with all their boasting,' he wrote to the King on October 24th. The Dutch armada, which had in fact sailed a few days earlier, was even then limping, scattered and battered by a fearful gale, back to its home ports. The extent to which the Gunfleet anchorage could be described as 'at sea' was to be defined all too clearly a very few days later when William, in one of the most breathtaking displays of nerve and of leadership in European history, brought the expedition out again to face weather that had already justified his most persistent critics.

To tell the story of the descent on England and to trace the role of the Royal Navy in the Revolution of 1688 lies outside the scope of this book. Both tasks have been admirably executed in works whose titles are echoed in the preceding sentence.[14] But it is over the ground bass of these events that the crescendo of Pepys's official career reaches our ears. It was he, if anyone, who activated the country's defence. James, physically and mentally, was not the man he once had been. Moodiness, indolence, timidity even, are too widely reported of him to be dismissed as malicious, out of character though they are. Dartmouth as Commander-in-Chief of the Fleet was thorough and professional: perhaps sometimes too thorough and professional in his insistence on obtaining for the ships under his command stores and equipment that a more forceful commander would either have commandeered or foregone. The politicians on whom James had relied were in disarray: alienated, discredited or disaffected. The one man who was trying to galvanise the King and the navy into effective action was Pepys, hurrying between Windsor and Westminster, between Westminster and London, keeping the dockyard up to the mark, overseeing the Navy Board (two of whose members, Berry and Booth, had been appointed to commands afloat), hustling the slopsellers, chivvying the victuallers, remonstrating strongly (and with only too much reason) with Dartmouth in his capacity as Chief of the Ordnance Board over the alarming deficiencies in that crucial department. All, and more, that could have been expected of the greatest naval administrator England had ever known was done. All, and more, that could be done by his colleagues Deane and Hewer, brought under his daily eye and hand to concert pitch, was done. But when all was done, it was not enough. Pepys was not cut out to be a Cromwell or a Chatham: he was not a politician, still less a war leader, and did not think of himself as one. In the numbness of purpose, the failure of will, that characterised that nightmare autumn, his sheer thrust came nearest to supplying the resolution that should have been behind him. He deserved a chief of William's temper.

In his Herculean efforts to organise England's naval defence he took one initiative of a wholly political character. When Dartmouth was appointed to supersede the Papist Strickland Pepys was charged, as on the Tangier expedition five years earlier, with finding him a chaplain. Ken, his selection on that earlier occasion, had been one of the Seven Bishops whose successful defiance of the King had just laid his policy in ruins. Even if James could be brought to consider such an appointment a bishop was too venerable an ecclesiastical officer for such a post. But Pepys did the next best thing. In what was clearly a desperate attempt to reconstitute the Tory party of Church and King that James had so fatally divided, he wrote and pressed the job on the red-nosed Dr. Peachell, now happily restored to his Mastership. The fact that Ken had been preferred to a bishopric after holding the same office (*post hoc, propter hoc*) was twice discreetly alluded to. Peachell was startled, if flattered. 'I had a little itch to such a service 30 years agoe, but am now as old againe, and incumbred with businesse and therefore desire 24 Houres to consider & compare.'[15] Next day's Cambridge carrier brought his refusal.[16]

Besides the frantic bustle of mobilising the fleet (as usual the press gangs got hold of people who were legally immune: as usual Balty exceeded his powers, putting himself in the wrong with a short-tempered captain whom he had accused of malingering), besides the unremitting effort to keep the King steady and to get Dartmouth going, Pepys was also conducting an extensive and urgent correspondence over the General Election which the King had called for that autumn. He knew that he and Deane were by no means safe in their old constituency of Harwich. There was a plot to denounce them both as crypto-Catholics on the eve of the poll.[17] Sir Robert Holmes who controlled the Isle of Wight seats was not unhopeful of finding room for him and for Hewer too if need be. But that was reinsurance. Harwich must be fought and if possible won. The vast correspondence with Captain Langley, master of the packet boats and Mayor of Harwich, shows how much time such a campaign consumed. And there were other Admiralty boroughs, Rochester, Portsmouth, Dover, in which Pepys had valuable connections that might be called on by the King's hard-pressed supporters.

Private anxieties, family obligations, calls for help, do not disappear by sympathetic magic from the life of a busy man just because he is at his busiest. Of his Jackson nephews, John, as we have seen, was up at

Cambridge while his elder brother Samuel had just arrived back in late July from a cruise to the West Indies. The smattering of navigation he had picked up was not, as Pepys had evidently hoped, to be put to use in a naval career. Perhaps Pall, his mother, was already ailing. Certainly she died the following autumn and Samuel thereafter managed, not at all satisfactorily, the Brampton estate. What Mary Skinner's brothers were up to we do not know but it was probably mischief. By the following June their mother was imploring Pepys to rescind his decision to have nothing more to do with Peter: 'this Greaceless son of mine . . . o would to God that you had cane'd him, that you had Broken all his Bones Limb from Limb . . .'[18] Sir Samuel Morland, Pepys's first tutor, was still soliciting his old pupil's aid in obtaining a divorce from the coachman's daughter he had married without first verifying his belief that she 'was a very vertuous pious and sweet disposition'd Lady, and an heiress who had 500L per Ann. in Land of inheritance, and 4000L in ready Money . . .'[19] What she had in fact was the pox and a lover. Anyhow Sir Samuel thought that Pepys's constant attendance on the King in these days of crisis would give him an excellent opportunity of putting in a word with the Lord Chancellor. And then there were the usual troubles with servants. Since the offender was in this case black Pepys sent him aboard the ship that had brought Samuel Jackson back from the West Indies to be sold into slavery.[20]

On this buzz of activity fell the thunderclap of William's success. The whole Dutch armada had sailed down the Channel unopposed and had put the troops ashore in Torbay without losing a man. The English fleet, equal more or less in numbers, probably superior in quality, certainly so in striking power since it had no troop convoy to protect and could deny the enemy his bases while having the run of its own, had been windbound, as James and Pepys had warned its Admiral, behind the Gunfleet. Dartmouth, numbed by the magnitude of the disaster, could still hardly credit the fact. That James, his cause ruined by disregard of his repeated advice, could still spare the feelings of a loyal and affectionate servant touches the ignominy of defeat with nobility and pathos.

> . . . 'tis the greatest happynes of my life that yr Ma^ty is sattisfyed with my endeavers tho' they have proved so unlucky hitherto, 'tis strange that such mad proceedings should have such sucess at this time a yeare . . .[21]

William had landed on November 5th.* Dartmouth's letter here quoted

---

* It is worth remembering that England was still using the Old Style in dating: the modern notation would have made it November 15th.

was written on the 11th. Even as he wrote the first desertions from James's army had taken place. By the end of the month the trickle had become a flood, headed by his Commander-in-Chief, his other son-in-law and his nephew. The fleet, when at last it had struggled out to sea, had proved, not surprisingly, unreliable to the point of ineffectiveness. It had hardly got into the Channel before it was separated by violent weather and prevented from re-uniting by an unseasonable calm. Individual captains seized the chance of joining the winning side. Those who remained loyal saw no point in fighting a lost battle. Like the Parliamentary captains at the Restoration they knew that they had the safety of their country in their hands and counted it their first charge.

Pepys, as before in moments of public danger, showed the coolness, the tenacity, the constancy that underpinned the warmth and quickness so much more conspicuous in the everyday conduct of life. As long as James was in business he was in business with him. The sinking of the heart that so experienced and so penetrating an observer must have felt was no excuse for not doing one's job. Reports, requests, entreaties, flowed in from admirals, captains and local commanders at their wit's end what to do or how to do it. Instructions, encouragement, answers at least constructive where possible and rational where not, flowed out. To Dartmouth in particular he showed a magnanimity equal to the King's.

I am yet under some fears of your taking too much to heart your late misfortune . . . pray be fully at ease in this matter, depending upon't that if I knew the least cause for the contrary I would tell you of it. For so upon my faith I would . . . Once more therefore pray be at peace with yourself.[22]

Immediately news of the invasion had reached London James prepared to leave for the west in order to take personal command of the army. On November 17th he had his will solemnly witnessed by the Lord Chancellor, the two Secretaries of State, two Catholic peers and four senior officials of whom Pepys signed first in order of precedence. Early in the afternoon he left for Windsor, the first stage on his journey west. Pepys accompanied him there and secured from him a testimonial of his services to both Charles II and himself and a recommendation to the Lords of the Treasury to do him 'full right' in respect of any sums that might be due to him either as Secretary of the Admiralty or in his past capacity as Treasurer of Tangier. The grand total, according to Pepys's calculations, amounted to £28,007. 2s. 1¼d. It was never paid. Years after his death Hewer, his executor, and John Jackson, his heir, were still keeping up a spirited action with the Treasury.[23] The shade of Pepys, we may be sure, would have approved their refusal to take no for an answer: it would equally have approved the prudent guardianship of public funds that dismissed specious claims from persons already adequately provided for.

After the King's departure Pepys continued as before directing the affairs of the navy, seeking especially to maintain the closest contact with Dartmouth, corresponding with the English consuls in the Mediterranean, gathering intelligence, stiffening morale, maintaining discipline. But the play was over: the stage invaded by the audience: the other actors trooping back in search of parts in the next production. Within ten days the King was back in London a broken man. His health had given way, his army had lost its credibility with the desertion of its general (an act that shocked at least one of William's commanders), there was nothing left in his role but to make an exit. Even this was muffed: and high tragedy closed with the botchings of an under-rehearsed farce. Nervously and physically the King was in no state for so taxing a final scene.

When James, at his second attempt, at last succeeded in leaving the country, it was nearly Christmas. The political uncertainty had already threatened the stability of public order in the capital. Anti-Catholic rioters had burnt down the Spanish embassy and attacked chapels where mass was said. Looting and lynching were in the air. For Pepys who had held high office under the fallen régime and who had great possessions it was a time of anxiety acuter even than the days when the Dutch had been in the Medway. Then, at least, it had been possible to transfer his gold to the safety of Brampton, incompetent though Elizabeth and his father had been over burying it in the garden. In the fire there had been time to take the Diary and other books and papers out to Bethnal Green, even to see to the protection of his wine and Parmesan cheese. But revolutionary anarchy was much more frightening. On December 18th James left Whitehall for Rochester at midday and William arrived at St. James's that afternoon. At least the library, the pictures and the manuscript collections at York Buildings were safe from the mob.

Pepys submitted to the *de facto* Government as became a great public servant, without toadying and without embarrassment. On December 19th he had an audience of the Prince of Orange (as William was styled until, on February 13th, 1689, he and Mary jointly accepted the Crown offered by Parliament). Like his friends and fellow civil servants Blathwayt, Southwell and the rest he was continued in office: but unlike them he found his bitterest political and professional enemies high in the King's favour. Russell and Herbert, the two senior sea officers who had managed the naval side of the Revolution, personified everything that Pepys had spent his life in opposing. They were gentlemen captains of the most formidable type and they knew, as well as Pepys, that there was not room for both themselves and the Secretary in the direction of the service. Besides that there were the strongest personal antipathies: Russell was brother-in-law to Harbord who had done his best to bring Pepys to the block at the time of the Popish Plot; Herbert as Dartmouth's predecessor in command at Tangier had done all he could to harm the men and measures that Pepys from his earliest days as Clerk of the Acts had tried to promote. Both men had often received the sharp letters of inquiry or reproof by which Pepys tried to maintain discipline. No doubt both saw in the Revolution a golden opportunity to be rid of him once and for all. A fighting service, in their eyes, was the proper sphere in which the aristocracy should shine: it had no business with jumped-up bureaucrats.

William, to judge from the men he did retain in office, would perhaps have preferred to keep him; but he had first of all to keep faith with the men who had brought him to the throne. Meanwhile he was at war with France and Pepys's knowledge of the day-to-day state of the fleet as well as his unrivalled grasp of English sea-power made him indispensable to the Government.

What did Pepys think? At first, it seems clear, he recognised that he was at the mercy of Russell, Herbert and the rest. The endorsement of the letter Will Hewer wrote him on the day of his audience with William, 'a letter of great tendernesse at a time of difficulty', even if made after the event speaks a mood of profound resignation. Unlike James, Pepys found light in his darkness. It was no small thing to read these words from a man who had been his closest subordinate and colleague for twenty-eight years.

. . . I know you will chearefully acquiesce in what ever circumstance God-Almighty shall think most propper for you, which I hope may prove more to your satisfaction than you can imagine; you may rest assured that I am wholly yours, and that you shall never want the utmost of my constant, faithfull and personall service, the utmost I can doe being inconsiderable to what your kindness & favour to me has and does oblige me to; And therefore as all I have proceeded from you soe all I have & am, is and shalbe, at your service.[24]

As the days went by he found himself treated with at least the same outward correctness that he had shown to his new masters. Did he begin to hope of holding on? Certainly he made strenuous efforts to secure a seat in the new Parliament at the General Election held in January. As before he was warned of treachery at Harwich and urged to appear in person. Both he and Sir Anthony Deane were defeated and on February 20th he resigned his office. His presence was apparently still necessary for another two days — his last official letter is dated the 22nd — and on March 9th he was ordered to hand over all books and papers belonging to his office to Phineas Bowles, a man of little weight who had been serving as Dartmouth's secretary until chosen as Pepys's successor.

Not, of course, that he was in any true sense Pepys's successor. Herbert and the rest were going to make very sure of that. Both his salary and his status were cut down to a size that declared the uniqueness of Pepys.

22

Retirement

To abandon the practice of a profession in which unrivalled, even unprecedented, mastery has been generally conceded can never be easy. Pepys, as his letters and his *Naval Minutes** show, felt resentment, anger, frustration, cynicism, but never despair. His nature was altogether too positive: he was too interested in justifying himself or in venting the scorn he felt for his successors to have time for self-pity. And in any case there was still more than enough to employ his inexhaustible energies. His books, his pictures, his collections: the Royal Society and the delights of conversation and correspondence with learned men: his family, his friends, his dependants: above all, the towering literary monument for which through all his working life he had been amassing material, his *Navalia*. Bitter as the first taste might be there was much to be said for retirement. His health would not have stood the pace of executive life much longer: the colleagues he left behind were, almost all, highly uncongenial: the men with whom it had been a pleasure to work, Pearse, Hewer and Deane, left office with him. These were all good reasons for accepting the situation and making the best of it. And Pepys was nothing if not rational. But over and above all this was the quality touched on in the first chapter of this book, the instinct at the heart of his life so perfectly expressed by his friend and contemporary the poet Dryden:

* A collection of notes made during his two periods of retirement and preserved in his library. Published by the N.R.S. in 1926.

From Harmony, from Heavenly Harmony
This Universal Frame began.

No man had a truer ear for the pitch of experience or a more natural sense of its rhythms.

In the savage world of seventeenth-century politics it was not always easy to glide peacefully from Westminster or Whitehall to a bookish retirement. Pepys knew from experience that the first moments out of office are those of intensest danger. It is the opportunity for revenge, for plunder, and for eliminating a rival beyond recall. 'Stone-dead hath no fellow.' The pithy political doctrine of the Earl of Essex, expounded to the young Mr. Hyde as they walked up and down the bowling-green in Piccadilly while Strafford's life hung in the balance and the storm-clouds gathered for the Civil War, was no relic of a picturesque if violent past. Pepys had been a boy of eight when the remark had been made. In the course of his life he had several times witnessed its practical application, most notably in the Popish Plot (of which, with reason, he believed himself to have been an intended victim) and in the subsequent reprisals of the Government. Some of the men who had tried to have him executed had reappeared with William; Harbord, Admiral Russell's brother-in-law, and Major Wildman, whose record in cloak-and-dagger work stretched back over three decades. When Pepys laid down his office he knew with a veteran's certainty that an attack was coming. The only questions would be those of timing, direction and force.

He had in this tactically weak and exposed position two of the veteran's advantages: he knew that attacks, even in intimidatingly superior numbers, do not always succeed; and he knew how to handle his weapons. He had beaten off enemies much stronger than himself by his unrivalled mastery of documentation. The first essential therefore was to prepare a defence of his Secretaryship, to organise his papers so that reinforcements could be rushed to whatever point was chosen for attack. No doubt, as at the time of the Plot, his enemies would try to strike at him through his friends and protégés. He would only be in a position to relieve them if the flag was still flying over his own citadel. This immediate task resulted in his only published book *Memoires . . . of the Royal Navy . . . For Ten Years, Determin'd December* 1688 (London, 1690). As its title makes plain this is the classic *pièce justificative* of Pepys's Second Secretaryship and of the Special Commission on which Deane, Hewer and Balty had served. Since its subject-matter has already been discussed in Chapter XX nothing more needs to be said about it here except to reiterate that it succeeded entirely both in its immediate purpose of defeating the formidable Parliamentary attack mounted in 1691–2 and, at a longer perspective, in establishing his own achievement above the tideline of envy and fashion.

As at the time of the Brooke House Committee twenty years earlier Pepys recognised the supreme advantage he enjoyed through mastery of his records. Repeated requests to hand over his Letter Books from his ex-subordinate and ultimate successor, Josiah Burchett, had still met with no success as late as 1700.[1] He had surrendered, not without a tussle, a complete and well-arranged set of official papers (keeping, of course, duplicates for himself) between March and July 1689. But he was not going to part with a scrap of evidence that the strictest interpretation of the law did not oblige him to.[2]

His conduct of the Secretaryship, defended in depth by his filing system, might stand a direct assault. But no one could doubt, and he would have been proud to own, his loyalty to James II. This exposed him for the rest of his life to the suspicions and the occasional interference of the Government. Unlike William's ministers most of whom reinsured themselves by secret correspondence with the Jacobite court Pepys would have scorned to face both ways. Such transparency makes a man vulnerable. It was easy to have him arrested, along with Deane and Hewer, as 'suspected of dangerous and treasonable practices against his Majestye's Government'. All three were taken into custody on May 4th, 1689, and not released until the beginning of July. Pepys was again arrested in June 1690 but on this occasion he was allowed bail after only five days. In October the proceedings against him were dropped and he celebrated the formal restoration of his freedom by inviting his bailors to dinner. All of them, Sir Peter Palavicini, James Houblon, Robert Blackborne and Joseph Martin, were city men with strong connections either with the East India Company or with the Mediterranean. Exactly the men, in short, on whom the traditional Whig interest was founded. So far as is known Pepys suffered no further direct political persecution: but he certainly believed that his correspondence was read; his private papers were, apparently, subject to random seizure and search; and when, as late as 1699, he sent his nephew John Jackson on the Grand Tour he would have so dearly loved to have undertaken himself, the Government kept an eye on Jackson's contacts abroad.[3]

Even after his first arrest Pepys seems not altogether to have abandoned the possibility of a return to public life. Immediately on hearing of the proclamation for a new Parliament in February 1690 he wrote to his old friend Sir Robert Holmes and to the great Tory magnate of the west, Sir Edward Seymour, to solicit a seat. Nothing came of it. Doubtless his second arrest in the following June convinced him that nothing could. It

is however characteristic of his concern for justice and of his strong sense
of duty that he remained ready to expose himself to the snubs, the insolence, even the vindictiveness of his supplanters whenever it seemed that a
man might be penalised for having enjoyed his favour in the past. Such
favour, he had always impressed on its beneficiaries, was absolutely con-
ditional on efficiency and honesty. It was in the logic of his position to
stand up for them against malice and jealousy. As Sir Arthur Bryant has
shown his last days in office were much occupied in the protection both of
old servants and of promising young men whom he did not wish to suffer
through his fall.

In April and May 1689 he exerted himself, without success, to secure
employment for Balty 'after neare 30 Years Service in the Navy, without
Reproach, through many offices of Trust'.[4] Balty's misfortunes were compounded by a total breach with Pepys towards the end of May. The cause,
though unknown, was almost certainly a row over the position occupied
by Mary Skinner.

> I understand [wrote Balty on May 28th] that by the malisious
> inventive ill offices of a female Beast, which you keepe, I am like
> allsoe to lye under your Anger and disgrace (to me more insuportable
> than the former) but I hope, and humbly pray, (though she tould me
> imprudently and arogantly, you scorned to see me) that with your
> Generous Usuall goodness, wisdome, manhood and former kindness
> you will not damn him Unheard whoe shoold Joy to hazard (as in duty
> bound) his dearest Bludd for your Service.'[5]

Pepys would not accept such language from anyone. He never, so far as
we know, wrote or spoke to him again. It seems that he relieved his wants
through an allowance. Balty certainly thanks him for something of the kind
two years later when afflicted 'with Such Sickness and tormenting paines
all over my body, with the adition of the Yellow Jandis and other distempers . . . as but two days agoe, it was thought, I shoold never more
have seene light in this world.'[6] But he rallied, recovering all his stylistic
powers in an appeal for cast-off clothes.

A happier outcome rewarded Pepys's efforts on behalf of his cousin
Charles, master joiner at Chatham Dockyard. On November 10th, 1689,
Charles Pepys wrote in great distress at finding that he was about to be
replaced by his own foreman. Pepys wrote at once to his old friend
Edward Gregory, Commissioner at Chatham, and to Sir John Lowther,
the only member of the new Admiralty Commission whom he respected
and liked, pleading '. . . that as farr as you reasonably may you will require

other crimes to be alledg'd and proved against him (& such I never yet
heard of) besides that of his name and Relationship to your most faithful
and humble servant.'[7] Their intervention was prompt and decisive. On
the 23rd Charles Pepys wrote in exultation still vibrant, still breathless,
after three centuries.

Sr
I had my warrant delivered to me on ye 21st instant of ye ad[ty] and
I hastened to ye Roy[ll] navie bord and gat my warrant entred and signed
by 3 Comm[rs] and so soone as that was done I went to ye River and
tooke a boate that brought me to Graves end and as soon as I came to
Graves end I tooke Coche that brought mee whom [home] in ye
King's yard in Chatham by 3 a Cloke in the morning and at seven a
Cloke I mett ye Comm[r] [Pepys's friend, Edward Gregory] & ye Mr
shipwrighte whitche wisht mee mutche joy of my renued warrant thaye
asqued mee how yr honor did and wear glade to hiere yr honor was
well . . .

They were not alone in this: even in his headlong self-concern Charles
Pepys goes on to say how his cousin's ex-clerks in the Admiralty remembered him kindly. Did Pepys, as he read the letter, catch an echo of his
own frantic haste to get a warrant sealed and entered thirty years earlier?
He answered it in one of the last of those many, many letters of a senior
official (though such he was no longer) to a junior in which kindness,
wisdom and justice combine with an irrepressible itch to improve the
occasion.

Cousin Pepys,
Tis matter of great content to me to find by your letter of ye 23rd
that you are once more settled in yr. Employment. I pray God to give
you Health long to enjoy yr. Benefit & to execute well ye Duty of it;
& very glad I am that in ye Present condicon of Affaires with mee I
have been able to give you any assistance towards the obtaining thereof.
But at ye same time you are not to impute so much of it to me as to
make you forget what you owe to Comm[r] Gregory, for without his
timely & hearty appearance at my desire for you by his letter to ye
Navy Board all I did, or could at this time have done on your behalfe
would have signifyed nothing.
Therefore let me advise you by no means to fail in your dutiful
acknowledgments to him of this happy friendship to you . . . And this I
the rather press you in from ye Error which I find you were fallen into,
when at your last being with me you took ye liberty of complaining so

particularly of ye want of sincerity in those of your seeming Friends at Chatham, as if at ye same time that they were giving you good words they were undermining you behind yr back, in getting yr Employment away for another Man. Whom you meant, I know not. But if yr doubts did reach to ye Comm^r he has given you a very good Proof of yr mistake, worthy to be always remembered by you.

But above all, let me recommend it to you to avoid ye thinking that whatever it is that you owe either to him or me on this occasion, either he or I would have stirred one step for you upon the single Score of yr Relation to me had it not been seconded with ye Opinion we both have of yr Desire, as well as Ability to perform ye Worke of yr Place & that you will not only continue to expresse the same by all ways of Diligence, Sobriety & Faithfulness, but that you will rectify that Lownesse of Spirit & Backwardnesse in appearing in ye Execution of yr Duty, as a Warrant Officer, which (without any other Crime) had, but for ye seasonable kindnesse of Commr Gregory certainly undone you: yr submitting yrself to be imposed upon in yr Office by yr Inferior having given him an Opportunity of carrying away ye credit of all that was done, & you to be lookt upon as a Cypher . . .[8]

The younger generation did not always profit from such exhortation as they should. Pepys's heir, his nephew Samuel Jackson, abandoned the sea officer's career designed for him and was ultimately disinherited in favour of his younger and more docile brother John for marrying a lady whom Pepys thought unsuitable. The young Skinners, Mary's brothers, write with such bland impudence that Pepys was once moved to open his reply with the awe-inspiring form of address 'Young Man'. Even this failed of its effect: although they pass out of his correspondence for a time, Peter reappears, his insouciance untarnished, in a begging letter of delicious cant and flattery written only a few months before the end.[9] A third brother, Corbett, pursued a blameless career in the Excise, in which Pepys ultimately obtained him promotion.[10]

Pepys had enough troubles of his own during this time. Apart from his running battle with the Admiralty over his official correspondence and over the possession of York Buildings, apart from the threat of sudden arrest or seizure of his papers on suspicion of Jacobite plotting, he and Sir Josiah Child the East India Company Director were jointly charged before a Committee of the House of Commons of a high misdemeanour in 'sending the Phoenix man of war, to the East Indies, to seiz the ships and goods belonging to the subjects of England.'[11] What had happened was this. The Phoenix had been sent out at the end of 1684 to suppress a successful *coup d'état* in the Bombay Presidency led by an ex-Cromwellian officer against the hated rule of the East India Company's governor, Sir John Child (brother of Josiah). On the way out the *Phoenix* caught the *Bristol*, an interloper, that is an English vessel trading in violation of the East India Company's monopoly, in the Mozambique channel. As the *Bristol's* captain had accidentally shot himself the *Phoenix* put a prize crew aboard and sailed in company for Bombay. Unfortunately the *Bristol* was leaking badly and sank a fortnight later. While she was on the point of foundering the *Phoenix's* captain looted twenty bales of chintz. After he had arrived at Bombay he had her retrospectively condemned as prize.

These events took place in May and June 1685. Neither Pepys nor anybody else in England knew anything about them until nearly a year later: and the *Phoenix* herself did not enter home waters until August 1687. It was not until 1689 that the owners of the *Bristol* petitioned Parliament for redress against the captain of the *Phoenix* and against those, Sir Josiah Child for the East India Company and Pepys for the Admiralty, who had signed his instructions. Ordinarily such a charge would have been negligible. But in the spring and summer of 1689 Pepys clearly thought it dangerous. The monopolies of the Chartered Companies were identified with the Stuart dynasty. It was easy to represent them as the economic counterpart of political tyranny: it was simple to show that their enforcement was a violation of the liberty of the subject: and how convenient that Mr. Pepys, the lackey of Stuart absolutism, should be caught red-handed at this fell work. The Committee reported on July 18th 'that Mr Pepys by signing the said Instructions . . . [is] guilty of high mis-demeanour . . .' But James Houblon went to see the great lawyer Pollexfen, whose name Pepys put first in his list of its members, and was able to reassure his friend. Pollexfen would remove the sting: 'in ye Report he will cause the word "signed" to be altered and instead of it put "counter-signed."'[12]

In the same month Pepys was ordered to appear before the House of Commons Committee for inquiring into the affairs of Ireland and the fleet. James had landed at Kinsale in March and had ridden in triumph to Dublin. Londonderry, still unrelieved from sea, was at the last gasp of the most famous siege in British history. Why were there only nineteen ships with Herbert in Bantry Bay? But this was Pepys's home ground. He produced at once a complete statement of the strength and disposition of every ship in sea pay as at November 5th (the day William landed), December 18th (the day James left) and on February 20th, his own last day in office.

In spite of his apprehensions Pepys emerged substantially unscathed from the Revolution. He had lost office, but how much longer would age and health have allowed him to hold it? He felt vulnerable and insecure, but could he look back on a single decade of his life in which he had not experienced these unpleasant sensations even more acutely? He did not like losing a large income, but who does? His occasional assertions of poverty, voiced in the plangent tones peculiar to the very rich, are amply contradicted by his style of life, by his eager purchase of books, prints, manuscripts and pictures, by his liberal patronage of scholars, by his benefactions to Christ's Hospital and the University of Oxford, by his hospitality and by his generosity. The long evening of Pepys's life was as rich, as comfortable and, from all the evidence, as happy as his friends could have wished.

At the beginning of his retirement he appears to have considered setting up as a country gentleman. Early in 1690 his old friend Richard Cumberland sent a long and careful description of Walcott House,* not far from Stamford, to Pepys's cousin Dr. Gale. 'I guesse,' he wrote, 'that your Occasion of enquireing about it may bee in behalfe of some purchaser.' Since the letter has come to rest among Pepys's personal papers it seems probable that he was the interested party. But why in that case did he not write to Cumberland direct? His friend had certainly taken pains, covering two sides of a large sheet. 'The house is very beautiful being adorned with a large lanterne as it were on the top . . . Those who are critical about the matter say the house is too large & good for the small estate in land which adjoins it . . . The land about is healthy and most convenient for the pleasure of hunting . . .'[13] Pepys had made a present of his hack to Wynne Houblon in the preceding summer[14] so that this was hardly a temptation.

Wisely such an uprooting was not tried. He remained at York Buildings until the spring of 1700 when, for reasons of health, he paid a long visit to Will Hewer's house at Clapham. In the following spring he settled there for the two years of life that were left to him. He had known the house since it was built by Gauden the victualler and had described it approvingly in his Diary entry for July 25th, 1663. It was so near his friends in London and Westminster, so close to John Evelyn's country house, first at Sayes Court, Deptford and then, after 1694, at Wotton, near Dorking, that he often stayed there even before it became his last home.

York Buildings for the last decade of the century became what another age, another language and another sex would have termed a *salon*. It was a

* Pulled down in the nineteenth century.

centre of the literary, artistic and intellectual life of the capital. Here dined each week the 'Saturday Academists', a small group of Fellows of the Royal Society. To the library came scholars, historians, antiquaries and connoisseurs. Alike in its contents and its methods of arrangement it expressed the personality that formed it as freshly, as strikingly, as the Diary which is its most famous possession. As its cataloguer has well written:

> Were the Diary non-existent, and were no other source of knowledge available, a judgment of Pepys's character formed upon a consideration of the contents of his library would reveal him to have been a man of great breadth of interest and catholicity of taste, an inquisitive scholar conversant with more languages than his own, and a person in whom a love of order and neatness in detail was paramount[15]

No other collection preserves more perfectly the impress of its maker. Among the long meditated and carefully drafted instructions embodied in a codicil to his will Pepys enjoined that except for making good obvious deficiencies at the time of his death 'thenceforward noe Additions' should be made. Every volume was to have its individual number, each was to contain his bookplate and to bear on its outside covers his crest or cypher stamped in gold, except of course where this would spoil one of the exquisitely designed and executed bindings in which he took such pleasure. Everything was catalogued within an inch of its life (the books had been bought for use, not show) but they were to take their place in his presses according to their height, not their subject-matter. On this Pepys refined in his eighth instruction: 'That their placing as to heighth be strictly reviewed and where found requiring it more nicely adjusted.' Just as Pepys himself needed a stool to reach the higher shelves (visible in the illustration facing p. 209) so the books that were not as tall as their neighbours were mounted on wooden blocks faced with leather to match their bindings. A work on navigation rubs shoulders with a classical author, a French historian reposes beside an English poet, a collection of contemporary pamphlets adjoins a law manual. The extraordinary balance and complexity of that deceptively clear mind can here be apprehended through sight and touch. From theology, not so massively represented as in most seventeenth-century libraries, to gay, even licentious poetry (Rochester's *Poems* which Pepys at one time thought written 'in a style unfit to mix with my other books' bear on the spine the slightly shame-faced legend 'Rochester's Life'),[16] from children's books to Atlases, from Economics to Travel, every category of a well-found library is supplied. And yet the

[handwritten annotations in margin]

May. 31. 266g.

Pepys's Bookplate.

flavour of one man's taste, one man's mind, is not lost in a bland compre-
hensiveness. It is, naturally, most marked in the special collections, the
Navalia and the ballads, distant echoes of summer evenings with Elizabeth
and her maid singing catches on the leads of the old Navy Office. The
prints, especially the portraits, to which Evelyn's connoisseurship and
John Jackson's journeyings were tributary streams, exemplify the fascinated interest in people that is in its turn the root of his own fascination for us.

From Pepys's study was conducted a correspondence that ranged over
every field then subject to speculative intelligence or rational inquiry and
even opened some — ecology, for example — that belong more to the twentieth century than the seventeenth. The embellishment of the library with
a gallery of portraits, the improvement, both by acquisition and by prun-
ing, of the book collection, the cataloguing of the manuscripts and the
sorting of a lifetime's accumulation of letters and papers went on continuously. Pepys was assisted in these tasks by two or three clerks, one of
whom Paul Lorrain, a Huguenot refugee, took orders, becoming in 1700
prison chaplain at Newgate. For twenty years he earned considerable sums

and a minor literary reputation by publishing the authorised confessions
of men and women on the point of execution. This grisly output was
supplemented by a small work of his own entitled 'The Dying Man's
Assistant'. Pepys, characteristically, used his influence with the Archbishop of Canterbury to forward his ordination. But, from his own point
of view it was a nuisance, inhibiting '. . . the use I should have to make
of him relateing to my books, papers and clerkelike services, other than
bare sitting at his deske upon solemne works only.'[17]

For the rest, the household went on much as before. Mary Skinner
still presided over a housekeeper, a porter, two footmen, a coachman, a
cook, a laundry-maid and a housemaid.[18] Invitations to dinner were accepted
with an alacrity that suggests good food and drink, less elaborate perhaps
than the gourmandising of younger days and sharper appetites. Dryden is
bidden to 'a cold Chicken and a Sallade', Dr. Gale to 'a dish of tripes',
Sir James Houblon to 'a piece of mutton' or 'a jole of ling' [best end of
cod], and a Baron of the Exchequer to 'a tansey', the lightest of light
refreshments.[19] But if grossness was eschewed, so was austerity. John
Evelyn, his favourite and most constant guest from Wotton at the end of
August 1692, wrote:

> Here is wood and water, meadows and mountaines, the Dryads and
> the Hamadryads; but here's no Mr Pepys, no Dr Gale. Nothing of all
> the cheere in the parlor that I tast; all's insipid, and all will be so to
> me 'til I see and injoy you againe . . . *O Fortunate Mr Pepys!* who knows,
> possesses, and injoyes all that's worth the seeking after. Let me live
> among your inclinations and I shall be happy.[20]

Deep though the pleasure it gave him, Pepys left this letter unanswered
for a fortnight. The reason was that he had gone to ground. The continued
suspicions of the Government, the unpredictable searches to which he
had been several times subjected had convinced him of the danger he was
in by preserving so many of his papers. Until he knew what was lying
about for his enemies to pick up he could not be easy. At the end of June
he took a house near the Houblons in Epping Forest, put it about that he
was spending the summer in the country – and disappeared. In reality
he shut himself up in York Buildings, not stirring outside, or even coming
downstairs, for the best part of three months. As usual he achieved what
he set out to do. But at a certain cost (besides the £30 on the house that
had been rented as a blind):

my constant poreing, and sitting so long still in one posture, without any divertings or exercize, haveing for about a month past brought a humour down into one of my leggs, not only to the swelling it to allmost the size of both, but with the giving mee mighty pains, and disabling mee to this day to putt on a shooe on that foot.[21]

Pepys's troubles with the new régime were, in fact, pretty well over. His most dangerous enemy, Admiral Herbert, had been disgraced after the Battle of Beachy Head; Russell, who survived in high command, was perhaps too calculating to indulge the caprice of revenge. Politically there was much less to be feared from men who openly refused to take the oath of allegiance to William and Mary on the grounds that they had already sworn themselves to James — non-jurors as they were called — then from those whose Jacobitism, real or pretended, was secret. Pepys grumbled at paying the double capitation tax imposed on this scruple, but he was never afterwards arrested. If the Secretaryship of the Admiralty was successively in the hands of two clerks with whom he had quarrelled, James Sotherne and Josiah Burchett (the miserable Bowles had not lasted long), there were other clerks such as Richard Gibson who kept their old chief informed and had the sense to avail themselves of his knowledge, his experience and his mastery of official draughtsmanship. When Gibson showed him a copy of a memorial he had drawn up for the King on the state of the navy Pepys noted approvingly that his proposals for victualling the navy were the same as those he had himself offered to Sir William Coventry in his famous New Year letter in 1666. Perhaps this was not altogether surprising since Gibson had, as Pepys acknowledges in the Diary, helped to frame his own ideas on the subject.

His true administrative heir did not, however, come from his most intimate circle of personal assistants but from the system and the tradition that he had shaped. Charles Sergison, who was Clerk of the Acts at the Navy Office from 1690 to 1719, a single-handed tenure of nearly thirty years except for the period 1702–6 when he shared the post with Pepys's old clerk Samuel Atkins, upheld the standards, voiced the very opinions, fought the familiar battles of his great predecessor. He had entered the Navy Office in 1675 as Chief Clerk to Thomas Hayter and Pepys's brother John who were then joined in the Clerkship of the Acts. He continued to serve as Chief Clerk under their successor James Sotherne until, at the beginning of 1690, Sotherne was appointed Secretary of the Admiralty and Sergison stepped into his shoes. How much he had imbibed of the true Pepysian spirit may be gauged from the terms in which, on May 24th, 1699, he and another civilian member of the board pressed William III to release them from office:

. . . we had struggled with many difficulties such as remote and deficient funds, stubborn and refractory officers, insulting superiors, such as rather countenanced than discouraged the loose discipline of the Navy, gratified their own passions and neglected everything else. But nevertheless by our adherence to the ancient rules and methods of the Navy, regularity of our payments and constant diligence and attendance we have overcome them all.[22]

Pepys was never entirely cold-shouldered by the official world he had left. On December 30th, 1689, he received a printed summons to attend the King and Queen on New Year's Day with the 'Mathematicall Boys' of Christ's Hospital. Although endorsed (twice) in his own hand 'went not',[23] his services to that foundation were recognised in April 1699 by the freedom of the City. He protested to Compton, Bishop of London, who asked him to recommend an impoverished cavalier for a clerkship in the Admiralty, that his name would only harm such a cause with Sotherne. Yet he was invited to Trinity House dinners, though no longer one of the Brethren, and from time to time dined with the Navy Board.[24]

Common sense and good feeling triumphed again when he was appointed a member of the Grand Committee for Greenwich Hospital in December 1694. The act of vision that was to transform the decaying Tudor palace of Placentia with its lovelier accretions, the Queen's House and the King's Pavilion, into the supreme composition of English architecture is enhanced by its association with Pepys. Evelyn, the greatest connoisseur of his age and an ex-Commissioner for the Sick and Wounded, was an inevitable choice for a position of control. But it was Pepys that Sir Christopher Wren took with him when he went down to view the site and discuss practicalities in late October or early November, and it was to Pepys that he outlined his first conception of making it the English answer to the Invalides. No one could have received the idea more eagerly. To achieve it, Pepys pointed out, Parliamentary finance was essential. Royal bounty and private charity would never prove adequate to so grand a design.

Once the danger of political persecution had receded, Pepys settled down to the enjoyment of those possessions and inclinations over which Evelyn had rhapsodised. His activity was almost entirely intellectual: his travels few and short: correspondence, conversation and reading made up the business of life. Nothing very much happened to him. He was held up by highwaymen at Michaelmas 1693 while on his way to Chelsea in a coach with Mary Skinner, John Jackson and several ladies. Pepys handed over his valuables without fuss and 'conjured them to be Civil to the Ladies, and not to Affright them, which they were'.[25] In the summer of 1694 and again in the spring of 1697 he was dangerously ill. From time to time his studies were interrupted by domestic broils (his housekeeper, Mrs. Fane, was so touchy that at last he insisted on her dismissal) or by friends in need. In March and April 1695 he was '. . . concern'd in a most tiresome, vexatious and yet foolish Sollicitation in Parliament for these last 6 or 7 Weekes, that has not left mee one thought free till the houre of its Prorogation . . . in behalfe of a friend that is nearest to my selfe.'[26] The House of Commons was at this time pursuing allegations of widespread corruption which culminated in the impeachment of Pepys's old ministerial colleague, Danby, now Duke of Leeds. Among the bodies particularly under attack was the East India Company with which Will Hewer had always been connected through his uncle Robert Blackborne and where, after his services were no longer required by the Admiralty, he had himself found employment, becoming in 1704 Deputy Governor.[27] The opportunity to repay Hewer's staunchness cannot altogether have come amiss.

But in old age the proportions of experience naturally shift from the direct to the vicarious. A reflective mind is offered fresh scope both by the confinements and the liberties of the condition:

> The soul's dark cottage, battered and decayed
> Lets in new light through chinks that time hath made.[28]

Pepys accepted the limitations imposed by age and health with the stoicism he had always professed and practised. For a man so interested in his own symptoms he was notably free from hypochondria. The inquiries of his friends are answered with serene assurances that cannot always have been easy to give. Even when in the spring of 1700 the wound from his lithotomy of forty years earlier became dangerously inflamed, necessitating three further operations and a great deal of pain and discomfort, he waited till it was all over before alarming his nephew, then on the Grand Tour, with the news:

> But I have great hopes given mee that what has been since done upon the third breach will prove thoroughly effectuall; I being (I thank God) once more upon my legs, and though my long lying in bed will cost me possibly some time for the removal of my weakness, yet I am in no doubt of recovering my first state very soon . . .[29]

It is no mean spirit that rises so gracefully over the temptations to self-pity.

The freedom conferred by exclusion from affairs was the best of blessings. All his life Pepys had strained to reduce phenomena, physical or psychological, to order because only by that way lay any hope of understanding. By setting down his experience, the totality of it, in a diary he had equipped himself to make sense of it. By preserving everything he could lay hands on in the way of nautical archives, he had equipped himself to reduce the naval universe to a harmonious rationality. The art of the shipwright 'their knowledge lying in their hands confusedly', the cheating of the purser, the economics of sea-power, the correct method of mustering stores, the promotion of hydrography, the virtues of Eastland plank, all the thousand and one topics central or outlying on which Pepys had been amassing material were to be resumed, digested and related in the Navalia which Evelyn awaited with such pleasing awe. And the Diary and the Navalia were but the exemplars of a curiosity that extended to everything it could cognise and of a belief that all phenomena were ultimately capable of rational explanation. He retained the intellectual appetite of a young man: he had spent a great part of his maturity in provisioning for a long voyage. It would not be his fault if he did not touch the happy Isles and see the great Achilles whom he knew.

23

Mens cujusque is est quisque

As a frontispiece to the *Memoires* Pepys printed an engraving of himself with his motto below it. He could not conceal his delight when it came to his ears that the Admiralty, imagining the words to be his own, had been pleased to criticise their sense and style. He wrote to Hewer:

> I could be well contented Mr Sotherne were told . . . that whatever reckoning I may make of his learning, I owne too great an esteem for that of my Lord of Pembroke's to think it possible for him to misplace upon me the honour of answering for a sentence soe much above my ambition of fathering, or the authority of any man else to censure but he (if any such there be) that would be thought a Latinist orator and philosopher fit to stand-up with Cicero, whose very words these are in that excellent and most divine chapter his Somnium Scipionis [Scipio's Dream] viz:
>
> Tu vero enitere; et sic habeto, te non esse mortalem, sed corpus hoc. Nec enim is es, quem forma ista declarat; sed *Mens cujusque is est quisque*, non ea figura, quae digito demonstrari potest.
>
> A thought derived to him from Plato, and wrought-upon after him by St Paul.
>
> I am, Your most affectionate servant,
>
> S.P.

No translation can do justice either to the passage or to the phrase that Pepys adopted for his motto, perpetuating its association with his name both by his book-plates and by the inscription on the front of his library. But, as this letter shows, it held so profound a meaning for him that not to translate would be the worse treachery:

Fight the good fight; and always call to mind that it is not you who are mortal, but this body of ours. For your true being is not discerned by perceiving your physical appearance. But 'what a man's mind is, that is what he is', not that individual human shape that we identify through our senses.

For Pepys, the *mens*, the mind, the intellect, reason, was the quality that set man above the beasts that perish and thus, implicit in the phrase if not in logic, his passport to immortality. It was the surest mark of the Divine hand, the thread to follow through the labyrinth in which generations of theologians had imprisoned their victims. In the ten pages of 'Notes from Discourses touching Religion'[1] this theme dwarfs every other. All his life Pepys had looked on atheism with horror. On the other hand there is little suggestion of piety and much to suggest the opposite. A man who goes to church to pinch the bottoms of pretty girls and emerges to pay his weekly visit to his whore can hardly be thought devout. Add to this a cool and sceptical turn of mind, a strong anti-clericalism, an even stronger distaste for religious enthusiasm based on bitter experience of its more frightening manifestations, and it would be plausible to represent Pepys as a sensible, comfortable materialist who conformed to the conventional observances of a religion that had its uses as a social sanction but who privately thought it all great nonsense. To discredit such an interpretation it is enough to read the letter quoted at the beginning of this chapter. There is no mistaking the language of the heart. And the circle in which Pepys passed the last decades of his life, Evelyn, James Houblon, Dr. Gale, Sir William Petty, were men who shared in differing degrees both his belief in God and his learned, critical, often irreverent, scepticism towards ecclesiastical pretensions.

To Pepys and to Petty, in particular, scepticism was a religious obligation. How else was the mass of superstition, hypocrisy, cant, ignorance and plain muddle to be cleared away? Was not this the essence of what the Royal Society was doing in the natural sciences? God had created the world and all that was in it. Religion, rightly understood, imposed on the *mens* the duty of making sense of everything, because every rational explanation of phenomena would uncover another sentence of the divine palimpsest. That is why the recovery and preservation of medieval manuscripts was pursued with the same zest as inquiry into hydrostatics or economics or the laws of chance or demography or the second sight. Knowledge, like God himself, was indivisible. What Pepys had done in the navy he would, had he but world enough and time, have done to the whole of life. Chance, as he truly remarked, brought him into the navy. But whatever he had done he would have instilled order and method, at first because he loved beauty but at last because he loved truth. Next door to Pepys's notes already referred to is a manuscript dialogue on Liberty of Conscience endorsed in Pepys's own hand: '1687. Sir Wm Petty's Paper written at my desire & given mee by himselfe a little before his Death.' Like the notes that precede it its tone is of candid inquiry, never of assertion or dogmatism. Both men (and this is true also of Pepys's other religious mentor, Dr. Gale) are entirely free from sectarianism: indeed in comparing the character and effects of Protestantism and Roman Catholicism they are more alive to the shortcomings of their own persuasion. Pepys even goes so far as to speculate whether a religious minority may not be a good thing in itself: 'It is said that we should live more carefully had we Catholicks amongst us then we doe now. As ye French Protestants were said to doe.'

If some choice souls have been disconcerted by the lack of the numinous in Pepys's religion, they have perhaps overlooked its seriousness and solidity. The cast of his mind was practical, workmanlike, matter-of-fact. The question 'Which, if any, is the true Church' was intellectually analogous to 'What price ought the Navy Board to pay for tallow.'

It is urged by some that ye present quarrell about Religion has sprung only from ye Priests, those on the Protestant side only beating downe ye Markett and pretending to serve ye people in a cheaper, not better, forme of worship than those of Rome; whereas ye latter are as obstinate in keeping up their price as ye others are concern'd to keep themselves in ye present Employment and power they have gott themselves into, tho' at a lower rate.

This is the tone in which Pepys and his friends talked. They were not sneering at religion any more than people discussing the motives and policies of a Communist Government are deriding Marxism. Any institutionalised system of ideas creates a network of interests. A few pages later Pepys notes:

D[r] G[ale] observes that places and business of proffitt are not disposed of & managed with grosser methods & Degrees of Coruption in the meanest & worst Societyes of Mankind than in ye Universityes.

It was precisely because he loved learning and adored his University that Gale, Fellow of Trinity, Cambridge, Regius Professor of Greek, High Master of St. Paul's, Fellow of the Royal Society and one of the most eminent scholars of his age, used such language. The universities were then, and long remained, closed clerical corporations. To him, as to Pepys, the offence of the clergy was double: their laziness and greed, bad in themselves, usurped the main resources available for the pursuit of knowledge: 'ye entered not in yourselves and them that were entering in ye hindered.'

It was therefore an essentially religious spirit that sustained the vigorous curiosity of the aging Pepys as it had animated the founders of the Royal Society.[2] Into the Notes touching Religion crowd questions and statements that foreshadow the preoccupations of the next two and a half centuries. 'When all is done reason must govern all since our very faith must be a reasonable faith.' 'Q. how farr mankind may be said to be made up of Different speecies, and where ye Brute ends & Man begins with the consequences thereof.' The age of Pope and the age of Darwin flash into focus. 'Consult Sir Wm Petty about ye N^o of Men in ye World etc.' We are in our own age of anxiety. And there is more than a hint of the modern school of linguistic philosophy in:

Sir Wm Petty's saying . . . that much ye greatest part of all humane understanding is lost by our discoursing and writeing of matters nonsensically, that is in words subject to more sences than one, to ye rendering disputations Infinite upon every Proposition that can be made in any Science whether divinity, Law etc.

Sometimes it seems that Pepys and his circle anticipated every intellectual attitude familiar to our world. When the Reverend Jeremiah Wells writes to him about a book entitled, 'Men Before Adam' we begin to wonder whether we are in the seventeenth century or the nineteenth. Neither archaeology nor natural science contributed to the arguments of this particular work which was based on internal criticism of the Bible.[3] But more often we recognise ideas and methods of a striking modernity. Dr. Goade's weather forecasts (based on astrology) are tested against observation. For January 27th the guarded prediction 'Curious briske winds & Frosty' was a pale reflection of observed reality: 'M[orning]: blak frost, with some drops of rain, a hard gale. A[fternoon]: more wind likely to snow.'[4] Pepys's historical researches suggest the idea of constructing a comparative price index: 'Confer with Sir James Houblon, M[r] Neale, Master of the Mint, etc. about the different par of our moneys compared with common commodities in different ages.'[5] The impact of Graunt and Petty's brilliant work on population statistics can be felt in half a dozen of his fields of interest: history, geography, economics, even, as we have seen, theology. The experiments in weighing and measuring on which Newton and Boyle and Hooke were rearing the topless towers of modern physics were beyond Pepys's competence but not beyond his intuition. Charles II and Samuel Butler might guffaw at the Royal Society:

> To measure wind and weigh the air,
> And turn a circle to a square;
> To make a powder of the sun,
> By which all doctors should b'undone;
> To find the north-west passage out,
> Although the farthest way about.[6]

Pepys had early recognised mensuration for a tool as diverse in its application and as revolutionary in its results as the wheel. His own mathematical limitations were not allowed to inhibit the play of mind. In November and December 1693 the project for raising money by a national lottery occasioned a long correspondence with Newton on the mathematical probabilities of dicing.[7] In the autumn of 1698 Dr. John Wallis, the Savilian Professor of Geometry at Oxford answered a letter of inquiry with a long disquisition on the mathematical expression of the relation of notes in music.[8] Wallis, like Pepys's old tutor Samuel Morland, had won early and brilliant success in the intelligence service by his skill as a cryptographer. Even in his learned retirement the Government of William III employed him to decipher the intercepted correspondence of the Jacobites.

But Wallis and mathematics were by no means the only connections that Pepys had formed with the University of Oxford. Through his interest in medieval manuscripts and through his friendship with Dr. Hickes, the master-builder of English historical scholarship, he had been drawn into an Oxonian circle, of whom Dr. Charlett, the Master of University College, was the busiest, most self-important and Humphrey Wanley the most learned and distinguished. The extraordinary story of this apparently incompatible group of combative individualists who nevertheless worked in complete harmony has been brilliantly told in

Professor David Douglas's *English Scholars*. Through Hickes and Charlett Pepys met and befriended the rising scholars, Wanley, the greatest of English palaeographers, Tanner, whose manuscript collections have enriched the Bodleian, and Gibson, to whose edition of Camden's *Britannia* Pepys contributed 'the account of the Arsenals for the Royal Navy in Kent with the additions to Portsmouth and Harwich so far as they relate to the Royal Navy.'[9] Through Evelyn he also met and helped forward the young Richard Bentley, greatest of English classical scholars and most tyrannical of Masters of Trinity. All these circles intersected. Evelyn was himself an antiquary of great erudition: Bentley was a Fellow of the Royal Society, as was Dr. Gale, who again combined classical and patristic scholarship with medieval studies. The cross-fertilisation of intellectual disciplines was never more fruitful than among the friends of Pepys.

To a heartening extent the spirit of inquiry transcended the divisions of politics and churchmanship. Apart from old friends in the city like the Houblons Pepys was on good terms with John Locke, the official philosopher of Whiggism, and with Lord Somers, its most skilful tactician. More surprising still, his friend Hickes who defied the Government in his inflexible refusal to take the oaths and whose loyalty to James II had been subjected to the agonising trial of a brother's execution, extended the same courtesy and respect to fellow scholars who conformed as to his nonjuring associates. Alone among Pepys's learned correspondents Dr. Thomas Smith, the Cottonian librarian seems to have been something of a bigot.[10]

The new scholarship, like the new science, could only grow from the publishing of results and the pooling of knowledge. In January 1693, Pepys in exchanging general information with Dr. Plot, the Professor of Chemistry at Oxford best known for his history of Staffordshire, sketched the idea of a National Bibliography.[11] Two years later he was writing to Evelyn in praise of the great survey of the manuscripts in English and Irish libraries that finally issued from the Oxford University Press in 1697:

> . . . I mean, the reducing into less room what poor mankind is now to turn-over soe many cumbersome, jejune, and not seldom unintelligible volumes for, and when that's done, not have 5, perhaps not one year, to reckon upon of his whole life for the sedate applying and enjoying those sorry pittances of seeming knowledge that he possibly has been 50 in collecting. What a debt were this to lay upon mankind![12]

Pepys, perhaps out of modesty, had declined an editorial invitation to
contribute the catalogue of his own collection. Evelyn told him, what he
must have known, how important it was 'for the very greate variety of the
choycest subjects, no where else to be found in England'.[13] The Anthony
Roll the most beautiful and the most valuable naval document of
Henry VIII's time presented to Pepys by Charles II in 1680 alone would
prove his case. Was it, perhaps, caution? As Edward Browne was to write
in a letter to Dr. Gale preserved among Pepys's papers:

> I do not very well like the printing of our English Mss. at Oxford;
> 'tis a dangerous thing, and may prove of fatal consequence to us some
> time or other, as the University of Heydelburg found to their cost,
> after they had set the Pope a longing for their Mss. upon their publish-
> ing a copy of 'em . . . I and you will make a good use of this book of
> Mss., Dr Gale, but there be those who will not.

To some extent Pepys had anticipated these disadvantages in his letter
to Dr. Charlett of August 4th, 1694, where it is not theft so much as
'the unreasonable Importunitys (and Interruptions too, where a Man
is his owne only Library-Keeper)' that he fears.[14] None the less he
complied: no less than 120 of his manuscripts are listed in the second
volume.

The many-sidedness of Pepys at an age when most men are grassing
over what they no longer have the energy to cultivate has still to be
remembered. His scientific and scholarly pursuits did not distract him
from the arts. He collected prints as avidly as ever. He was the patron and
friend of Kneller and, in the last year of his life, commissioned him to
paint the magnificent portrait of Dr. Wallis which he presented to the
University of Oxford. If his musical evenings were more sedate and less
frequent than in the days of the Diary, they were eagerly attended by men
of taste. On May 30th, 1698, Evelyn records dining 'at Mr Pepyss,
where I heard that rare Voice, Mr Pate, who was lately come from Italy,
reputed the most excellent singer England ever had: he sang indeede
many rare Italian Recitatives, &c: & several compositions of the last Mr
Pursal, esteemed the best composer of any Englishman hitherto.' His
great valediction to the art is contained in the letter he wrote to Dr. Charlett
on November 5th, 1700. Charlett had asked him to comment on a proposed scheme for educating the nobility and gentry. Pepys in reply con-
fines himself to two omissions, music and drawing. This studied passage

complements the spontaneity of what he had written in the Diary a generation earlier:

> *Musick*, a science peculiarly productive of a pleasure that no state of life, publick or private, secular or sacred; no difference of age or season; no temper of mind or condition of health exempt from present anguish; nor, lastly, distinction of quality, renders either improper, untimely or unentertaining.[15]

The modes are different, the theme the same.

A few weeks later Evelyn again dined with Pepys to meet another Englishman whose supremacy was even less disputable. William Dampier who had, as Evelyn remarks, 'ben a famous Buccaneere', had published the year before his *A New Voyage Round the World*. 'He brought a map, of his observations of the Course of the winds in the South Sea, & assured us that the Maps hithertoo extant, were all false as to the Pacific-sea . . .' Dampier's claims, which led to his being granted a captain's commission in the Royal Navy and the command of a fifth-rate for a further voyage of exploration, were in no way exaggerated. As his most recent biographer has written 'He was the only explorer of any note during that century. He alone could provide descriptions of the flora and fauna of unknown parts of the world. He worked out the wind system of the southern hemisphere. He illustrated his journal with drawings of exotic plants and fruits and described the habits of strange beasts and savages.'[16]

The charm of Pepys's company and conversation is evident from every source. ''Tis never any drudgery to wait on Mr Pepys,' wrote Humphrey Wanley, a scholar more apt to offend than to compliment, 'whose conversation, I think, is more nearly akin to what we are taught to hope for in Heaven, than that of anybody else I know.'[17] The increase of his learning did not make him pedantic. To the end of his life his curiosity was as readily stirred by the things that interest the unlearned as by the questions propounded by savants. Ghost stories and anecdotes of second sight found in him an absorbed if critical listener. The supernatural had on occasion obtruded itself on his official consciousness as when on April 11th, 1672, the Commissioner at Harwich reported that:

> . . . on Munday night last about 10 of ye clocke at night [the *Merlin* yacht] being at anchor in above 10 fathom water, on a sudden the yacht fell into a shivering and trembling; in soemuch that som thought she had strucke; a souldier and a seaman being upon the Decke the Souldier cryes out they shoot cross barre shot. The Sprit fell from the Mast and all ye Iron rings were broken in small pieces.[18]

Fortunately such visitations were rare. Another correspondent credited
Pepys with first-hand psychic experience:

> Sir a gentlewoman of my Acquaintance, tould mee shee had it for a
> great certainty from the family of the Montagues, that as you were one
> night playing late upon some Musicall instrument (together with your
> friends) there Sudainly appeared a Humane feminine Shape and
> Vanished. And after that sometime, walking in the Studdie, you
> Espied the Appearing person Demanded of her if at such time shee
> were not in Such a place. Shee answered no But shee Dream'd shee
> was and Heard Excellent musick.[19]

Pepys evidently knew the story from another source since he endorsed the
letter 'about the Vision appearing (to Mr Mallard) at his playing by night
on the viall'.

In the middle of the Revolution of 1688 James Houblon sent his
friend an account of the apparition at Cork of a murder victim to the
Protestant (and English) maid-servant of one of his Protestant business
associates. The 'specter' showed the maid where to dig for his bones which
were found the next morning to the excitement of all.[20] It seems improbable that Pepys was much impressed: certainly there is no sign that he
followed the story up.

A few years earlier on passage to Tangier, Pepys had been 'very hot'
in opposing Dr. Ken's belief in the existence of spirits. His investigation
of the matter in his retirement led him to qualify this opinion, or rather
to admit the existence of phenomena that could not in the present state of
knowledge be satisfactorily explained. The two very long letters that
weighed with him, one from Lord Reay and the other from Hickes,
deal entirely with manifestations of the second sight in Scotland, especially in the Highlands, and Islands. Hickes had been chaplain to the Duke
of Lauderdale when he was High Commissioner of Scotland in the late
1670s. It is clear from Hickes's letter that the Duke, a highly educated
man of the world, unromantic to the point of cynicism, accepted absolutely the evidence for second sight and even witchcraft that Hickes
was in two minds about. In this he agreed with educated Scottish
opinion: 'I never met with any learned man, either among their divines
or lawyers, who doubted of the thing.'[21] Pepys himself reserved his position: '. . . as to the business of the second sight, I little expected to have
been ever brought so near to a conviction of the reality of it as by your
Lordship's and the Lord Tarbutt's authoritys I must already own myself
to be,' he wrote to Lord Reay.[22] To compare Pepys's critical assessment of

such evidence with that of his slightly older contemporary John Aubrey is to turn from modern science to folk lore. Yet both men, and their many common friends in the Royal Society, would have valued both the older and the newer approach.

The last case in which Pepys took an interest was that of his old friend, Dr. Gale, who died in his Deanery at York in the spring of 1702. A month or two later before any successor had been installed the Vicar Choral who was reading the Second Lesson at Evensong saw in the Dean's stall a robed dignitary constructed on the ample lines of its late familiar occupant. On leaving the lectern the vicar bowed. The figure made no acknowledgment. Small wonder, since it was that of a canon residentiary who had cut it too fine to get into his own stall and had slipped into the Dean's. The vicar, however, construed its embarrassed immobility as evidence of its being Dean Gale's ghost: or at any rate thought it a story worth telling after drinking too much at a Lord Mayor's banquet. The Dean's son, Roger, exploded it in answer to Pepys's inquiry, 'to a person that had rather hear truth than strange storys'.[23]

The correspondence that most perfectly unfolds the mind and temper of the post-official Pepys is that with Evelyn. The letters range easily over all that is doing in the learned world: the praiseworthy efforts of the Virtuosi of Oxford in gathering and printing manuscripts, the progress and careers of the young scholars they were encouraging, the meetings of the Royal Society, the travels abroad of their young friends and relations. At any moment they turn aside to raise a point of scholarship or connoisseurship, to relate a piece of gossip, to discuss (pungently and never at length) the political situation or the conduct of the war. Men of learning and men of the world, they touch every note except flippancy or self-pity. The reader of this book will be tediously familiar with Pepys's ailments; a glance down the relevant column of Dr. Esmond de Beer's index to his magisterial edition of Evelyn's Diary reveals a scarcely less dismaying clinical history. Both men make the most of what is left to them: both urge the other on. 'Why don't you give us a part or two?' Evelyn wrote when the Navalia had still, by the end of 1696, failed to appear. 'Time flies a pace, my friend. 'Tis evening with us; do not expect perfection on this side of life. If it be the very best, as I am sure it is, nothing can be better; no man out-throws you.'[24] Posterity may regret that this excellent advice was not taken. But Pepys, perhaps, had had enough of ambition, though he could never be idle. Writing from Clapham in August 1700 he tells Evelyn that his doctor has forbidden him to bring his books ' "What then," will you say too, "are you a doing?" Why truely nothing that will bear nameing, and yet am not (I think) idle; for who can that has so much (of past and to come) to think on as I have? And thinking, I take it, is working.'[25] Death, never far from their thoughts, is serenely accepted. Evelyn, whose piety was deep and lifelong looked forward to their arrival:

> in those regions of peace and love and lasting friendships, and where those whose refined and exalted nature makes capable of the sublimest mysterys, and aspire after experimental knowledge (truely so called), shall be filled; and there without danger tast of the Fruite of the Tree (which cost our unhapy parents so deare); shall meete with no prohibition of what is desierable, no serpent to deceive, none to be deceived. This is, Sir, the state of that *Royal Society* above, and of those who shall be the worthy members of it.

Pepys acclaimed a Beatific Vision so congenial to his own.

> What then should I have to say to the whole of that glorious matter that was so enclosed in your last? Why truly, neither more nor lesse than that it looks to me like a seraphick *How d'ye* from one already entred into the regions you talk of in it, and who has sent me this for a *viaticum* towards my speeding thither after him.[26]

The letter had begun with this sentence:

> *Dover-Streete* at the topp and *J. Evelyn* at the bottom had alone been a sight equal in the pleasure of it to all I have had before me in my 2 or 3 months by-work of sorting and binding together my nephew's Roman marketings . . .

John Jackson had returned in August 1701 from a two years Grand Tour, planned, financed and followed by his uncle with far greater zest and far acuter perceptions than those of the traveller himself. The account of the tour given by J. R. Tanner in his introduction to the *Correspondence* is too long to quote and too happy to mangle. Perhaps it was Tanner's years as a College Tutor that enabled him to hit off exactly the staid, worthy, complacent dullness of the young man and to contrast it, by implication, with the glittering sprightliness of the old one.

Evelyn supplied the inspiration of the journey. Pepys never tires of telling his friend how he towers above his contemporaries by having added a European to an English education. John Jackson was to receive the benefits of which Pepys felt the lack and which he constantly recommended to friends like Dr. Gale who had sons to bring up. The details of the route, the arrangements for letters of introduction and the provision of foreign exchange were seen to by the Houblons. Besides the chief aims of civilising John Jackson and acquiring books, prints and manuscripts an important subsidiary objective was to witness the opening of the Jubilee Year of 1700 in St. Peter's. Leaving London on October 13th, 1699, Jackson was in time to see the deputy appointed by the Pope open the Holy Door on Christmas Eve. The Pope's illness raised hopes that he might be in Rome for a papal election. Captain Hatton, dining with Pepys, commissioned Jackson to obtain a form book for the big race, 'a Historicall List of the Names, Countrys, Ages, Characters & Interests of all ye Praesent Cardinalls; in order to ye employing Conjectures touching ye Choice to bee made . . .'[27] Pepys had earlier passed on a request from 'my Lord Clarendon who you know is a great saladist and curious' that his nephew should dust his letters with Roman lettuce-seed.

To get from London to Rome Jackson had ridden in one October day to New Shoreham, where contrary winds kept him the best part of a week. To his complaints of boredom and low company Pepys pointed out that he was better off waiting ashore than 'beating it to noe purpose at sea'. Landing at Honfleur after a hair-raising voyage in which an alcoholic master ran aground three times, Jackson and his servant passed by way of Rouen to Paris and on to Lyon and Geneva. His aptitude for the delights of travel may be gauged by his writing from Lyon: 'I must not omitt observing to you that I have not yet mett with a dropp of good wine; even in Burgundy itselfe it was hardly tolerable.' From Geneva he crossed the Mont Cenis to Turin and found, at last, in Genoa a town he actually enjoyed. 'But the difficultys wee found in getting away very much allayed this passion of mine.' He had hoped to get a felucca to Leghorn but had to follow the coast road instead. In Rome he conscientiously did what was expected of him: saw the sights, listened, rather glumly, to the singing in the Sistine chapel, obtained both an audience of the Pope (who had rallied a little) and, after much difficulty, transcripts of Henry VIII's letters in the Vatican Library. He obediently sanded his letters with lettuce-seed, he avoided living with English people so as to improve his Italian, and lolloped docilely through the hoops that his enthusiastic ringmaster set up for him by every post.

Naples he disapproved on moral grounds; at Venice he was indisposed. Only on his way back to Genoa to take ship for Provence and Spain was he moved to delight by the intensive culture of the Po valley, attributing it (wrongly) to the natural fertility of the land instead of the remarkable irrigation begun in the twelfth century. In the Midi he visited Montpellier and found 'no manner of amusement or conversation, but dangerous, very dangerous play among the ladys of quality, and idle chatt and ramping among the grisettes'. Spain was expensive but Houblon's trading partner Sir William Hodges entertained him so long and so handsomely that a useful economy was effected. Anticipating this possibility Pepys had specifically warned his nephew to establish himself in lodgings 'that you may be actually fixt therein before you appear to him, that so you may go to him only as a traveller, recommended to him (as before) for moneys and advice as such, without the least appearance, either of designing him other trouble, or drawing on Sir James Houblon or myself any further obligations for the same.' When he heard from Hodges (not from Jackson) that he was not only established as a guest in his house but had let him go to all sorts of trouble to arrange an extended tour in Spain 'a most formal and elaborate tour that I never heard undertaken in Spaine by any private gentleman that was not led to it either by being in the train of some Embassador or by business as a merchant or otherwise' he was very angry. The affectionate curiosity of his side of the correspondence suddenly merges into the tone, half menace, half reproof, that that peccant sea-officers knew so well. Poor Jackson! He had tried to follow Pepys's instructions but Hodges, the Old Wardle of Cadiz, would not take no for an answer. Pepys accepted the situation, grudgingly at first but soon lost sight of his resentment in his anxiety that his nephew should see a bull-fight. All in all Spain was a success: certainly it shone by contrast with Portugal from which country Jackson at last took ship for home.

Throughout the tour Pepys not only told him what to see and do but took great care to form his manners. He must not cadge from Sir William Hodges: he had been very remiss in not writing to thank the Houblons for all the trouble they have taken on his behalf: besides writing himself, 'You should furnish mee with something to say to those friends of ours who have endeavoured to oblige us by theyr recommendatory letters on your behalfe; whatever the fruite of them may have really proved to you.' Pepys cannot have learned his own charming manners from his father and mother. He had acquired them by living on intimate terms with the Mountagu family and as the friend of such men as Sir William Coventry and John Evelyn. For all the affectionate pride he took in his nephew's acquirements — a pride nowhere more evident than in the care taken by his closest friends to say how gifted, how cultivated Mr. Jackson was — he was too much of a realist to credit him with his own powers of observing and assimilating. And Jackson seems to have been well fitted for the part assigned to him. It was the only family relationship that has left no trace of any quarrel.

Pepys's natural tenderness of heart checked by the early frosts of selfishness and competition flowered abundantly in age. Affection so freely given was generously returned. The staunchness of Hewer, the gentleness of Mary Skinner, the simplicity of John Jackson upheld him when the dark days came. In October 1700 Sir James Houblon died, 'one of the longest as well as most approved friends till now left mee in the world'. Dr. Gale, disappointed a second time of the Mastership of Trinity, died in his hated northern Deanery in April 1702. Evelyn, frail and a good twelve years older than Pepys, was the only survivor of his intimate circle. Ill health was closing in. It must have meant much at such a time to receive the offer of an old married servant to leave her own home and help nurse him if need be.[28] To the end he retained his intellectual curiosity. Only a few months before his death he asked John Houghton, the political economist, to send him his notes on population, national income and the avoidance of war. 'Honoured Sir,' replied Houghton, 'if these cogitations shall pass muster, and find a place among the meanest of your Collections, I will not despare but that once in a thousand years it may come among statesmen to be considered whether there may not be a better way for one kingdome to humble another than by killing the people.'[29] The honour paid to Pepys's spirit of rational humanity was richly deserved.

In his last, most golden season, Pepys did not turn inward. If he devoted the bulk of his time to perfecting his collections, arranging and re-arranging them, to the satisfaction of intellectual and artistic tastes and to the cultivation of his many friendships, he did not neglect his duty to his neighbour. His papers include schemes for redeeming the English captives at Algiers, for improving and extending the naval welfare system of the Chatham Chest.[30] He was a benefactor to Christ's Hospital and to the French Church at the Savoy.[31] He was ready to give practical help to refugees from religious persecution.[32] Quite simply he was a good man. When after much pain and discomfort it was clear that he was dying it was of other people, not himself, that he thought. His last letter was an appeal to Sir George Rooke, Commander-in-Chief and Admiralty Commissioner, on behalf of Balty, still without any relief after all his years of service. The letter immediately preceding it written by John Jackson at Pepys's dictation answers a French refugee's request that a grandchild be nominated to a place at Christ's Hospital. Its courtesy, its care and its constructiveness would be notable even from a man who was not on his deathbed.

Whether Pepys saw Balty and was reconciled to him we do not know. Evelyn, himself barely recovered from a broken shin that had taken a long time to heal, called to say good-bye on May 14th, 'which much affected me'. John Jackson, Mary Skinner, and Hewer were in constant attendance and Hickes gave him the Last Sacraments. Jackson's account of his uncle's affection and tranquillity while in great physical distress is very moving.[33] Hickes who conducted the funeral as well as attending the deathbed, wrote to their common friend Charlett:

> The greatness of his behaviour, in his long and sharp tryall before his death, was in every respect answerable to his great life; and I believe no man ever went out of this world with greater contempt of it, or a more lively faith in every thing that was revealed of the world to come. I administered the Holy Sacrament twice in his illness to him, and had administered it a third time, but for a sudden fit of illness that happened at the appointed time of administering of it. Twice I gave him the absolution of the Church, which he desired, and received with all reverence and comfort; and I never attended any sick or dying person that dyed with so much Christian greatnesse of mind, or a more lively sense of immortality, or so much fortitude and patience, in so long and sharp a tryall, or greater resignation to the will, which he most devoutly acknowledged to be the wisdom of God; and I doubt not but he is now a very blessed spirit, according to his motto, *Mens cujusque is est quisque.*[34]

So circumstantial an account from a scholar of such integrity leaves nothing more to be said about Pepys's final position on matters of religion. He died early in the morning of May 26th, 1703. John Jackson, obedient, we may be sure, to some earlier injunction, noted that it was exactly '47 minutes past 3 . . . by his gold watch'.

His best epitaph was written, fittingly, in a diary. For all their familiarity, Evelyn's words will bear repetition:

> This [day] dyed Mr Sam. Pepys, a very worthy, Industrious & curious person, none in England exceeding him in the knowledge of the Navy, in which he had passed thro all the most considerable Offices . . . all which he performed with greate Integrity: when K: James the 2d went out of England he layed down his Office, & would serve no more . . .
>
> [He] was universaly beloved, Hospitable, Generous, Learned in many things, skill'd in Musick, a very greate Cherisher of Learned men, of whom he had the Conversation . . .
>
> Mr Pepys had ben for neere 40 years, so my particular Friend, that

he now sent me Compleat Mourning: desiring me to be one to hold up the Pall at his magnificent Obsequies; but my present Indisposition hindred me from doing him this last Office.

On June 4th he was laid beside Elizabeth in front of the altar at St Olave's. The funeral took place in the evening, a practice then common in the fashionable world to symbolise the ending of a day. Elizabeth's bust looked down on a gathering representative of almost every stage and facet of her husband's career. Balty was there, supported by one of his daughters. The second Earl of Sandwich and his brother the Dean of Durham sat next to them. A host of Pepys relations and connections echo the pages of the Diary. His doctors, his banker, his book-binder, his lawyer: the Clapham household, the Hewer clan, the President and many of the Fellows of the Royal Society, the Dean of Christ Church and the Master of Trinity, even the venerable Dr. Wallis swell the crowd. The Board of Admiralty were there in force and both the Archbishop of Canterbury and the Bishop of London, though it was the non-juror Hickes who took the service. As in his life, so at the commendation of his soul to God there was room for the people who had loved and served him as well as for the famous and the talented.

Appendix

———

The drafting of this letter, signed by Lord Brouncker, Sir John Mennes, Thomas Middleton, Samuel Pepys and John Cox, is fully described in the *Diary* (April 17th and 18th, 1669). The text here printed follows that printed (with modernized spelling) by J. R. Tanner in *Further Correspondence . . .* (pp. 230–5) from the office copy in the Letter Book now in the National Maritime Museum (LBK/8, ff. 589–93). The original has recently come to light among the papers of Pepys's sometime colleague, Sir Thomas Osborne, later Earl of Danby and Duke of Leeds. It is now to be found in the Duke of Leeds MSS in the custody of the Yorkshire Archaeological Society (DD5/12/10). The original, of course, contains the phrase about the outbreak of the civil war which the Duke of York asked Pepys to alter. I have also restored the characteristic parenthesis round the phrase 'as one body'.

The Navy Board to James, Duke of York.

17 April, 1669.

These are, in pursuance of your Highness's late commands, humbly to present your Highness with an account, as well as what occurs to us touching the ancient, as of what methods we are ourselves governed by in the present administration of those affairs of his Majesty's which fall within the cognizance of the Office of the Navy, and which (for the better explication of what follows) may be summarily comprised in the five ensuing particulars.

1. The well and husbandly building, equipping, manning, victualling, safe mooring, repairing, and preserving in harbour his Majesty's ships.

2. The seasonable, uninterested, and circumspect buying, preserving, and employing his stores.

3. The timely and reasonable demanding, together with the rightful and orderly dispensing, of his treasure.

4. The strict and timely calling to account all persons chargeable under or from this Office with any his Majesty's said treasure or stores.

5. Lastly, the seeing all orders of his Majesty's and the Lord High Admiral's duly executed, both by its own members and all inferior officers, as well in these as what other particulars shall come before it conducing to his Majesty's naval service.

Which being the standing duties of this Office, your Highness may be pleased to know that his Majesty's Royal predecessors, having until the time of King Henry the 8th served themselves in most occasions of sea service, both in peace and war, with fleets supplied them from the Cinque Ports and other hired ships, there was then but small use of, and consequently at this day little to be found touching any settled Office of the Navy within that time.

But when under that prince the Crown (from reasons then occurring) found it necessary to improve its naval strength, both in the build and force of its ships, beyond what was at that time to be found among merchantmen, then it was that the King becoming a builder himself, and in order thereto entering into a great expense in fitting of yards, storehouses, and wharfs, buying of stores, entertaining variety of workmen and labourers, and this with with such effect as in his lifetime to raise his Royal Navy to thirty ships of burthen and forty smaller vessels, it was found necessary that this action should be brought under some settled œconomy, and the same accordingly done by an establishment of proper officers for managing each part thereof, and all submitted to the superintendency of four Principal Officers, under the names of Treasurer, Comptroller, Surveyor, and Clerk of the Navy, who by the due execution of the distinct duties severally allotted them, stood (as one body) jointly entrusted with the performance of the whole work above mentioned.

This (may it please your Royal Highness) is the first method wherein under the Lord High Admiral we find the ministerial part of the Navy put; and under this it was that it continued more than 100 years, viz., until Anno 1642, without any other interruption than what was given it by an experiment made towards the end of King James of having several parts thereof managed by Commission,* touching the proceedings and issue whereof we conceive it unnecessary to say more here than that after 10 years proof of the fruits of that alteration it was found requisite to resume not only the old constitution but as many of the old hands as had survived that suspension.

In the year 1642, *upon the rupture between his late Majesty and the Parliament,*† his Majesty was pleased to forbid the Principal Officers of his Navy to pay the said Parliament any obedience or continue further acting in their employments; and being therein obeyed by all but the Surveyor,‡ the Parliament (as themselves declare in their Ordinance on that behalf) is compelled to supply the absence of those Officers by erecting a Commission,§ wherein what was before by proper distributions charged upon particular members, under the care and control of the whole, is now committed to the management of the whole promiscuously.

This Commission by successive changes (answerable to those in the hands that made them) continued till the happy Restoration of his present Majesty; when upon debate, first before your Royal Highness and then his Majesty in Council, touching the best method of settling the affairs of the Navy, and therein consideration being had as well of the approved method of ancient times as of the difference and disproportion between the naval action now and what it was formerly, to the rendering both the distinct and common work of the Principal Officers thereof much more difficult than heretofore, it was concluded most suitable to the present condition of the Navy that to these ancient, stated Officers there should be added (as there hath for the most part been an equal number of) Assistant Commissioners 'who' (as your Royal Highness hath in a late letter been pleased to observe) 'by being not limited to any, and yet furnished with power of acting and controlling every part both of the particular and common duties of the Office, have full opportunity given them as well of understanding the defects of the whole and applying their assistance where it may be most useful, as also of being able to remonstrate to your Highness where

---

* The Commission of 1618.

† *Marginal note*: 'Memorandum, That upon my reading my first draught of this letter to his Royal Highness, he liked well of the same, directing only these words to be altered thus, *The beginning of the late Rebellion*, and so it went from the Board to him.'

‡ Batten, who had been Surveyor of the Navy since 1638, at first adhered to the Parliament.

§ The Commission of the Navy appointed by the Ordinance of 15 September, 1642.

(through neglect, insufficiency, or want of further assistance) any part of the work of the said Office lies unprovided for.'

And this (may it please your Royal Highness) is the constitution according to which the Office was then first settled and now remains. Wherein as being supported both by Officers under special trusts and Commissioners qualified for the care and control of the whole, his Majesty is secured no less in the advantages flowing from the ancient method than of what are thought peculiar to that of the late times under a Commission.

That which offers itself next to your Royal Highness is the consideration of the rules by which the hands thus entrusted do govern themselves. About which we think it not needful to observe more to your Royal Highness than that, though it appears that the distinct duties of each officer and underofficer of the Navy have been in all times ascertained, yet we do not find that the same were formally digested into one body till the time of the Earl of Northumberland, who caused them to be collected, and confirming them with his hand as Admiral enjoined them upon the Officers of the Navy for their future government. The course your Royal Highness also hath been pleased to take, not only by a review, ratifying, and improvement of those orders of the Earl of Northumberland soon after the last settlement of this Office, but by several other subsequent acts, and particularly those sprung from that general inquisition into the methods and management of this Office which your Royal Highness hath been pleased to make since the close of the late War,*

Touching which, though we shall not so far undertake for their perfection as to think them proof against all the possible evils and abuses which time and the restless invention of ill men may produce in a matter not only so copious as this of the Navy but where the necessities arising from want of their due have driven many persons to the invention of and adventuring upon such practices as naught but those necessities could probably have urged them to; yet dare we not (may it please your Royal Highness) be so far unfaithful to his Majesty and our own observation as not to say that, as the rules and methods of the present administration of this Office carry in them no less than the result of all the long and chargeable experience of times past, so do they contain remedies sufficient to obviate the evils met with in the Navy at this day, if answered with suitable endeavours in us who are to execute them, and we furnished with the means requisite for the enabling us thereto.

---

* On the Duke of York's revised Instructions of 28 January, 1662, based on those of the Earl of Northumberland issued in 1640, see *Catalogue of Pepysian MSS.*, i, 20. The 'other subsequent acts' are described in *ibid.*, i, 21ff.

Of which, as we shall (each of us for himself) most readily embrace any course of examination as to the former, so the frequency and expressiveness wherewith we have from time to time declared and inculcated our wants, with the untimeliness and insufficiency with which these wants have been ever answered, are too legible that we should doubt of our justification in what concerns the latter.

We have nothing to add but the acquainting your Highness with our having annexed to this letter a copy of your Highness's aforesaid books of instructions, with the additional rules established by your Highness during the late War, for regulating our payments and methodizing the accounts thereof, as also the Orders of Council conferring special parts of the Comptroller's work on others of our number and giving him further assistance in the auditing the accounts of storekeepers. Which papers comprehending a complete view of the general administration of this Office, we have (for avoiding prolixity) spared the adding those other particular orders which your Highness hath occasionally been led to the establishing, and which, though of no less importance to the weal of the Navy, yet being for the most part only supplemental to the said book, easy reference may be had thereto in any case wherein his Majesty or his Highness shall upon its perusal think fit to call for any further information.

Notes

Shorthand Letters	*Shorthand Letters of Samuel Pepys*, transcribed and edited by Edwin Chappell (C.U.P., 1933).
Howarth	*Letters and the Second Diary of Samuel Pepys*, ed. R. G. Howarth (1932).
H.T.H.	*The Letters of Samuel Pepys and his Family Circle*, ed. Helen Truesdell Heath (O.U.P., 1955).
D.	Pepys's Diary.

At the moment of going to press the definitive edition of R. C. Latham and W. Matthews has reached December 31st, 1667. For entries after that date I have used Wheatley's edition. For the convenience of the reader all references to the Diary are given by date of entry.

ABBREVIATIONS

Adm.	Admiralty Library.
C.S.P. Dom.	*Calendar of State Papers, Domestic.*
D.N.B.	*Dictionary of National Biography.*
E.H.R.	*English Historical Review.*
LBK	Letterbook in National Maritime Museum Pressmark LBK/8.
M.M.	*Mariners Mirror.*
N.M.M.	National Maritime Museum.
N.R.S.	Navy Records Society.
P.L.	Pepys Library.
Rawl.	Rawlinson MSS. in the Bodleian Library.

NOTES

CHAPTER I

1 Cat. Pepysian MSS., i, 4.

2. *Loc. cit.*, p. xx.

3 F. R. Harris, *Edward Mountagu, 1st Earl of Sandwich* (London, 1912), i, 137.

4 Rawl. MS. A.185, printed in A. Bryant, *Years of Peril*, 410–11.

5 D. 6 Sept. 64.

6 D. 27 Feb. 68.

7 D. 30 July 66.

8 W. T. Costello, S.J., *The Scholastic Curriculum at early seventeenth-century Cambridge* (Harvard U.P., 1958), 142.

9 This conjecture is supported by D. 26 June 62, '. . . comes Mr Nicholson, my old fellow-student at Magdalene, and we played three or four things upon the violin and basse . . .'

10 G. P. H. Pawson, *The Cambridge Platonists* (London, 1930), 19 ff.

11 Quot. *D.N.B.* article on Anthony Tuckney.

12 Costello, *op. cit.*, 48.

13 John Hall, *An Humble Motion to the Parliament of England concerning the Advancement of Learning and Reformation of the Universities* (London, 1649), quoted by Mullinger, iii, 372–3. Spelling and punctuation here modernised.

14 D. 30 Jan. 64.

CHAPTER II

1 Clarendon, *Rebellion*, xv, 57. J. R. Powell, *The Letters of Robert Blake* (N.R.S., 1937), *Robert Blake, General-at-Sea* (1972).

2 On all this see Violet A. Rowe, *Sir Henry Vane the Younger* (1970), a most valuable and original biography.

3 Professor Aylmer has recently pointed out (*History*, lvi, June 1971, pp. 186–7) that Mountagu was a member of the Army Committee that voted a large advance of money to Cromwell in continuance of his military pay in May 1647 when his membership of Parliament should have disqualified him from holding any military appointment.

4 D. 25 Feb. 67.

5 Rawl. MS. A.185, ff. 206–13, printed in A. Bryant, *Years of Peril*, 405–13.

6 *The Diary of John Evelyn*, ed. E. S. de Beer (O.U.P., 6 vols., 1955 and O.S.A., 1 vol., 1959). 3 May 50 (description of lithotomies at La Charité in Paris) and 10 June 69 (Pepys's visit to Richard Evelyn. This is the first mention of Pepys in Evelyn's Diary: Evelyn first appears in Pepys's Diary on 9 Sept. 65).

CHAPTER III

1 D. 10 Mar. 66.

2 Quot. Anthony Powell, *John Aubrey and His Friends* (London, 1948), 93.

3 D. 7 Nov. 60.

4 Alan Macfarlane, *The Family Life of Ralph Josselin* (C.U.P., 1970), 170.

5 In the title of a work published in 1672, *Microscopium statisticum quo status imperii Romano-Germanici repraesentatur*, cited by Roger Mols S.J. in *Fontana Economic History of Europe*, ii, 35.

6 D. 11 Feb. 60.

7 Godfrey Davis, *The Restoration of Charles II 1658–1660* (1955), 283.

8 David Underdown, *Royalist Conspiracy in England 1649–1660* (Yale, 1960), 310–11. For Mountagu's conduct at the Sound (p. 50) see Harris, *op. cit.*, i, 143 ff.

CHAPTER IV

1 D. 8–9 Mar. 60.

2 D., ed. Latham and Matthews, i, 86, n. 2. J. R. Powell (ed.), *The Letters of Robert Blake* (1937), *passim*.

3 D. 25 Jun. 60 and 30 Jan. 66.

CHAPTER V

1 He appears to have helped himself to £500. D. 4 Apr. 68; *Further Correspondence*, 188–9.

2 D. 5 July 60.

3 N.M.M., LBK/8, f. 20.

4 D. 8–9 Aug. 62.

5 D. 14 June 67.

6 D. 20 Aug. 62.

7 Rawl. MS. A.174, f. 239.

8 *Ibid.*, f. 482.

9 D. 7 June 62.

CHAPTER VI

1 D. 30 Sept. 62.

3 D. 29 Apr. 60.

3 D. 1 July 60.

4 D. 2 May 63.

5 R. W. Chapman (ed.), *Journal of a Tour to the Hebrides* (O.U.P., 1970), 246.

6 D. 8 Dec. 67.

7 *Naval Minutes*, 2.

8 D. 25 Apr. 62.

9 J. R. Tanner, *Mr. Pepys*, p. 98.

10 D. 31 July 62.

11 D. 26 Nov. 65.

12 'The Present Ill State of my Health', Rawl. MS. A.185, ff. 206–13, printed in A. Bryant, *Years of Peril*, 412.

13 D. 19 Jan. 63.

14 D. 9 Feb. 66.

15 D. 9 Nov. 65.

16 D. 21 June 66.

17 D. 5 Sept. 64.

18 D. 12 July 66.

19 D. 13 June 66.

20 H.T.H., pp. xxi–xxii.

21 D. 24 Apr. 63.

22 D. 8 June 62.

CHAPTER VII

1 D. 1 July 63.

2 'The Medical History of Mr. and Mrs. Samuel Pepys' in *Pepys Club: Occasional Papers*, i, 86.

3 D. 9 July 63.

4 *Further Correspondence*, 91.

5 *Cat. Pepysian MSS.*, i, 274–5.

6 D. 17 July 63.

7 D. 27 Feb. 64.

8 D. 23 Jan. 65.

9 D. 12 Sept. 66.

10 P.L. 2853, Adty. Letters, vi, 428–9.

11 Bryant, *Years of Peril*, 372.

12 Bryant, *Saviour of the Navy*, 166.

13 *Ibid.*, 386.

14 E.g. D. 6 Sept. 64.

15 D. 9 Sept. 63.

16 D. 14 June 64.

CHAPTER VIII

1 D. 30 Sept. 61; 3 Nov. 61.

2 *Brief Lives*, ed. Lawson Dick, 240.

3 For envy and contempt see the Diary *passim*; for hatred see, e.g., Rawl. MS. A.185 ff. 13–26.

4 D. 19 Jan. 63.

5 D. 29 May 64.

6 'Pepys and Shakespeare' (especially p. 18) in *Pepys Club: Occasional Papers*, ii.

7 D. 31 Dec. 64.

8 D. 20 Jan. 65.

9 D. 15 July 60.

10 D. 29 July 65.

11 D. 9 Nov. 61.

12 D. 31 Oct. 63.

13 D. 14 Aug. 65.

14 D. 15 June 63.

15 D. 17 Nov. 63.

16 D. 26 May 63.

17 D. 4 Feb. 65.

CHAPTER IX

1 D. 24 Apr. 65.

2 D. 10 Sept. 64.

3 Bernard Pool, *Navy Board Contracts 1660–1832* (1966), 38.

4 D. 30 Mar. 63.

5 Chappell, *Shorthand Letters*, pp. 29–30 and Kaufman, *Conscientious Cavalier: Colonel Bullen Reymes M.P., F.R.S.* (1962), *passim*.

6 Kaufman, *op. cit.*, 191–8. Curiously there is no reference to this mission in Miss E. M. G. Routh's excellent book on Tangier.

7 *Further Correspondence*, 122–3, 8 Mar. 66.

8 This seems the inescapable inference from D. 30 July and 7 Aug.

9 D. 6 Mar. 63.

10 LBK, ff. 46–7, 7 Mar. 63.

11 For Holmes in general and this incident in particular see the author's *Man of War* (London, 1969).

12 D. 24 Mar. 63.

13 Rawl. MS. A.195 f. 53^v.

14 *Further Correspondence*, 290.

15 *Ibid.*, 2.

16 D. 28 Apr. 65.

CHAPTER X

1 It is perhaps still necessary to repeat that Holmes did *not*, as stated in the *D.N.B.*, capture New Amsterdam and rename it New York. For the history of this *canard* see the author's *Man of War*, 209.

2 D. 10 Oct. 64.

3 D. 3 June 64.

4 D. 4 Nov. 64.

5 Ogg, i, 285 puts it at 98.

6 LBK, f. 149, 24 and 25 Jan. 65.

7 D. 7 Apr. 65.

8 E.g. LBK, ff. 305, 323, 332 and, especially, the postscript of 28 Dec. 65, f. 335.

9 LBK, f. 248, 8 Oct. 65.

10 Rawl. MS. A.174, f. 468.

11 LBK, ff. 176, 182.

12 D. 21 Sept. 64.
13 D. 30 Aug. 65.
14 Howarth, 24–5.
15 Sandwich, *Journal*, 234.

CHAPTER XI

1 Sandwich, *Journal*, 248.
2 D. 7 Sept. 65.
3 D. 9 Sept. 65.
4 Chappell, *Shorthand Letters*, 61.
5 Penn, *Memorials*, ii, 365.
6 *Further Correspondence*, 51.
7 *Naval Minutes*, 250.
8 Cat. Pepysian MSS., i, 154.
9 *The Rupert and Monck Letter Book 1666*, ed. J. R. Powell and E. K. Timings (N.R.S., 1969), 142.
10 *Ibid.*, 287.
11 In his introduction to the *Journals of Sir Thomas Allin*, vol. ii (N.R.S., 1940), where the best and fairest account of the question is to be found.
12 *The Rupert and Monck Letter Book*, 57.
13 See, e.g., D. 1 July 66.
14 LBK, f. 389.
15 *The Rupert and Monck Letter Book*, 94.
16 D. 12 July 66.
17 Reproduced in *The Rupert and Monck Letter Book* and in *Man of War*. On the authorship of the draft see my note in *M.M.*, 57, 215. For the best description of the battle see Dr. R. C. Anderson's introduction to vol. ii of *The Journals of Sir Thomas Allin*, xxvii ff.
18 D. 21 July 66.

CHAPTER XII

1 For examples of both (on consecutive days) see D. 28 and 29 Oct. 66.
2 D. 7 Oct. 66.
3 See on all this P. G. Rogers, *The Dutch in the Medway* (1970) and A. W. Tedder, *The Navy of the Restoration* (Cambridge, 1916).
4 D. 16 Dec. 66.
5 Quot. Rogers, *op. cit.*, 75.
6 Coventry MSS. xcvii, f. 69.
7 D. 10 June 67.
8 D. 11 June 67.
9 Coventry MSS. xcvii, f. 75, 11 June 67.
10 Monck's report quot. Rogers, 87.
11 D. 13 June 67.
12 For this connection see Marvell, *Poems and Letters*, 2 vols. ed Margoliouth (Oxford, 1927), *passim*.
13 D. 9 July 67.
14 E.g. 29 July 67.
15 D. 12 July and 9 Aug. 67.
16 D. 22 July 67.

CHAPTER XIII

1 D. 2 Sept. 66.
2 LBK, f. 404, 25 Aug. 66.
3 *Ibid.*, f. 435.
4 D. 27 Sept. 67.
5 D. 9 Nov. 67.
6 The Deborah Egmont from whom Sir Arthur Bryant prints a letter to Pepys dated 30 January 1689 (*Saviour of the Navy*, Appendix E, p. 400) was not the same person as Deb. Willett. See the author's note in the *T.L.S.* 15 Feb. 1974, p. 164.
7 D. 25 Feb. 68.
8 Coventry Papers, xcvii, f. 111.

CHAPTER XIV

1 D'Arcy Power, 'Why Samuel Pepys Discontinued his Diary', in *Occasional Papers*, i, 63–77.
2 *Further Correspondence*, 239.
3 Bryant, *Years of Peril*, 406–7.
4 D. 31 Mar. 69.
5 D. 18 Jan. 69.
6 N.M.M., LBK, f. 632. For a fuller discussion of the charges in their relation to Pepys see Pool, *Navy Board Contracts*; Bryant, *Years of Peril*; and J. R. Tanner, *Further Correspondence*.
7 *Diary of John Evelyn*, ed. de Beer, iii, 232.
8 D. 12 Dec. 67.
9 P.L. 2874 (the sixth volume of Pepys's Miscellanies which contains the Brooke House Journal), ff. 388–90. In future references this document will be cited as J.
10 J., 393.
11 J., 396.
12 J., 413.
13 J., 480–5.
14 J., 427.
15 J., 425.
16 Bryant, *Years of Peril*, 32.
17 J., 469.
18 J., 477.
19 J., 497.
20 D. 1 Mar. 68.
21 E.g. LBK, f. 423.
22 J., 471.
23 J., 473.
24 J., 496.
25 J., 501.

CHAPTER XV

1 For Pepys's unsleeping vigilance towards this officer's misdemeanours see Tanner, Cat. Pepysian MSS., *passim*, but especially iv, lxix–lxx. For his relation to Penn see Penn, *Memorials*, ii, 559–60. James's confidence in him may be judged by his bringing him out of retirement to command an armed merchantman in the Bristol Channel during Monmouth's Rebellion. P.L. 2858, ff. 209–10.

2 Rawl. MS. A.174, f. 239.

3 Michael Lewis, *The Navy of Britain* (1948), 362.

4 Later reduced to one or two meetings a week. See on all this J. R. Tanner's introduction to Cat. Pepysian MSS. i–iv, *passim*.

5 See, e.g., LBK, f. 760, 6 Jan. 77.

6 *Naval Minutes*, 71.

7 *Works of George Savile, Marquess of Halifax*, ed. Raleigh (Oxford, 1912), 193.

8 Howarth, 64.

9 Quot. Tanner, *Mr. Pepys*, 118n., from Lucas-Dubreton, *Petite Vie de Samuel Pepys, Londinien* (Paris, 1923).

10 On 15 Dec. 76, *Diary of Robert Hooke* (1672–80), ed. Robinson and Adams (1935), 262.

11 *Diary*, ed. de Beer, iii, 559.

12 *Ibid.*, 570.

13 Cat. Pepysian MSS., iv, 542.

14 P.L. 2849, Adty. Letters, ii, 130, 11 Sept. 73.

15 *Further Correspondence*, 272–3, quot. B. M. Ranft, 'The Political Career of Samuel Pepys', *Journal of Modern History*, xxiv, No. 4, 368–75, who corrects Tanner's conjecture as to the addressee of this letter.

CHAPTER XVI

1 *Diary*, ed. de Beer, v, 538.

2 *Naval Minutes*, 316.

3 See on all this Stuart Mountfield, 'Captain Greenville Collins and Mr. Pepys', *M.M.*, Vol. 56, No. 1, 85–97.

4 Letter Book of J. Gauden, Adm. MS. *passim*, but notably f. 45.

5 *Naval Minutes*, 176–7.

6 *Ibid.*, 62.

7 *Ibid.*, 300.

8 LBK, f. 737, 8 May 76.

9 *Naval Minutes*, 26.

10 *Samuel Pepys and the Royal Navy*, 70.

11 *Naval Minutes*, 418.

12 *Ibid.*, 158.

13 *Ibid.*, 187–8. Although Pepys here specifically names Danby as one who *had* taken out a pardon this was in fact a last-minute expedient of the King's. See Andrew Browning, *Danby* (Glasgow, 1951), i, 317n.

14 Cat. Pepysian MSS., i, 196; iii, 92 and *Naval Minutes*, 322. See also Chappell's article on this officer, *M.M.* (1934), 115–19.

15 Rawl. MS. A.185, f. 110. For the excesses of Captain Ashby in the *Rose* on the same service see *ibid.*, f. 299.

16 For all this see Rawl. MS. A.181, f. 210 and ff. 340–83 where the Captain's name is usually spelled Roydon. Pepys in his Register of Sea Officers spells it Royden. See further pp. 253 and 282.

17 Rawl. MS. A.177, ff. 1–76.

18 *Ibid.*, A.181, ff. 130–93.

19 Cat. Pepysian MSS., i, 202–5.

20 *Ibid.*, iv, 535–6, 543–4.

21 Quot. *ibid.*, i, 203.

22 See examples cited in *Years of Peril*, 134–5.
23 Rawl. MS. A.185, f. 281.
24 LBK, ff. 753–4.
25 Cat. Pepysian MSS., iii, 298.
26 *Further Correspondence*, 310.
27 *Naval Minutes*, 146.
28 *Ibid.*, 323.

CHAPTER XVII

1 For all this see J. J. Keevil, *Medicine and the Navy*, ii, *passim*, but especially 84 ff. and 131–47.
2 Cat. Pepysian MSS., iv, 135.
3 J. R. Tanner reads 'horse cloth'. The MS. is P.L. 2867, f. 416.
4 John Ehrman, *The Navy in the War of William III*, 239–40.
5 Quot. Lloyd, *The British Seaman* (1968), 107.
6 E. Coxere, *Adventures by Sea*, ed. Meyerstein (1945), 71.
7 P.L. 2862, Adty. Letters, xv, f. 226.
8 Cat. Pepysian MSS., iii, 68.
9 LBK, f. 772 and Adty. Letters, vi, f. 116.
10 *Naval Minutes*, 268.
11 Smith, *The Navy and its Chaplains in the Days of Sail* (Toronto, 1961), 21.
12 *Ibid.*, 22.
13 C.S.P. Dom. 28 Nov. 65. Pepys here supports the application for chaplain's pay from an unordained member of the ship's company who had supplied this function in the *Coast* frigate.
14 Cat. Pepysian MSS., i, 205. See also Adty. Letters, x, ff. 353–4.
15 LBK, ff. 816–18.
16 Michael Lewis, *England Sea Officers* (1939), 264.
17 Rawl. MS. A.185, ff. 265–6.

CHAPTER XVIII

1 See on all this John Kenyon, *The Popish Plot* (1972), *passim*.
2 Quot. Bryant, *Years of Peril*, as epigraph to his chapter 'The Trial of Atkins' which gives much the fullest and best account available.
3 *Years of Peril*, 203–9.
4 H.T.H., 36.
5 LBK, f. 885.
6 Howarth, 80.
7 Rawl. MS. A.181, f. 197.
8 H.T.H., 176.
9 LBK, f. 893, 29 Apr. 79.
10 Howarth, 83, 86.
11 *Years of Peril*, 284.
12 H.T.H., 115.
13 *Ibid.*, 74.
14 *Years of Peril*, 279 ff.
15 *Naval Minutes*, 71–2.

CHAPTER XIX

1 24 Sept. 1680; H.T.H., 164–8.

2 H.T.H., 188.

3 Rawl. MS. A. 183, f. 140.

4 Howarth, 126.

5 *Ibid.*, 115–18.

6 *Ibid.*, 145–8.

7 Rawl. MS. A. 178, f. 235

8 *Ibid.*, f. 120.

9 *Ibid.*, A. 179, ff. 24, 30.

10 Ibid., A. 178, f. 34. Sir Arthur Bryant reads 'inkbottle'.

11 Howarth, 120.

12 *Ibid.*, 129.

13 H.T.H., 204–5.

14 All Souls MS., 317.

15 *Ibid.*, f. 10.

16 *Ibid.*, f. 52.

17 See on this Sir Stephen Gaselee's paper on 'The Spanish Books in the Library of Samuel Pepys', *Pepys Club: Occasional Papers*, ii, 117 ff.

18 *Tangier Papers*, 7, where the editor has guessed 'Sir Nicholas Acland' for a difficult reading.

19 Quot. Routh, *Tangier*, 196.

20 Quot. Routh, *Tangier*, 280.

21 *Tangier Papers*, 25–6.

22 Rawl. MS. A. 196 (2 foliations: (1) f. 102; (2) f. 105).

CHAPTER XX

1 Rawl. MS. A. 171, 1 f. 203.

2 *Ibid.*, f. 217.

3 *Ibid.*, 102, 274–5, 287.

4 *Ibid.*, A. 189, f. 125.

5 *Tangier Papers*, 119.

6 *Ibid.*, 122.

7 *Ibid.*, 191.

8 As late as December 1688, in the last weeks of his official life, Pepys was forced to admit that the question was 'Not yet settl'd'. Rawl. MS. A. 186 ff. 29 v, 30.

9 *Tangier Papers*, 121.

10 Rawl. MS. A. 190, f. 236.

11 *Tangier Papers*, 182.

12 *Diary*, ed. de Beer, iv, 477.

13 Quot. Bryant, *Saviour of the Navy*, 124.

14 *Years of Peril*, 336.

15 Howarth, 127–8.

16 Ehrman, 206–7.

17 Rawl. MS. A. 170, f. 217.

18 Cat. Pepysian MSS., i, 90.

19 Rawl. MS. A. 189, f. 146; Cat. Pepysian MSS., i, 345.

20 *Ibid.*, f. 107.

21 *Ibid.*, f. 199.
22 Rawl. MS. A.179, ff. 5 A & B. Sir Arthur Bryant has read '25 per cent' for 25s. 6d.
23 *Ibid.*, ff. 102–3.
24 *Ibid.*, f. 5B.

CHAPTER XXI

1 *Diary*, 19 Sept. 85.
2 *Ibid.*, 5 May 86.
3 Rawl. MS. A.189, f. 21.
4 *Diary*, 16 Sept. 85.
5 Howarth, 177.
6 *Ibid.*
7 Rawl. MS. A. 186, f. 89. Sir Arthur Bryant (*Saviour of the Navy*, 263) has confused the writer with Pepys's old tutor at Magdalene, Joseph Hill. Abraham was the eldest brother of Thomas, the Lisbon merchant.
8 This was surely the letter whose arrival is so dramatically described by Macaulay (iii, 1105): 'It is said that, when the King had read it, the blood left his cheeks, and he remained some time speechless.' Macaulay and the authorities he cites appear to have misdated it by a month: hence the cautious scepticism of Ehrman, *op. cit.*, 214 n. 6 as to its existence.
9 Quot. Tanner, *E.H.R.* (1893), 'The Naval Preparation of James II in 1688', 272–3.
10 Rawl. MS. A.186, f. 288 ff.
11 Pepys to Captain Smith of the *Falcon*, quot. Bryant, *Saviour of the Navy*, 258.
12 Rawl. MS. A.179, f. 44. For Holmes in general see the author's *Man of War*.
13 *Ibid.*, A.186, ff. 227–9, 308–9.
14 John Carswell, *The Descent on England* (1969) and E. B. Powley, *The English Navy in the Revolution of 1688* (1928).
15 Howarth, 194–5.
16 Rawl. MS. A.179, f. 107.
17 *Ibid.*, f. 179.
18 Howarth, 200–1.
19 *Ibid.*, 175–6, 192.
20 Bryant, *Saviour of the Navy*, 270.
21 Rawl. MS. A.186, f. 396. Dartmouth to James II (holograph) 11 Nov. 88.
22 Quot. Bryant, *Saviour of the Navy*, 305.
23 As late as 1712–14, see N.M.M. MSS. AGC/XX.
24 Howarth, 198.

CHAPTER XXII

1 *Correspondence*, i, 354.
2 See on all this Ehrman, 283 ff., and the same author's article in *M.M.*, Vol. 34, No. 4, 255–70.
3 *Correspondence*, i, 57, 60; *Mr. Pepys*, 270.
4 H.T.H., 224–6.
5 *Ibid.*, 223.
6 *Ibid.*, 229.
7 Rawl. MS. A.170, f. 124.
8 *Ibid.*, f. 26 and 26ᵛ.
9 *Correspondence*, ii, 290–1.

10 *Ibid.*, ii, 156, 188, 190. In his introduction (i, xxxvii) J. R. Tanner inexplicably overlooks Daniel, the most interesting of the three, and debits Mary with only two brothers.

11 Rawl. MS. A.170, ff. 147-69.

12 *Ibid.*, f. 169 and f. 161.

13 *Ibid.*, f. 11.

14 Howarth, 189.

15 F. Sidgwick, *A Descriptive Catalogue of the Library of Samuel Pepys* (1914), Part II, pp. i-ii.

16 *Occasional Papers*, ii, 62.

17 *Correspondence*, i, 200.

18 *Mr. Pepys*, 272.

19 Howarth, 281; *Correspondence*, i, 61; i, 36; i, 137.

20 *Correspondence*, i, 59.

21 *Ibid.*, i, 61.

22 *Sergison Papers*, ed. Merriman (N.R.S., 1950), 6. Sergison probably owed his entry to the office to his being a cousin of Will Hewer's. Smith, *Life, Journals and Correspondence of Samuel Pepys* (1841), ii, 120.

23 Rawl. MS. A.170, f. 100.

24 *Naval Minutes*, 389.

25 *Pepysiana*, 46.

26 Howarth, 257.

27 *Occasional Papers*, ii, 73.

28 These lines first appear in the fifth edition of Waller's *Poems* (1686): Pepys possessed a copy, still in his library, of the fourth (1682).

29 Howarth, 296.

CHAPTER XXIII

1 Rawl. MS. A.171, f. 217 ff.

2 See on this R. K. Merton, *Science, Technology and Society in Seventeenth Century England* (1938: re-issued Harper Torchbooks 1970), esp. pp. 113-14.

3 Rawl. MS. A.183, f. 1.

4 *Ibid.*, A.178, f. 25.

5 *Naval Minutes*, 297.

6 Quot. Marjorie Hope Nicolson, *Pepys's Diary and the New Science* (Charlottesville, Va., 1965), 139.

7 *Correspondence*, i, 72-94.

8 *Ibid.*, i, 155-65.

9 Quot. Douglas, *English Scholars* (1939), 335.

10 E.g. Howarth, 344-6.

11 *Naval Minutes*, 282.

12 *Correspondence*, i, 97. The work in question was *Catalogi librorum manuscriptorum Angliae et Hiberniae in unum collecti* (1697).

13 *Correspondence*, i, 103.

14 *Ibid.*, i, 141; Howarth, 243-6.

15 *Correspondence*, ii, 109.

16 Evelyn, *Diary*, v, 295; Christopher Lloyd, *William Dampier* (1966), 13.

17 Howarth, 331.

18 Rawl. MS. A.174, f. 394.

19 Howarth, 52–3.

20 Rawl. MS. A.186, ff. 110–11.

21 *Correspondence*, i, 367–76.

22 *Ibid.*, i, 241.

23 *Ibid.*, ii, 304–5.

24 *Ibid.*, i, 134–5.

25 *Ibid.*, ii, 35.

26 *Ibid.*, ii, 238–41.

27 N.M.M. MSS. 52/056. In *Correspondence*, where all unattributed quotations referring to Jackson's tour may be found, this letter is printed from a copy.

28 *Correspondence*, ii, 302.

29 *Ibid.*, ii, 263–5.

30 Rawl. MS. A.171, ff. 61^v–62^v.

31 *Occasional Papers*, ii, 66.

32 For the case of Dégalénière, see *Correspondence passim*. An earlier instance may be found in LBK/797.

33 *Correspondence*, ii, 312–14.

34 *Diary*, ed. Wheatley, Vol. i, lii.

Chronology

1633	23 Feb.	Pepys born in Salisbury Court off Fleet Street.
	3 Mar.	Baptised in St. Bride's Church.
c. 1644		At Huntingdon Grammar School.
c. 1646–50		At St. Paul's School.
1650	21 June	Entered on the books of Trinity Hall, Cambridge.
	1 Oct.	Transferred to Magdalene College.
1651	Mar.	Began residence at Cambridge.
1654	Mar.	Took his B.A.
?1654		Employed as some kind of steward to his cousin Edward Mountagu in London. The date at which this arrangement began is not known.
1655	1 Dec.	Married Elizabeth St. Michel.
1656	10 Oct.	Began to live with her as man and wife.
?1656		Employed part-time as a clerk to George Downing in the Exchequer. Again the beginnings of this cannot be accurately dated but it was certainly before Cromwell's death in September 1658.
1658	26 Mar.	Cut for the stone.
	c. Aug.	Set up house in Axe Yard, Westminster.
1659	May	Sent out briefly with letters to Mountagu in the Baltic. Becomes one of his master's principal London correspondents.
1660	1 Jan.	Begins the Diary.
	Mar.	Joins the Fleet as secretary to Mountagu, General at Sea charged with bringing over Charles II from Holland.
	25 May	Witnesses the King's landing at Dover.

	28 June	Resigns Exchequer clerkship.
	29 June	Appointed Clerk of the Acts.
	17 July	Moves to Navy Office house in Seething Lane.
	23 July	Sworn in as Clerk of the Privy Seal.
	24 Sept.	Sworn in as a J.P.
1661	July	Death of uncle Robert Pepys.
		Pepys visits Brampton which he has inherited from him.
1662	15 Feb.	Admitted a Younger Brother of Trinity House.
	17 Aug.	Resigns Clerkship of Privy Seal.
	Nov.	Appointed to the Tangier Commission.
1664	15 Mar.	Death of his brother Tom.
1665	15 Feb.	Elected a Fellow of the Royal Society.
	22 Feb.	Second Dutch War breaks out.
	20 Mar.	Appointed Treasurer for Tangier.
	5 July	Moves his household (but not himself) to Woolwich to avoid the plague.
	27 Oct.	Appointed Surveyor-General of the Victualling.
	Sept.–Dec.	Prize Goods Scandal. Sandwich disgraced and sent as Ambassador to Madrid.
1666	7 Jan.	Brought his household back to London.
	1–4 June	The Four Days Battle.
	25 July	St. James's Day Fight.
	2 Sept.	Fire of London breaks out.
1667	25 Mar.	Death of his mother.
	June	The Dutch in the Medway. Pepys withdraws his gold and sends it with Elizabeth and his father to Brampton for safety.
	28 July	Resigns Surveyorship of Victualling.
	31 July	End of the War.
	Oct.	Visits Brampton to dig up his buried treasure.
	22 Oct.	Defends the Navy Office before Parliamentary Committee.
1668	27 Feb.	Marriage of his sister Paulina to John Jackson.
	5 Mar.	Defends the Navy Office before the House of Commons.
	May–June	Jaunts to Cambridge and to Oxford and the West.
	25 Oct.	Elizabeth discovers his relations with Deb.
1669	Spring	Increasingly troubled with his eyes.
	31 May	Closes the Diary in fear of blindness.
	June–Oct.	Obtains leave for a tour to Holland, France and Flanders at the end of which Elizabeth is taken ill.
	10 Nov.	Death of Elizabeth.
1670	Jan.–Feb.	Brooke House Committee.
	30 Mar.	His brother John appointed Clerk to Trinity House.
1672	24 Jan.	Pepys admitted an Elder Brother of Trinity House.
	Mar.	Outbreak of Third Dutch War.
	7 June	Death of Sandwich at Battle of Solebay.
1673	29 Jan.	Fire at Navy Office in Seething Lane. Pepys moves to Winchester Street.
	Mar.	Test Act excludes Roman Catholics from office.

	June	Duke of York in consequence forced to resign as Lord High Admiral. Pepys appointed Secretary of the Admiralty. Succeeded as Clerk of the Acts by his brother John and his clerk Thomas Hayter.
	Oct.	Elected M.P. for Castle Rising. Attempt to unseat him for alleged Roman Catholicism.
1674	Feb.	End of Third Dutch War.
		Moved from Winchester Street to Admiralty Office at Derby House.
1676	1 Feb.	Appointed a Governor of Christ's Hospital.
	22 May	Elected Master of Trinity House.
1677	Spring	Death of his brother John.
	8 Aug.	Elected Master of the Clothworkers Company.
1679	Feb.	His clerk Samuel Atkins acquitted of murdering Sir Edmund Berry Godfrey.
	Mar.	Elected M.P. for Harwich in first Parliament of 1679.
	Apr.	Dissolution of Admiralty Commission and appointment of a new Board hostile to Pepys.
	May	Fall of Pepys. Resigns Secretaryship of Admiralty, Treasurership of Tangier (in which Hewer succeeds him) and is sent to the Tower.
	July	Released on bail: goes to live with Hewer at York Buildings, near the Watergate.
1680	Feb.	Relieved of bail.
	June	Proceedings abandoned.
	?Aug.–Sept.	Death of his brother-in-law John Jackson.
	Oct.	Death of his father.
1682	Spring	Visits Edinburgh and Newcastle in attendance on Duke of York.
1683	30 July	Leaves London to accompany Dartmouth on expedition to Tangier as his Secretary.
	Dec.	Leaves Tangier to travel in Spain.
1684	Mar.	Returns to England.
	June	Re-appointed Secretary to the Admiralty.
	30 Nov.	Elected President of the Royal Society.
1685	Feb.	Death of Charles II.
	Apr.	Pepys elected M.P. for Harwich.
		Walked in James II's coronation procession as a Baron of the Cinque Ports.
		Appointed a Deputy Lieutenant for Huntingdonshire.
	July	Master of Trinity House for second time.
1686	Mar.	Special Commission begins to sit.
1688	Oct.	Special Commission dissolved.
	Nov.	William of Orange lands at Torbay.
	Dec.	James II flees to France.
1689	Jan.	Pepys defeated at Harwich in elections for the Convention Parliament.

	20 Feb.	Resigns Secretaryship of the Admiralty.
	May–July	Imprisoned in the Gatehouse.
	Aug.	Resigns the Trinity House.
1690	June	Again imprisoned in the Gatehouse.
	Dec.	Published his *Memoires of the Royal Navy 1679–88*.
1693	Sept.	Robbed by highwaymen while driving to Chelsea.
1694	Aug.	Recovering from a serious illness.
1697	Apr.	Again seriously ill.
1699	Oct.	Pepys's nephew John Jackson sets out on his Grand Tour.
1700	?May	Visits Hewer's house at Clapham to recover his health.
	?Dec.	Returns to York Buildings.
1701	?June	Final retirement to Clapham.
	Aug.	Return of John Jackson from the Grand Tour.
1702	Sept.	Presents portrait of Dr. Wallis to the University of Oxford.
	Oct.	Receives the thanks of the University.
1703	26 May	Death of Pepys at Clapham.
	4 June	Burial in St. Olave's, Hart Street.

Index

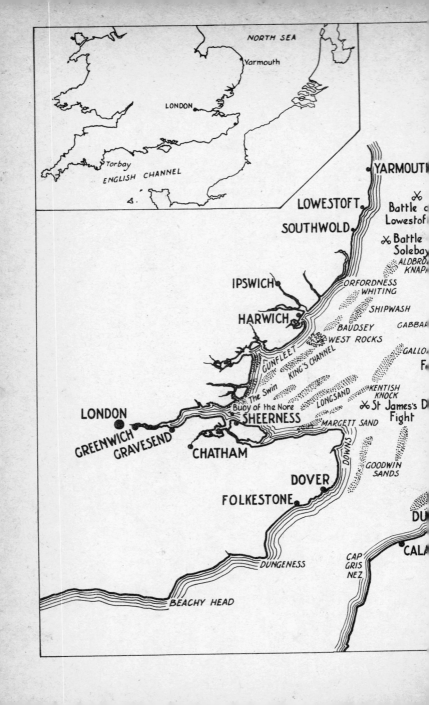

NORTH SEA

Yarmouth

LONDON

Torbay

ENGLISH CHANNEL

YARMOUTH

LOWESTOFT

✕ Battle of Lowestoft

SOUTHWOLD

✕ Battle Solebay

ALDBRO
KNAP

IPSWICH

ORFORDNESS
WHITING

SHIPWASH

HARWICH

GABBAR

BAUDSEY
WEST ROCKS

GALLO

GUNFLEET

KING'S CHANNEL

F

The Swin

KENTISH
KNOCK

LONGSAND

✕ St James's Day Fight

Buoy of the Nore

LONDON

SHEERNESS

MARGETT SAND

GREENWICH
GRAVESEND

CHATHAM

DOWNS

GOODWIN
SANDS

DOVER

FOLKESTONE

DU

CALA

DUNGENESS

CAP
GRIS
NEZ

BEACHY HEAD

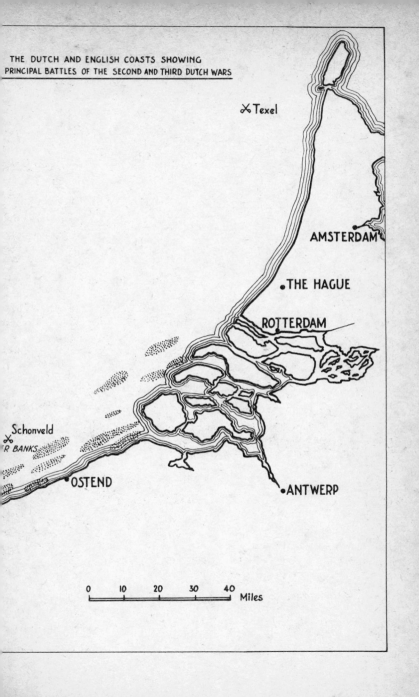

THE DUTCH AND ENGLISH COASTS SHOWING
PRINCIPAL BATTLES OF THE SECOND AND THIRD DUTCH WARS

⋊ Texel

AMSTERDAM

•THE HAGUE

ROTTERDAM

Schonveld
⋊
R BANKS

•OSTEND

•ANTWERP

0   10   20   30   40   Miles